To ma cherie and our lovely family!
Thank you so much for your help
and for always being there!
May Allah (SWT) bless you all!
Je vous aime!
Salima

MUSLIM POLITICAL PARTICIPATION IN EUROPE

MUSLIM POLITICAL PARTICIPATION IN EUROPE

• • •

EDITED BY

JØRGEN S. NIELSEN

EDINBURGH
University Press

© in this edition Edinburgh University Press, 2013
© in the individual contributions is retained by the authors

Edinburgh University Press Ltd
22 George Square, Edinburgh EH8 9LF
www.euppublishing.com

Typeset in 10/12.5pt Sabon by
Servis Filmsetting Ltd, Stockport, Cheshire, and
printed and bound in Great Britain by
CPI Group (UK) Ltd, Croydon CR0 4YY

A CIP record for this book is available from the British Library

ISBN 978 0 7486 4694 4 (hardback)
ISBN 978 0 7486 4695 1 (webready PDF)
ISBN 978 0 7486 7753 5 (epub)
ISBN 978 0 7486 7752 8 (Amazon ebook)

The right of the contributors to be identified as authors of this work
has been asserted in accordance with the Copyright, Designs and
Patents Act 1988.

CONTENTS

TABLES AND FIGURES

Tables

Figures

INTRODUCTION

Jørgen S. Nielsen

In the media and among politicians in recent years it has been common to point to tendencies among Muslim communities which seek to either isolate themselves from the surrounding society or seek actively to position themselves in public opposition to it. This especially happens around national elections when isolationist tendencies are interpreted as a sign of a deep incompatibility between Islam and democracy while oppositional voices are interpreted as proof of such incompatibility. At several recent general elections in the United Kingdom, party election posters in some districts of Muslim residential con-centration, certain districts of, for example, Birmingham and Bradford, have been defaced with slogans calling on Muslims not to vote in a *kafir* system. While John Bowen's study on Islam in France (Bowen 2010) does not directly investigate Muslim activity during elections his account identifies a sector, especially among young Muslims, that withdraws from society into their own religio-cultural enclaves. At the other end of the spectrum have been the instances of political parties seeking to attract a Muslim vote (see Didero and Peace in this volume)

In fact the participation of Muslims in European political processes is not a straightforward issue. Firstly, at least in the case of Muslims of immigrant origin (mostly in the west), there is the matter of getting access to voting and to standing for election, usually associated with the acquisition of citizenship. Traditionally, this has been linked to a certain number of years of residence, sometimes linked to fulfilling other conditions. Britain and France used to have quite open regimes based on birth in the country, in Britain's case twinned with a system whereby citizens of the Commonwealth and the Republic of Ireland had political rights without having to acquire UK nationality. At the other end of the spectrum, Germany's concept of citizenship meant that until the late 1990s, it was very difficult for anyone not of German descent to acquire citizenship. Whatever the regime, a further obstacle has been the reluctance of many countries to allow dual citizenship, so people who were reluctant to make a complete break with their country of origin – or whose country of origin did not allow them to make the break – found themselves excluded.

Secondly, having acquired the right to vote, the more substantial issue is the decision whether to vote and, even more substantially, whether to stand for election – locally, nationally, and for which party? The general pattern seems to have been that Muslims have stood for election in local contests earlier than in national contests. Given that the practical issues which concerned them during the early phases of settlement tended to be issues which were determined locally, this would seem to make sense. This process seems to have applied also in countries such as France which traditionally had a very central-ised form of government, possibly because it was precisely during these years that substantial parts of government were being delegated partly to the depart-ments but also to the newly established regions. As the process of settlement deepened during the 1980s and into the 1990s, it began to impinge more on issues which were managed at the level of central government. In Britain this shift coincided with the growing move of government powers from the local to the central decision-making processes characteristic of the Conservative government led by Margaret Thatcher from 1979 to 1990.

In this development it is also apparent that those very few individuals who entered national politics in the early phases did not regard a Muslim identity as of any significance. They were activists in trades unions, and the overview which Sinno provides of 'Muslim' members of European parliaments for 2006 shows that they are overwhelmingly towards the left-hand end of the politi-cal spectrum (Sinno 2009: 72–5). The early activation of immigrants of South Asian origin in the UK was often through the Indian and the Pakistani Workers Associations, with strong Marxist sympathies, through their association with the trades unions, and thus with the Labour Party. By this route many elected local government councils had a significant number of members whose origins lay in the Muslim world, already by the late 1970s. Although a similar process took place rather later in West Germany, and because of the difficulties asso-ciated with attaining citizenship the focus for elections tended to be local 'migrant advisory councils', it was here also that secular activists first moved into politics – although they often were Kemalists rather than leftists, and their links tended to be with the Social Democrats.

This started to change during the 1980s and particularly during the 1990s as Islam moved up the levels of public awareness – and increasingly of con-troversy in public and then political discussions. In part, it could be argued, this was driven by international political developments. Already in 1979 the revolution in Iran had drawn a link between Islam and politics, and this at a time when the Lebanese civil war, which broke out in 1975, was increas-ingly (and simplistically) being analysed as a conflict based on confessional rivalries, especially between Muslims and Christians. During the 1980s violent opposition movements to certain Arab regimes (Syria and Egypt especially) were marking themselves as Islamic. These events contributed to the growing number of refugees knocking at Europe's doors and, together with tendencies among the already immigrated communities sympathetic to such movements, were creating the kinds of active links which had characterised aspects of the Turkish unrest leading up to the military coup in September 1980. Such political mobilisation, linking movements between émigré communities with the country of origin, became a critical dimension of the Algerian civil war in its relations with certain parts of the Algerian communities in France.

How deep this link spread remains a contested issue. But it contributed to the beginning securitisation of discussions about the integration of Muslims in Europe. A report published in early 1992 by the then Dutch Internal Security Services suggested:

> Although it only appears occasionally in western Europe, the terrorism carried out by Islamic fundamentalist groups must still be feared, especially when its activities are under the influence of a state such as Iran. Terror violence arising out of a mixture of ideological and separatist elements also appears, still mainly abroad, out of conflicts around groups such as Sikhs and Tamils. Through the presence of representatives of these Asian populations in the Netherlands, the BVD remains attentive to the possible implications for our security. (Netherlands 1992, quoted in Nielsen 1994)

These beginnings of a securitisation of Islam in Europe coincided with the period when the children of the immigrant generation were coming of age, especially in Britain and France – this process ran up to a decade later in other parts of Europe due to the fact that, in very general terms, the process of family reunion had run that much later.[1] A growing number of young people of Muslim background were starting to engage in domestic politics already from the late 1980s, as they came out of schools and colleges and entered the labour market. It was difficult to get a hearing in the traditional local political networks for all kinds of reasons, including racism and the reluctance of existing holders of power to sponsor a totally new population sector within their organisations. One alternative route was to take to the street. The first instances of young people choosing to go this way were the 'affairs' of 1989: Rushdie in the spring in Britain and headscarves in France in the autumn. There is little doubt that the Dutch security assessment of 1992 had these events in mind.

By now it was becoming clear that there were other routes to political participation than traditional European election processes, local or national. The affairs of 1989 had been an expression of a process of collective mobilisation finding alternative routes to influence than voting and standing for election. The outbreak of war in the Gulf following the Iraqi invasion of Kuwait in the summer of 1990 was the first of a number of international political issues which were adopted as 'Muslim' issues, especially by these new generations. Not that their parents had not been interested in international developments, but they tended overwhelmingly to be those of the country of origin: Pakistanis followed developments in Kashmir very closely, Turks followed developments in Turkey, as we had seen during the 1980s, and Algerians looked to Algeria, as we saw in the 1990s. Their children retained those interests but they attached themselves to broader concerns felt to be Muslim. The US- and UK-led invasion to expel Iraq from Kuwait in early 1991 led many young Muslims to join forces with other groups protesting the war, something of a rehearsal for the much stronger and much more visible convergence of interest groups coming together in 'Stop the War' alliances when Iraq itself was invaded in March 2003, most notably in the massive demonstration in London on 15 February that year. Throughout the 1990s, the war in Bosnia in connection with the collapse of Yugoslavia, followed by the war in Kosovo, as well as events in the northern Caucasus (especially Chechnya), had strengthened the sense of a group of Muslim causes which mobilised young people and even, in the minds of some, raised questions about their future security in Europe.

In parallel with the slow progress through the formal political system of parties and elections and the rather faster, but also more provocative, progress in public campaigning under some form of Muslim identity, Muslim organisations were developing their experience and networks, strengthening their ability to participate in and have an impact on their environment. Many of these organisations had grown out of movements and organisations with long experience in the countries of origin. They had often cut their teeth on opposition to European colonial powers. Among them the Muslim Brotherhood (among Arabs), the Deobandis, Brelwis and Jama'at-i-Islami (among South Asians), the Tablighi-Jamaat (of Indian origin but very adeptly crossing over ethnic boundaries), and Milli Görüş, Süleymancis and the Diyanet (among Turks, the last representing the Turkish government) were some of the most noticeable organisations. But while they were of overseas origin, they gradually metamorphosed (at varying speeds, to varying degrees, and in different ways) under the impact of their new environments and to meet the demands of their European constituencies (see e.g. Maréchal 2008; Masud 2000). But with the passage of time the internal processes of many of these organisations, and of the Muslim communities more broadly, themselves became subject to internal challengers as newer generations demanded a say.

There remain sections of Muslim communities that have maintained separation from the various political processes which have been summarised. There are those, especially among the immigrant generations, which hardly ever connected with their new surroundings beyond the strictly economic – in employment, receiving various forms of social welfare support, etc. – or in the receipt of basic services, mainly medical care. In cities with larger interrelated ethnic communities there are levels of collective support mechanisms which are difficult to quantify and which are largely invisible to the outsider. But there is another section, especially among younger educated people, which has deliberately sought to isolate itself from what are perceived as the corrupting, even infidel influences of society at large. Often lumped together by observers under the heading 'Salafi', they are not an organised group, at least not in any formal sense, but are informal networks which often identify themselves by a common attachment to one or other learned religious authority. The attachment is usually loose, and attachments can change, often without too much difficulty, although in some instances such a network can take on the character of a person-centred cult in which expectations of loyalty can be strong.

In setting out to explore the various dimensions of Muslim political participation outlined above, the starting point for the first part of the book is a series of five case studies of specific experiences in electoral politics. The case of Muslims' political participation in Belgium represents its own distinct situation in Europe but research on this issue is scarce. Fatima Zibouh considers that, from a post-migration angle, analysis of political participation has been mainly focused on foreign origin, and more specifically on ethnic origins: Italian, Maghrebi, Turkish, or sub-Saharan. The lack of research on the political participation of Muslims might be explained by a francophone Belgian national context that is strongly influenced by the French republican tradition which tends to ignore the individual's ethno-cultural distinctiveness. Several factors, such as easy access to Belgian citizenship, or the high demographic concentration of Turkish and Moroccan minorities in a few municipalities, make the Muslim community in Belgium a highly valuable asset at each election. In this chapter political participation is, firstly, tackled from a conventional theoretical point of view. Secondly, the analysis focuses on both the political participation of elected political representatives of Muslim origin, who represent 20% of all the elected body of the Region of Bruxelles-Capitale (Brussels), and the voting behaviour of Muslim citizens – through the so-called ethnic vote. Finally, social network sociology is used as a theoretical framework. This allows Zibouh to tackle the mobilisation of religious social networks, through the role of mosques and Muslim associations during political campaigns.

A very different kind of locality is investigated by Maike Didero, who bases her analysis on the structurationist theories of Bordieu and Giddens. In June 2009 the Confederation for Peace and Fairness (BFF) registered for the municipal council elections in the city of Bonn. This was the first case in Germany of a local voter association founded exclusively by Muslims. In spite of their Muslim membership, however, the BFF's founders fervently insist on not being a Muslim party. Reasons for its foundation may be found in the enabling and at the same time constraining structures inherent in both the German political system and the present public discourse on Islam and integration. At the same time, the BFF's creation cannot be explained without highlighting the activities of the individual members. Due to their personal capabilities and resources they were able launch a successful election campaign in an extremely short period of time and to win two seats on the city council. The duality of structure and agency as displayed in the example of the BFF is at the core of structurationist theories by Bourdieu and Giddens. This chapter therefore introduces an analytical framework based on these theories. It serves to explain the emergence of this new political actor, the strategies employed by its members and the reasons for their success. Looking at the historical development of discourses and legal institutions in Germany, as structuring and structured by activities in the political field, will help explain why the creation of this 'non-Muslim' party seems a paradox to many German citizens and was thus heavily opposed.

Jonatan Bäckelie and Göran Larsson analyse young Swedish Muslims' attitudes towards democratic processes in relation to Swedish political parties. Based on a survey among approximately 250 young Muslims that are affiliated to the Swedish youth organisation SUM (Sweden's Young Muslims), the chapter outlines how young Muslims position themselves in relation to the political left-right spectrum. The analysis is located in relation to the general situation of Muslims in Sweden and to the public discussion about Muslims in local and national elections. The survey's findings lead us to conclude that the political left-right spectrum is hardly relevant to this group of young Muslims. While the majority of the respondents self-identify as either somewhat or clearly to the left, in seven out of twenty-five specific political proposals the group show a clear sentiment towards what could be called conservative values (usually considered to be located to the right of the political spectrum). The chapter shows that no party seems to fully correspond to the full range of sentiments held by the majority of respondents, effectively leaving them without a fully representative political alternative. If anything is a problem for this group of respondents, it is not a lack of interest or knowledge about politics, but rather one of representation.

Moving to the edge of the former Soviet Union, one encounters several distinct attitudes among Lithuania's Muslims towards participation in democratic political processes, which roughly correspond to the four constitutive components of the Lithuanian Muslim community. Egdūnas Račius shows that the patterns of the Lithuanian Tatars and Soviet-time colonists' political participation (first of all in the form of voter profile but also in the forms of other conventional and unconventional political participation) are hardly distinguishable from those of the majority of citizens. Ultimately, of the four groups of Lithuania's Muslims the most interesting are Lithuanian citizens who have converted to Islam because their attitudes towards participation in political processes can be presumed to have been shaped and influenced by numerous experiences and factors of both an internal and an external nature, major among which are different levels of personal and group socialisation and access to and the influence of 'Islamic' texts and other (especially on-line) material. As converts are usually very keen on painstakingly observing the rules and regulations of their newly adopted religion, as they see them, it is to be expected that the 'Islamic factor' should have a profound influence on how converts perceive democracy as a political system *per se*, its compatibility with Islam, and finally their personal decision to take or not to take part in the democratic political process.

Britain and France are often presented as opposites, one with a strong communitarian multicultural heritage and the other with the individualist foundations of state secularism. In both countries Salima Bouyarden points out that Islam is itself a multicultural religion in the sense that it is followed by many different ethnic and national groups. The organisation of the Muslim communities of these countries is today still in process. This chapter on British and French Muslim communities investigates how these two multicultural societies located in two different systems are working. What are the different aspects of present Muslim political participation on both local and national levels? An analysis of their respective histories shows how relations between the younger generation and their voting patterns, their political engagement and their Muslim identity has been influenced by the past. In this context Bouyarden then focuses, through an investigation of the emergence of Muslim women in politics, on their motivations and the difficulties they might have encountered, on whether one can talk of the existence of a 'Muslim vote'.

But political participation is not just about voting, as previously indicated. In many countries in the world, there are parliamentary assemblies where everyone has a vote but voting is organised by some form of ethnic, national or religious communal categorisation. This may be by tradition rather than by formal requirement, as in Malaysia where certain parties are conventionally defined as Malay, Tamil or Chinese. Or it may be a formal dimension of the electoral system, as in Pakistan or Iran where there are reserved seats for specific religious minority communities. Or it may be as in the Lebanese system, where the vote is free but for confessionally allocated seats in the National Assembly. In Europe, the idea of a 'Muslim vote' has on occasion tempted both existing political parties and Muslim individuals or organisations into seeking to mobilise it. They have often, though not always, discovered that it has been more imaginary than real. However, it emerges that the political processes are such that there are other ways of having an impact on local and national politics other than purely through elections – as any organiser of public demonstrations knows. The second part of the volume takes a closer look at cases illustrating this.

Franck Frégosi's analysis of the larger picture seeks to demystify the subject. He reminds us of the truism that the Muslims of Europe, just as elsewhere in the world, have different visions of their religion, of what is Islam, sometimes they are almost opposed. Their attitudes towards religion range from the strictest ways of practising it to a critical attitude towards the ritual practices.

While some young Muslims are deeply religious because they believe in being concerned citizens and are politically active, numerous others do not use their faith as the only prism through which they look at their everyday lives and are active within society. Being a Muslim does not necessarily mean having a life centred only on religion; therefore Muslims do not only mobilise to achieve religious goals. In this chapter Frégosi compares these various mobilisations of people with Muslim backgrounds in order to underline the main diverging and converging lines between them in terms of social involvement (conflicted or consensual mobilisation), related or not to claims of citizenship (minority or civic mobilisation), and political partnerships with other social and political forces. He rather provocatively perhaps points also to those individuals of Muslim background who have become activists against Islam. One may ask, at what point can Muslims in the minority environment cease being Muslims, or can they not escape?

The Danish cartoons controversy of 2005–6 was a test of how Muslims might act on the political stage on an issue which touched them deeply. Lasse Lindekilde discusses the level of political integration displayed by the Danish Muslims engaged in the controversy. Conceptualising political integration as a multi-dimensional phenomenon distinguishing three aspects of political integration – a) political trust in democratic institutions, b) adherence to liberal-democratic values such as freedom of speech and secularism, and c) political participation in the polis – the chapter tests the degree of political integration of Danish Muslims against a unique database on political claims-making by the Danish Muslims involved in the cartoons controversy. In contrast to the widespread public perception of the controversy, the chapter argues that the Danish Muslims involved in public claims-making displayed a considerable degree of political integration. Despite the public uproar concerning the so-called 'imam delegations' seeking support in the Muslim world, Danish Muslims actually demonstrated considerable trust in democratic institutions, relying mainly on procedural forms of claims-making and turning to internationalisation of the issue only as a last resort. Furthermore, Lindekilde argues that the claims-making of Danish Muslim activists revealed alternative interpretations of fundamental liberal-democratic values and also displayed significant adherence to the basic principles of these values through commitment to non-violence and the translation of religious despair into a secular, rights-based mode of justification. Finally, the chapter argues that the level of political participation of Danish Muslims was particularly high during the cartoons controversy and that this high level of political claims-making and mobilisation should be understood as active citizenship rather than 'cultural backlash'.

In the aftermath of the terrorist attack in the US in September 2001, Madrid in 2003 and London in 2005, a new emphasis on national identity and national belonging has increasingly replaced multicultural approaches dismissed under the accusation of having nurtured homegrown terrorists. Muslims have been the main target of counterterrorism policies aimed at monitoring and governing the 'Islamic threat'. In this polarised environment, characterised by a mounting anti-Islamic atmosphere, it has become very difficult for Muslims to work and be recognised as a part of European society. This is particularly true for Muslim women activists, who struggle against, on the one hand, stereotypical perceptions of Muslim women while also having to cope with traditions of male social dominance in both Muslim and non-Muslim communities. Alessia Belli analyses the growing political visibility of Muslim women in Italy and the UK. The lens of gender offers a privileged insight into the two political systems and stimulates an interesting debate on national identity. The study sets out to counter mainstream research approaches on Muslims in Europe that focus on deviant behaviours and terrorism-related issues. Instead of blindly following the 'domestication of Islam' agenda pursued by many European governments, this research looks at and tries to understand the interesting dynamics involving Muslims that are taking place across Europe.

The last chapter in this section adopts a local focus in its examination of internal debates about political participation among Muslims in the city and *banlieues* of Lyon, France. Drawing upon ethnographic research and interviews conducted in mosque communities and Islamic associations, Fareen Parvez argues that beliefs about political participation in the form of state engagement differ across class and religious ideology. Middle-class Muslim activists participate in a politics of recognition, directly engaging the state and viewing political participation as a form of minority integration. Practising an avowedly 'mainstream' or 'moderate' Islam, they are critical of the growth of Salafist Islam in Lyon's banlieues and the lack of political participation. At the other end of this spectrum, the poor Salafist Muslims in this study viewed political engagement as both profane and dangerous, after years of state surveillance and social and economic exclusion. In the aftermath of the collapse of civil societies in their neighbourhoods, they practise a form of antipolitics, whereby they have valorised private life instead of public life, retreating into moral parallel communities, withdrawn from the state. Further, they feel that major Islamic associations are loyal foremost to the state and do not represent 'Islam of the banlieues.' In elaborating these various dynamics, Parvez also explores the different stakes involved in being viewed as political actors. Paradoxically, it is precisely poor Muslims' withdrawal from politics and distance from the state that contributes to their top-down politicisation. This set of arguments departs from existing literature by privileging the role of the state, local histories, and class relations – rather than struggles over immigrant identity.

Moving from the border region between individual and collective manifestations of participation, the third part of this book provides four case studies of how more institutionally based routes of participation can function. The concept of institution here is broad, covering not only formal institutions but also collective actors with a deep-rooted history of collective identity as well as newer communities which have established a strong local identity. Certainly, the political participation analysed in these chapters relates to the wider polity, but it also relates to other Muslim actors (nationally and internationally) and also to contesting internal actors seeking to play a part in how the shared collective locates and presents itself to the wider public.

Some Muslim organisations have sought to find a Europe-level role without much success in practice. The image of Muslim representation in Europe has been aided by international organisations like the European Council for Fatwa and Research (ECFR), whose prestigious network of scholars purportedly addresses the concerns of western Muslims while acting as one of the few representative voices of European Islam. Adil Hussain Khan argues that this image of a unified 'European Islam' does indeed, at first glance, appear to be an impressive accomplishment for Europe's Muslim communities. But it is not the outcome of local efforts from European Muslims at grassroots level. Rather, organisations like the ECFR are the result of a top-down approach intended to project an image of European Islam. This is reflected in the non-European majority membership of the Council. Headquartered in Dublin, despite Ireland having one of the smallest Muslim populations in Western Europe, the relationship between such an ambitious international Islamic institution and the local community makes for tensions as the simultaneously local, continental, and international dimensions pull in different directions.

One of the oldest established Muslim communities in eastern central Europe is that of the Tatars, whose history dates back to the fourteenth century. They first settled in the Polish-Lithuanian Commonwealth in the fourteenth century as prisoners of war and refugees, and later mercenaries brought by the Lithuanian Duke to fight the enemies of the country. Agata S. Nalborczyk recounts how, in return for military service under the command of Lithuanian princes, Tatars were granted land together with a social status similar to that of the local nobility. They were also granted the right to practise their religion, erect mosques and serve under their own military banners. Subsequently, they remained an integral part of the social and military structures of the country, and this narrative remains a strong dimension of the public identification of Tatars with the Polish nation. It was therefore natural that during the Danish cartoons affair, the Polish state authorities supported Muslim protests against publishing the cartoons, and stressed Tatar loyalty as Polish citizens. Nalborczyk argues that the historical role of the Tatars was the reason for their continued strong acceptance as integrated and active citizens by present-day Polish society and by the state authorities.

A very different strong community identity is that of the Alevis, a community with a deep heterodox tradition in central and eastern Anatolia. As Deniz Koşulu shows, the political marginalisation of the community in the Turkish republic since the collapse of the Ottoman empire has created the foundation for a renewal and a degree of re-invention, as Turkish official restraints have been withdrawn in recent decades, and émigré communities in western Europe have taken advantage of the greater space for maneouvre which the political environments there afford. With a focus on France, the author shows how different strategies are being tested both internally within the community and externally in relation to the authorities with a view to maximising the political and other benefits perceived to be available.

Leicester, a medium-sized city in the East Midlands is on the way to becoming one of the first British cities where former migrants will be a larger group than the native population, a prospect which seems not to be particularly panicking the city's general population. Carolina Ivanescu looks at how the Muslim community, not the largest of the immigrant-origin communities in the city (that is the Hindu community), has absorbed the experiences of the changing British – and local – discourses of ethnic minority. The original quite crude racialised efforts to keep out South Asians expelled from East Africa in the 1960s, which failed, gave way gradually to a local understanding of plural citizenship, in which religion and ethnicity are actively mobilised, and in which concepts of civil religion are engaged both by the communities and by local government.

It is unfortunately the case that the various aspects of these complex issues are discussed in public – and too often by researchers – as if the current state of affairs is the end of an historical process. Change and development in the past we can deal with but we find it rather more difficult to take on board that we are actually in the middle of a process, a process which continues, and whose character (let alone whose results) we can only vaguely foresee. To underline this point, the last two case studies, in part four of the book, look at boundaries, at developments which look forward rather than back.

Tim Peace examines the processes and realities of Muslim participation in both local and national politics in Britain through a case study of the Respect Party. This party is unique in Europe as it is the first party dominated by Muslim leaders that has achieved any notable electoral success. Formed in 2004 in the wake of the mobilisation of Muslims against the war in Iraq, it has had occasional electoral success both nationally and locally despite an electoral system in Britain that effectively penalises minor parties. Constituencies with high numbers of ethnic minorities have in the past always represented 'safe seats' for the Labour Party. The paper details how the Respect Party has played a key role in drastically reducing this support, particularly amongst Muslim voters. It also shows how Respect has changed the 'rules of the game' and forced mainstream parties to re-think their electoral strategies in response to its success. It is argued that relationships with civil society organisations have been one of the crucial factors in helping Respect to achieve this success. As a party that evolved directly from a social movement, it could rely on the pre-existing networks that had been built up with various sections of civil society as a solid base for support. It has also been active in cultivating links with mosques, faith-based organisations, community groups and trade unions. Most recently, at a by-election in Bradford in early 2012, it appears that the party has also become a route for dissatisfaction among a younger genera-tion of Muslims, significantly including women on a large scale, against their parents' attempts to keep control of the political system locally.

In a sketch on the German elections the Turkish-German comedian Fatih Cevikollu makes fun of ethnic minorities. He repeatedly interrupts his perfor-mance to affront the audience for laughing at his racist jokes. Riem Spielhaus takes up the ways in which comedy as subversion can challenge open and hidden racism and senses of superiority while turning the surveillance of Muslims against the spectators. Most surveys on political participation con-centrate on active and passive elective participation, the measurement of trust in legal and political institutions, adherence to liberal-democratic values, degrees of organisation, and protest movements. This chapter, however, looks at a different field of politics: political satire and other subversive strate-gies that allow subalterns to address injustice, discrimination and structural exclusion from the political field. In an atmosphere of suspicion and verbal taboos, political satire is gaining ground by addressing and criticising attempts at domestication and securitisation. Ironically – especially after the cartoon crisis – Muslim comedy and satire has entered mainstream entertainment in European countries and North America. Muslims' contributions to politically grounded satire, the field of humour, of absurdity, ridicule and subversion is worth examining in terms of content and as political strategies for addressing the unspeakable.

In sum, the evidence of these case studies emphasises the multiplicity of experiences and circumstances which impact on the political participation of Muslims in European society. The question of whether Muslims want to take part in the political processes – or even deserve to, if one listens to certain neo-nationalist tendencies – fades into insignificance once one scratches just a little bit below the surface of public debate. The wealth of different tactics and strat-egies chosen, and sometimes activated simultaneously, are evidence enough of both the will and the ability. A countervailing force remains, however – the extent to which the majority is willing to accept and recognise this, for clearly many of the tactical choices made by Muslims individually and collectively are constrained and focused by what the majority allows as legitimate.

The chapters in this volume were originally presented at a conference held in Copenhagen in October 2010 organised by the Centre for European Islamic Thought, a project of the Danish National Research Foundation. In preparing the conference and this volume, I am particularly grateful to my two admin-istrative assistants Line Stæhr and Emil Saggau. Cooperation with colleagues at Edinburgh University Press has, as I have come to expect, been exemplary.

Finally my thanks go to the chapter authors for their re-working of their writings, and for their patience in waiting for the editorial process to finish. I trust they will accept my apologies for any mistakes which inadvertently may have escaped my attention.

Copenhagen, July 2012

Note

1. In Britain non-European labour recruitment was first restricted in the first Commonwealth Immigration Act, of 1962, while similar measures were introduced in most of mainland western Europe in connection with the economic downturn of 1973–4, usually associated with the sharp rise in oil prices starting in 1972. The restrictions in labour immigration resulted in a marked increase in family reunion.

References

Bowen, J. R. (2010), *Can Islam be French? Pluralism and Pragmatism in a Secularist State*, Princeton: Princeton University Press.

Maréchal, B. (2008), *The Muslim Brothers in Europe: Roots and Discourse*, Leiden: Brill.

Masud, M. K. (ed.) (2000), *Travellers in Faith: Studies of the Tablighi Jama'at as a Transnational Islamic Movements for Faith Renewal*, Leiden: Brill.

Netherlands, Binnenlandse Veiligheidsdienst (1992), *Ontwikkelingen op het gebied van de binnenlandse veiligheid*, 11 February.

Nielsen, J. S. (1994), 'Will religious fundamentalism become increasingly violent?', *International Journal on Group Rights*, vol. 2, pp. 197–209.

Sinno, A. H. (2009), 'Muslim underrepresentation in American politics', in Abdulkader H. Sinno, *Muslims in Western Politics*, Bloomington: Indiana University Press, pp. 69–95.

PART ONE

• • •

LAYING FOUNDATIONS: NATIONAL AND LOCAL ELECTIONS

2

MUSLIM POLITICAL PARTICIPATION IN BELGIUM: AN EXCEPTIONAL POLITICAL REPRESENTATION IN EUROPE

Fatima Zibouh

1. Introduction

Compared with other major European cities, the Brussels-Capital Region has a unique configuration in terms of the political representation of elected representatives descended from diverse ethnocultural groups, and in particular Muslim elected representatives. Nearly one out of five members of the Parliament of the Brussels-Capital Region is of Muslim origin. This is all the more unique given that, for the first time in Brussels and in the entire European Union, one of the seats in the Brussels Parliament is held by a Muslim member who wears a headscarf (Mahinur Ozdemir).

This political representation lies within the scope of a city where more than 50% of the inhabitants are foreigners or of foreign origin. It is, however, difficult to have precise figures regarding the number of Muslims in the capital. Nevertheless, their presence is significant enough – especially in certain municipalities of Brussels – to have a relative impact on electoral results.

The objective of this chapter is to understand the explanatory factors regarding this political representation, which is quite unusual in Europe, by formulating the hypothesis of the deciding influence of institutional parameters combined with the demographic evolution and community mobilisation of Muslims.

Political participation covers a large scope including different modes of individual or collective action. This chapter is aimed at examining the political participation of Muslims – in the conventional sense[1] (Mayer and Perrineau 1992) – in the Brussels Region, and more precisely its political representation through the examination of the evolution of the electoral behaviour of Belgian Muslim citizens and elected representatives in the Brussels regional elections. We shall not discuss the political representation of Muslim elected representatives at municipal level (deputy mayors and municipal councillors) in order to focus more on the mandates of regional members.

The present chapter is based on documentary work as well as an empirical approach carried out using interviews which were conducted with Brussels MPs and community stakeholders mobilised before the elections as well as an ethnographic observation of the election campaign, and will examine this question in five parts. Firstly, an evaluation of the literature on the political participation of Muslims in Belgium will be carried out, underlining the gaps in terms of work dedicated to this specific question. Secondly, given the sensitive nature of this subject, we shall explain the process of ethnicification of the Muslim identity and define what is meant by the term 'Muslim'. Thirdly, we shall examine the different trends in the voting behaviour of Muslims in France and in Belgium via the question of the existence of a possible 'Muslim vote'. Fourthly, we shall study the evolution of the political representation of Muslim elected representatives in the capital by making a quantitative analysis since the creation of the Brussels-Capital Region. Fifthly, we shall present explanatory factors enabling a better understanding of the special character of the political representation of Muslim MPs in the Brussels Region. Finally, we shall conclude with a few recommendations, taking into consideration a prospective dimension of the political participation of Muslims in Brussels.

2. Evaluation of the literature on the political participation of Muslims in Belgium

The academic literature in the area of the political participation of people of foreign origin in Belgium began in the 1990s. By focusing on the relationship between ethnic group and political authority, Martiniello (1992) was among the first in Belgium to question the role played by political stakeholders in the integration of ethnic communities. Work regarding political participation in Belgium was then carried out by taking into consideration foreign origin in general (Martiniello 1998; Lambert 1999; Réa 2002; Jacobs, Martiniello, Réa 2002; Jacobs, Bousetta, Réa, Martiniello, Swyngedouw 2006; Réa, Jacobs, Teney, Delwit 2010) or a specific national origin: Italian (Martiniello 1992), Moroccan (Bousetta 2001), Turkish (Manço and Manço 1992), sub-Saharan (Kagné 2001) and Maghrebian (Zibouh 2010).

However, as regards the study of the political participation of Muslims in particular, there are few in-depth analyses of the question, whereas the situation in Belgium is quite unique with respect to this dimension (Zibouh 2011). These gaps could be explained among others by the Belgian francophone national context, which is strongly influenced by the French republican tradition which tends to erase the ethnocultural differences of people, whereas in Flanders,[2] the Netherlands or English-speaking countries, cultural or religious diversity is recognised more easily (Jacobs and Réa 2005). In the Netherlands, for some time now they have spoken of the 'Political participation and identities of Muslims in non-Muslim states' (Shadid and van Koningsveld 1996). In the literature from English-speaking countries, it has also been easier to speak of 'Muslims' Place in the American Public Square' (Bukhari Nyang, Ahmad, Esposito, 2004) and 'Muslims in Westerns Politics' (Sinno 2009). Recently in France, there have been a few surveys regarding the voting behaviour of Muslims (Dargent 2003, 2010; Brouard, Tiberj 2005). In Belgium, more specific analyses have been conducted with respect to the cooperation between Muslims and local authorities in a municipality of Brussels (Manço, Kanmaz 2005), the challenge of the Muslim vote (Sandri, De Decker 2008) and the role played by the political leadership of Muslims in the management of Islam at local level (Torrekens 2009).

3.   The process of ethnicification of the Muslim identity

Generally speaking, many works exist on various subjects with a direct or indirect link with Islam in Belgium, but Muslims in Belgium have not been the object of quantitative, systematic and in-depth studies. Furthermore, the lack of official data related to religious belonging makes it difficult to establish representative quotas and samples to study the Muslim community in Belgium.

In this framework, it is still difficult to speak of the political participation of Muslims. However, in what is said by politicians and in the news as well as in academic literature, we can identify an evolution in the denomination of people with a Moroccan, Turkish or Pakistani background, who are considered more and more as Muslims in the sociological sense of the term. Generally speaking, otherness is no longer defined as Arab, Moroccan or Turkish, but rather according to an assigned Muslim identity. We have thus witnessed a process of ethnicification of the term Muslim in current public debates (Fassin and Fassin 2006), although the perfectly rigorous demonstration of this hypothesis remains to be carried out.

Despite this categorisation, one must avoid making improper generalisations when studying certain groups of individuals, by not essentialising different forms of belonging which have unchanging traits. The Muslim community is far from forming a monolithic group, due to its ethnic, socio-economic, linguistic and cultural diversity, among others.

The ethnographic observations made during election campaigns show that the claims of Muslims do not necessarily concern common political stances, yet there are certain shared themes such as the fight against discrimination. Even if there is a risk of essentialising people of Muslim ancestry or who are from Muslim countries (Kateb 2004), we have chosen not to use the definition of the term Muslim in a strictly religious sense only, but rather to have a more general sociological interpretation. Therefore, the term 'Muslim' will not necessarily be defined as an identity which is exclusively religious. We take up the suggestion by A. H. Sinno (2009), who applies the term Muslim to elected representatives who define themselves as being Muslim by faith, and/or who have at least one parent who is Muslim by faith, and/or who belong to a group which is considered as being traditionally Muslim:

> I do not consider "Muslim" to necessarily indicate a religious identity, but an identity that may have religious, racial, political, or cultural dimensions. (. . .). I therefore consider a parliamentarian to be Muslim if he or she is Muslim by faith or has at least one parent who is Muslim by faith or belongs to a group that is traditionally Muslim. (Sinno 2009: 70)

Secularised or agnostic Muslims, or even atheists of Muslim culture,[3] will therefore be included in this categorisation.

4.   Studies of the electoral behaviour of Muslims

An analysis of the political participation of candidates and Muslim elected representatives on the political scene without an understanding of the voting behaviour of electors does not allow an in-depth examination of the transformations in the political configuration of representative authorities. This type of approach involves examining the question of the vote conditioned by community belonging and, more precisely, in this case of the 'Muslim vote', which implies that a Muslim elector would vote for a Muslim candidate or that a group of Muslims would urge people to vote for a particular Muslim or non-Muslim candidate. Here we may detect the danger of social determinism (Lazarsfeld, Berelson, Gaudet 1944: 27)[4] and the essentialisation of the act of voting which reduces the motivations of electors to the assertion of their religious identity. In reality, ethnicity or religiosity should only be considered as variables similar to others such as voting according to geographic proximity, age or gender, for example.

4.1.   *Studies on the electoral behaviour of French Muslims*

Research on the political behaviour of Muslims is relatively recent and not very well developed in Belgium. In France, however, Muxel (1988) examined the question of the weight of the religious variable among young people from an immigrant background. Jocelyne Cesari (2001) has also corroborated the hypothesis of the left-wing vote of French Muslims. One of the first studies which truly examined the voting behaviour of French citizens of Muslim faith via an extensive survey (Dargent 2003) shows that these electors are more interested in politics and vote left wing. Furthermore, based on CEVIPOF data[5] from large samples – representative of registered electors and selected according to quotas – Dargent (2009) shows that during the second round of the French presidential elections in 2007 this firm attachment to the left meant that 95% of Muslims voted for Ségolène Royal compared with 5% for Nicolas Sarkozy. By means of an extensive survey conducted in 2005 based on a large sample that was representative of French people of north African, African and Turkish origin, Brouard and Tiberj (2005) also highlighted the massive left-wing vote of Muslims.

4.2.   Studies on the electoral behaviour of Belgian Muslims

What is the situation in Belgium and, more specifically, in Brussels? During the 2004 regional elections, CEVIPOL conducted an extensive survey at the exit of polling stations in order to study the voting behaviour of Belgians. This study is quite interesting given the fact that it also examined the vote of electors of Muslim faith (who described themselves as such in the questionnaire) in this framework. The results thus showed that 45.7% of the Muslim electorate voted for the PS (Socialist Party), 13.3% for the MR (Mouvement Réformateur – Liberal Alliance Party) and 7.1% for the CDH (Centre Démocrate Humaniste – Christian Democratic Party), (Sandri, De Decker 2008: 44).

The same study was repeated for the 2007 legislative elections. Of the 2,807 people interviewed randomly, 1,319 lived in Brussels. Although the question-naire was used on the eve of federal elections, the results from the Brussels Region were isolated. Some interesting information may be drawn from this survey. Firstly, the percentage of respondents who declared that they were of Muslim faith is estimated to be 11.8% (compared with 3.8% in Wallonia). Secondly, generally speaking, the firm attachment to the left of citizens of Muslim faith was confirmed. Thus, at the 2007 legislative elections, 42.3% of Muslims residing in Brussels voted for the Socialist Party (PS), 16.7% for the Centre Démocrate Humaniste (CDH), 14.7% for the Mouvement Réformateur (MR) and 12.2% for Ecolo. The Socialist Party therefore accounts for a large section of the Muslim electorate. Thirdly, according to this survey, whether or not Belgian citizens of Muslim faith practise their religion does not have a strong impact on their voting behaviour. Fourthly, the variable related to religious belonging or practice is not enough to explain the vote of the Muslim electorate. Other determining factors related to an often relatively low socio-professional status, age (more than half of the Muslims interviewed were under 34) and level of education (lower than the average of the other groups) may also explain the firm attachment to the left (Sandri and de Decker 2008).

Without isolating the religious variable, the voting intentions at the 2007 federal elections of secondary school students in Brussels from an immigrant background were also studied (Teney and Jacobs 2009) by establishing the possible electoral particularities of these new electors. A large quantitative survey among 1,283 students, which took their origin into consideration, showed a tendency for young people of Moroccan and Turkish origin to vote for the Socialist Party.

Generally speaking, all of these surveys – both French and Belgian – show that the degree of religious practice is not a determining variable in the Muslim vote. However, socio-economic status plays a more determining role. This being the case, it would be useful to elaborate extensive surveys which would take the strictly religious dimension into account, by integrating the variable which consists in knowing whether a Muslim elector would vote for a candidate based on his or her Muslim faith.

4.3.   Studies on the 'Muslim vote' in particular?

While there is less interest in the question of the Catholic vote in the area of political research, it is interesting to note that the question of the Muslim vote is becoming part of the public debate. However, the observation of certain practices leads one to think that the role played by the particularity of this type of vote is much less than what one might imagine. The observation of certain electoral choices of Muslim citizens tends to be focused on themes related to the fight against discrimination rather than on the Muslim character of candidates.

The hypothesis regarding the practice of the preferential vote via the ethnic (or Muslim) vote could explain the high level of political representation of Muslim elected representatives. This explanatory element would not be enough on its own, however, otherwise the results of the successive failures of Muslim religious parties would be paradoxical. The explanatory factors are discussed in the last part of this chapter, but above all it should be underlined that voting is an individual act influenced by several parameters, and that the electoral weight of the political party of candidates also constitutes an important dimension in the voter's choice.

5.   Quantitative approaches regarding the evolution of the political representation of Muslims in the Brussels-Capital Region

In order to have a general idea of the political representation of Muslim MPs in the Brussels-Capital Region, it is useful to develop a quantitative approach to allow a better understanding of the evolution. Given the lack of official data which take into consideration ethnic, cultural and religious affiliations, Muslim elected representatives are first identified according to an onomastic approach. But a name does not necessarily indicate a belonging to a group or an affiliation of any type, especially since Islam does not concern only Turkish or Moroccan immigrants. Identification is also based on the self-definition of elected representatives as being Muslim or of Muslim culture, as well as on the direct or indirect activation of the reference to Islam in their speeches and their electoral practice. The patronymic approach is therefore combined with a biographical analysis of Brussels regional MPs. Based on this methodology, we obtain the following findings:

Table 2.1 Muslim MPs in the Brussels-Capital Region (1989–2009)

Election	PS	MR	CDH	ECOLO	SPA-SPIRIT	Total	% of the total number of seats
1989	0	0	0	0	0	0	0%
1995	3	0	0	1	0	4	5.3%
1999	4	2	0	2	1	9	12%
2004	13	2	1	0	1	17	19.1%
2009	11	1	3	3	1	20	22.5%

This table presents the five elections held at regional level since the creation of the Brussels-Capital Region (BCR). The political parties presented are those which had at least one Muslim MP during these five terms, who was either French- or Dutch-speaking. Only the people who were members of the Brussels Parliament are considered here. Some of them were not elected directly, but ended up having seats as substitutes. Others were elected but did not take up their seats due to the allocation of executive mandates or a change in their parliamentary function involving other plenary assemblies such as the Senate. Furthermore, some of them left their party during the election period. Beyond these individual considerations, this table presents all of the Muslim MPs who had a seat in the Brussels Parliament, either for a short or a long period of time. Finally, the percentage of the total number of seats in the Parliament of the BCR was calculated on an evolving basis, due to the increase in the number of seats (75 until 1999 and 89 since 2004).

Based on these figures, it is interesting to note that the number of Muslim MPs in the Parliament of the BCR rose from 0% in 1989 to 22.5% in 2009, i.e. more than one Brussels MP out of five. The 2004 elections represented a true turning point linked to the changes in the electoral code as well as to other factors, which we shall discuss below. The more significant presence of this category of elected representatives in the Socialist Party should also be noted. This being the case, it is important to put this number into perspective, considering the general score of the party, which made a breakthrough in the 2004 elections. Certain personal victories are inevitably related to the size of the parties these candidates belong to (Bousetta 1998). Furthermore, certain observers did not hesitate to establish a correlation between this victory and the presence of several candidates of foreign origin on the list of the Socialist Party. Although there was a slight decrease in this tendency within the Socialist Party for the 2009 elections, a greater mix was observed for the electoral lists of the other political parties, which could explain the general increase in the number of Muslim MPs.

Based on these data, how can we evaluate the level of representation of Muslim electors? According to Pitkin (1972), political representation must be a 'mirror' of the different groups and movements that make up society. In this respect, Marques Pereira and Nolasco (2001: 28) propose three basic elements to define a 'mirror representation' of the different groups which make up society: firstly, institutional instruments specifying the social composition of the different groups which make up the electorate; secondly, a political will on behalf of the electorate to vote for candidates who are like them; and thirdly, a diversified political representation on the electoral lists. The authors also add a system of proportional representation in order to favour political representation which mirrors society.

In this perspective, the body of elected representatives must be representative of the different political and sociological characteristics of the electorate. Martiniello (1998) defines political representation as being 'statistically correct when the percentage of elected representatives of immigrant origin reflects the percentage of the population of foreign origin in the electorate'. Given the lack of reliable estimates regarding the size of the Muslim community in the Brussels-Capital Region, it is difficult to evaluate its representation. Let us also mention the fact that a proportion of the Muslim community does not have the right to vote because of the conditions to become elector (nationals of other countries may vote in municipal elections if they fulfil certain conditions).

We shall not analyse the different profiles of its members, yet we must mention the significant diversity which exists in this category. In terms of religious practice, this includes everything from regular visits to the mosque to atheism and agnosticism. The profiles are also quite varied in terms of academic capital and careers. The mobilised fields of action are also very different and are far from being representative of a unified group in terms of specific claims.

Finally, it should be mentioned that for the first time since the 2004 Brussels regional elections, two elected socialist representatives of Muslim background were given government positions at regional and community level. Furthermore, these mandates were renewed following the 2009 elections. These were Fadila Laanan, Minister for Culture, Audiovisual and Youth of the French-speaking Community (the competence for youth was replaced in 2009 by Health and Equal Opportunities) and Emir Kir, with the function of Brussels State Secretary for Public Cleansing and Monuments and Sites (modified in 2009 to be included within the remit of Public Cleansing and Urbanism) and Minister for Social Action, Family and Sports (widened in 2009 to become Professional Training, Culture, School Transport and International Relations).

6. Explanatory factors of the political representation of Muslims in the Brussels Region

Our quantitative approach shows that the Brussels-Capital Region has a relatively significant political representation of elected representatives from diverse backgrounds compared with the Flemish and Walloon Regions, as well as with other European cities. The combination of a certain number of institutional and demographic parameters as well as common structuring might explain this particularity.

6.1.   *Institutional factors*

Firstly, Belgium makes use of a system of proportional representation for voting, which allows a more faithful representation of the different movements which make up the electorate compared with majority voting systems. A second important factor which contributes to the emergence of Muslim elected representatives is related to the weighting by half of the devolutive effect of the top box (or preferential voting). The effects of this new measure could be measured effectively for the 2000 municipal elections and the 2004 Brussels regional elections, which were marked by a greater representation of elected representatives from diverse backgrounds. Thirdly, the laws on nationality (1984, 1991, 1998 and 2000) have allowed more than 200,000 naturalisations since 1989 (Deboosere et al. 2009) in the Brussels-Capital Region alone. The change of nationality has of course given these people the right to vote. Finally, the fact that voting is obligatory in Belgium has often been omitted from the explanatory elements which allow an understanding of the special political configuration of people from an immigrant background in Brussels. Several studies show that disadvantaged people are often the ones who do not vote. The fact that voting is obligatory in Belgium forces these people from an immigrant background – who are often in disadvantaged socio-economic conditions – to vote, with a financial penalty if they fail to do so. But all of these factors are defined by the federal legislator and apply to the three regions. They therefore do not explain the specific situation in Brussels. It is therefore necessary to question the influence of demographic factors and community structuring.

6.2.   *Demographic factors*

The Brussels-Capital Region is characterised by quite exceptional diversity and multilingualism, in that more than half of the population are foreign or of foreign origin. Furthermore, certain areas of the capital have a high concentration of Muslim populations, in particular of Moroccan and Turkish origin. This concentration has an impact on the geographical distribution of votes and is therefore a determining element in understanding the political representation of Muslim elected representatives.

Generally speaking, we do not have reliable figures regarding the Muslim population in Brussels. The last census in 2001 was only able to take into consideration the nationality of origin of the population, and not religious belonging. Some indications do however provide approximations. Manço and Kanmaz (2004) estimate the Muslim population in the Brussels Region to be 162,000 – i.e. 39% of the total number of Muslims in Belgium – and therefore 16.5% of the total population of Brussels.[6] Furthermore, sociologist Jan Hertogen recently published figures which were much debated. According to him, there are 235,782 Muslims living in Brussels, i.e. close to 22%[7] of the population of Brussels. The debate which followed this announcement illustrates the challenge of clear scientific and methodological criteria. When dealing with such a sensitive subject, a rigorous statistical policy should be developed by means of a major survey, with a large enough and random representative sample. But, generally speaking, the abovementioned figures allow us to assume a more or less balanced political representation in the Parliament of the Brussels-Capital Region, in terms of the number of Muslim electors.

6.3. Factors related to community mobilisation

In addition to institutional and demographic factors, one must also question the role played by the collective action of this category of the electorate in political participation, in particular through community mobilisation, which is particularly concentrated in the Brussels Region (Jacobs, Phalet and Swyngedouw 2004; Lambert 2004). As an example, Torrekens (2007) refined the analysis of this demographic concentration at a more local level, by examining the presence of Muslim associations in certain neighbourhoods of Brussels. She showed that two-thirds of Muslim and cultural associations are concentrated in Schaerbeek, Molenbeek and Brussels City. Furthermore, studies (Jacobs, Phalet and Swyngedouw 2006) show that there are differences in the community involvement of people of Moroccan and Turkish origin, which appears to be more pronounced and better structured among the latter. This could be one of the reasons for the favourable results of candidates of Turkish origin. Let us mention that during the last elections, the second highest score of the Socialist Party was obtained by a candidate of Turkish origin, Emir Kir, just after that of the Minister-President of the Brussels-Capital Region, Charles Picqué. This clearly indicates the importance of taking into account the diversity within this category of the population when referring to the community or political mobilisation of the Muslim community. The absence of leadership and strong community structures in the Muslim community therefore explains why collective action and, more precisely, the influence of the structuring community of the latter are not the major factors in the political participation of Muslim elected representatives in the Brussels Region.

6.4. Effect of the interaction between explanatory factors

What could explain the particularity of the Brussels-Capital Region, given that it is not the only city which experiences significant population growth and relatively significant community mobilisation of immigrant populations, and that the institutional mechanisms apply throughout the country? The answer lies mainly in the interaction between these different explanatory factors which, together, result in this unique political representation of Muslims in the Belgian capital. But the particularity of Brussels lies above all in the structures of political opportunities and in its formal institutional dimension (Giugni 1995), or more precisely the 'structures of opportunities for political participation' (Martiniello 1997) mobilised by people from an immigrant background. In this respect, Maxwell (2010) illustrates the importance of the influence of national or regional institutions on political participation. As institutions become more open to the political mobilisation of people from an immigrant background, political participation gets stronger. He thus explains that in the French case, the republican framework discourages the political mobilisation of minorities. In this context, minorities have fewer opportunities to build networks that may mobilise participation in the face of socio-economic disadvantages. The characteristics of the political and social context in Brussels, which we have discussed, together with community mobilisation, allow a better understanding of how all of these factors – which are explained above – determine the access of certain groups to formal and state levels of authority. Furthermore, it is important to emphasise the role played, with respect to a relatively new electorate, by political parties[8] that want to include Muslim candidates on their electoral lists in order to win the most votes, in particular in certain neighbourhoods of Brussels.

7. Conclusion

This chapter has provided a review of the evolution of the political participation of Muslims in the Parliament of the Brussels-Capital Region. We have tried to understand the voting behaviour of Muslim citizens by examining a series of studies that have taken into consideration the different variables which explain the vote by this category of the population. We notice that the results are not always sufficient given that they are centred on one or more particular dimensions of voting behaviour. The challenge would be to develop studies which would make use of several variables: ethnic origin, choice based on conviction or philosophy, gender, age, level of education, socio-economic status and place of residence. In this perspective, we have noticed that quantitative analyses have become crucial in order to obtain reliable data on the Muslim community of Brussels and Belgium. This is all the more true as the same group asks the most questions about interculturality in the public debate. These data would also allow the prejudices which exist with respect to this minority to be overcome. These tools are also absolutely essential in order to allow a better evaluation of public policies.

As regards the political will of Muslim electors, we must differentiate between the mobilisations and community structures of people of Moroccan origin and those of Turkish origin. Our ethnographic observations show that among people of Moroccan origin, there is a lack of true community organisation that would have enough influence to define voting directives. Among those of Turkish origin, however, these modes of community action are relatively efficient, in particular as regards supporting a candidate. Nevertheless, there is no trace of any list of demands with claims specific to the Muslim community. Despite the lack of a strong community structuring of Muslims (with differences according to origin), the political representation of Muslims is ensured thanks to other institutional mechanisms as well as the diversity of the profiles of candidates on the electoral lists of certain political parties.

Generally speaking, in this chapter we have tried to illustrate the importance of political opportunity structures (Meyer 2004) favouring the political participation of Muslims. In Belgium and in Brussels in particular, these political opportunity structures are more favourable to the emergence of Muslim political representatives and, generally speaking, to those from diverse backgrounds. Nevertheless, the institutional factors would not have exclusive effects if we did not consider the demographic realities as well as the community density of the Brussels Region. With equal mobilisation, institutional political contexts increase or reduce the chances of success of certain collective mobilisations. Nevertheless, these political opportunity structures in Belgium should not underestimate the role played by the political stakeholders as well as by the electorate. On the contrary, the interaction between institutional and demographic factors, urban realities as well as social stakeholders and, to a lesser extent, the mobilisation of community networks can explain the political representation of elected representatives from diverse backgrounds in the Brussels Region.

In this perspective of 'mirror representation', it is useful to bear in mind that more than a quarter of the population of Brussels (26%) does not have Belgian nationality or the right to vote, given that only nationals are allowed to vote in the Brussels regional elections. Even if the question is not currently on the political agenda, it would be useful to revive the debate on extending the right to vote to include the regional elections, in order to ensure the representation of a significant part of the population of Brussels.

A prospective approach to political participation, which takes into consideration the demographic evolution of the population of Brussels, allows us to assume that the political representation of Muslim elected representatives will become a bigger stake, even if it maintains a certain stability. We must bear in mind that the most disadvantaged municipalities in the capital have the highest growth rates (Deboosere, Willaert 2005), in particular Molenbeek and Saint-Josse, and that 25% of youths in Brussels are of Muslim origin (Bousetta, Maréchal 2003), and will therefore represent an electorate which cannot be ignored in future legislatures.

In the years to come, however, the real debate will not be about the number of Muslim MPs in the Parliament of the Brussels-Capital Region, but rather about examining how the latter will uphold the interests of the entire population of Brussels, while using their difference to the benefit of neighbourhoods or categories of the population which are disadvantaged and strongly affected by discrimination. The political participation of Muslims is far from being a threat to social cohesion, and instead reinforces democratic principles by allowing individuals who have been kept in the background of political institutions for so long to be true stakeholders in political decision making.

Notes

1. More precisely, this refers to forms of political participation centred on elections (voting, running, campaigning, etc.). For a more complete definition of political participation, see E. Van Haute, 2009.
2. It should be noted that there are not many studies on the political participation of Muslims in Flanders either. This should certainly be considered in the Belgian historical and political context, which has an influence on the difficulties of isolating religious and linguistic variables in censuses and surveys.
3. Those who identified themselves as non-religious Muslims indicated that Islam is more of a cultural identity and that their ethnic minority identity is more important to them than being 'Muslim'. One councillor described herself as a 'cultural Muslim' (Sinno 2009: 116).
4. According to the Columbia school, one of the most determining variables in electoral choice is religious belonging (Lazarsfeld, Berelson, Gaudet 1944).
5. Available at <http://www.cevipof.com/PEF/2007/PEF2007.htm#p3> (last accessed 30 March 2012).
6. Despite the methodological note explaining the approach, these figures may be criticised given the lack of precise data provided by the authors.
7. The detailed figures may be obtained online on Jan Hertogen's website at <http://www.npdata.be> (last accessed 30 March 2012).
8. It is interesting to note that certain leading lights of the liberal party (MR) attribute the electoral failure of the 2009 and 2010 elections to the fact that candidates from diverse backgrounds were not taken into consideration enough. See the interview by Olivier Maingain: *'Le MR doit s'ouvrir aux candidats issus de l'immigration'*, La Dernière Heure, 15 June 2010.

References

Bousetta, H. (1998), 'Le paradoxe anversois. Entre racisme politique et ouvertures multiculturelles', *Revue Européenne des Migrations Internationales*, (14) 2, pp. 151–72.
Bousetta, H., and B. Maréchal (2003), 'L'islam et les musulmans en Belgique. Enjeux

locaux et cadres de réflexions globaux', study report, Brussels: Fondation Roi Baudouin.

Brouard, S., and V. Tiberj (2005), *Français comme les autres? Les citoyens d'origine maghrébine, africaine et turque*, Paris: Presses de Sciences Po.

Bukhari, Z. H., S. S. Nyang, M. Ahmad and J. L. Esposito (ed.) (2004), *Muslims' Place in the American Public Square: Hopes, Fears, and Aspirations*, Lanham: Rowman and Littlefield.

Cesary, J. (2001), 'Attitudes politiques et culture religieuse de la population musulmane issue de l'immigration', in R. Leveau and C. Wihtol De Wenden (eds), *L'islam en France et en Allemagne: identités et citoyennetés*, Paris: La Documentation Française.

Dargent, C. (2003), *Les musulmans déclarés en France: affirmation religieuse, subordination sociale et progressisme politique*, Paris: Cahiers du CEVIPOF (34).

Dargent, C. (2010), 'Musulmans versus catholiques: un nouveau clivage culturel et politique?', à la ST 42, *Des valeurs politiques en mutation: analyse quantitative comparée*, Congrès International des Associations Francophone de Science Politique, 7 September 2009, available at <http://www.con gresafsp2009.fr/sec4onsthema4ques/st42/st42dargent.pdf> (last accessed 13 December 2010).

Dargent, C. (2010), 'La population musulmane de France: de l'ombre à la lumière?', in *Revue Française de Sociologie*, vol. 51 (2), pp. 219–46.

De Decker, N. and G. Sandri (2008), 'Le vote des catholiques', in P. Delwit and E. Van Haute (ed.), *Le vote des Belges (Bruxelles-Wallonie, 10 Juin 2007)*, Brussels: Université Libre de Bruxelles, pp. 25–37.

Deboosere, P. and D. Willaert (2005), *Atlas des quartiers de la population de la Région de Bruxelles-Capitale au début du 21ème siècle*, Institut Bruxellois de Statistique et d'Analyse, no. 42, Bruxelles: Iris Edition.

Deboosere, P., T. Eggerickx, E. Van Hecke and B. Wayens (2009), 'Citizens' Forum of Brussels. The population of Brussels: a demographic overview', in *Brussels Studies*, Synopsis number 3, 12 January 2009 (corr. 17 March 2009), available at <www. brusselsstudies.be> (last accessed 15 December 2010).

Delwit, P. and De Waele J.-M. (2000), *Le mode de scrutin fait-il l'élection?*, Brussels: Editions Libre de Bruxelles.

Fassin, D. and E. Fassin (ed.) (2006), *De la question sociale à la question raciale? Représenter la société française*, Paris: La Découverte.

Fassin, D. (ed.) (2010), *Les nouvelles frontières de la société française*, Paris: La Découverte.

Geisser, V. (1997), *Ethnicité Républicaine. Les élites d'origine maghrébine dans le système politique français*, Paris: Presses de Sciences Po.

Giugni, M. (1995), *Entre stratégie et opportunité: Les nouveaux mouvements sociaux en Suisse*, Zurich: Seismo.

Jacobs, D., M. Martiniello and A. Réa (2002), 'Changing Patterns of Political

Participation of Citizens of Immigrant Origin in the Brussels Capital Region: The October 2000 Elections', in *Journal of International Migration and Integration*, vol. 3 (2), pp. 201–40.

Jacobs, D. and A. Réa (2005), 'Construction et importation des classements ethniques. Allochtones et immigrés aux Pays-Bas et en Belgique', in *Revue Européenne des Migrations Internationales*, vol. 21 (2), pp. 35–59.

Jacobs, D., H. Bousetta, A. Rea, M. Martiniello and M. Swyngedouw (2006), *Qui sont les candidats aux élections bruxelloises? Le profil des candidats à l'élection au parlement de la Région de Bruxelles-Capitale du 13 juin 2004*, Louvain-La-Neuve: Academia-Bruylant.

Jacobs, D., L. Phalet and M. Swyngedouw (2006), 'Political Participation and Associational Life of Turkish Residents in the Capital of Europe', in *Turkish Studies*, vol. 7 (1), pp. 145–61.

Kagne, B. (2001), 'Immigration, stratégies identitaires et mobilisations politiques des Africains en Belgique', in G. Gosselin and J.-P. Lavaud , *Ethnicité et mobilisations sociales*, Paris: L'Harmattan, Logiques Sociales.

Kateb, K. (2004), 'De l'étranger à l'immigré et de l'ethnique au religieux: les chiffres en question?', in Y.-C. Zarka, S. Taussig and C. Fleury (eds), (sous la dir. de), *L'islam en France*, Paris: PUF, coll. 'Cités', Quadriges.

Lambert, P.-Y. (1999), *La participation politique des allochtones en Belgique*, Louvain-La-Neuve: Academia-Bruylant.

Lambert, S. (2004), '"Elus d'origine étrangère" et vie associative: quelles ressources pour la démocratie en Belgique francophone?', in J. Gatugu, S. Amoranitis S. and A. Manço (eds) , *La vie associative des migrants: quelles (re)connaissances? Réponses européennes et canadiennes*, Paris: L'Harmattan, coll. Compétences interculturelles.

Lavau, G. (1953), *Partis politiques et réalités sociales*, Paris: Armand Colin.

Lazarsfeld, P. F., B. Berelson and H. Gaudet (1944), *The People's Choice*, New York: Columbia University Press.

Manço, A. and U. Manço (1992), *Turcs de Belgique: Identités et trajectoires d'une minorité,* Brussels: Info-Turk.

Manço, U. and M. Kanmaz (2004), 'Belgique. Intégration des musulmans et reconnaissance du culte islamique: un essai de bilan', in U. Manço (ed), *Reconnaissance et discrimination. Présence de l'islam en Europe occidentale et en Amérique du Nord*, Paris: L'Harmattan.

Manço, U. and M. Kanmaz (2005), 'From Conflict to Co-operation Between Muslims and Local Authorities in a Brussels Borough: Schaerbeek', in *Journal of Ethnic and Migration Studies*, vol. 31, no. 6, pp. 1105–23.

Marques Pereira, B. and P. Nolasco (2001), *La représentation politique des femmes en Amérique latine*, Paris: L'Harmattan.

Martiniello, M. (1998), 'Les élus d'origine étrangère à Bruxelles: une nouvelle étape de la participation politique des populations d'origine immigrée', in *Revue Européenne des Migrations Internationales*, vol. 14 (2), pp. 123–49.

Martiniello, M. (1992), *Leadership et pouvoir dans les communautés d'origine immigrée*, Paris: L'Harmattan.

Martiniello, M. (1997), 'Quelle participation politique?', in Collectif, *La Belgique et ses immigrés. Les politiques manquées*, Brussels: De Boeck Université.

Mayer, N. and P.Perrineau (1992), *Les comportements politiques,* Paris: Armand Colin.

Meyer, D. S. (2004), *Protest and Political Opportunities*, Annual Review of Sociology, 30: 125–45.

Muxel, A. (1988), 'Les attitudes socio-politiques des jeunes issus de l'immigration maghrébine en région parisienne', in *Revue française de science politique*, 38(6), pp. 925–40.

Pitkin, H. F. (1972), *The Concept of Representation*, Berkeley: University of California Press.

Réa, A. (2002), *La représentation politique des Belges d'origine étrangère aux élections communales de 2000: le cas de Bruxelles*, Les Cahiers du CEVIPOL, available at <www.ulb.ac.be/soco/cevipol> (last accessed 26 January 2011).

Réa, A., D. Jacobs, C. Teney and P. Delwit, (2010), 'Les comportements électoraux des minorités ethniques à Bruxelles', *Revue Française de Science Politique*, vol. 60 (4) August pp. 691–718.

Sandri, G. and N. De Decker (2008), 'Le vote des musulmans', in P. Delwit and E. Van Haute (ed.), *Le vote des Belges (Bruxelles-Wallonie, 10 juin 2007)*, Brussels: Université Libre de Bruxelles.

Shadid, W. A. R. and P. S. Van Koningsveld (1996), *Political participation and identities of Muslims in non-Muslim states*, Kampen: Kok Pharos.

Sinno, A. H. (2009), 'Muslim underrepresentation in American Politics', in A. H. Sinno (ed.), *Muslims in Western Politics,* Bloomington: Indiana University Press.

Teney, C. and D. Jacobs (2009), 'Students in Brussels from an immigrant background and their first vote. An analysis of voting intentions for the 2007 federal elections', in *Brussels Studies,* no. 24, 30 March 2009, available at <www.brusselstudies.be> (last accessed 21 March 2011).

Torrekens, C. (2007), 'Concentration of Muslim populations and structure of Muslim associations in Brussels', *Brussels Studies*, no. 4, 5 March 2007, available at <www.brusselsstudies.be> (last accessed 4 February 2011).

Torrekens, C. (2009), *L'islam à Bruxelles*, Brussels: Editions de l'Université Libre de Bruxelles.

Van Haute, E. (2009), *Adhérer à un parti. Aux sources de la participation politique*, Brussels: Editions de l'Université de Bruxelles.

Van Heelsum, A. (2001), *Marokkaanse Organisaties in Nederland, een netwerkanalyse*, Amsterdam: Het Spinhuis.

Zibouh, F. (2007), 'Le droit de vote des étrangers aux élections municipales de 2006 en Belgique', in *Migrations Société*, (November–December) vol. 19 (114), pp. 141–50.

Zibouh, F. (2010), *La participation politique des élus d'origine maghrébine.*

Elections régionales bruxelloises et stratégies électorales, Louvain-La-Neuve: Academia-Bruylant.

Zibouh, F. (2010), 'Ethnic Diversity in political parties' organisational structures: a Belgian case study, in ENARgy (September), *Participation et représentation politique des minorités ethniques: du vœu pieu à la réalité*, pp. 6–7.

Zibouh, F. (2012), 'La participation politique des musulmans en Belgique', in B. Maréchal, *L'islam de Belgique*, Louvain-La-Neuve: Academia-Bruylant.

MUSLIM POLITICAL PARTICIPATION IN GERMANY: A STRUCTURATIONIST APPROACH

Maike Didero

1. Introduction: setting the stage[1]

The 2009 local council elections in the German State of North-Rhine-Westphalia brought about a significant innovation: for the first time citizens with a migration background came to the fore as founders of local voter associations. Among these newly founded voter associations, the Bündnis für Frieden und Fairness (Confederation for peace and fairness, BFF) stands out for two reasons: first of all, because it immediately won two seats on the city council, although it was founded only two months prior to the elections. Secondly, it is unusual because it was founded exclusively by Muslims. This fact triggered attention by media far beyond the local scope and raised fierce debates about the legitimacy of such a political organisation.

This chapter argues that while the emergence of these new political actors can be explained by looking at political and social structures and discourses, the astonishing success of the BFF can only be explained if we take into account both structures and individual agency, considering both as forces for change in a reciprocal and iterative process (Moser 2006: 69). A structurationist approach has therefore been chosen for the analysis at hand. It will be presented in detail in the following section. A third section then outlines the main characteristics of the German political field which frame immigrants' political participation on the one hand and Muslims' political participation on the other hand. The fourth section deals in more detail with the BFF and analyses the reasons for its success. Finally the paper discusses whether the founding of the BFF is indeed a sign of fragmentation – as claimed by many political opponents – or whether it can instead be interpreted as a sign of integration and a positive contribution to democracy in Germany.

2.   Theoretical background: a structurationist approach

Within the context of social theorising, a structurationist approach aims to overcome the structure/agency debate by arguing that it is neither the structures that determine what people do, nor the people who shape structures according to their free will. The two most prominent representatives of this school of thought are Pierre Bourdieu and Anthony Giddens. The analytical framework developed for the research question at hand draws on the thoughts of both authors. The advantage of employing elements from both theoretical frameworks derives from the fact that they provide complementary perspectives on the duality of structure and agency: while Giddens pursues a more top-down perspective, Bourdieu develops his viewpoint using an ethnographic, bottom-up approach. For the purpose of this paper, Giddens's theory of structuration will be used to take into account the role of rules and institutions. Bourdieu's theory of practices will be used to differentiate between different types of capital and to analyse the specifics of the political field.

2.1.   Giddens

Giddens' theory of structuration is based on the assumption that structures have to be conceived of as results of human agency (Giddens 1997: 290). The relationship between structure and agency is one of duality: structures frame actions but at the same time can be changed through action. Importantly, structures constrain and enable actions at the same time (Giddens 1997: 78). According to Giddens' approach, human beings are conceived as competent agents who are capable of reflexivity, even though a large proportion of day-to-day activities are governed by tacit, practical knowledge (Giddens 2008: 6). Actions are framed by the structures defined as 'rules and resources recursively implicated in social reproduction' (Giddens 2008: xxxi). Rules include normative elements and codes of signification. Resources refer to capabilities or forms of transformative capacity which generate command over objects or goods (allocative resources) or other persons (authoritative resources) (Giddens 2008: 33). These resources include knowledge about and awareness of social rules and one's own resources (cf. Tröger 2003: 29).

   Giddens' classification of institutions differs from traditional definitions in that he distinguishes between symbolic orders and political, economic and legal institutions. However, in his endeavour to resist 'substantivist' concepts, he conceives each of these institutional orders as being based on a specific relationship between signification, domination and legitimisation (Giddens 2008: 33). The order and relationship of the three dimensions vary: while symbolic orders rely mainly on signification, legal institutions are primarily based on legitimation and political institutions are related to domination. Giddens also stresses the importance of time/space relation. He argues that social interaction is contextual – that it is situated and positioned in time and space – and yet transcended by the 'stretching' of social relations across time and space (Giddens 2008: 35–6). These concepts allow for discussing the founding of BFF as an event facilitated by its situation within a specific time/space context and scrutinising the relationship between symbolic discourse (symbolic orders) and legal orders as part of the structural context for this decision.

2.2.   Bourdieu

Two sub-sets of Bourdieu's theory of praxis are of particular relevance to the topic of this article: the concept of social field, and his theory of habitus. Bourdieu defines a field as a social space, where agents strive to maintain or improve their relative positions. An actor's position in a specific field is determined by the type and amount of capital that he or she possesses. Types of capital include economic capital (financial resources, all forms of material wealth that can be converted to money), social capital (factual and potential resources that can be derived from the existence of a social network or by belonging to a social group; Bourdieu 1983: 183–98) and cultural capital (basically a person's personal knowledge, abilities and education). And finally there is symbolic capital, which denotes the chances to gain and retain social prestige and recognition (Fuchs-Heinritz and König 2005). The forms of capital are all interrelated in that they can be converted from one form to another. Since each field is endowed with specific rules which define the value of a specific type of capital in a field, actors can hold different positions in different social fields.

A habitus, according to Bourdieu, is a set of dispositions which people acquire during their socialisation process and which guides their future actions and behaviour. As a result of past actions and experiences the habitus is thus at the same time structured and structuring (Bourdieu et al. 1982: 280). Being acquired in relation to a specific social field, the habitus enables actors to develop a 'sense for the game', thereby tacitly knowing how to behave in a certain social field.

One of these social fields is the political field. This field is defined as 'the site of a competition for power [. . .] [and] the monopoly of the right to speak and act in the name of some or all of the non-professionals' (Bourdieu 1991: 199). Political actors' ability to mobilise social groups depends on their political capital or authority. This specific sort of symbolic capital can be derived either from a person's individual reputation and prestige (personal political capital), or it can be delegated by a political organisation to its individual members (delegated political capital). In order to benefit from delegated political capital, an actor has to be 'instituted' by a political party. An investiture – for example being nominated as an election candidate – usually requires the candidate to have invested time and/or money in this organisation prior to the nomination (Bourdieu 1991: 194–5; 2001: 102).

Bourdieu defines the political field as a 'singular game', or 'microcosm', embedded in a larger 'social macrocosm' (Bourdieu 2001: 20–41). This means that political actors are embedded in power relationships within the political field as well as within the larger social field. Yet the barrier between the political and the social field remains essential: actors inside the political field are the 'ordained', the active agents, who have gained the right to represent the 'laic' outside the political field (Bourdieu 1991: 171). The most important instruments for entering the political field are leisure time and cultural capital (Bourdieu 1991: 172). On an even more basic level, however, an individual first of all needs to feel entitled to a political opinion. This feeling of entitlement depends on a specific social status and habitus (Bourdieu 2001: 9).

2.3.   An analytical framework

Drawing on the theoretical input by Giddens and Bourdieu as described above, as well as on some helpful insights presented by Koopmans (2005) in his study on contested citizenship, we can now develop a comprehensive framework. It will serve to structure the analysis and elucidate the reasons for the foundation of the BFF, the circumstances of its foundation and its success at the ballots.

The political field (Figure 3.1) includes both individual and collective actors. In Germany, the political parties are viewed as being among the most important collective actors in the political field (cf. Sontheimer and Bleek 2002: 195–265; Korte 2009: 9–11). Individual party members and the parties among themselves compete with each other for the power to represent the 'laic outsiders' in the social field. In these struggles for influence and power the political actors can draw either on different forms of personal capital (cultural, social, economic or symbolic), and/or can use the political capital delegated by a political party. Bourdieu stresses that these struggles are not simply about legislation or the distribution of 'real power'. 'The monopoly of the elaboration and diffusion of the legitimate principle of division of the social world and as a result of the mobilisation of groups' is equally contested (Bourdieu 1991: 181). The political field is hence a major arena in which hegemonic discourses are being established and challenged.

Future practices and decisions in the political field are then framed by these symbolic orders (discourses) on the one hand, and legal institutions (laws and regulations) on the other hand: legal institutions legitimise or constrain specific political practices. However, they can in turn be shaped and changed by the actors in the political field, for example, through legislation. On the other hand, what the actors are able to say or think is highly contingent on the hegemonic discourses prevalent at a specific time. Koopmans points out that these discursive opportunities are important in that they 'determine which collective identities and substantive demands have a high likelihood to gain *visibility* in the mass media, to *resonate* with the claims of other collective

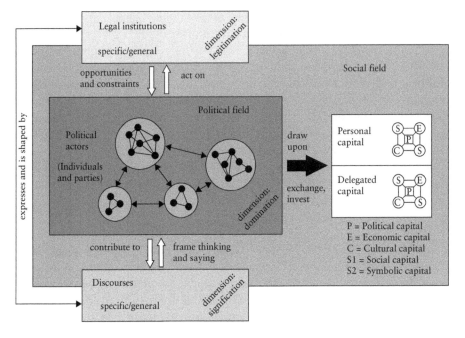

Figure 3.1 The political field in Germany – an analytical framework

actors and to achieve *legitimacy* in the public discourse' (Koopmans 2005: 19). Hegemonic discourses gain in importance if they are transformed – or 'materialised' – into laws or regulations which then serve as a framework for future decisions and actions. At the same time, however, due to the power they are invested with, and by means of their individual public speech acts, political actors can contribute to enhancing the perceivability of certain discourses while silencing others.

3.   The political field in Germany

Bourdieu points out that the political field itself is always the (contingent) result of historical processes (Bourdieu 2001: 102). The following section thus outlines the emergence of the laws and discourses which functioned as enabling and constraining structures in the foundation of the BFF in 2009. Since approximately half of the BFF's founding members have been born abroad, a first sub-chapter presents the conditions for immigrants' political participation in Germany. Media coverage on the BFF on the other hand focused on its 'Muslim' character. Hence a second sub-chapter looks into what it means to be perceived as Muslim in German politics today.

3.1. A question of participation: migration and citizenship in Germany

As the political scientist Koopmans argues, different configurations and conceptions of citizenship and nationhood are crucial when trying to explain political mobilisation by immigrants or on behalf of them or against them (Koopmans 2005: 6, 17). In Germany, since the actual foundation of the German state in 1871, national identity has been based on an ethno-linguistic concept of citizenship as opposed to a political or civic concept of community (Brubaker 1992: 180–2). Belonging to the nation is thus construed to be a question of having the 'right blood' and parental lineage (cf. Oberndörfer 2009: 127–42). The establishment of *jus sanguinis* as the legal base for the allocation of citizenship was an obvious consequence.[2]

This specific configuration of discursive and legal structures heavily influenced Germany's post-World War II immigration policy (Oberndörfer 2009: 129). For example, until 1993 immigrants defined as 'ethnic Germans' were not only able to immigrate more or less freely, but were also given German citizenship on arrival without having to comply to the stipulations of the German naturalisation law (e.g. interdiction of dual-citizenship) (Wüst 2003: 30). In addition, the eastern European re-settlers were also provided with a well-developed set of integration measures (German Federal Agency for Civic Education, 1978).

However, the immigrant workers recruited from 1953 to 1973 faced a completely different situation. They were perceived to be a reserve labour force of 'temporary mobile labour units' which was supposed to return home during economic recessions (Castels 1985: 519; Treibel 1999: 56). This is why work migrants were neither offered any consistent integration measures, nor attributed a realistic chance of obtaining German citizenship. With naturalisation being granted on legal discretion only until 1990 (Koopmans 2005: 6, 17), Germany had one of the lowest naturalisation rates in Europe (Wüst 2003: 30). Low naturalisation rates and the commonly-held idea of return-migration meant that the political participation of immigrants was no issue; immigrants were neither perceived as potential voters nor as a political force. If they did have any claims to make, they were supposed to contact established political bodies, such as trade unions (Miller 2008: 148–82) or members of local or national parliaments and their administrations (cf. Schiffauer 2007: 112–13).

A very basic level of self-representation was provided only in larger cities where 'local councils for foreign nationals' were established. Elected by all the non-German residents in a city, these councils were supposed to inform and advise municipal councils about the immigrant population's needs and claims. However, their function remained mainly symbolic, as they were denied any kind of real decision-making power (cf. Koopmans 2005: 65).

A review of the political field in the period up to the beginning of the 1990s reveals a clear segregation: in line with the main discursive and legal gap between (ethnically defined) nationals and foreigners, these two groups were represented by separate political bodies. The power to decide on the 'rules of the game' remained entirely in the hands of the established political elite, who saw immigrants as being 'mere objects to be managed' (Peter 2010: 123).

A major shift took place after the change in government in 1998. The ruling coalition comprising the SPD (social democrats) and the Green Party for the first time acknowledged Germany's status as an immigration country and the need for integration policies. The government decided to reform citizenship and naturalisation laws in order to solve the problem of a growing number of 'denizens' (Hammar 1995) – long-term residents without any political rights (Hailbronner 2010). In 2000, accompanied by fervent, controversial discussion, a new citizenship law (StAG) finally replaced the law from 1913 (RuStAG). Breaking with former traditions, for the first time in Germany citizenship is awarded according to the principles of a – modified – *jus soli.*[3] Since the turn of the millennium, naturalisation has been both facilitated and hindered: while the minimum residency period has been reduced to eight years, a new language and knowledge test has been introduced as an additional hurdle (cf. Spindler 2002: 56).[4] Although naturalisation rates remain on a modest level, modified legislation translates to increasing diversity among German citizens: From 2000 to 2010, 1.4 million inhabitants have been naturalised (Statistisches Bundesamt 2011: 15), and 400,000 children have obtained German citizenship according to the new *jus soli* option model (BAMF 2011).

In terms of discourse, a significant shift following the reforms in citizenship law has been perceivable: since 2005 the central statistical agency has no longer distinguished between foreign nationals and German nationals only, but also shows information on persons 'with a migration background'. This extremely broad category includes non-German nationals (German and foreign born) and foreign-born Germans, as well as children of whom at least one parent is either foreign-born or a foreign national (Statistisches Bundesamt 2009: 324–32).

An additional change in the political field concerns the political representation of foreign nationals. In the early 1990s, EU citizens obtained an (active and passive) right to vote in municipal elections. As a result, many of them lost interest in the 'foreigner councils'. In addition, the councils have been criticised for 'a lack of resources, the often non-representative character of their constituencies and their negligible role in local political life' (Nordbruch 2011; cf. Copur 2005; Roth 2009: 201–2). Today these councils are losing their democratic legitimation since they are being increasingly shunned by their constituencies. In North-Rhine-Westphalia, for example, the average election participation rate for the councils reached an all-time low of only 11% in 2010 (LAGA NRW 2010).

3.2.   *A question of representation: Islam and Muslims in Germany*

A second important shift in the political field concerns the 'principles of division'. As Bourdieu points out, these are discursively constructed categories which have to be interpreted as contingent results of symbolic battles (Bourdieu 1987: 158). However, these principles are ever more powerful and persuasive if they are 'backed up' by objective (existing) differences and inequalities in society. The trouble when talking about Muslims in Germany arises from the fact that – unlike in the US for example – the majority of Germany's 3.8 to 4.3 million Muslim inhabitants are indeed foreign-born or second generation immigrants (cf. Azzaoui 2009: 1–8; Haug et al. 2009: 116–17).[5] Consequently there are people who do fall into both categories and who can be called 'Muslim immigrants'. The question is: why should this matter?

It is indeed noticeable that although a substantial number of Muslims have been living in Germany since the 1960s, until very recently the religious background of immigrants was no issue – neither in public discourses, nor in science or politics (cf. Peter 2010: 127; Shooman and Spielhaus 2010: 198; Tiesler 2007; Spielhaus 2011). So why and how did this new nexus of discourses on immigration and Islam emerge? Why are immigrants today first and foremost perceived as Muslim immigrants (Shooman and Spielhaus 2010: 198)?

The German cultural anthropologist Werner Schiffauer argues that the emergence of religion as a new principle of division is not incidental. It happens at a time when an increasing number of immigrants (who do not correspond to an ethnic conception of 'Germanness') have gained legal rights and formal equality. According to Schiffauer, this is deeply troubling for German society. The process is a major challenge to 'the self-understanding that defines belonging to national community' (Koopmans 2005: 23) and might also affect the social position of the dominant majority (Peter 2010: 119; Schiffauer 2007: 112). Referring to religion instead of nationality to define out-groups now legitimates the (discursive) exclusion of those who – by law – are fully-fledged German citizens, bestowed with all social and political rights.

The visibility of this new category of division is, however, also due to the increased presence of Muslim believers and Muslim institutions in Germany. Contrary to the labour migrants of the 1970s, who conceived of their religious institutions as temporary arrangements (Azzaoui 2011: 250f), today a substantial number of Muslims feel at home in Germany and consequently aim to regularise and normalise religious practices – for example by turning 'back yard mosques' into purpose-built mosques. This legitimate wish has, however, been interpreted by the majority population as an illegitimate 'land grab', making mosque building operations a contentious issue (cf. Schmitt 2003;

Beinhauer-Köhler et al. 2009). Similar fervent public disputes concern the wearing of a headscarf as a visible sign of religious practice (Amir-Moazami 2007; Yurdakul 2006). The emergence of a substantial religious minority also poses a challenge to the relationship between the church and the state in Germany. According to the principle of 'positive neutrality' (Oebbecke 2010: 3), religious communities officially recognised by the German state are endowed with wide-ranging legal and fiscal privileges. In addition, they may obtain the right to provide religious education in national schools. Muslim representatives have increasingly claimed this official recognition as a 'religious community', which would put them on par with the Lutheran and Roman Catholic Church and the Jewish community in Germany (Peter 2010: 125; cf. Heinrich Böll Stiftung 2010; Azzaoui 2011: 247–76 on the complex legal framework and Bodenstein 2010, 55–68; Thielmann 2010: 169–95 on organisational structures).

These pertinent discussions on the formal and legal integration of Islam in the German legal system unfortunately coincide with the increased presence of Islam in international politics and discourse. Although 9/11 is often cited as a watershed event in this context, various researchers have demonstrated that the current image of Islam in the media only exacerbates a well established perception of Islam as an inherently political and dangerous ideology (Cesari 2010: 2; Hafez 2002; Brema 2010; Schiffer 2004). In Europe this 'lasting trauma' of Islam (Said 1978) has recently been reactivated by a number of events and debates. The Madrid and London bombings as well as the cartoon controversy are examples in case (cf. Spielhaus 2011: 65f for overview). This led to an 'Islamisation' of debates on migration and citizenship (Tiesler 2007: 24–31; Butterwegge 2007: 57) and contributed to the image of European Muslims as the 'enemy within' (Schiffauer 2006: 94, 116; Shooman and Spielhaus 2010: 203). The consequence is dire. In Germany today 'foreigners' are perceived as 'Muslims'. 'Muslims' in turn are equated with 'foreigners'. And both groups are inevitably associated with terrorism, extremism and the suppression of women's rights.

However, on the other hand, these events have 'shocked German policy makers out of their disinterest in Muslims' (Jonker 2006: 145). Even if it is within a security framework (cf. Peter 2010), they are finally showing themselves willing to tackle the question of the role and status of Islam in Germany. Previously, Muslim claimants wishing to clarify issues related to religious practices had to take these issues to court (Azzaoui 2011: 255). Although this is common practice and a basic democratic right, Muslim plaintiffs have been delegitimised in that they have been shown up as newcomers who are to adapt to existing regulations instead of challenging them (Schiffauer 2007: 122–4). The 'German Islam Conference', convened in 2006, offered a novel forum to discuss these issues with policy makers and signalled the recognition of Islam and Muslims as an irreducible part of Germany (Schäuble 2006). The conference proceedings nonetheless speak less of a harmonic process of 'welcoming Muslims into the nation' (Peter 2010: 125) than of a harsh power struggle between political and religious representatives (Azzaoui 2011). A major point of conflict has been the question of who is entitled to represent 'German Muslims' (Nordbruch 2011: 17f). Government officials argued that the four major Islam organisations were not representative for Muslims in Germany and therefore invited a majority of unaffiliated (Schäuble 2006: 5f), or even 'secular' Muslims (Islamkonferenz 2010). While this invitation policy corresponds to the government's aim to discuss issues related to religious *and* social integration, Muslim participants and observers have justly criticised that the issues debated as well as the invitation policy reinforce the conflation of ethnic and religious categories (Azzaoui 2011: 260; Krüger-Potratz and Schiffauer 2011). Although Muslim participants have been disenchanted by the slow pace and lack of concrete outcomes of the first and second Islam conference (Islam still lacks the status of a religious community) (cf. Azzaoui 2011: 260–1), it seems that at least in North-Rhine Westphalia (NRW), the tiresome struggle and the (legal) recommendations issued by the Islam Conference (de Wall 2008; Deutsche Islamkonferenz 2011) have facilitated a pragmatic compromise. Islamic religious education might be offered in state schools as early as 2012 (Landesregierung NRW 2011a,b; cf. Søvik 2008, 241–66 for information on the process and problems related to the introduction of Islamic Education in NRW).

4. The case of the BFF

4.1. *Context of foundation*

The BFF was founded at a time when a growing number of immigrants have obtained the right to vote, but are not yet represented accordingly as active participants in the political field. Recent studies and surveys (Wüst Heinz 2009: 201–18; Schönwälder 2010; Schönwälder and Kofri 2010) suggest that the number and proportion of (post-war) immigrants and their descendants in legislative bodies – although having increased substantially throughout the last two decades – still remain far from attaining statistical representativeness.[6] Whether such reversed representativeness is necessary or advisable touches on the question of whether we are speaking about a relevant and/or mobilised social group (Bourdieu 1998). Schönwälder (2010: 30f) argues that first and second generation immigrants are a socially relevant group, sharing a number of common interests and specific expertise, which up to now have not been reflected adequately in the political field. As shown above, German politics on immigration and integration has indeed until very recently been dominated by anti-migration (and recently anti-Muslim) narrations rather than by concerns about diversity, equality and anti-discrimination issues (cf. Nordbruch 2011 on public debates).[7] This is related to the fact that in 2009, only 39% of immigrant voters in NRW were able to cite a party representing their political opinions and interests (Schönwälder 2010: 29–35). 'Feeling represented' and being able to identify with a political actor is arguably not only a question of party affiliation or agreement on certain issues, but is likely also to be influenced by the voter's personal attributes or habitus (Falter 2005: 239–40). This explains why, in a 2009 survey among respondents of Turkish origin, when asked for party preferences the Social Democrats (SPD) ranked first (55%), and the Green party second (23%). But when asked whom they would elect as chancellor (a hypothetical question) the Green Party chairman Cem Özdemir ranked first (25%) and the SPD candidate Frank-Walter Steinmeier came in second (20%) (Data4U 2009).

While this nationwide gap between a growing pool of immigrant voters and the lack of political (visible) representation constituted a significant opportunity, there are more reasons for the BFF being founded on a local level and, more specifically, in the city of Bonn.

Firstly, with the German political system and the political parties being organised federally, it is the local level which provides the most common 'entrance' for newcomers to the political field (Sinanoglu and Volkert 2011). In addition to the possibility of running for municipal council elections as a candidate for the established German national parties, citizens in North-Rhine Westphalia can also create their own voter associations (*Wählergemeinschaften*). Since the minimum 5% of the votes required for membership in local councils was abolished in 1999, these small independent lists have a realistic chance to win seats on the council (Korte 2009). In addition, the minimum voting age was reduced from 18 to 16 years for the 2009 municipal council elections (Korte 2009). As Schönwälder and Kofri (2010: 11f) point out, younger age groups are more ethnically diverse than older age groups and have certainly contributed to the BFF's electoral success (Stadt Bonn 2009b).

In Bonn, a very specific institution facilitated and triggered the foundation of the BFF. Responding to political demands for a unique contact institution, members of the Muslim communities in Bonn founded the 'Muslim Council of the city of Bonn' in early 2006. This umbrella organisation is exceptional in that it includes all nine mosque associations located in Bonn, thereby representing a large variety of Islamic denominations, and also uniting members from various linguistic and regional backgrounds (Arabic, Turkish, Bosnian).[8] The council's aims are to support Muslims in Bonn through counselling services, to facilitate networking and contact among Muslim organisations, and to function as a unique representational body for Muslim interest vis-à-vis local political institutions (RMB 2006). While counselling and networking worked well, and local politicians appreciated the council members as partners for dialogue and discussion, major Muslim demands – such as the go-ahead for the construction of a new mosque building – were still unmet in 2009 after three years of lobbying (Preuß 2009 and interviews).

In this context several members of the Muslim Council in Bonn were approached by local politicians offering them the opportunity to run for the integration council on the respective party's ticket. The Muslim Council Chairman Haluk Yildiz explains that they declined this offer because they no longer wanted to be relegated to symbolic politics, they wanted to enter the political sphere as equal political actors (Preuß 2009 and own interview). Consequently, they proposed that they run as candidates in the municipal council elections instead. Unfortunately, municipal council elections in NRW operate on the basis of closed lists (Schönwälder and Kofri 2010: 12), which means that seats are usually heavily contested in the larger cities. Since political newcomers usually have to give way to long-time party members (Korte 2009), the parties were not able to offer any top positions on the list to the Muslim council members.[9]

The proposal however awakened Muslim Council members to their potential for political participation and representation. Having found out that Bonn is home to 30,000 immigrants and their descendants, the Muslim council speaker estimated that this corresponded to a large enough number of potential voters. In mid-June 2009 several members of the Muslim Council decided to found their own voter association. Instead of restricting their political ambitions and modestly awaiting their turn to be selected by one of the parties, they decided to take the fast track to political power, simply relying on their own personal political capital. Even though they had only twelve days left, they managed to collect 450 signatures, decide on an electoral platform and recruit candidates for all but one of the electoral wards in Bonn just in time to register for the elections. Even more astonishingly, in the elections on 30 August 2010, they collected 2.11% of the votes, which gained them two seats on the council.

4.2.   Conditions for success – agency

Even though the foundation of the BFF was facilitated and promoted by the series of external structural opportunities and constraints described above, its creation cannot be explained without highlighting the activities of individual activists: the BFF founders did not only take up available opportunities. They were also willing to take action and disposed of sufficient allocative and authoritative resources to mobilise their electorate.

Firstly, the well established Muslim Council and its member associations provided social capital that the BFF could draw upon to mobilise a large number of potential candidates in a very short time. Both this institutionalised network and the founders' private social capital provided additional support that could be activated in order to organise and finance the election campaign. In addition, member mosque associations offered important platforms for campaign activities. The small group of founders' limited personal resources were increased and enhanced by a strategic choice of candidates according to their cultural capital: while incorporated capital in the form of a perfect command of the German language was a minimum requirement, many candidates had also acquired a large amount of institutionalised capital in the form of formal and professional certificates (28% had a university degree – a proportion below the average of the established parties but above that of the other local voter associations; Stadt Bonn 2009a). In addition, among the BFF founders there were many candidates who already enjoyed a high level of respect and recognition (symbolic capital). Whenever possible, the electoral wards were attributed to a candidate already well known in the respective quarter, for example due to his or her previous voluntary or professional social commitment.

As stated at the beginning, knowledge of the rules is in itself an important resource: in this case, the BFF founders' bureaucratic competence enabled them to gather information about the specific laws and regulations concerning the foundation of a voter association and to comply with these laws and regulations in a very short time. An additional factor contributing to the BFF's success is the habitus of its candidates who feel at home and 'fit in' with an average middle-class electorate while at the same time retaining compassionate ties to the inhabitants of the more marginalised quarters in Bonn. They thus enjoy a high level of trust among local residents from diverse social backgrounds.

The party's claim to diversity is also reflected in its choice of candidates: Firstly, with 25% female candidates, the BFF comes close to the average of the smaller parties in Bonn, and matches the share of the Christian Democrats (CDU). Secondly, with an astonishing 50% of foreign-born candidates (Stadt Bonn 2009a), the BFF is also widely diverse with regard to country of birth and/or linguistic competencies (including Turkish and various Arabic dialects) (Stadt Bonn 2009b). Arguably, this was an important asset for the BFF in their aim of addressing a large and diverse electorate. Whereas candidates were able to furnish information on the voter association and their programme in a number of languages, the BFF very deliberately designed campaign posters primarily in German. This choice of language, as well as the very professional and mainstream 'look and feel' of the posters clearly showed that the BFF did not aim at establishing themselves in a 'political niche economy'.[10] Instead they wanted to appeal to a typical mainstream voter.

Both the BFF's campaign material and their electoral platform indicate a highly developed sensitivity to the German political context and its hegemonic discourses: since many German people have an aversion to the use of foreign languages in the public sphere, the BFF's focus on the German language helped to counteract, at least partly, the fear of 'parallel societies'. The same holds true for their slogans, for example 'Uniting instead of dividing', which are fully in line with the German consensus-oriented political culture that is suspicious of any kind of particularistic interest (Sontheimer and Bleek 2002: 184). The association's name and its slogan 'Justice is the way, peace the aim' indicate the BFF's acute 'sense for the game' in that they reflect general concerns about segregation in general and the idea of a violent and aggressive Islam in particular, while at the same time voicing clear and self-confident claims of non-discrimination and social justice. This dual perspective is reflected in the BFF's election platform, which combines a specific focus on integration policies and a broad range of social, cultural and environmental issues. Close attention is paid to the situation of children, youths, families, women and elderly people, with claims focusing on welfare support as well as on measures facilitating broader access to the work force, for example enhanced and extended child-care facilities or antidiscrimination measures (BFF 2009).

4.3. *Reactions in the political field: political participation contested*

Bourdieu (2001: 89) draws our attention to the fact that political parties 'exist only in relation to other parties, and any attempt at defining who they are and what they proclaim would be in vain if it did not take into account who their competitors are in this same field and what these competitors proclaim' (translation MD). The following part therefore looks at the relations between the BFF as a political 'newcomer' and established political actors.

The BFF's foundation evoked a wide range of reactions. From among the local political parties, the Green and the Left (*die Linke*) parties displayed a rather positive attitude, welcoming the BFF as a legitimate new adversary in the political field. This might seem surprising since these two parties targeted the same electorate as the BFF. However, both parties harbour a high esteem for bottom-up democracy driven by and depending on the commitment of individual citizens. In contrast to the religion-averse Left Party, the Green Party shows a certain concern for these issues: they established a nation-wide subgroup for Muslim members (Grüne Muslime) and have offered substantial support to the mosque building process in Bonn (Vallender 2009).

Representatives of the Social and Christian Democrats, by contrast, criticised the BFF as disintegrative and disruptive (Preuß 2009). This attitude is psychologically easy to explain: being large catch-all institutions representing a 'common good', these parties are not interested in an increased number of competitors who could endanger their dominant positions in the political field. Similar criticism was voiced by a representative of the North-Rhine Westphalia association of integration councils (LAGA), which can be assumed to be in a similar position of competitiveness vis-à-vis the political newcomer (Bosse 2009).

The BFF, like many other voter associations founded by immigrants and their children, faced accusations of opening up social divisions (Hummel 2009). Members and candidates have been advised to become part of established parties instead of founding their own parties.[11] Although this argument does fall in line with the general consensus-oriented culture in Germany, it is surprising that other political newcomers – such as the IT-related 'Pirate Party' – have not likewise been reprimanded. An explanation is given by Schiffauer, who postulates that in Germany, identification with a 'general and common good' is taken for granted for 'old citizens' (or ethnic Germans). 'New citizens' (or citizens considered to be ethnically different) first need to prove this in order to gain not only the (legal) right, but also the (discursive) legitimation to participate in politics (Schiffauer 2007: 116). Interestingly, even the (extreme) right-wing newspaper *Junge Freiheit* (JF) (Schwarz 2009) follows this line of argument. In an interview with BFF Chairman Haluk Yildiz, the JF journalist accuses the BFF of hiding their concern for minority politics behind a facade of common-good rhetoric. According to this view, integration is a problem for immigrants only and does not concern society at large.

Most articles on the BFF were however less concerned with the issue of integration. They heralded the creation of a new 'Muslim party', despite the BFF's platform's lack of reference to religious issues. The BFF candidates tried to refute this opinion. They insisted on being 'just' Muslims and interested in politics (like any Christian Democrat). Yet they were unable to escape this opinion.

The first reason for this is that they were challenged by 'Pro-Bonn'. This local voter association was also founded in 2009. It is one of several political spin-offs rooted in the anti-mosque movement of 'Pro-Köln'. The 'Pro-Movement' has since developed to become a catchment for former members of extreme right-wing parties (Häusler 2008; Inhoffen et al. 2011).[12] Pro-Bonn staged a fierce election campaign 'against Islamisation and foreign infiltration', including verbal attacks against Muslims and anti-mosque signs sprouting everywhere in the city (SWR 2009). The BFF tried to counter this by drawing on the German consensus delegitimising extreme right-wing politics. Members participated in a demonstration organised by an anti-extremist network, (Maul 2009), and designed additional campaign posters, depicting a potato, an eggplant and a garlic bulb and featuring the slogans 'at home in Bonn' and 'no chance for the right'. However, the anti-Muslim tenor of the Pro-Bonn campaign forced the BFF to take a stand on religious issues as well. Muslim voters consequently perceived the BFF as an actor who would defend their religious freedom, which was jeopardised by Pro-Bonn in particular and an Islam-sceptic public opinion in general. This fear helped to mobilise voters and contributed to the BFF's success at the ballot box – certainly against Pro-Bonn's original intentions.

The second reason why the religious frame is so difficult to fend off relates to the two elected candidates: Haluk Yildiz is chairman of both the BFF and the Muslim Council. Hülya Dogan, the second council member, is the first veiled women to hold office in a German parliament (Preuß 2009). In the context of a well established discourse on Islam as a dangerous political ideology this very obvious display of religiousness and religious activism has been interpreted as an illegitimate intrusion of religion into politics, and thus served to delegitimise the BFF's political commitment. An article on the BFF and the Cologne voter association ABI in the conservative newspaper *Welt am Sonntag* is entitled 'Politics in the spirit of the Qur'an', followed by the leading question: 'Should we be afraid of these parties?' (Stoldt 2009). Stoldt substantiates his criticism by pointing to the dark prophecies concerning Germany's Islamisation propagated by 'professional Islam critics'.

These individual critics (cf. Schneiders 2009; Rommelspacher 2009), as well as various Islam-hostile websites (cf. Schiffer 2009: 341ff for overview) have recently fomented the German fear of Islam as a politicising religion. One of the authors writing regularly for several of these websites dedicated an entire twelve-page article to a wholesale assault on the BFF (Eussner 2009). Gudrun Eussner purports that the term fairness in the BFF's name has been chosen to avoid the term 'justice' (as in the Turkish 'party for justice and development' AKP). Using the mechanism of linguistic presupposition, she claims that the BFF is a 'party for Islam and justice' and concludes that the BFF has taken up its 'political work in the AKP's sense aiming at the Islamisation of German society' (Eussner 2009). Although Eussner has to concede that a majority of the BFF's campaign statements are in line with a 'traditional left-wing orientation', she uses the argument of wilful deception ('*taqiyya*' – a common trope in anti-Islamic blogs see Shooman and Spielhaus 2010: 213–14) to reason indirectly that all the BFF's propositions relate to Islamic claims. In her reading, the BFF call for equal treatment and non-discrimination of women, regardless of their (ethnic) background, religious or political beliefs (BFF 2009), which can be found in similar form in article 3, paragraph 3 of the German constitution (Grundgesetz), is translated as a 'call for shawl, headscarf, hijab, chador, niqab, burka and burkini, whenever unfortunate Muslim women want to don these 'by their own choice'. In keeping with the generalised conspiracy and subversion theories typical for this type of Internet document (cf. Schiffauer 2007: 130), Eussner's article presents any item of information collected on the BFF's programme and its candidates as being doubtful and potentially dangerous. For example, she accuses some candidates of 'concealing' their places of birth – only because she cannot 'verify' these places on Google Maps.

Although one might want to dismiss this article (and similar contributions on the weblogs 'Politically Incorrect' (PI) and 'Achse des Guten') as singular cases of far-fetched conspiracy fantasies, Shooman and Spielhaus (2010: 220) warn that 'Islam-hostile websites such as the Politically Incorrect weblog should not be downplayed as a marginal phenomenon, because of their high access numbers[13] and their function as platforms to network and exchange narratives'.[14] This call for awareness is specified and promoted by recently published information revealing the relations between authors publishing on

PI and members of two populist right-wing parties (the 'Pro-Movement' and 'die Freiheit') (Geyer and Schindler 2011).

5. Conclusion: a sign of integration or fragmentation?

What lessons can be drawn from the case study described above? Firstly, it seems obvious that a new group (a new class in Bourdieu's terms) of immigrants has emerged in Germany. Post-war migrants, who have long been considered political objects, increasingly feel that they have a right to participate in German politics and shape German society. Instead of remaining '*laic* clients' on the outside, they strive to enter the political field themselves in order to influence political decisions (rules and regulations) as well as public discourses and principles of division. As shown through the example of the BFF, a certain number of immigrants and their descendants not only feel entitled to participate, but have the resources and the habitus enabling them to do so – whether as members of established parties or on their own ticket.

Secondly, the relationship between the political and religious field is currently being re-negotiated. Muslim stakeholders are increasingly dissatisfied with a situation in which Islam is denied the privileges enjoyed by Christian churches. Since the rules of the game are set in the political field, Muslim actors seek to gain influence – whether in a traditional manner through lobbying or by entering the political field as participating actors.

However, as shown in Section 3.2, any actor wishing to enter the political field is faced with a specific hegemonic discourse. Foreigners being equated with Muslims and both being perceived as social out-groups, any political organisation which knowingly positions itself with relation to both of these categories needs to be aware of the severe headwinds it will face. In order to cope with this problem and to dissipate fears and accusations of disunity and segregation, the BFF resorted to talking about peace, unity and social cohesion. Yet beyond this rhetoric, the question remains: are political opponents right when they accuse the BFF and similar voter associations of contributing to separation and social disintegration?

In line with a political culture which cherishes the ideal of consensus oriented politics and believes in the existence of a 'common good', the BFF is interpreted as an illegitimate segregationist party. From a different perspective, however, it can be argued that civil commitment and an interest in political affairs – such as that shown by the BFF founders – is a prerequisite for a functioning, vibrant democratic system. Currently only 4% of German citizens are party members (Korte 2009), 90% of Germans see no sense in being politically active, and 94% of them are convinced that they have no influence whatsoever on decisions in the political field (Decker et al. 2010: 198–9). Therefore one could hold the view that any individual who does share the illusion – that is the collective belief in the meaningfulness of the respective 'game' (cf. Bourdieu

1998: 140–2) – and does wish to enter the political field should be welcome to do so. The BFF in particular was able to mobilise a larger number of young, first-time voters and citizens who were not in the habit of using their vote. This could indeed be considered a valuable contribution to the legitimacy of the German political system.

Nonetheless, two critical questions need to be raised: Firstly, while the BFF's strategy and positioning worked well in a very specific local situation, it is doubtful whether this success can be reproduced on other political levels. In 2010, the 'Association for Innovation and Justice' – a merger between the BFF and two other voter associations – fell well below the 5% threshold and thus failed to gain entry into the state parliament in NRW. Actors wishing to influence state and national politics are thus well advised to work their way upward inside the large established parties instead. Recently all the major parties have begun to realise that it is necessary to open up to ethnically diverse candidates (Schönwälder 2010: 29) – a process to which the new voter organisations might or might not have contributed. Since the end of the last decade party members 'with a migration background' ascending to the highest ranks in party politics and executive bodies have become a novel, but increasingly well established phenomenon.[15] Their prominent position in the political field provides them with the power to effectively influence and change structures to a much larger extent than a small voter association might ever be able to do. For example, in her first three months in office Bilkey Öney, state minister for integration in Baden Wurttemberg, initiated legislation on dual citizenship and abolished the widely contested 'test of consciousness' for Muslims applying for naturalisation in Baden-Wurttemberg (Allgöwer 2011).

A second open question remains as to whether a political actor such as the BFF which juggles with religious and social issues and terminologies will not corroborate the conflation of ethnic and religious categories described above. The BFF's declared aim to normalise the participation of visible and practising Muslims in the German political field might work out in the long run. However, at present it seems as if the visible and obvious religious affiliation of the BFF's candidates, and the observation that they do lobby for the interests of Muslim believers in a municipal council, for example with regard to the mosque building or the contentious question of mixed-gender swimming lessons, might rather increase the distrust they and other Muslim actors in the political field are faced with. The widespread criticism of the Pope's speech in the German parliament in September 2011 is indicative of a situation in which German society is becoming increasingly wary of the 'positive neutrality' that used to shape state-church relationships. Thus, although Christian Democrats might (still) be able to assert their religious identity and base political claims on this identity, the day when Muslim politicians will be able to do the same is yet to come. Until then, politicians are well-advised to do what Omid Nouripour (the only Member of Parliament to have registered as 'Muslim' in the Parliament handbook) and others do, namely declare their religion to be a private and not a political issue.

Notes

1. The findings presented in this paper are based on interviews with four members of the BFF, participant observation during the election campaign, as well as an analysis of online and offline media coverage of the local council elections of 2009. This fieldwork is part of a larger research project on the image of Islam and the everyday lives of Arab Muslims in Germany, funded by the DFG (German Research Foundation).
2. The 1913 'Reich citizenship law' (RuStAG) was re-installed after WW II (cf. Brubaker 1992 for the various pragmatic reasons for this decision). It was amended for the first time in 1990 and finally replaced by a new citizenship law (StAG) in 2000.
3. Today, children born in Germany to foreign parents who have lived in Germany for at least eight years and have an unlimited residence permit, receive German citizenship at birth (article 4 paragraph 3 StAG). In response to the conservative opposition's lobbying against possible dual nationality and the state elections in Hessen won inter alia due to this agenda, all German citizens having obtained dual citizenship at birth on the basis of *the jus soli* regulation have to decide on only one of their citizenships when they reach the legal age of consent (article 29 StAG) (exceptions are made for cases in which naturalisation would not be impeded by dual citizenship, i.e. for EU citizens – cf. article 12 StAG).
4. Amendments in 2005 and 2007 introduced advantages for naturalisation with participation in an integration course (articles 10 to 12 StAG) and obligatory tests on the German political and social system (article 10 paragraph 7 StAG).
5. Numbers are rough estimates since information on religion has not yet been included in regular statistical data collection mechanisms in Germany.
6. In 2008, a share of 10% of citizens 'with migration background' corresponded to only 2% of members of Parliament and 2.3% of state parliament members with a migration background (Wüst 2009: 201–18). In 2009 a share of 13–20% of first and second generation immigrants in the NRW electorate corresponded to a share of only 4% immigrants in the municipal councils (Schönwälder and Kofri 2010). Representativeness however varies by party with the Left and Green party offering more opportunities for migrants than Social or Christian Democrats or the Liberal party (Schönwälder and Kofri 2010; Sinanoglu and Volkert 2011).
7. Here again a difference in political orientation is noticeable: anti-migration issues are regularly picked up by conservative politicians, i.e. Roland Koch 1999; Jürgen Rüttger 2000; Horst Seehofer 2011, while the Green and the Left parties try to develop and establish alternative narratives and ideologies.
8. Similar councils have been founded in Hamburg in 1999 (cf. Spielhaus 2011 for a detailed account), in Munich (2003) and in Dortmund (2007).

9. Olbricht's analysis of the 2011 state elections in Bremen using an open-list system reveals that this mechanism increases the chance of immigrant candidates and/or political newcomers getting a seat in parliament. In this case, rather than depending completely on their 'institution' by the party, candidates can also bring in their personal political capital to advance their position on the list.

10. An example for such a niche strategy is provided by the 'Alternative citizens initiative', a voter association founded at the same time in neighbouring Cologne: they presented (male) candidates of Turkish origin only, with campaign materials equally designed in Turkish (available at <http://www.zeit.de/online/2009/36/waehlergemeinschaft-migranten-koeln> (last accessed 6 August 2012)). Nevertheless, their meagre result of only 0.04% of the votes in the municipal council elections in 2009 is also to be attributed to their lack of a previously established organisational structure and the fact that due to their lack of candidates, they were present in only six electoral wards, available at <http://www.stadt-koeln.de/wahlen/kommunalwahl/2009/wahlpraesentation> (last accessed 6 August 2012).

11. For example a member of a local voter association in Gelsenkirchen, speaking about a new voter organisation founded by members of the local integration council: 'In our city numerous political parties and voter associations do exist. Politically interested voters are always welcome there. An active engagement in these parties and associations would be a sign of successful integration. The foundation of an 'own' list on the contrary is from the viewpoint of the UB-GE a sign of Self-Separation (Abgrenzung) from the native majority society'. Available at <http://www.ub-ge.de/news.php?id=9> (last accessed 21 April 2010).

12. Although right-wing populism has been less successful in Germany than in other European countries (Decker Hartleb 2006: 191–215), a change in strategy can currently be observed, with parties everywhere in Europe rallying around a common anti-Islamic platform (Geden 2009: 92–107).

13. A Google research for 'Bündnis für Frieden und Fairness' (19 August 2011) underlines the high visibility of these platforms, three of which feature on the first page, one of them (PI) among the top three hits.

14. Recent findings available at <http://www.fr-online.de/die-neue-rechte/-politically-incorrect--im-netz-der-islamfeinde,10834438,10835026.html> (last accessed 6 August 2012).

15. Examples include: Cem Özedemir, first member of parliament in 1994, Chairman of the Green party since November 2008; Phillip Rösler, Federal Minister for Health and Labour since 2009, available at <http://www.bmwi.de/DE/Ministerium/minister-und-staatssekretaere.html> (last accessed 6 August 2012) and Chairman of the Liberal party (FDP); Aygül Özkan, State Minister for Integration in Lower Saxony (CDU) – heralded as the first 'Muslim' minister, available at <www.ms.niedersachsen.de> (last accessed 6 August 2012); and Bilkay Öney SPD, State Minister for integration in Baden-Württemberg since 2011, available at <www.integrationsministerium-bw.de> (last accessed 6 August 2012).

References

Allgöwer, R. (2011), *Integrationsministerin Bilkay Öney. Freundin des offenen Worts,* available at <http://www.stuttgarter-zeitung.de/inhalt.integrationsministerin-bilkay-oeney-freundin-des-offenen-worts.79361412-f1df-478a-a6bc-cbfc4bd71aa6.html> (last accessed 10 November 2011).

Amir-Moazami, S. (2007), *Politisierte Religion: der Kopftuchstreit in Deutschland und Frankreich,* Bielefeld: transcript.

Azzaoui, M. (2009), *Similarities in Difference: The Challenge of Muslim Integration in Germany and the United States,* available at <www.aicgs.org/documents/pubs/issuebrief33.pdf> (last accessed 10 November 2011).

Azzaoui, M. (2011), 'Muslimische Gemeinschaften in Deutschland zwischen Religionspolitik und Religionsverfassungsrecht – Schieflagen und Perspektiven', in H. Meyer, K. Schubert (eds), *Politik und Islam,* Wiesbaden: VS Verlag, pp. 247–76.

BAMF (2011), *Integrationsreport,* available at <www.bamf.de/SharedDocs/Anlagen/DE/Downloads/Infothek/Forschung/Integrationsreport/Einbuergerung/einbuergerung-tabelle-3-4-xls.html> (last accessed 12 September 2011).

Beinhauer-Köhler, B., C. Leggewie et al. (2009), *Moscheen in Deutschland. Religiöse Heimat und gesellschaftliche Herausforderung,* München: Beck.

BFF (2009), Wahlprogramm, available at <www.bffbonn.bff-bonn.de/uploads/media/BFF_Wahlprogramm_2009.pdf> (last accessed 10 November 2011).

Bodenstein, M. (2010), 'Organisational Developments towards Legal and Political Recognition of Muslims in Germany', in A. Kreienbrink (ed.), *Muslim Organisations and the State, European Perspectives,* Nürnberg: Bundesamt für Migration und Flüchtlinge, pp. 55–68.

Bosse, M. and M. Teigeler (2009), *Wählervereinigung mit muslimischen Wurzeln,* <www . domradio . de / aktuell / 56264 / waehlervereinigung - mit - muslimischen - wurzeln.html> (last accessed 10 November 2011).

Bourdieu, P. (1982), *Die feinen Unterschiede. Kritik der gesellschaftlichen Urteilskraft,* Frankfurt am Main: Suhrkamp.

Bourdieu, P. (1983), 'Ökonomisches Kapital, kulturelles Kapital, soziales Kapital,' in R. Kreckel (ed.), *Soziale Ungleichheiten,* Göttingen: Schwartz, pp. 183–98.

Bourdieu, P. (1987), *Choses dites,* Paris: Les Editions de Minuit.

Bourdieu, P. (1991), *Language and symbolic power,* Cambridge: Polity Press.

Bourdieu, P. (1998), *Praktische Vernunft,* Frankfurt am Main: Suhrkamp.

Bourdieu, P. (2001), *Das politische Feld. Zur Kritik der politischen Vernunft,* Konstanz: UVK.

Brema, N. (2010), *Friedliche Religion oder Bedrohung. Eine Analyse der Darstellung des Islams in DER SPIEGEL – 1998–2008,* Saarbrücken: VDM.

Brubaker, R. (1992), *Citizenship and nationhood in France and Germany,* Cambridge, MA: Harvard University Press.

Butterwegge, C. (2007), *Benehmt euch. Ihr seid hier nicht zu Hause',* available at <www.zeit.de/2007/45/Migranten-in-Medien> (last accessed 10 November 2011).

Castels, S. (1985), 'The Guests who stayed – The Debate on "Foreigners Policy" in the German Federal Republic', *International Migration Review*, no. 71, pp. 517–34.

Cesari, J. (2010), 'Securitization of Islam in Europe', in J. Cesari (ed.), *Muslims in the West after 9/11. Religion, politics, and law*, London: Routledge, pp. 9–27.

City of Bonn (2009a), *299 Kandidaten für das neue Stadtparlament,* available at <www2.bonn.de/statistik_wahlen/dl/Wahlstatistik/kw/kw2009Kandidaten.pdf> (last accessed 10 November 2011).

City of Bonn (2009b), *Kommunalwahl 30. August 2009 in Bonn. Wie wählten Jung und Alt, Männer und Frauen?* available at <www2.bonn.de/statistik_wahlen/dl/ Wahlstatistik/kw/kw2009Repraesent.pdf> (last accessed 10 November 2011).

Copur, B. (2005), *Debatte: Reform der Ausländerbeiräte. Integrationsausschüsse statt nur Integrationsräte als Mogelpackung.* Pro: 'Modell Essen'. Heinrich Böll Stiftung, available at <www.kommunale-info.de/index.html?/infothek/2560.asp> (last accessed 26 May 2010).

Data4U (2009), *Pressemitteilung 003/2009. Erstmals Wahlabsichten türkischer Migranten repräsentativ befragt,* available at <www.data4u-online.de/downloads/ pressemitteilung-data4u-0309.pdf> (last accessed 10 November 2011).

Decker, F. and F. Hartleb (2006), 'Populismus auf schwierigem Terrain. Die rechten und linken Herausfordererparteien in der Bundesrepublik', in F. Decker (ed.), *Populismus*, Wiesbaden: VS Verlag, pp. 191–215.

Decker, O., M. Weißmann, J. Kiess and E. Brähler (2010), *Die Mitte in der Krise – Präsentation,* available at <www.fes-gegen-rechtsextremismus.de/pdf_10/101013_ praesentation.pdf> (last accessed 15 October 2010).

Deutsche Islamkonferenz (2011), *Islamischer Religionsunterricht in Deutschland Perspektiven und Herausforderungen,* available at <http://www.deutsche-islam-konferenz . de / cln _ 101 / SharedDocs / Anlagen / DE / DIK / Downloads / Sonstiges / Dokumentation_20IRU-Tagung_202011,templateId=raw,property=publication File.pdf/ Dokumentation% 20IRU-Tagung%202011.pdf> (last accessed 27 September 2011).

Eussner, Gudrun (2009), *Islam ist Frieden. Gib dem FRIEDEN deine Stimme!* available at <www.eussner.net/artikel_2009-08-18_00-08-13.html> (last accessed 10 November 2011).

Falter, J. W. and H. Schoen (eds) (2005), *Handbuch Wahlforschung*, Wiesbaden: VS Verlag.

Fuchs-Heinritz, W. and A. König (2005), *Pierre Bourdieu. Eine Einführung*, Konstanz: UVK.

Geden, O. (2009), 'Die Renaissance des Rechtspopulismus in Westeuropa', *Internationale Politik und Gesellschaft*, no. 2, pp. 92–107.

German Federal Agency for Civic Education (bpb) (ed.), (1978), *Als Deutsche unter Deutschen leben. Eingliederung der Aussiedler,* Bonn: Bonner Universitäts-Buchdruckerei.

Geyer, S. and J. Schindler (2011), *Im Netz der Islamfeinde*, available at <www.fr-online.de/die-neue-rechte/-politically-incorrect--im-netz-der-islamfeinde,10834438,1083502.htm> (last accessed 10 November 2011).

Giddens, A. (1997), *Die Konstitution der Gesellschaft. Grundzüge einer Theorie der Strukturierung*, Frankfurt am Main: Campus.

Giddens, A. (2008), *The constitution of society. Outline of the theory of structuration*, Cambridge: Polity Press.

Hafez, K. (2002), *Das Nahost- und Islambild der deutschen überregionalen Presse*, Baden-Baden: Nomos.

Hailbronner, K. (2010), *Integration und Staatsangehörigkeit. 53. Bitburger Gespräche*, available at <www.irp.uni-trier.de/typo3/fileadmin/template/pdf/53BG_Hailbronner.pdf> (last accessed 20 May 2010).

Hammar, T. (ed.) (1995), *European Immigration Policy*, Cambridge: Cambridge University Press.

Haug, S., S. Müssig and A. Stichs (2009), *Muslimisches Leben in Deutschland. Im Auftrag der Deutschen Islam Konferenz*, Nürnberg: Bundesamt für Migration und Flüchtlinge.

Häusler, A. (ed.) (2008), *Rechtspopulismus als 'Bürgerbewegung'. Kampagnen gegen Islam und Moscheebau und kommunale Gegenstrategien*, Wiesbaden: VS Verlag.

Heinrich Böll Stiftung (ed.), (2010), *Muslimische Gemeinschaften zwischen Recht und Politik*, available at <www.migration-boell.de/downloads/integration/Dossier_Muslimische_Gemeinschaften.pdf> (last accessed 10 November 2011).

Hummel, U. (2009), *Muslim group fields candidates in local elections*, available at <www.dw-world.de/dw/article/0,,4600025,00.html> (last accessed 10 November 2011).

Inhoffen, L. et al. (2011), *Bonner Ratsherr Ernst war in der NPD*, available at <www.general-anzeiger-bonn.de/index.php?k=loka&itemid=10490&detailid=870480> (last accessed 10 November 2011).

Jonker, G. (2006), 'Islamist or Pietist? Muslim Responses to the German Security Framework' in G. Jonker, V. Amiraux (eds), *Politics of visibility. Young Muslims in European public spaces*, Bielefeld: Transcript, pp. 123–50.

Koopmans, R. (2005), *Contested citizenship. Immigration and cultural diversity in Europe*, Minneapolis, MN: University of Minnesota Press.

Korte, K.-R. (2009), *Wahlen in Nordrhein-Westfalen*, Schwalbach: Wochenschau-Verlag.

Krüger-Potratz, M. and W. Schiffauer (eds) (2011), *Migrationsreport 2010*, Frankfurt am Main: Campus.

LAGA NRW (2010), *Pressemitteilung vom 8. Februar 2010. Beteiligung an Integrationsratswahlen konstant*, available at <www.integrationsratswahlennrw.de/data/pressemitteilung_08.02..pdf> (last accessed 10 November 2011).

Landesregierung NRW (2011a), *Landesregierung und Muslime erzielen Durchbruch auf dem Weg zum islamischen Religionsunterricht*, available at (www.schulministerium.nrw.de/BP/Presse/Meldungen/Pressemitteilungen/pm_22_02_11_pdf.pdf> (last accessed 10 November 2011).

Landesregierung NRW (2011b), *Löhrmann: Wir führen den islamischen Religionsunterricht Schritt für Schritt ein*, available at <www.schulministerium. nrw.de/BP/Presse/Meldungen/Pressemitteilungen/pm_06_05_2011_pdf.pdf> (last accessed 10 November 2011).

Maul, U. (2009), *Geballter Protest gegen 'Gefahr von rechts'*, available at <www. rundschau-online.de/html/artikel/1246895316549.shtml> (last accessed 10 November 2011).

Miller, J. (2008), *Postwar negotiations: The first generation of Turkish Guest workers in West Germany*, New Brunswick, NJ: Rutgers University Press.

Moser, M. (2006), *Rural Primary Schools: Mapping conflict between the community and the market*, University of Lancaster.

Nordbruch, G. (2011), *Germany: Migration, Islam and National Identity*, available at <http://static.sdu.dk/mediafiles/E/C/4{EC494903-F28A-4260-862D-C718526E80AB}11096N.pdf> (last accessed 26 September 2011).

Oberndörfer, D. (2009), 'Einwanderung wider Willen. Deutschland zwischen historischer Abwehrhaltung und unausweichlicher Öffnung gegenüber (muslimischen) Fremden', in T. G. Schneiders (ed.), *Islamfeindlichkeit. Wenn die Grenzen der Kritik verschwimmen*, Wiesbaden: VS Verlag, pp. 127–42.

Oebbecke, J. (2010), *Der Islam als Herausforderung für das deutsche Religionsrecht*, pp. 3–7, available at <www.migration-boell.de/downloads/integration/Dossier_Muslimische_Gemeinschaften.pdf> (last accessed 10 November 2011).

Olbricht, R. (2011), *Politische Parteiengründung durch Migranten: Förderung der (politischen Integration von Einwanderern oder zunehmende gesellschaftliche Spaltung? Das Beispiel der Bremer Integrationspartei (BIP)*. Unpublished Master thesis, University of Bremen, Bremen.

Peter, F. (2010), 'Welcoming Muslims into the nation: tolerance, politics and integration in Germany'. in J. Cesari (ed.), *Muslims in the West after 9/11. Religion, politics, and law*, London: Routledge, pp. 119–44.

Preuß, Roland (2009), Mit dem Kopftuch im Parlament. In Bonn stellt erstmals eine Migrantenpartei zwei Stadträte – der Kampf neue Moscheen hat die Muslime starkgemacht, in: Süddeutsche Zeitung, 28 September 2009.

RMB (2006), *Rat der Muslime in Bonn*, available at <www.muslimrat-bonn.de/uploads/media/RMB-Flyer.pdf> (last accessed 10 November 2011).

Rommelspacher, B. (2009), 'Islamkritik und antimuslimische Positionen am Beispiel von Necla Kelek und Seyran Ateş', in T. G. Schneiders (ed.), *Islamfeindlichkeit*, Wiesbaden: VS Verlag, pp. 433–456.

Roth, R. (2009), 'Integration durch politische Partizipation und bürgerschaftliches Engagement', in F. Gesemann, R. Roth (eds), *Lokale Integrationspolitik in der Einwanderungsgesellschaft*, Wiesbaden: VS Verlag, pp. 195–216.

Said, E. W. (1978), *Orientalism*, New York: Vintage Books.

Schäuble, W. (2006), *Regierungserklärung des Bundesministers des Innern, Dr Wolfgang Schäuble, zur Deutschen Islamkonferenzvor dem Deutschen Bundestag am 28 September 2006 in Berlin,* available at <http://www.bundesregierung.de/ Content/DE/Bulletin/2001_2007/2006/09/_Anlagen/93-1-bmi-islamkonferenz-bt. pdf?__blob=publicationFile&v=1> (last accessed 6 August 2012).

Schiffauer, W. (2006), 'Enemies within the gates. The debate about the citizenship of Muslims in Germany', in T. Modood (ed.), *Multiculturalism, Muslims and citizenship,* London: Routledge, pp. 94–116.

Schiffauer, W. (2007), 'Der unheimliche Muslim – Staatsbürgerschaft und zivilgesellschaftliche Ängste', in M. Wohlrab-Sahr, L. Tezcan (eds), *Konfliktfeld Islam in Europa,* Baden-Baden: Nomos, pp. 111–33.

Schiffer, S. (2004), *Die Darstellung des Islams in der Presse. Sprache, Bilder, Suggestionen; eine Auswahl von Techniken und Beispielen,* Würzburg: Ergon.

Schiffer, S. (2009), 'Grenzenloser Hass im Internet', in T. G. Schneiders (ed.), *Islamfeindlichkeit. Wenn die Grenzen der Kritik verschwimmen,* Wiesbaden: VS Verlag, pp. 341–62.

Schmitt, T. (2003), *Moscheen in Deutschland. Konflikte um ihre Errichtung und Nutzung,* Flensburg: Dt. Akad. für Landeskunde.

Schneiders, T. G. (2009), 'Die Schattenseite der Islamkritik. Darlegung und Analyse der Argumentationsstrategien von Henryk M. Broder, Ralph Giordano, Necla Keleck, Alice Schwarzer und anderen', in T. G. Schneiders (ed.), *Islamfeindlichkeit,* Wiesbaden: VS Verlag, pp. 403–32.

Schönwälder, K. (2010), 'Einwanderer in Räten und Parlamenten', *APuZ,* no. 4647, pp. 29–35.

Schönwälder, K. and C. Kofri (2010), *Diversity in Germany's Political Life? Immigrants in City Councils,* Max Planck Institute for the Study of Religious and Ethnic Diversity, Göttingen, <www.mmg.mpg.de/workingpapers> (last accessed 10 November 2011).

Schwarz, M. (2009), '*Wir sind keine islamische Partei',* available at <www.jun gefreiheit.de/Single-News-Display-mit-Komm.154+M53cd3d6ca8f.0.html> (last accessed 10 November 2011).

Shooman, Y. and R. Spielhaus (2010), 'The concept of the Muslim enemy in the public discourse', in J. Cesari (ed.), *Muslims in the West after 9/11. Religion, politics, and law,* London: Routledge, pp. 189–228.

Sinanoglu, C. and D. Volkert (2011), *Politische Partizipation und die Präsenz von Menschen mit Migrationshintergrund in den Räten deutscher Großstädte: Vielfalt oder Einfalt?* Stiftung, H. B., available at <www.migration-boell.de/web/integra tion/47_3012.asp> (last accessed 7 November 2011).

Sontheimer, K. and W. Bleek (2002), *Grundzüge des politischen Systems Deutschlands,* Bonn: Bundeszentrale für Politische Bildung.

Søvik, M. (2008), 'Islamic Instruction in German Public Schools: The Case of North-Rhine-Westphalia', in A. Al-Hamarneh, J. Thielmann (eds), *Islam and Muslims in Germany,* Leiden: Brill, pp. 241–66.

Spielhaus, R. (2011), *Wer ist hier Muslim? Die Entwicklung eines islamischen*

Bewusstseins in Deutschland zwischen Selbstidentifikation und Fremdzuschreibung, Würzburg: Ergon.

Spindler, H. (2002), 'Das neue Staatsangehörigkeitsrecht: Ziele, Inhalte der Vorschriften und Umsetzung', in H. Storz, C. Reißlandt (eds), *Staatsbürgerschaft im Einwanderungsland Deutschland*, Opladen: Leske + Budrich, pp. 53–70.

Statistisches Bundesamt (2009), *Bevölkerung und Erwerbstätigkeit. Bevölkerung mit Migrationshintergrund Ergebnisse des Mikrozensus 2005*, available at <www. destatis.de/jetspeed/portal/cms/Sites/destatis/Internet/DE/Content/Publikationen/ Fachveroeffentlichungen/Bevoelkerung/MigrationIntegration/Migrationshintergru nd2010220057004,property=file.pdf> (last accessed 10 November 2011).

Statistisches Bundesamt (2011), *Fachserie 1, Reihe 2.1 Einbürgerungen 2010*, available at <www.destatis.de/jetspeed/portal/cms/Sites/destatis/Internet/DE/ Content/Publikationen/Fachveroeffentlichungen/Bevoelkerung/MigrationIntegra tion/Einbuergerungen2010210107004,property=file.pdf> (last accessed 10 November 2011).

Stoldt, T.-R. (2009), *Politik aus dem Geist des Korans*, available at <www.welt.de/ die-welt/vermischtes/article4425463/Politik-aus-dem-Geist-des-Korans.html> (last accessed 10 November 2011).

SWR (2009), *Muslime mit Sitzen im Bonner Stadtrat*, available at <www.swr.de/inter- national/de/-/id=233334/nid=233334/did=5314048/1i717gd/index.html> (last accessed 10 November 2011).

Thielmann, J. (2010), 'The Turkish Bias and Some Blind Spots: Research on Muslims in Germany' in A. Kreienbrink (ed.), *Muslim Organisations and the State. European Perspectives*, Nürnberg: Bundesamt für Migration und Flüchtlinge, pp. 169–95.

Tiesler, N. C. (2007), 'Europäisierung des Islam und Islamisierung der Debatten', *APuZ*, no. 2627, pp. 24–31.

Treibel, A. (1999), *Migration in modernen Gesellschaften. Soziale Folgen von Einwanderung, Gastarbeit und Flucht*, Weinheim, München: Juventa.

Tröger, S. (2003), 'Akteure in ihrer Lebensgestaltung (livelihood) zu Zeiten sozialer Transformation', *Geographica Helvetica*, vol. 58, no. 1, pp. 24–34.

Vallender, F. (2009), *Moscheeverein soll Pläne ändern*, available at <www.general- anzeiger-bonn.de/index.php?k=loka&itemid=10490&detailid=643911> (last accessed 10 November 2011).

Wall, H. de (2008), *Verfassungsrechtliche Rahmenbedingungen eines islamischen Religionsunterrichts*, available at <www.deutsche-islam-konferenz.de/cln_ 101/SharedDocs/Anlagen/DE/DIK/Downloads/DokumentePlenum/ 2008-IRU- zwischenresumee-der-dik,templateId=raw,property=publicationFile.pdf/2008- IRU-zwischenresumee-der-dik.pdf> (last accessed 27 September 2011).

Wüst, A. (2003), '*Das Wahlverhalten eingebürgerter Personen in Deuschland*', *APuZ*, no. 52, pp. 29–39.

Wüst, A. and D. Heinz (2009), Die politische Repräsentation von Migranten in Deutschland', in M. Linden, W. Thaa (eds), *Die politische Repräsentation von Fremden und Armen*, Baden-Baden: Nomos, pp. 201–18.

Yurdakul, G. (2006), 'Secular versus Islamist: The Headscarf Debate in Germany', in G. Jonker, V. Amiraux (eds), *Politics of visibility. Young Muslims in European public spaces*, Bielefeld: Transcript, pp. 151–68.

4

POLITICAL OPINIONS AND PARTICIPATION AMONG YOUNG MUSLIMS IN SWEDEN: A CASE STUDY[1]

Jonatan Bäckelie and Göran Larsson

In April 2009 Sweden's largest Sunni Muslim youth organisation, Sweden's Young Muslims[2] (SUM), organised their 16th annual youth conference. Based on a survey distributed at the conference, this chapter aims to document and analyse political opinion and political participation among young organised Muslims in Sweden and relate the respondents' answers to the political left and right scale. For this purpose – well aware of competing and alternative definitions – we do not apply an external definition of 'young' or 'Muslim', but rather assume that those attending a conference for young Muslims see themselves as fitting the bill.

Before we go into the specific survey we would like to offer some more general comments on the composition of Sweden's Muslim population. Like most countries in Europe, the Swedish population has been altered because of international migration (workforce migration, family reunification migration and asylum seekers) and more generally by globalisation processes. Compared to the nineteenth century and early twentieth century, Sweden is today a multi-cultural and multi-religious society and the Swedish constitution and the state places great stress on freedom of religion and pluralism. For example, when writing this chapter (autumn 2012) the Swedish state supports six Muslim umbrella organisations with economic subsidies, and religious groups are often seen as important interlocutors for the state. However, this recognition does not clash with the fact that the state of Sweden aims at neutrality when it comes to religious affairs. This policy has been questioned by various actors and it is often argued that the state is unaware of the fact that it is embedded in its own Swedish Christian heritage.[3] Nevertheless, the state argues that religious and other voluntary organisations are vital for an open democratic society, and it is because of this belief that the state is willing to support religious organisations.

When it comes to Muslims in Sweden we want to stress that this community is highly heterogeneous, and today it is not possible to say that one ethnic or linguistic group is in a dominant position. Although it is possible to identify Muslims from all parts of the larger Muslim world in Sweden today, it would be incorrect to view all Muslims in Sweden as practitioners of Islam on a regular basis. According to estimations made by both Muslims and academics the number of Muslims in Sweden is close to 400,000 out of Sweden's 9.1 million inhabitants. However, according to the governmental body that hands out state support for religious organisations (SST) the number of 'active, believing' Muslims is closer to 110,000. These figures are merely estimations as there are no official statistical data on religious affiliation in Sweden today (for constitutional reasons).

This backdrop indicates two things. First, the Muslim community in Sweden is very heterogeneous; secondly, it is not correct to say that all Muslims in Sweden should be portrayed as religious. Rather it is probable that only a minority of Swedish Muslims are active practitioners of Islam. The large majority of people with a Muslim cultural background in Sweden are Sunni Muslims and this group also dominates the youth organisation that we have taken as a starting point for our discussions.

Before turning to our case study it is first necessary to say a few words about the political context in Sweden. In order to sit in parliament in Sweden it is necessary for a party to get 4% of the voters' support. When our survey was distributed seven parties held seats in the parliament: S = Social Democrats; L = Left Party; GP = Green Party; C = Centre Party; LP = Liberal Party; M = Moderates; and CD = Christian Democrats. Besides these seven parties, our survey also touches on two parties that were outside the parliament in 2009. These are SD = Sweden Democrats and P = Pirate Party. Since our study was conducted, the SD party has entered the parliament and among many things have contributed to a heated debate about immigration and Islam/Muslims. At the time of the study (and when writing this) Sweden was governed by a coalition consisting of M, C, LP and CD. With this background it is now time to turn to our case study.

1.   The Youth Conference

Between 10 and 13 April 2009, Sweden's Young Muslims (SUM) arranged a youth conference for the 16th time at Åsö gymnasie- och vuxenskola at Skanstull in central Stockholm. According to the organisation approximately 1200 people attended the conference, out of which around fifty were volunteer workers. The programme consisted mainly of lectures by Swedish and international Muslim leaders, but also included music performances, panel discussions, a support night for Palestine, and other activities. Amongst the lecturers were Sheikh Mohamed Dini, Khalid Yassin (both from the US) and Daniel Stridsman (deputy vice-chancellor of the Al-Azhar School, which is a

Muslim independent school) on topics relating to Islam and the Muslim presence in Sweden.

Mohamed Dini's lectures emphasised balance between material and spiritual aspects of life and encouraged the youngsters not to view life in black and white terms. Furthermore, Dini also had Q & A sessions where the youngsters could receive advice in practical questions such as what is allowed and not: 'Can I kill a wasp because I'm scared?', 'Can I ask a guy/girl about their MSN-details [i.e. how to contact an individual via a chat client] if my intentions are pure?', 'What should I do in order to get my former friend to stop spreading rumours about me?' and so on. Dini attained a noticeable following that approached him with questions in between and in relation to the lectures. For instance, it took him half an hour to walk from the auditorium to the canteen only 40 meters away because he was repeatedly stopped by people who had questions and feedback.

If Dini's approach was that of a low-key priest, then Khalid Yassin was closer to a charismatic evangelical preacher. Yassin held two lectures, one under the title 'Islam and Modernity', where Yassin claimed that Muslims were behind practically all important discoveries and scientific advances.[4] At the first lecture he invited a convert up on stage, but also decided that the young man should be given a new name, something that happened without being discussed with either SUM or the convert himself. This could be interpreted as openness from SUM's side in terms of allowing several different theological approaches, or it could likewise be interpreted as though Yassin acted on his own in a way that didn't correspond to SUM's expectations.

Apart from lectures the conference also included panel discussions on society and politics. Among the participants where minister of parliament Mehmet Kaplan (GP, Green Party) and the candidate member of the EU parliament Ardalan Shekarabi (S, Social Democrat) in a discussion titled 'The Muslim perspective in the political debate'. Kaplan was optimistic and talked about how the election of Barack Obama 2009 constituted a change which reached outside of the borders of the USA. The election of Obama, Kaplan argued, shows that people who feel alienated from society to some extent now are beginning to feel as though there may be a way to regain power and influence and a belief in change. Shekarabi, on the other hand, was more cautious and emphasised that the 'Muslim perspective' could be lost in societal debate as electoral turnout is low in areas where the population consists to a large degree of immigrants, along with the increasing support of right-wing party the Sweden Democrats. Both Kaplan and Shekarabi stressed that those who 'hate Muslims' don't distinguish between practising Muslims and secular or anti-religious people of Muslim decent. Instead, the question is reduced to the 'issue with the Muslims' much like the 'issue with the Jews' in the 1930s.[5]

Besides lectures, Q & As and panel discussions, prayers were part of the programme, along with gender segregated sporting activities such as African dancing and football. The school's restrooms, which were usually unisex, were separated into ones for 'brothers' and 'sisters'. At the lectures in the auditorium men and women were seated in separate rows, although the division was not between men on one side and women on the other, although measures with that intention were taken (with separate entrances).

Lectures were held in Swedish and English, where Arabic featured frequently, mainly without translation. In addition several languages were spoken at the conference, such as Norwegian, Turkish and sign language. Out of the 1200 participants a relatively large group came from Norway.[6] These were excluded in our survey as its focus is on how Swedish Muslims relate to their political system. With the Norwegians excluded, the estimate is that almost a quarter of the Swedish participants partook in the survey. The questionnaire, containing eighty-three questions, had been brought in 500 copies to the conference, meaning that it was not possible to get answers from all participants. Out of the 500, 269 questionnaires were returned, which gives a response frequency of 53.8%. It is, of course, hard to estimate the percentage of women vis-à-vis men at the conference, but women seem to have been in the majority. This corresponds to the returned questionnaires where approximately 70% were answered by women, 30% by men. The majority of the attending women had some kind of headscarf, a handful had a fully covering veil or *niqab*. Of the men, a minority had loose fitting full-length garments while the majority had 'regular' clothes. The conference main sponsors were Studieförbundet Ibn Rushd,[7] Islamic Relief, Tele2 Comviq, and Sweden's Islamic Schools.[8]

2.   Conducting the survey

In this section we will account for how Bäckelie collected the data during the conference. There was a room next to the canteen where a number of tables were put up in order to sell art (calligraphy) based on Qur'an quotations, but also Muslim swimwear,[9] and a range of hats, scarves and other articles in support of Palestine. The board of SUM also had a table of their own both for selling books, pens, mugs, and to be of general assistance. In order to carry out the survey Bäckelie had been provided with a table in this room, on and behind which signs saying 'What do you think about Swedish Politics? Partake in an important survey!' were put up, in order to attract attention. The bulk of the Friday was quiet and most visitors to the room were in fact looking for the registration desk. It soon became obvious that the signs weren't sufficiently inspiring to attract a stampede of youngsters to make their way to the table. Therefore the strategy was abandoned in favour of approaching the young people gathering outside in the sunshine. It turned out to be fairly hard to catch the youngsters' attention enough to make them break away from their friends entirely. To fill out the survey without interruption would take about fifteen minutes, but doing so at the same time as hanging out took a considerably longer time, sometimes doubling or even tripling the time. When choosing between socialising with friends or filling out a questionnaire many participants tired of the questionnaire, resulting in a number of them only being filled out to a certain extent. This results in a varying response frequency on different questions (which will be discussed more below).

The up-side of personally handing out the questionnaire was that it meant that it was possible to engage groups and individuals that maybe wouldn't have sought the questionnaire out by themselves. When asked to take part in the questionnaire many replied 'But I don't know anything about politics', and so it was possible to explain that this was not a case of who-knows-most, but rather that all replies were equally valuable regardless of whether one loves, hates or feel absolutely indifferent to politics.

Friday and Saturday were relatively successful in getting answered questionnaires returned by female participants. The 'brothers', however, turned out to be more reluctant. Fortunately some of the members of SUM's board were kind enough to encourage people to answer the questionnaire, vouch for its validity and even hand out a number of questionnaires themselves, which was very generous of them. There was also a rumour circulating that the survey was being conducted on behalf of the Swedish Secret Police (Säpo), which added to the reluctance. To the extent such concerns were aired in the presence of either SUM's board members or MP Mehmet Kaplan (who we had contact with prior to the conference), the rumours could be countered. A small number of people did not want to answer the questions as they felt it might reflect badly on Swedish Muslims. Some of the participants, in other words, seemed aware that some personal views may differ radically from what the majority of society may think on that topic, and that this could fan a fear of expressing political judgments built on religious conviction in the public space.

3. The results

Below we show the results of the survey. As previously noted, not all of the questions were answered in the 269 returned questionnaires, meaning that the number of respondents differs from one question to the next. This means that 100% of the population is not the same total on every question. For example, on the question of sex, 245 individuals answered this question, which means that 245 individuals make out 100% on that particular question. Displaying the results in this format was chosen in order to maximise the possibility of comparison with a similar study conducted by Magnus Hagevi (see below), using the same way of accounting for the results.

Of the respondents 177 were female (72.2%) and 68 were men (27.8%). When it comes to citizenship 183 individuals (74.7%) stated that they were Swedish, 12 individuals (4.9%) were citizens from another country and 50 individuals (20.4%) held dual citizenship (in Sweden and another country).

More than half of the participants (144 individuals, 59.3%) came from the greater Stockholm area, 38 individuals (15.6%) came from the rest of the surrounding Svealand region, 25 individuals (10.3%) came from the greater Gothenburg area (Gothenburg being the second largest city in Sweden), 14 individuals (5.7%) came from Malmö-Lund area (Malmö being the third largest city in Sweden and very close to Lund). Fifteen individuals (6.2%) came from other places in the Götaland region. Six individuals (2.5%) were from the Norrland region. One person (0.4%) was Swedish but lived in Oslo.

As noted above, Social Democratic representative Ardalan Shekarabi claimed, during the conference's socio-political panel discussion, that electoral turnout in municipalities considered to have a predominantly immigrant population is only at around 15% in total. There is reason to comment on this. Apart from the discussion below it should be noted that there are some branches within Islam where participation in democratic processes is perceived as non-Islamic, as democracy gives sovereignty to the people instead of Allah.[10] An organisation with this perspective is Hizb ut-Tahrir (Hizb ut-Tahrir 2009). This perspective, however, has very little or nothing in common with either the view of the respondents or the view of SUM, as it was expressed during the conference.

Coming back to Shekarabi's claim, this could be interpreted as though Muslims in general are uninterested in politics (because Shekarabi touches on this as relevant in this particular forum). Moreover it can be interpreted as though the respondents are mainly living in areas predominantly populated by immigrants (and are identified as part of this group). There are a number of comments to be offered here. On electoral turnout it can be noted that in Bergsjön, a suburb of Gothenburg that fits Shekarabi's description, the turnout in local elections (as immigrants without citizenship are allowed to vote locally but not in national elections) were in total 32.6% in 1994, and 19.8% in 1998. In Gunnared (another similar area) in Gothenburg, the equivalent numbers in 1994 and 1998 were 34.5% and 23.8% respectively (Jonsson 1999: 8). Shekarabi's estimate does not coincide with the turnout in Stockholm suburb Botkyrka in 2006, where 76% voted in the election to national parliament and 71% voted in the local election (these elections are held on the same day). This can be compared with Olsson and Dahlgren's numbers stating that the general turnout in Swedish elections is around 80% (Olsson and Dahlgren 2009: 34). At the same time the trend seems to be decreasing rather than increasing turnout, so from this perspective Shekarabi's bleak outlook may have some relevance. It is however problematic to claim that the conference participants only live in the said areas. Based on the data there is a wide spread between various living accommodation (houses, rental apartments, etc.) and in the type of area they reside in (suburbs with a predominantly immigrant population, 'well off' suburbs, city centre, etc.). This survey has not been able to draw any such particular conclusion on the basis of our demographic data.

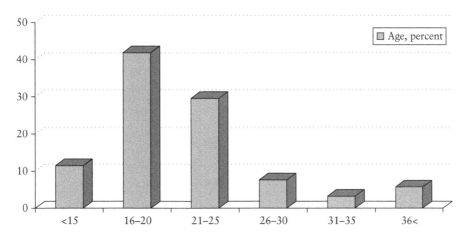

Figure 4.1 Age of respondents

Table 4.1 How often do you pray five times a day?

	Individuals	Percent
Every day	171	70.7
Most days every week	33	13.6
1–2 days a week	11	4.5
Sometime every month	9	3.8
More seldom	11	4.5
Never	7	2.9
Total	242	100

Figure 4.1 shows the spread of age, divided into categories >15 years, 16–20, 21–5, 26–30, 31–5 and 36<. The majority (174 individuals) belonged to the categories 16–20 and 21–5 years old; together these made up 71.6%. Twenty-eight individuals (11.5%) were 15 or younger, 102 individuals (42%) were between 16–20, 72 individuals (29.6%) between 21–5, 19 individuals (7.8%) were between 26–30, 8 individuals (3.3%) were between 31–5 and 14 individuals (5.8%) were 36 or older.

Although religious commitment would appear to be a given for those who choose to participate in a Muslim youth conference (at least given the spiritual content of this conference), it is relevant although hard to measure to what extent participants are practising Muslims, given that there are multiple definitions of who 'counts' as a Muslim and what we mean by religiosity.[11] Aware of the methodological problems, we asked the following questions: 'How often do you pray five times a day?' and 'Do you fast during Ramadan?'. These answers are displayed in Tables 4.1 and 4.2.

Table 4.2 Do you fast during Ramadan?

	Individuals	Percent
Yes	241	98
No	5	2
Total	246	100

Table 4.3 General interest in politics

	Individuals	Percent
Very interested	59	21.9
Somewhat interested	119	44.2
Not particularly interested	71	26.4
Not interested at all	20	7.5
Total	269	100

A total of 171 individuals (70.7%) stated that they prayed five times every day, 33 individuals (13.6%) prayed five times a day most days of the week, 11 individuals (4.5%) between one and two days a week, 9 individuals (3.8%) monthly, 11 individuals (4.5%) more seldom, and 7 individuals (2.9%) stated that they never pray five times a day. Furthermore, 241 individuals (98%) stated that they fast during Ramadan, and only 5 individuals (2%) stated that they did not.

Given that SUM has the intention of promoting and constructing a Swedish Muslim identity (Larsson 2003), where the primary language of Islam in Sweden is Swedish, not Arabic, it was interesting to investigate whether or not the respondents understood Arabic. Some 164 individuals (70.7%) answered yes and 68 individuals (29.3%) answered no. Thirty-seven questionnaires were deemed invalid as respondents had ticked both boxes or written remarks such as 'a little' or had ticked in between the boxes.

To comment further on electoral behaviour based on the numbers discussed earlier it may be interesting to note that 36 individuals (13.4%) were members of a political party, its youth branch or women's organisation. This adds to the complexity and shows a variety of relations within the survey population, rather than confirming any general image of Muslims equating with immigrants residing in a poor suburb, uninterested in politics.

On the issue of 'General interest in politics' (Table 4.3), 59 individuals (21.9%) said they were very interested, 119 individuals (44.2%) claimed to be somewhat interested, 71 individuals (26.4%) said they were not particularly interested, and 20 individuals (7.5%) said that they were not interested in politics in general at all.

Table 4.4 Confidence in politicians

	Individuals	Percent
Very high confidence	7	2.7
Fairly high confidence	74	28
Fairly low confidence	138	52.3
Very low confidence	45	17
Total	264	100

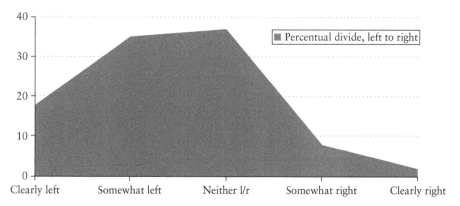

Figure 4.2 Self-identification along the left–right scale

Moreover, the respondents were asked about their 'Confidence in politicians' (Table 4.4) On this issue 7 individuals (2.7%) said they had a high degree of confidence in Swedish politicians, 74 individuals (28%) felt relatively confident in them, 138 individual (52.3%) said they had fairly little confidence in them, and 45 individuals (17%) said they had very little confidence in Swedish politicians, generally speaking. Confidence in political leaders does not automatically correspond to ethnic or religious belonging, but according to media reports from 2010 seven out of ten Swedes had high or relatively high confidence in political leaders (Stiernstedt 2010).

The next question was 'Sometimes it is said that political opinions can be placed along a left-right scale. Where would you place yourself on such a scale?' (Figure 4.2). Here 45 individuals (17.9%) placed themselves 'clearly to the left', 88 individuals (35.1%) placed themselves 'somewhat to the left', 93 individuals (37%) placed themselves 'neither right nor left', 20 individuals (8%) placed themselves 'somewhat to the right', and five individuals (2%) placed themselves 'clearly to the right'. In sum a little more than a third identified themselves as neither left nor right, 53% identified themselves as left to varying extent, and merely 10% identified themselves as right to some extent.

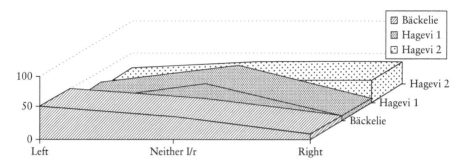

Figure 4.3 Self-identification on the left–right scale (percent), compared to two selections from Hagevi

Regarding the discussion about different ways to measure religious commitment, it is possible to compare these results with the category of Muslims which political scientist Magnus Hagevi calls 'Salat-praying Muslims' (meaning those who regularly adhere to the five obligatory prayers), in his *Politisk Opinion och Religiositet i Västra Götaland* (2009a). Out of Hagevi's population 12% identify themselves as 'clearly to the left', 20% as 'somewhat to the left', 60% as 'neither right nor left', 6% as 'somewhat to the right' and 2% as 'clearly to the right' (Hagevi 2009a: 219). This result can also be compared to Hagevi's category 'regular attendants to their religion's services' (in general, not only Muslims). There 9% identified themselves as 'clearly to the left', 18% stated 'somewhat left', 36% 'neither left nor right', 28% 'somewhat to the right' and 9% as 'clearly to the right' (Hagevi 2009a: 142). In Figure 4.3 the alternatives have been grouped into 'left', 'right' and 'neither left nor right', subsuming 'somewhat' and 'clearly' into the same group. Here the two selections from Hagevi are compared to Bäckelie. Hagevi 1 refers to *Salat-bedjande muslimer* (Hagevi's term for those Muslims who observe the five daily prayers), a group with 256 respondents. Hagevi 2 means 'regular attendants of religious services', a group with 382 respondents.

It should be noted that the results from our study are more complex than what is shown here. It proves hard to place the respondents on a left-right scale as this does not strictly coincide with either support of a political party or opinions regarding specific questions. This will be discussed further below, especially when attitudes towards specific topics do not correspond with how the favoured party position themselves on that same topic. Trying to circle the respondents' views with the help of a left-right scale therefore risk being misguiding. This is something that we wish to emphasise as one of the primary findings of our work.

When respondents were asked 'What party do you favour today?' the answer was the following: 118 individuals (54.6%) favoured S, which makes

Table 4.5 Which party do you currently favour?

	Individuals	Percent
S	118	54.6
GP	60	27.8
L	19	8.8
M	15	6.9
C	2	0.9
CD	1	0.5
P	1	0.5
LP	0	0
SD	0	0
Total	216	100

it the most favoured Swedish party (Table 4.5). After S came GP, which 60 individuals (27.8%) favoured. After this followed L, favoured by 19 individuals (8.8%); M: 15 individuals (6.9%); C: two individuals (0.9), and CD: one individual (0.5%). None of the respondents favoured either LP or SD. The question was also open to entering a party of your own choice, here one respondent (0.5%) named P, the Swedish Pirate party. Many questionnaires had to be excluded because respondents had ticked several boxes, indicating they favoured two or several parties equally.

According to Hagevi (2009a), S was also the most favoured party amongst *salat*-praying Muslims: 64% of them favoured S. The second largest party here was L, with 19%, and then GP, with 10%. LP received 4%, M: 3%, whilst CD, C and SD received 0% each (Hagevi 2009a: 184).[12]

This can be compared to the sympathies of those categorised as regular attendants of religious services. Here S was the most favoured party with 31%, followed by CD: 30%, LP: 12%, M and C with 10% each, and L with 3% (Table 4.5) (Hagevi 2009a: 131).

In Table 4.6 'Bäckelie' stands for this survey whilst *salat*-praying Muslims (consisting of 215 respondents) are named 'Hagevi 1', and regular attendants of religious services (359 respondents) are named 'Hagevi 2'. The Hagevi results are displayed in percentages. However, given that the support for CD and C are so small in our study, this would be misrepresented in percentages. Therefore, our results are displayed with decimals.

To deepen the discussion about left and right, the respondents were asked 'Do you consider yourself a convinced supporter of this party?' and could choose from the alternatives 'yes, very convinced', 'yes, somewhat convinced' and 'no'.

Table 4.7 shows that of those favouring S, 23.9% said they were 'very convinced', 51.3% were 'somewhat convinced', and 24.8% were 'unconvinced'. The corresponding numbers regarding GP were 18.6% 'very', 47.5%

Table 4.6 Favoured party, compared to two selections from Hagevi (percent)

	Bäckelie	Hagevi 1	Hagevi 2
S	54.6	64	31
GP	27.8	10	4
L	8.8	19	3
M	6.9	3	10
C	0.9	0	10
CD	0.5	0	30
P	0.5	0	0
LP	0	4	12
SD	0	0	0
Total	100	100	100

Table 4.7 Do you consider yourself a convinced supporter of this party?

Party	divide, percent				
	Yes, very	Yes, somewhat	No	Total	Individuals
S	23.9	51.3	24.8	100	113
GP	18.6	47.5	33.9	100	59
L	15.8	36.8	47.4	100	19
M	33.3	33.3	33.3	99.9	15
C	0	50	50	100	2
CD	0	0	100	100	1
P	0	0	100	100	1
LP	–	–	–	–	0
SD	–	–	–	–	0

'somewhat', and 33.9% 'unconvinced'. For L the numbers read 15.8% 'very', 36.8% 'somewhat', and 47.4% 'unconvinced'. The Moderates had an even distribution of five respondents (33.3%) per alternative (which explains the sum of 99.9% instead of 100%). None of the other bourgeois parties, or SD or P for that matter, had any convinced supporters.

The respondents were asked to rate a number of proposals stemming from political and public debate. The respondents could choose between the alternatives 'very good proposal', 'fairly good proposal', 'neither good nor bad proposal', 'fairly bad proposal', 'very bad proposal', or alternatively 'not familiar with this debate'. Because the questionnaires were not read mechanically it was possible to read the comments that had sometimes been written in the margin. One proposal was 'Start a Swedish imam education' to which one respondent had replied 'under whose direction?'. By the proposal 'The state should do more to protect morals' one respondent pointed out that Muslim and Swedish morals do not necessarily coincide. In order to take a stand on a proposal regarding protecting morals, the issue is primarily what kind of morals one refers to – the one of the respondent or that of the societal majority. Likewise, the imam comment can be perceived in a way where respondents are of the sentiment that such an education is neither good nor bad per se, solely based on what country the education is offered in.[13]

Among the specific questions that respondents reacted to there are a few that are worth noting. This is due to the fact that the respondents' position does not coincide with the position of S, GP and L – the parties that were supported by approximately 90% of the respondents. In other words, the sentiments expressed here can be said to be pretty far from a left-orientated sentiment (in a Swedish context at the very least). It should be said that the respondents are generally in support of the position of the parties mentioned above. It is not a case of saying that one supports the left although one is in fact supporting a 'clearly right' perspective. Instead it is a matter of seven (out of twenty-five) questions where respondents' opinions deviate. The questions of particular interests are therefore not the questions that – to little surprise – coincide with the official party positions of S, GP and L, but rather the minority of questions where respondents have listed S, GP or L as their favoured party even though the parties' positions differ from the individual's on a number of topics. The questions highlighted may tell us something about how young Muslims relate to left and right, what meaning such signifiers could have, and if ideological markers really are important. The particular questions we analyse further from this perspective are the following:

- Lower taxes.
- Tougher sentencing for criminals.
- Marks for conduct in public schools.
- Introduce capital punishment for murder.
- Give homosexuals the right to marry.
- Limit the right to free abortion.
- The state should do more to protect morals.

The proposals to lower taxes, tougher sentencing for criminals, introducing capital punishment for murder, marks for conduct, are traditionally proposals that tend to come from the political right. To limit the right to free abortion, and to not let homosexuals marry was at the time of writing not supported by any party in parliament[14] apart from a minority within CD. To agree with the proposal that the state should do more to protect morals should equally be considered a position to the 'right' on the political scale. Tables 4.8–4.14 are laid out as follows: The upper half of the table shows the respondents' sentiments in percentage terms, the lower one displays the result as individuals. The favoured party is placed on the column to the left, and then the split between percent/individuals amongst those who – for instance – have said they favour L are listed horizontally on that same row.

Table 4.8 Favoured party versus 'lower taxes', percentage (top),
individuals (bottom)

Favoured party	Very good	Fairly good	Neither good/ bad	Fairly bad	Very bad	Don't know	Total
L	27.8	33.3	11.1	11.1	16.7	0	100
S	30.5	25.7	17.1	11.4	10.5	4.8	100
GP	15.4	28.8	27	17.3	9.6	1.9	100
M	9.1	36.3	9.1	18.2	9.1	18.2	100
Average	26.3	26.3	19.9	12.7	10.6	4.2	100

Favoured party	Very good	Fairly good	Neither good/ bad	Fairly bad	Very bad	Don't know	Individuals
L	5	6	2	2	3	0	18
S	32	27	18	12	11	5	105
GP	8	15	14	9	5	1	52
M	1	4	1	2	1	2	11

Table 4.8 displays the positions on the proposal 'Favoured party versus "lower taxes", percentage (top), individuals (bottom)'. Out of those 18 individuals who favoured L and in addition answered this question, 5 individuals (27.8%) thought it was a 'very good' proposal to lower taxes, 6 individuals (33.3%) thought it 'fairly good', two individuals (11.1%) thought it 'neither good nor bad', the same number thought it was 'fairly bad', and three individuals (16.7%) of those who favoured L thought it was a 'very bad' proposal.

As Table 4.9, 'Favoured party versus "tougher sentencing for criminals", percentage (top), individuals (bottom)', shows, those respondents who favoured L were the most positive to the proposal 'tougher sentencing for criminals'; 94.1% of the respondents chose either the alternative 'very good' or 'fairly good' proposal. This can be compared with how the respondents answered in general on the question; then 78.1% were positive. The respondents favouring GP were also more positive than this, with 83.4% in support of this. No respondents favouring L thought it was either a 'fairly bad' or 'very bad' proposal, in comparison to 7.2% of the respondents over all. It should however be noted that the number of individuals favouring L is low, which makes for a greater variation.

On the issue of 'Favoured party versus "marks for conduct in school", percentage (top), individuals (bottom)' (Table 4.10), the results for individual parties keep close to the average numbers. Out of all respondents 51.9% thought the proposal was either 'very good' or 'fairly good', while 21.1% thought the proposal was either 'fairly bad' or 'very bad'. M and L differed the most from this sentiment with 70.2% of respondents in favour of M and

Table 4.9 Favoured party versus 'tougher sentencing for criminals', percentage (top), individuals (bottom)

Favoured party	Very good	Fairly good	Neither good/ bad	Fairly bad	Very bad	Don't know	Total
L	64.7	29.4	5.9	0	0	0	100
S	42.7	27.2	20.4	8.7	0	1	100
GP	38.9	42.6	13	1.8	3.7	0	100
M	50.1	33.3	0	8.3	8.3	0	100
Average	48.6	29.5	13.9	5.1	2.1	0.8	100

Favoured party	Very good	Fairly good	Neither good/ bad	Fairly bad	Very bad	Don't know	Individuals
L	11	5	1	0	0	0	17
S	44	28	21	9	0	1	103
GP	21	23	7	1	2	0	54
M	6	4	0	1	1	0	12

Table 4.10 Favoured party versus 'marks for conduct in school', percentage (top), individuals (bottom)

Favoured party	Very good	Fairly good	Neither good/ bad	Fairly bad	Very bad	Don't know	Total
L	11.1	50	22.2	11.1	5.6	0	100
S	27.6	24.8	26.7	4.7	13.3	2.9	100
GP	22.7	24.5	32.1	9.4	11.3	0	100
M	54.5	18.2	27.3	0	0	0	100
Average	28.7	23.2	25.3	9.7	11.4	1.7	100

Favoured party	Very good	Fairly good	Neither good/ bad	Fairly bad	Very bad	Don't know	Individuals
L	2	9	4	2	1	0	18
S	29	26	28	5	14	3	105
GP	12	13	17	5	6	0	53
M	6	2	3	0	0	0	11

61.1% of respondents favouring L being positive towards the proposal. On this specific question it is not a question of L standing out, but rather it is surprising that the respondents overall are positive to such an extent.

Out of the respondents 32.9% were positive towards 'introduce capital punishment for murder' (Table 4.11). For instance, 16.7% of those who favoured L were negative toward the proposal. The respondents favouring M were the most supportive, with 50% in favour. The same number for L was 38.9%, 26.6% among S supporters, and 37% of those in favour of GP.

Table 4.11 Favoured party versus 'introduce capital punishment for murder', percentage (top), individuals (bottom)

Favoured party	Very good	Fairly good	Neither good/ bad	Fairly bad	Very bad	Don't know	Percent
L	33.3	5.6	44.4	11.1	5.6	0	100
S	12.8	13.8	22	14.7	32.1	4.6	100
GP	18.5	18.5	14.8	11.1	33.4	3.7	100
M	41.7	8.3	8.3	8.3	33.4	0	100
Average	18.1	14.8	21.8	12.8	28.4	4.1	100

Favoured party	Very good	Fairly good	Neither good/ bad	Fairly bad	Very bad	Don't know	Individuals
L	6	1	8	2	1	0	18
S	14	15	24	16	35	5	109
GP	10	10	8	6	18	2	54
M	5	1	1	1	4	0	12

Table 4.12 Favoured party versus 'give homosexuals right to marry', percentage (top), individuals (bottom)

Favoured party	Very good	Fairly good	Neither good/ bad	Fairly bad	Very bad	Don't know	Total
L	0	11.8	17.6	11.8	47	11.8	100
S	4.7	6.6	24.5	11.3	44.4	8.5	100
GP	7.4	1.8	14.8	5.6	64.8	5.6	100
M	0	0	7.7	0	69.2	23.1	100
Average	4.1	5	21.9	9.1	51.6	8.3	100

Favoured party	Very good	Fairly good	Neither good/ bad	Fairly bad	Very bad	Don't know	Individuals
L	0	2	3	2	8	2	17
S	5	7	26	12	47	9	106
GP	4	1	8	3	35	3	54
M	0	0	1	0	9	3	13

In Table 4.12, 'Favoured party versus "give homosexuals right to marry", percentage (top), individuals (bottom)', somewhat of an opposite relation occurs. Here, it may be seen as surprising that such a number of respondents were negative towards the proposal 'give homosexuals the right to marry'[15] at the same time as they list either S, GP or L as their favourite party. Out of the total survey population 9.1% were positive towards the proposal, whilst 60.7% were negative. Respondents favouring L had the highest frequency in support of the proposal, where 11.8% thought it was a 'fairly good' proposal

Table 4.13 Favoured party versus 'limit the right to free abortion', percentage (top), individuals (bottom)

Favoured party	Very good	Fairly good	Neither good/ bad	Fairly bad	Very bad	Don't know	Total
L	33.4	22.2	11.1	11.1	22.2	0	100
S	27.6	17.1	27.6	6.7	12.4	8.6	100
GP	30.8	23.1	17.3	9.6	17.3	1.9	100
M	25	0	33.3	0	33.3	8.4	100
Average	29	18.1	23.1	7.5	16	6.3	100

Favoured party	Very good	Fairly good	Neither good/ bad	Fairly bad	Very bad	Don't know	Individuals
L	6	4	2	2	4	0	18
S	29	18	29	7	13	9	105
GP	16	12	9	5	9	1	52
M	3	0	4	0	4	1	12

(no respondent favouring L thought it was a 'very good' proposal). The most negative sentiment was found among GP supporters, with 70.4%. The same number for S supporters was 55.7%. No respondent favouring M was in favour of the proposal. It should also be noted that an unusual number of respondents ticked the 'not familiar with this debate' box, compared to the frequency on the other questions (which in the tables are shown as 'don't know'). This brings us back to the question of those reluctant to take part in the survey, discussed earlier.

As Table 4.13, 'Favoured party versus "limit the right to free abortion", percentage (top), individuals (bottom)', demonstrates, 47.1% of the respondents were positive towards the proposal to 'limit the right to free abortion'. The highest number of respondents positive to the proposal was L supporters with 55.6%, followed by GP with 53.9%. 23.5% of the respondents were negative to the proposal. L, GP, and M ranked above this with L and M at 33.3% negative towards the proposal each, and 26.9% of GP supporters were negative towards the proposal.

Often, the importance of law-making on a moral basis is perceived as common amongst conservative parties on the right of the political scale. This can however be problematised since the left in Sweden have called on moral grounds for law-making, for instance when it comes to current legislation on prostitution.[16] In this survey 63.2% of the respondents were positive to the proposal the 'state should do more to protect morals' (Table 4.14, Favoured party versus 'state should protect morals', percentage (top), individuals (bottom)), whereas 7.2% were negative. This can be compared with 77.7% favouring L, who thought the proposal was either 'very good' or 'fairly good'.

Table 4.14 Favoured party versus 'state should protect morals', percentage (top), individuals (bottom)

Favoured party	Very good	Fairly good	Neither good/ bad	Fairly bad	Very bad	Don't know	Total
L	44.4	33.3	16.7	0	0	5.6	100
S	35.3	24.5	15.7	3.9	2.9	17.7	100
GP	51.9	16.7	14.8	3.7	3.7	9.2	100
M	25	33.3	25	0	0	16.7	100
Average	41.7	21.5	16.9	3.8	3.4	12.7	100

Favoured party	Very good	Fairly good	Neither good/ bad	Fairly bad	Very bad	Don't know	Individuals
L	8	6	3	0	0	1	18
S	36	25	16	4	3	18	102
GP	28	9	8	2	2	5	54
M	3	4	3	0	0	2	12

The corresponding number of GP supporters was 68.6%, also placing itself above the average of the survey population. S and M came in slightly under the average at 59.8% and 58.3% respectively. No respondents favouring L or M thought the proposal was either 'very' or 'fairly' bad. The corresponding number for S was 6.8%, and for GP it was 7.4% (compared to the 7.2% average).

Tables 4.8–4.14 show the differences between the respondents' views on particular topics, compared to the position of the parties the respondents favour. Highlighting these results can be understood in different ways. It is true that it is not possible to say what the average person voting for the Left Party thinks about 'lowering taxes'. But it is no stretch to think that people in support of L understand that much of the party's politics rests on (in an international comparative perspective) very high levels of monetary redistribution, meaning high taxes. This policy of redistribution is undoubtedly central to the party programme and the party's ideological profile. The overall image emerging from the results in these tables, suggests that there is no party that fully represents the 'whole package' of political views held by the main bulk of the respondents in our survey.

4. Conclusion

Previous research on religion and political attitudes has shown that religious practitioners tend to vote more to the right than to the left (Inglehart 2004: 201; Hagevi 2002: 65). Such results seem to not correspond very well with our findings.

To what extent the respondents relate to the political left-right scale in Sweden was measured with the help of three different types of questions; by asking the respondents to identify themselves along the left-right scale, by stating what party they favoured (and whether or not they were convinced supporters of this party), and finally by responding to a number of specific questions taken from political and societal debate.

The three parties – S, GP and L – who are positioned left of centre gained the most support. The most supported party was S (54.6%), followed by GP (27.8%) and L (8.8%), meaning that a total of 91.2% of the respondents favoured a party left of centre. As should be clear, parties right of centre received miniscule support in comparison. Apart from M, which received support from 6.9% of the respondents, there is close to no support for the other bourgeois parties. One of 269 respondents favoured CD, two favoured C, and no one favoured LP.

Given the lack of support for right-of-centre parties, Hagevi's earlier research can be commented on. Hagevi writes: 'perhaps this group is not one in favour of neoliberalism but rather classical conservatism' (Hagevi 2002: 65). Both our and Hagevi's later research (2009a, 2009b) suggests that it is not a case of Muslim practitioners being inclined to vote to the right, rather the distinction of understanding different right-of-centre movements, such as neoliberal and conservative, as separate from each other.

Based on our research it can be said that although bourgeois parties receive little support, there is a row of particular topics where the respondents are inclined to agree with sentiments supported by parties to the right, rather than to the left of the political spectrum. Proposals that 'popped out' of a 'leftist profile' is that many respondents were positive towards lowering taxes, tougher sentencing for criminals, marks/grades for conduct in school, introducing capital punishment for murder, limiting the right to free abortion, the state should do more to protect morals, and a negative attitude toward the proposal to give homosexuals the right to marry. As has been noted, over 90% of the respondents supported left-of-centre parties. Looking at the correlation between favoured party and sentiments on these topics still gives the same image.

The survey's respondents do not seem to find a political alternative that caters to all of their sentiments. If this is something particular for this group of young Muslims or for young people in general can be discussed and would benefit from further research. Based on our findings we however wish to indicate that the division in left vs right seems to be a substantial part in contributing to the problem. For instance, there is nothing to say that conservative views on moral questions (such as regarding abortion rights or marks/grades for conduct) are incompatible with politics with a high level of redistribution.

If we, despite this, use a left-right rhetoric, the following question emerges: What makes people who are oriented towards the right in questions regarding morals and values to – to such a large extent – vote almost exclusively for parties positioned to the left? The respondents show a fair degree of consensus with values that are only represented in the Swedish parliament by factions of CD, a party only one respondent favours. It could be possible to interpret this in, at least, two ways. The first is to interpret the results as though these questions regarding morals and values are not a top priority for the respondents. If the respondents felt these questions were more important, it is perhaps possible that the right-of-centre parties (and particularly CD) would receive greater support. The second way to interpret the results is that these questions are important, but that the respondents for one or several reasons find supporting right-of-centre parties as something inconceivable. The survey strengthens the hypothesis that a division of political parties along a left-right scale does not represent the political opinions held by young Swedish Muslims in a satisfactory way. Differently put, young Muslims are politically interested and informed, but they do not relate to the left-right scale of Swedish politics to a particularly large extent.

Notes

1. An earlier version of this text was published in Swedish (Bäckelie and Larsson 2011) and if nothing else is indicated the data for the chapter is taken from Bäckelie 2010. We would like to express our gratitude to Studentlitteratur for their approval of our English version of the text.
2. In Swedish: Sveriges Unga Muslimer.
3. See Bäckelie 2011 for a discussion of the Swedish state's relationship with religion in general, and Islam in particular.
4. Cf. Stenberg (1996).
5. For instance, see a debate article by SD leader Jimmie Åkesson (2009).
6. See Jacobsen (2006) for an introduction to young Muslims in Norway.
7. An organisation offering non-degree education for adults.
8. In Swedish: Sveriges Islamiska Skolor.
9. For a discussion on this see Berglund (2008).
10. For an introduction to various Muslim perceptions and positions on democracy, see Esposito and Voll (1996).
11. Examples of how this is discussed and measured differently can be seen in Sander 1993; Inglehart 2004; Hagevi 2009a; Skoog 2001a; and Larsson and Sander 2007.
12. It can be noted that in Hagevi the *salat* group did only differ marginally from the group 'Muslim' in general. The greatest difference was that S was favoured by 72 people 'at the expense' of L: 14%, and GP: 8%.
13. A similar sentiment is offered in *Utbildningsdepartementets* Swedish Government Official Report: *Staten och imamerne: Religion, integration, autonomi* (SOU 2009: 52).
14. SD has since entered the Swedish parliament, and is expressing some sentiments towards restricting abortion.

15. A right, it should be added, that homosexuals have at the time of the study (and today).
16. This said, we do not suggest that all who are labelled 'left' have the same assessment. In Germany, for instance, leftists have gone in the opposite direction. See Dodillet (2009) for further discussion.

References

Åkesson, J. (2009), 'Muslimerna är vårt största utländska hot', *Aftonbladet*, 19 October.

Berglund, J. (2008), 'Muslim swim wear fashion at Amman Waves on the internet and live', *CyberOrient: Online journal of the virtual Middle East*, available at <http://www.cyberorient.net> (last accessed 20 July 2012).

Bäckelie, J. (2011), *Religion And Politics – A Valid Divide?: Confessionality In Politics And Higher Education*, available from <http://gupea.ub.gu.se/handle/2077/25887> (last accessed 20 July 2012), Göteborg: Göteborg University.

Bäckelie, J. (2010*), I Vilken Utsträckning Relaterar Unga Muslimer Till Vänster-Högerskalan I Svensk Politik?: En Fallstudie Från Sums Ungdomskonferens 2009*, available at <http://gupea.ub.gu.se/handle/2077/22096> (last accessed 20 July 2012), Göteborg: Göteborg University.

Bäckelie, J. and G. Larsson (2011), 'Unga muslimer och politik', in G. Larsson and S. Olsson (eds), *Islam och politik*, Lund: Studentlitteratur, pp. 143–71.

Dodillet, Susanne (2009), *Är sex arbete? Svensk och tysk prostitution sedan 1970–talet*, Stockholm: Vertigo.

Esposito, J. L. and J. O. Voll (1996), *Islam and Democracy*, New York: Oxford University Press.

Hagevi, M. (2002), 'Religiositet i Generation X', in Henrik Oscarsson (ed.) *Spår i framtiden. Ung SOM-undersökningen, Västsverige 2000*, Göteborg: SOM-institutet, pp. 39–78.

Hagevi, M. (2009a), *Politisk opinion och religiositet i Västra Götaland*, Lund: Sekel.

Hagevi, M. (2009b), 'Integrationen är ett fiasko', *Aftonbladet*, 6 August.

Hizb ut-Tahrir (2009), *About Us*, available at <http://english.hizbuttahrir.org/index.php/about-us> (last accessed 20 July 2012).

Inglehart, R. (2004), 'Religious Parties and Electoral Behavior', in R. Inglehart and P. Norris (eds) *Sacred and Secular: Religion and Politics Worldwide*, Cambridge: Cambridge University Press, pp. 196–212.

Jacobsen, C. M. (2006), *Staying on the straight path: religious identities and practices among young Muslims in Norway*, Bergen: Universitetet i Bergen.

Jonsson, C. (1999), *Allt färre röstar i invandrartäta områden*, Norrköping: Integrationsverket.

Larsson, G. and Å. Sander (2007), *Islam and Muslims in Sweden: Integration or Fragmentation? A Contextual Study*, Berlin: LIT.

Larsson, G. (2003), 'Att vara ung och muslim i Sverige', in G. Larsson (ed.) *Talande Tro: Ungdomar, religion och identitet*, Lund: Studentlitteratur, pp. 67–80.

Olsson, T. and P. Dahlgren (2009), 'Internet som resurs för unga medborgare. Är nätet AC/DC?', in T. Karlsohn (ed.) *Samhälle, teknik och lärande*, Stockholm: Carlsson, pp. 34–49.

Sander, Å. (1993), *I vilken utsträckning är den svenske muslimen religiös?* Göteborg: Centrum för Kulturkontakt och Internationell Migration.

Skog, M. (2001a), 'Sverigeräkningen 2000', in M. Skog (ed.) *Det religiösa Sverige: Gudstjänst- och andaktsliv under ett veckoslut kring millenieskiftet*, Örebro: Libris, pp. 15–28.

SOU (2009: 52), *Staten och imamerna. Religion, integration, autonomi*, Stockholm: Fritzes.

Stenberg, L. (1996), *The Islamization of science: four Muslim positions developing an Islamic modernity*, Lund: Lund University.

Stiernstedt, J. (2010), 'Högt förtroende för svenska politiker', *DN*, 22 September.

LITHUANIAN MUSLIMS' ATTITUDES TOWARD PARTICIPATION IN THE DEMOCRATIC POLITICAL PROCESS: THE CASE OF CONVERTS

Egdūnas Račius

1. Islam in Lithuania – the background

The last census (that of 2001, in which, among others, a question on religious identity was included) for which there is publicly available official statistics produced the following figures for Lithuanian inhabitants adhering to Islam: 2,860 Sunni Muslims or 0.1% of the total population, 1,679 of whom (or 58.7% of all Sunni Muslims) identified themselves as ethnic Tatars, 362 (12.6%) as Azerbaijanis, 185 (6.5%) as Lithuanians, 74 as Russians, 15 as Belarusians, 13 as Polish, five as Ukrainians and even four as Jewish (Department 2002: 204–5). There is no data available on Shi'is.

The biggest group of Lithuania's inhabitants with a Muslim background, the Lithuanian Tatars (3,235 in 2001, (Department 2002: 188–9)), have been living in the eastern part of today's Republic of Lithuania since the fourteenth century when they started settling in what then was the territory of the Grand Duchy of Lithuania (GDL, the lands of which are now divided among Lithuania, Belarus and Poland) as mercenaries and political immigrants (Račius 2009: 16–17).

Though precise data are not available, it can, from anecdotal evidence, be safely assumed that at no time in history did the Muslim population of the GDL exceed 100,000. Despite or because of the fact that Muslims have been only a tiny minority of the citizenry of the GDL, they enjoyed almost all the rights and freedoms that their Christian fellow citizens did. Upon settlement, the Tatar elite were raised to the nobility and given tracts of land as fief later to become personal property. Even more, Muslims in the GDL (and later, post-1569, the Republic of Two Nations – *Rzeczpospolita*) were never forced to abandon their faith either through coerced conversion or because of artificially created obstacles in practising their religion (such as bans, prohibitions, segregationist decrees, etc.). In the GDL/*Rzeczpospolita*, Muslims throughout the centuries were allowed to publicly observe all Islamic duties and rituals. It is believed that mosques on the territory of the GDL were being built as early as the late fourteenth or the beginning of the fifteenth century (Kričinskis 1993: 158). In the times of *Rzeczpospolita* (that is until the final partition of it in 1795) there might have been up to two dozen mosques (Kričinskis 1993: 161), as a rule with adjacent cemeteries.

In the aftermath of the First World War the Vilnius region was occupied by Poland and most of the Muslims of the GDL became Polish citizens, though over a thousand (Central Bureau 1925: 34) remained in the Republic of Lithuania as its citizens. Lithuanian Muslims with certain help from the state built the first brick mosque in the then capital Kaunas in the early 1930s. In Poland, an official Muslim organisation representing some two dozen Muslim congregations (comprising 6,000–7,000 Muslims (Miskiewicz 1990: 58–60)) was founded in 1925 with a seat of the mufti in Vilnius.[1] In general terms, both Polish and Lithuanian Muslim communities in the inter-war period not only enjoyed religious freedom but were very active in their socio-religious life – it was the time when numerous quasi-academic studies of the history of Muslims of the GDL, popular literature, religious tracts, study books and guidebooks were written and published. This all led to a revival of Tatar national consciousness and identity in which Islam played a prominent role.

Though over time Lithuanian Tatars had lost their mother tongue, they retained their religion and survived as a distinct ethno-cultural yet well integrated group. Today the Lithuanian state recognises Islam (albeit only in its Sunni Hanafi form) as one of the nine traditional confessions in Lithuania (Parliament 2009, available at <http://www3.lrs.lt/pls/inter3/dokpaieska. showdoc_l?p_id=385299> last accessed 16 December 2011).

Descendants of immigrants from the Muslim Central Asian and Caucasian republics who settled in Lithuania during the Soviet period made up most of the rest of the Muslims in Lithuania throughout the Soviet period and well into the period of independence (around 1,400 in 2001 (Department 2002: 188–9)). Though a substantial number of Lithuania's inhabitants with a Muslim background (around half of both 3,235 Tatars and 788 Azerbaijanis) did not indicate their affiliation to Islam in the 2001 census, many nonetheless may be considered nominal Muslims. This especially applies to ethnic Azeris, traditionally Shi'is, some of whom might have chosen not to identify with Sunnis but may still be observant Muslims.

By the end of 2011 there were up to 2,500 foreign nationals of Muslim background living in Lithuania on various grounds – asylum seekers (mainly Chechens), businessmen (mainly Kazakhs, Azerbaijanis, Turks, Uzbeks), exchange and programme students (chiefly from Lebanon and several other Arab countries, as well as Pakistan and Turkey), on family reunion grounds (Department of Migration data provided through personal communication).

In addition to the above groups, between 500 and 700 Lithuanian citizens have converted to Islam in the past two decades. Their children (who presumably are also Muslim) by now number at least several dozen.[2]

As a result, the total number of nominal Muslims (or, to be less prejudiced, people of Muslim background) in Lithuania by the beginning of 2012 could be as high as 8,000. However, as many of Lithuania's Muslims are highly secularised (Norvilaitė and Račius 2011), the number of those who are active believers, e.g. engage in religious rituals and adhere by religious injunctions on a daily basis, is far smaller. Converts presumably constitute a prominent share of those 'truly living' their religion.

The four groups of Lithuania's Muslims, though internally diverse, also differ among themselves significantly with regard to the level of identification with and loyalty to the state of Lithuania: there is plenty of evidence (in their periodical, *Lietuvos totoriai*, various other publications and numerous public statements by community leaders) that Lithuanian Tatars strongly identify with Lithuania as their sole homeland. The 'colonists', being also fully-fledged citizens of the country and fairly well integrated into society, also tend to be loyal to the state they chose to be citizens of – those who were not left Lithuania immediately after the collapse of the Soviet Union. As most of the immigrants, however, are relatively recent arrivals to the country, they still have to establish their relationship to it. Of all the groups, loyalty to the motherland and identification with it by Lithuanian converts to Islam is least investigated in research.

Hence, when considering the attitudes of Lithuania's Muslims toward participation in democratic political processes, one encounters several distinct tendencies roughly corresponding to the four constitutive components of the Lithuanian Muslim community. Lithuanian Tatars' participation in Lithuania's politics (primarily in the form of voting in elections, but also occasionally in standing for public office, and working as public servants at governmental institutions, e.g. MFA) appears to be very much in line with the majority's participation in politics. Though more in-depth and detailed research is needed, it can be presumed that the patterns of Tatar political participation, first of all in the form of voter profile but also in the forms of other conventional and unconventional political participation, is hardly distinguishable from those of the majority of citizens. This, however, remains a working hypothesis that calls for verification through research.

The level of Soviet-time immigrant Muslims' participation in Lithuanian politics also tends to be on a par with the rest of society. Some of them play a prominent role in political parties or in ethnic organisations, like the Azeris, which cultivate amicable relations with certain individual politicians or even political parties. However, very much as in the case of the Lithuanian Tatars, more profound research to reveal the spectrum of political attitudes and participation among this group of Lithuania's Muslims is desirable.

One can hardly talk of immigrant political participation in Lithuania as almost all of them are still not citizens of the country and Lithuanian legislation does not extend the right to vote on any level to foreign nationals. As for attitudes toward democracy in general, some immigrants support the idea of an alternative political system to democracy (as a rule, in connection with socio-political processes taking place in the Middle East and elsewhere in Muslim-majority lands) though there are also those who fully support democracy. In any case, immigrant Muslims make up a fraction of all the Muslims in Lithuania and are a group on the move – many, even if granted refugee status, have a propensity to stay in Lithuania only until they see a chance to relocate further West, while others are in the country on a temporary basis for the duration of their studies or for business purposes. Immigrant Muslims lack group consciousness and coherence and this prevents them from political mobilisation at community level.

Ultimately, of the four groups of Muslims in Lithuania the most interesting are Lithuanian citizens who have converted to Islam. The attitudes of this group towards participation in political processes could be presumed to have been shaped and influenced by numerous experiences and factors of both an internal and external nature, major among which are different levels of personal and group socialisation and access to and influence on one's worldview of 'Islamic' texts and other material from outside the borders of Lithuania. As converts are often (Račius, forthcoming) keen on painstakingly observing the rules and regulations of their newly adopted religion, it could be expected that the 'Islamic factor' could have a profound influence on how they perceive democracy as a political system per se, its compatibility with Islam, and finally their personal decision to take or not to take part in the democratic political process. But before proceeding with the analysis of these attitudes, it is worth briefly introducing Lithuanian converts to Islam.

2. Lithuanian converts to Islam: an attempt at a typology[3]

Conversion of Lithuanians (both ethnic and of other ethnic origins, like Polish, Russian) to Islam is a recent phenomenon – two decades ago there were virtually were no Lithuanian convert Muslims. And although no official data on the number of Lithuanian converts to Islam exist, it can be safely argued, based on long-term research, that today their number has passed 500 and continues to grow. Estimates given below are based on the fieldwork research of other authors (Norvilaitė 2011; Markevičiūtė 2009), survey of Internet and other sources (published media, conversations with Muslims) and private acquaintances of the author. The author has direct personal information on some 100 Lithuanian converts to Islam. Although it is too early to talk about any noteworthy tendencies, it is nonetheless already possible to offer a crude typology of Lithuanian converts to Islam.

One may speak of three types (or groups) of Lithuanian converts to Islam based on 'motivational experiences' forwarded by Lofland and Skonovd: intellectual, mystical, experimental, affectional, revivalist, and coercive (Lofland and Skonovd 1981: 373–85), to which later authors added several more 'motivational experiences', among them negativist (Lakhdar et al. 2007: 1–15). In the case of Lithuanian converts to Islam, affectional and experimental 'motivational experiences' evidently dominate.[4]

Relational converts

Probably the biggest group (up to 300 individuals) of converts are female Lithuanian citizens who have either married or maintain close personal relations with Muslims hailing from Muslim-majority countries. Most of these female converts may be assigned affectional 'motivational experience'. Or, to use Stefano Allievi's terminology, this type of conversion can be called 'relational' and 'conversion under these circumstances is a means to reach another aim (marriage), not an end in itself' (Allievi 2002: 1). Yet, many of such women married to Muslims become themselves devout Muslims though few gain any proper (and virtually none of them formal) religious education.

Discovery converts

The second group (between 150 and 250 individuals) of converts might tentatively be called 'adventurers' or 'romantics', what in part corresponds to the experimental 'motivational experience', though negativist 'motivational experience' is also often present. Usually these are young unmarried males and females. Many of them simply 'stumble' upon Islam by accidentally coming upon information on Islam on the World Wide Web or meeting Muslims while abroad and become fascinated with it. According to Allievi (Allievi 2002: 1), such conversions belong to a 'discovery of Islam' type. In the initial phase after their conversion converts of this type painstakingly aspire to become as Islamic as possible: constantly repeat Islamic formulas in Arabic, use religious symbols, don 'Islamic' attire.

Rational converts

The third, and by far the smallest (less than 50 individuals) group of converts might be called 'spiritual seekers' (with intellectual 'motivational experience') whose conversion, in Allievi's words, belongs to the 'rational' conversion type (Allievi 2002: 1). These are people who discovered Islam after having gone through several other religious traditions, movements and cults (in other words, with a 'conversion career'[5]). As a rule, they are married, middle-aged males with families and careers in Lithuania. Sometimes they manage to persuade their family members also to convert to Islam. Such converts plunge into religious self-study: they analyse the Qur'an and Hadith and devour religious texts in search for what they believe is the essence of Islam. Some of them are fascinated by what Jensen (Jensen 2006) calls 'ethical' Islam, in which the mystical dimension of Islam – Sufism – is paramount.

Based on the available sources one may speculate that currently the majority (possibly up to two-thirds) of Lithuanian converts to Islam are individuals younger than twenty-five years of age, a quarter between twenty-five and forty years, and less than a tenth older than forty. From a very simplified and schematised perspective one might provisionally say that a typical citizen of Lithuania who has converted to Islam is a young (up to twenty-five years old), very likely married, female.[6]

The fact of conversion to Islam in itself is not so much significant as the 'type' of Islam converts choose. Most of the Lithuanian converts to Islam appear to have opted for complete overhaul of their identity and have joined the ranks of Muslims who in the academic literature have been generally referred to as revivalists as opposed to traditionalists (e.g. Muslims adhering to one of the so-called 'classical dimensions' of Islam[7]). In their search for knowledge about their adopted religion, Lithuanian converts to Islam have been pulled into the whirlpool of the revivalist debates on the nature and composition of the 'true' Islam in abundance and easily accessible on the internet and through other advanced means of communication. Most of the converts who had been socialising on the online forum at islamas.lt[8] and continue to do so on its reincarnation at islam-ummah.lt themselves tend to lean toward a sort of revivalist-type (though not necessarily of Salafi kind), deterritorialised (Roy 2004: 18–20) (not seen as bound by locality and its culture), *ulama*-less quasi-legalist[9] (even neo-fundamentalist[10]) Islam (as opposed to the traditionalist Islam of the Lithuanian Tatars) with an expressed 'desire to follow the 'straight path', or even relocate it amidst the maze of alternatives generated through history' (Bunt 2003: 128). All this leads Lithuanian converts to Islam to identify first and foremost with the transnational Umma rather than the Lithuanian nation (which they see as very anti-Islamic[11]) and the state or even the indigenous Muslims of the land, the Lithuanian Tatars, of whom the neophytes have a very low opinion.[12]

3.   The state of democracy in Lithuania

The attitudes held by Lithuanian converts to Islam towards political participation should among other things be considered against the backdrop of the general state of democracy in Lithuania and its populace's opinion of it and actual participation in the political process.

Compared to western European countries, Lithuania is still a young democracy – the first democratic multiparty elections were held just over two decades ago. All the more, as a post-Soviet society, Lithuania had to undergo a complete overhaul of its socio-political system to make it (or at least to make it look like) a truly democratic one. The transition, however, is universally recognised as a success – in a mere fifteen years since regaining its independence, Lithuania became a fully-fledged member of the EU and NATO – the twin bastions of and champions for democracy, while Freedom House firmly places Lithuania within the basket of consolidated democracies (Freedom 2011).

Yet, though structurally as democratic as any nation could get to be, the Lithuanian state is far from being a paradise on earth – it still is economically a very poor place with poor public administration permeated by nepotism and corruption (Transparency 2009), all inherited from Soviet times. Ultimately, to the bulk of its citizens it matters less that they can choose at the polls from candidates representing some thirty political parties across the political left-to-right spectrum than low wages, high unemployment, minimal or non-existent social and health security benefits, poor public services, etc. Several recent opinion polls revealed that there is a clear disappointment with the workings of democracy in the country and long-term observations like Eurobarometer suggest a steadily worsening tendency: 'Although the Lithuanian poll in the last decade has never been satisfied with the way democracy works in their country, over the past two years, this figure has continued to decrease from 24% to 18%' (Eurobarometer 72, National Report 2010: 4). In 2004 it still stood at 33% (Ramonaitė 2006: 101).

A representative Eurobarometer 72 opinion poll conducted in late 2009 revealed that a staggering four fifths (79%) of Lithuanians indicated that they were not happy with how democracy works in the country, while those satisfied with the workings of democracy amounted to less than a fifth (18%) when the EU average satisfaction with democracy stood at 53% (Eurobarometer 72 BNS 2009). Similar findings were discovered in a later poll conducted early in the spring of 2010, the results of which suggested that some 76% of respondents 'expressed dissatisfaction with how democracy works in the country' and only a sixth (16%) claimed to be satisfied with how it works, while 8% were undecided (this suggesting that they were at least not completely satisfied) (ELTA 2010). Meanwhile, the multiparty system is said to be appreciated by just over half of Lithuania's citizens (Lrytas 2009).

Trust in public institutions among Lithuanians is not only exceptionally low but is also permanently worsening:

> The trend of recent years to mistrust the majority of state institutions remains the same. Only 15 percent of Lithuanians tend to trust their national government (19 percent in the spring of 2009), and only 7 percent trust their Parliament (10 percent in the spring of 2009). But perhaps the most important difference compared with the European Union average is the lack of trust in the justice and law enforcement

system. Almost three times fewer citizens trust these institutions in Lithuania (15 percent) than in the EU on average (43 percent). (Eurobarometer 72 2010: 5)

Lithuanians' disappointment with democracy and mistrust in elected officials is vividly attested to by ever lower figures of voter participation in elections. If Lithuanians started with an over 75% turnout at the first free elections to the Parliament of the newly independent Lithuanian state in 1992 and almost 79% turnout at the first Presidential elections in 1993 (Ramonaitė 2006: 92, 96), in the last Presidential elections of 2009 just over half (52%) of those eligible took part (Central 2009), while in the Parliamentary elections of 2008 – just 48% in the first and less than a third (some 32%) in the second round (Central 2008a, 2008b). The main argument for not voting in elections has been discovered to be 'getting disappointed with politics' (Žeruolis 1998; Ramonaitė 2006: 103).

Research (Žiliukaitė 2006) revealed that Lithuanians' apathy toward participation in politics extends beyond voting into the realms of other conventional and non-conventional forms of political participation – Lithuanians are among the least inclined of the Europeans to engage in petition signing, boycotts, lawful or unlawful demonstrations, etc. (Žiliukaitė 2006: 117), with just a sixth of Lithuanian citizens having some 'experience of participating in protest politics' (Žiliukaitė 2006: 116). It is argued that, contrary to Western societies where acts of protest have become a norm,

> inhabitants of Lithuania perceive acts of protest as a last resort measure which they would embark on if their life conditions got significantly worse or if there emerged a great threat to the political order of the country, and not as an activity partaking in which they could contribute to democratisation processes in the country (...) (Žiliukaitė 2006: 114)

4. Converts' position on participation in the democratic political process

In the context of general dissatisfaction and disappointment with democracy (or at least how it works) in the country, it could be expected that Lithuanian converts to Islam may be even less enthusiastic about democracy for several reasons: for once, most of them do not differ in their socialisation and personal experiences from non-Muslim citizens; having been moved (as many of them are) (Račius, forthcoming) into the vortex of Muslim revivalists' worldwide debates about the true nature of Islam as well as democracy, their perceived (in)compatibility, Muslims' rights and duties in a non-Muslim polity and similar, many converts could look at democracy and participation in it as something 'un-Islamic', which 'true' Muslims (as most converts strive to be(come)) should shun. Finally many, if not most, converts identify with the transnational Umma rather than the Lithuanian nation and polity and many of them have already emigrated or actively entertain the idea of emigrating from Lithuania. As Ramonaitė reasons:

> One could think that a person who is not satisfied with the current political system, but who is concerned about the fate of his country, will be more prone to taking part in elections than one who is more or less satisfied with the situation, but who does not feel the bond with the state. And contrarily, the one who is not only dissatisfied with how the political system works, but also does not feel to be his own country's citizen, should be least inclined to participate in elections. (Ramonaitė 2006: 104)

The last deduction could be expected to have a certain amount of truth in it with regard to Lithuanian converts to Islam. Upon closer inspection,[13] however, it becomes evident that the political attitudes of Lithuanian converts to Islam form a wide and colourful spectrum, with those in favour of democracy and taking part in the democratic political process being far from a minority.

4.1.   Which political system is better? Lithuanian Muslims' view of democracy

At the outset of this analysis of attitudes towards democracy and political participation among Lithuania's Muslims, one needs to underline that the few mosques in the country seem to play no noteworthy role in shaping Muslims' political outlook. This is so for several reasons. First of all, the imams of the mosques, who are all Lithuanian Tatars (plus a Turk at the Muftiate's *musalla*), in their *khutba*s avoid any political connotations. Secondly, the bulk of the attending worshippers are foreign nationals who, though they might be politically concerned, especially on foreign policy issues and international relations, have no right to take part in local politics and consequently tend to have little interest in it. Thirdly, the congregations attending Friday prayers are ethnically and thus culturally diverse with different (Russian-, Arabic- and Turkish-speaking) groups of worshippers not being able to communicate among themselves in a common vernacular.

In their daily lives Lithuanian converts to Islam (who, though presumably devout, generally do not frequent mosques) are not necessarily more politically active or concerned than immigrants or indigenous Muslims – 'to me on the whole politics is such a repulsive thing' (Dovilė), 'I am not interested in politics at all, though maybe it is wrong' (Rasa) – but when pressed they give it some thought.

Democratic political system
Most of the interviewed converts, contrary to expectations, were either ambivalent or even positively predisposed toward democracy. Answering the

question 'What political system is most acceptable to you?', Ieva, a female convert in her mid-20s and a Muslim of just one year replied: 'Democracy is acceptable (. . .), yes, democracy is perfect'; while Rasa, a female convert of four years in her early 30s, was ambivalent: 'probably democracy, but for [me as] a Muslim, I think that Shari'a would be best – the Islamic ruling.' Likewise, Aušra (mid-20s, a Muslim of two-and-a-half years), was undecided: 'Hm, I don't know. So democracy, perhaps.' A male convert in his late 30s, Sufijus, also subscribes to the idea of democratic elections, yet he longs for a strong leader with wide-ranging powers (and he sees Russia as a role model).

On the other hand, in the online forum at islamas.lt, a number of Lithuanian converts to Islam saw little value in democracy:

If people believe in God, are good and tolerant to each other, there will be no need for any democracy. Unfortunately, I do not much believe it will ever be that way. (Svecias_deivis)

or were even outspokenly critical of it:

In the democratic regimes only the art of lying and mass manipulation gets perfected. (Akayak)

Some doubt the reality of democracy:

And what that true democracy is? That is just a nice fairytale in the book, a utopian dream, which man will never be able to properly implement practically. (Khadeja)

My opinion is such that all this democracy and personal freedom, being proclaimed by western states, are only words and they are abiding by them when it suits the government itself. (Rimante)

Likewise, one of the interviewed converts was sceptical about the feasibility of democracy:

One needs to be very cautious in using [the term] democracy. As all this is declared: rights, freedoms, but in reality there is very little of that freedom. There is an illusion of that freedom. In reality you are being controlled everywhere without yourself knowing and there is very little of that freedom. That democracy, no . . . (Dovilé, early 20s, two years of being a Muslim)

Such reasoning on democracy, though coming from the lips and minds of converts to Islam, is easily recognisable in most Lithuanians no matter what their religious affiliation is. In other words, in being sceptical about democracy Lithuanian converts hardly express any original reservations distinct from those expressed by non-Muslim Lithuanians found in research on Lithuanians' attitudes toward democracy (Ramonaitė 2006).

Though many of the converts subscribe to the idea that for Muslims an Islamic political system is best, few find a truly Islamic political system to exist anywhere in the world at the moment. Still there are those who go so far as to favourably assess the Taliban regime:

> As for the Taliban regime (. . .) People tried to create an Islamic state, follow the Shari'a principles . . . maybe they overdid it in the end and went to a very far extreme – but nonetheless – that was much better from a moral and ethical perspective than in the so-called 'democratic' Western society. (Jurga)

Democracy and Islam

The debate about the perceived mutual exclusivity between democracy and Islam/Shari'a or absence thereof is directly tied to the discussion of the value of democracy as such. Most of the interviewed converts insist that the two are not incompatible:

> Say what you want, but the very aim of democracy is justice, and democracy is man-made. Islam is justice and it is even better than democracy, so Islam and democracy to me do not quarrel among themselves: to me it is even more just (than anything). (Svecias Halima)

Others said 'I cannot ever agree that there is no democracy in Islam . . .' (Sadiqqah) and 'Islam conforms to democratic principles' (Ieva). But, like Rasa, they might see the two as compatible 'not in all aspects', adding 'but probably [Islam] is most compatible with democracy' (Rasa). A sole interviewed convert was convinced that the two are mutually exclusive; 'I think (they are) incompatible' (Dovilė).

In conclusion, most of the interviewed converts did not see Islam and democracy as incompatible but still consider democracy to be a deficient political system and inferior to Islam. At the same time, converts are realistic about the prospects for Shari'a in Lithuania. Realising that an Islamic political system in Lithuania (and indeed elsewhere in Europe) is not a feasible prospect, many of the converts dream of relocating to a more Islamic (or at least Muslim-friendly) environment. Some, especially those most opposed to democracy, call for an outright new *hijra*:

> It is time for Muslims living in Europe [without doubt also in Lithuania] and other countries of developed democracies to consider hijra. I advise those from among us [Muslims] who think that by taking part in all sorts of elections in these countries one may change anything to shake off this perilous and contradictory to the Quran and Sunna conviction and ask Allah's forgiveness for straying. (Akayak)

Indeed, the notion of hijra – in the sense of not just a mere emigration but a religious act or even duty – is a common feature among converts. As indicated above, many of them have in fact already emigrated (albeit mostly to other non-Muslim countries in Europe and North America).

4.2.   To vote or not to vote?

Voting, one of the main elements of political participation in a democratic political system, pops up naturally in the deliberations on political participation among converts. The bulk of the interviewed converts claimed to take part in voting, albeit many of them see it as a mere formal duty: 'By and large I do not believe [in elections] but I go [to them] – I carry out my civil duty and that's it.' (Aušra), or

> I do take part because I hold it to be a civil duty to go but maybe because though it might be that among those suggested [on the ballot] no-one will suit me, nonetheless it is my duty, because if I do not go others will choose for me. (Ieva)

Sometimes fulfilling one's duty to vote one is 'not voting "for" but voting "against" somebody, so that the worse do not get elected, and the less bad gets elected.' (Dovilė). Some converts have a stronger sense of responsibility: 'One is to take part in all elections. After all, we are ourselves to elect the government, etc. We ourselves are responsible for who is in power. So we are obliged.' (Rasa) Yet others see it as a right: when asked, 'Will you take part in the next elections?' Dovilė confirmed: 'I will surely take part. One is to exercise one's right.' (Dovilė) Sufijus goes even further to almost endorse voting as an Islamic duty: 'Muslim people should take part in voting . . . Even according to Shari'a, you are to vote 'cause you are to think of your future.'

Such a strong sense of duty among converts sounds a bit odd when compared to the attitudes of Lithuanians as a whole towards participation in elections. Though a certain percentage of Lithuanians, who are not satisfied with politicians and how the democratic political system works in the country, nonetheless go to elections (to fulfil their civic duty), one might expect converts to feel less duty-bound, if only due to their divided loyalty, part of which is accorded to the imagined worldwide Muslim commonwealth. This would seem to be especially true in the case of those converts who have effectively emigrated from Lithuania.

Yet, at least some of the converts, for instance Ewrin, who has been living abroad for quite some time and might not see or feel any direct benefits from taking part in elections, still maintains that voting in Lithuanian elections is worthwhile:

I always vote, though I have not been living in Lithuania for the past eleven years, but my parents, relatives remain there, and I myself care about Lithuania's future, we cannot be so indifferent that if we do not live [in Lithuania] why should we burden ourselves.

She finds voting by mail most convenient and even recommends it to other converts residing abroad: 'I voted by mail, for I have been voting for long, maybe you could try looking up the embassy's webpage' (Ewrin). Another devout convert, well-read in Islamic material (judging by her numerous posts on islamas.lt forum and her personal blog), who has been living in the UK for an extended period of time, is adamant:

I always vote whenever I have a possibility. And this time I will vote in the first round for I will be in Lithuania, *inshaAllah*. *Alhamdullillah*, Islamic theologians do not think that voting is un-Islamic. For if it is haram to elect a non-Islamic government then it is haram to live in a country governed by a non-Islamic government, and abide by its non-Islamic laws. I never had the attitude that 'anyway, nothing will change'. Thank God that not a majority think so and that some still come to elections. (Rimante)

Some converts see Muslim participation in elections (and politics in a broader sense) beyond voting. For instance, Aušra reasoned: 'Muslims themselves get to governmental institutions through elections and represent their interests – that is even better and that system works very well.' However, so far a convert has not stood for an elected office and generally it is obvious that converts (and Lithuanian Muslims in general) lack the resources, engagement and recruitment to make this happen any time soon.

Although most of the interviewees had difficulties identifying their political views on the right-to-left spectrum, some were very resolute: 'I always vote for the right, for the conservatives, for to me [they] associate with religion, with conservative values, the family institution . . . ' (Aušra).

As for those, who opt to abstain from voting, the individual decision not to take part in the democratic political process can be circumscribed by several factors. As Hussain argues in the case of British Muslims (something that applies to Muslims in other European states),

We have seen that some British Muslims choose not to engage in the political process out of principle. There are however those who, due to their experiences, feel so frustrated with 'the system' that they end up losing confidence and faith in the political process altogether . . . It is surprising to see how many young (and not so young) people feel a sense of alienation. (Hussain 2004: 396)

Though the end result might be the same, the motivations stemming from 'out of principle' and 'due to experience' have different roots.

In the case of those Muslims who choose not to participate in the political process 'out of principle', 'universal' normative-theoretical arguments found in *fatwas* and the arguments of Muslim thinkers (both traditionalist and revivalist) are paramount. To such Muslims Islam and democracy are incompatible, and democracy is a deficient political system (if feasible at all). Those who adopt this stance consciously stand on the margins if not altogether outside the political system, no matter what it has to offer them. Consequently, in this 'out of principle' group, it is easy to find voices calling for absolute abstention from elections on purely religious grounds: 'I think that Muslims should not vote in the elections to government of non-Muslim countries of any level. It follows that by voting we accept supremacy of man-made laws over the God-given'. (Akayak) Consider also Umm safiyah's case. In one of the posts on the islamas.lt forum she reasoned: 'I do not know if it is haram to elect a non-Islamic government (I did not even ever inquire), but I think that if we elect such a government that means we support such a system. And this system is far from being perfect . . .' After reading a *fatwa* against Muslim participation in the democratic political process (Islam QA, available at <http://www.islam-qa.com/en/ref/107166/election>, last accessed 10 December 2011), recommended by another convert member of the forum, she made up her mind: 'I read the *fatwa*. I liked how at the very beginning it explained what kind of a system it [democracy] is, who created it and what it is based on. So, from my perspective, I will better abstain from voting.' (Umm safiyah)

Those converts whose decisions are instead informed by 'experience' (or rather the perception that nothing changes even if one takes part in elections), ground their choice in less religious and more personal arguments, like Siguliukas17, who like many non-Muslim Lithuanians snaps: 'I will not vote, for even when I was still living in Lithuania I would not vote. Do you think anything will change?' Some converts, like many non-Muslim Lithuanians, see a certain conspiracy behind the facade of democracy: 'as for voting, I do not see much sense. Corporations and governments will in any case rule over the people, though it should be the opposite . . . ' (Svecias dawood).

All in all, motives for (and certain reservations about) voting among Lithuanian converts to Islam do not differ significantly from those common among non-Muslim fellow citizens, though in the case of converts they might have religious overtones. Rejection of participation in elections sometimes has a clear religious basis – the perceived un- or even anti-Islamic nature of voting in a secular liberal democratic political system. Ultimately, those converts who do not go to the polls, next to the regular group have an extra argument to do so.

5. Conclusion

Attitudes of Lithuanian converts to Islam towards the democratic political system and participation in the democratic political process have been discovered to be shaped and influenced by a variety of factors, some of them shared with non-Muslim fellow citizens, others peculiar to converts. Taking into account the prevailing political mood (that of disappointment with how democracy works in the country and voter absenteeism), it is only natural to expect low convert interest and involvement in the political processes. Additionally, the influence of some of the 'Islamic' material (especially of that negatively predisposed toward democracy) on the worldview of converts could be further expected to make them apathetic, if not altogether hostile, towards democracy and taking part in democratic political process.

Yet, from a closer scrutiny of converts' attitudes on these issues it turns out that their opinion of democracy at times might be even very favourable and their participation in voting marked by a shared sense of duty, something that the bulk of non-Muslim Lithuanians lack. It appears that many, if not most, converts do care about the future of Lithuania, even if they are prone to a sense of helplessness. On the other hand, those who do not care and/or are especially negative about the Lithuanian nation and the state, might have long left it and fall outside the sight of the research either because of abstaining from expressing their views on islamas.lt and similar forums or declining to be interviewed.

A note needs to be added in regard to other forms of political participation: Lithuanian converts to Islam (and for that matter, other Muslims) hardly take part in any other types of political participation besides voting, though some of the interviewees indicated that they have taken part in such acts as petition signing and boycotting certain goods.

Finally, as Hussain argues,

> The discussion about political engagement partly impinges on the social, economic and political needs of the Muslim community, as well as on how established the Muslim community has become and is able to understand the opportunities available to articulate its needs, concerns and vision to the wider society. (Hussain 2004: 379)

In the case of Lithuanian Muslims in general and more specifically converts to Islam, political participation remains exclusively on an individual basis as a 'Lithuanian Muslim community' hardly exists as an entity with a practical sense of common background and shared expectations. Therefore, it remains to be seen if, when, and how such a community develops and if converts will play any prominent role in its evolution. Alternatively, converts could continue to be treated as a distinct 'community' in their own right and a cultural sub-group within the Lithuanian citizenry.

Notes

1. For further detail, see the article by Agata Nalborczyk in Chapter 12 of this volume.
2. These crude estimates are derived from observations of on-line Muslim internet forums and the personal experience of the author. A note has to be added here – many Lithuanian converts to Islam reside, temporarily or permanently, outside Lithuanian borders.
3. The below provided typology is to be treated as a crude extrapolation made on the basis of some two decades-long personal communication and observation of the evolution of Islam in Lithuania. For early findings, see Racius (2002); see also Račius (forthcoming).
4. A similar distribution was found in research on seventy British converts to Islam by Köse and Loewenthal (2000).
5. The expression 'conversion career' has been borrowed from Richardson (1978).
6. A similar situation was observed in Denmark where for a long time young female converts constituted the majority of Danish converts to Islam (Jensen 2006: 644).
7. Historically (classical) Islam comprised at least three distinct dimensions: one normative – 'legalistic' (Redfield's 'great tradition' (Redfield 1956), Gellner's 'high' Islam of the ulama (Gellner 1993: 23–39), and two cultural – 'mystical' and 'folk' (Redfield's 'little tradition', Gellner's 'low' folk). The normative and the cultural are mutually opposed, while the two cultural dimensions have much in common and are accommodating of each other.
8. Since its inception in the spring of 2004, the Forum had, by the spring of 2010, accumulated more than 45,000 entries on several dozen Islam-related topics, ranging from theological-dogmatic to practical and rituals-related issues, submitted by almost 700 registered members (of whom probably more than half were non-Muslim) and scores of occasional visitors (statistics taken from the main page of the online Islamas.lt forum at <http://www.islamas.lt/forumas/index php?act=idx> (last accessed 21 April 2010)). However, on 25 May 2010, after six full years in operation, the Forum was removed by its administrators 'due to server error (some hacking issue)', available at <http://www.islamas.lt/forumas/>.
9. Quazi-legalist Islam in this chapter is a term used to designate a hybrid sub-dimension of revivalist Islam common to contemporary converts to Islam in the West, the main features of which are longing for a non-denominational *fiqh* and unreserved hostility to folk Islam.
10. For the 'basic tenets of neofundamentalism' see Roy (2004), 243–47.
11. That Lithuanians are indeed rather anti-Islamic has been revealed by the results of a recent opinion poll: over a third of surveyed Lithuanians had negative opinions about Islam while less than 10% saw it in a favourable light. No other 'world' religion was perceived more negatively than Islam. See opinion poll results commissioned by the Ministry of Justice (2007), Jackevičius (2007).

12. On Lithuanian converts' opinions about the Lithuanian Tatars see Račius (forthcoming).
13. The main methodological tools employed in the research were:

- long-time scrutiny of online sources, among them, since 2004, the online forums of Lithuanian converts to Islam at <www.musulmonai.lt> and <www. islamas.lt>. Unfortunately, due to the recent closure (in 2008 and 2010 respectively) of both forums, the author can no longer provide proper references to the location of the citations of the converts' thoughts.
- a dozen semi-structured interviews (in the form of a questionnaire) with randomly chosen Lithuanian converts to Islam (conducted in the spring and summer of 2010 by Vaida Norvilaitė).

References

Allievi, S. (2002), 'Converts and the Making of European Islam', *ISIM Newsletter*, issue 11, pp. 1, 7.

Baltic News Service, *Demokratijos būkle šalyje nepatenkinti keturi iš penkių Lietuvos gyventojų*, 2009-12-14, available at <http://www.15min.lt/naujiena/aktualu/lietuva/demokratijos-bukle-salyje-nepatenkinti-keturi-is-penkiu-lietuvos-gyventoju-56-75663> (last accessed 10 April 2011).

Bunt, G. R. (2003), *Islam in the Digital Age: E-jihad, Online Fatwas and Cyber Islamic Environments*, (London: Pluto Press).

Central Bureau of Statistics (1925), *Lietuvos gyventojai: 1923 m. rugsėjo 17 d. surašymo duomenys* (Kaunas: Centrinis statistikos biuras).

Central Electoral Commission (2008a), *Voters turnout in constituencies*, available at <http://www.vrk.lt/2008_seimo_rinkimai/output_en/rinkimu_diena/rinkeju_akty vumas_ordereda1turas.html> (last accessed 15 December 2011).

Central Electoral Commission (2008b), *Voter turnout in the single-member constituencies at the second poll*, available at <http://www.vrk.lt/2008_seimo_rinkimai/output_en/rinkimu_diena2/rinkeju_aktyvumas_ordereda2turas.html> (last accessed 15 December 2011).

Central Electoral Commission (2009), *Patvirtinti galutiniai Respublikos Prezidento rinkimų rezultatai*, available at <http://www.vrk.lt/lt/naujienos/patvirtinti-galutiniai-rinkimu-respublikos-prezidento-rinkimu-rezultatai.html> (last accessed 15 December 2011).

Department of Statistics (2002), *Gyventojai pagal lytį, amžių, tautybę ir tikybą* (Vilnius: Statistikos departamentas).

ELTA, *Apklausa: nuomonė apie padėtį valstybėj giedrėja, apie demokratiją – rekordiškai bloga*, 2010-03-22, available at <http://www.ve.lt/?rub=1065924810&data=2010-03-22&id=1269251277> (last accessed 15 December 2011).

Eurobarometer 72, National Report, Executive Summary, Lithuania, available at <http://ec.europa.eu/public_opinion/archives/eb/eb72/eb72_lt_en_exec.pdf> (last accessed 15 December 2011).

Eurobarometer 72, available at <http://ec.europa.eu/public_opinion/archives/eb/eb72/eb72_fact_lt_en.pdf> (last accessed 15 December 2011).

Freedom House (2011), *Nations in Transit 2011. Democratization from Central Europe to Eurasia*, Lanham: Rowman and Littlefield.

Gellner, E. (1993), *Postmodernizmas, protas ir religija* (Vilnius: Pradai).

Hussain, D. (2004), 'Muslim Political Participation in Britain and the 'Europeanisation' of Fiqh', *Welt des Islams*, vol. 44, no. 3, pp. 376–401.

Islam QA, *Ruling on democracy and elections and participating in that system*, available at <http://www.islam-qa.com/en/ref/107166/election> (last accessed 10 December 2011).

Jackevičius, M. (2007), 'Lietuviai nepakantūs islamui, tačiau garbina krikščionybę', *Delfi.lt*, available at <http://www.delfi.lt/archive/article.php?id=15277252> (last accessed 15 December 2011).

Jensen, T. G. (2006), 'Religious Authority and Autonomy Intertwined: The Case of Converts to Islam in Denmark', *Muslim World*, vol. 96, no. 4, pp. 643–60.

Köse, A. and K. M. Loewenthal (2000), 'Conversion Motifs Among British Converts to Islam', *International Journal for the Psychology of Religion*, vol. 10, no. 2, pp. 101–10.

Kričinskis, S. (1993), *Lietuvos totoriai* (Vilnius: Mokslo ir enciklopedijų leidykla).

Lakhdar, M., G. Vinsonneau, M. J. Apter, E. Mullet (2007). 'Conversion to Islam Among French Adolescents and Adults: A Systematic Inventory of Motives', *International Journal for the Psychology of Religion*, vol. 17, no. 1, pp. 1–15.

Lofland, J. and N. Skonovd (1981), 'Conversion motifs', *Journal for the Scientific Study of Religion*, vol. 20, no. 4, pp. 373–85.

Lrytas.lt, *Demokratijos ir kapitalizmo re˙me˙ju˛ Lietuvoje per 18 metu˛ gerokai sumaže˙jo*, 2009-11-03, available at <http://www.lrytas.lt/-12572339101255889554-demokratijos-ir-kapitalizmo-r%C4%97m%C4%97j%C5%B3-lietuvoje-per-18-met%C5%B3-gerokai-suma%C5%BE%C4%97jo.htm?utm_source=rss&utm_medium=rss&utm_campaign=rss> (last accessed 15 December 2011).

Markevičiūtė, Dalia (2009). *Internal Linkages and External Adjustment of Muslim People in Lithuania*, unpublished MA thesis, Department of Social Sciences, Vytautas Magnus University.

Ministry of Justice, *Visuomenės požiūris į naujas religines grupes*, 2007-12-10, available at <http://tm.infolex.lt/?item=relig> (last accessed 15 December 2011).

Miskiewicz, A. (1990), *Tatarzy polscy 1918–1939. Zycie spoteczno-kulturalne i religijne* (Warsaw: PWN).

Norvilaitė, V. (2011), *Transnacionalumo apraiškos lietuvių musulmonų konvertitų diskurse*, unpublished MA thesis, Institute of International Relations and Political Science, Vilnius University.

Norvilaitė, V. and E. Račius (2011), 'Musulmonų bendruomenių reakcija į sekuliarizacijos procesą Lietuvoje', *Kultūra ir visuomenė*, vol. 2, no. 3, pp. 49–66.

Parliament, *Law on Religious Communities and Associations*, 4 October 1995, No I-1057 (as last amended on 22 December 2009, No XI-601), available at <http://

www3.lrs.lt/pls/inter3/dokpaieska.showdoc_l?p_id=385299> (last accessed 16 December 2011).

Racius, E. (2002), 'Islam in Lithuania: Changing Patterns of Religious and Social Life of Lithuanian Muslims', *Journal of Muslim Minority Affairs*, vol. 22, no. 1, pp. 176–84.

Račius, E. (2009), 'Islam in Lithuania', in G. Larsson (ed.), *Islam in the Nordic and Baltic Countries*, London and New York: Routledge, pp. 116–32.

Račius, E. (forthcoming), 'A 'virtual club' of Lithuanian converts to Islam', in G. Larsson and T. Hofmann (eds), *Muslims and the New Information and Communication Technologies: Theoretical, Methodological and Empirical perspectives*, New York: Springer.

Ramonaitė, A. (2006), 'Kodėl rinkėjai ne(be)balsuoja?', in R. Žiliukaitė, A. Ramonaitė et al., *Neatrasta galia: Lietuvos pilietinės visuomenės žemėlapis*, Vilnius: Versus aureus, pp. 92–112.

Redfield, R. (1956), *Peasant Society and Culture*, Chicago: University of Chicago Press.

Richardson, J. T. (ed.) (1978), *Conversion Careers: in and out of the New Religions*, Thousand Oaks, CA: Sage Publications.

Roy, O. (2004), *Globalised Islam: The Search for a New Ummah*, London: Hurst.

Transparency International, *Global Corruption Barometer 2009*, available at <http://www.transparency.org/policy_research/surveys_indices/gcb/2009> (last accessed 15 December 2011).

Žeruolis, D. (1998), 'Lithuania', in S. Berglund (ed.) *The Handbook of Political Changes in Eastern Europe*, Cheltenham: Edward Elgar, pp. 121–56.

Žiliukaitė, R. (2006), 'Protesto politika: kraštutinė priemonė ar įprasta praktika', in R. Žiliukaitė, A. Ramonaitė et al. *Neatrasta galia: Lietuvos pilietinės visuomenės žemėlapis*, Vilnius: Versus aureus, pp. 113–38.

POLITICAL PARTICIPATION OF EUROPEAN MUSLIMS IN FRANCE AND THE UNITED KINGDOM

Salima Bouyarden

Introduction

In Britain and France Islam is a faith encompassing many cultures, which has created very significant political issues in terms of the visibility and number of Muslims. The most recent official United Kingdom Census of 2001 estimated that there were 1.6 million Muslims in the UK, mainly of South Asian origin, representing 3% of the total population (Summerfield and Baljit 2005: 182).[1] Sean McLoughlin and Tahir Abbas reported that the Office for National Statistics estimate was 2.4 million Muslims in 2009 in the United-Kingdom (McLoughlin and Abbas 2010: 545). This places Islam, as in France, as the second main religion in the country. In France, where Muslims are mainly of North-African descent, it is more difficult to evaluate the exact number of Muslims since any census of the population on religious or ethnic criteria is forbidden. Despite this, one estimate has given a potential number of 4.1 million, and in 2007 the National Institute of Statistics estimated that Muslims represented 7.1% of the total population (Zwilling 2010: 184). At a European level, these figures place British and French Muslim communities as the third and the first largest in western Europe respectively.

The organisation of these communities is still in process. This chapter aims to identify the major features of the processes at work in these two communities. This chapter also aims to explore how these two multicultural communities, evolving in two different systems, are politically defining themselves by creating their own identity, and how they are building their sense of belonging by creating networks and identifying and laying claim to their rights.

What kind of political participation are they defining? Through our analysis of British and French Muslims' respective histories, we can assess the extent to which Muslim political participation – voting patterns, political engagement and Muslim identity, as well as the relationship between these factors – has been influenced by the past. The chapter will then focus on the new patterns of present French and British Muslim political participation, and the processes at work among these Muslim communities. Then we will discuss the emergence of Muslim women in politics, their motivations and the difficulties they might have encountered. The chapter will conclude with some discussion on the existence of a 'Muslim vote' and a 'Muslim lobby' in these two countries, and with the birth of a European Muslim civic participation.

Historical context

Before investigating in detail the present situation of Muslims in Europe, it is important to put this chapter into historical perspective and provide an overview of some key events and personalities influencing the creation and visibility of these communities.

The building of Muslim communities, whether in France or in Britain, has been a long and complex process which started predominantly at the time of the French and British Empires. Indeed, contrary to general thinking, Muslims were present in Britain and France long before the mass immigration of the 1970s to these countries. Among Muslim pioneers were *ayahs* (nannies), *munshis* (teachers at the court), *lascars* (sailors), soldiers and colonial workers,[2] all symbolising the power and wealth of their respective Empire.

In any discussion of early Muslim pioneers, it is important to note the presence of British and French names at the top of what I call 'the European Muslim family tree'. The earliest Muslims in Europe were not exclusively Arab or Asian, contrary to general expectation. Early converts to Islam played a significant role in Britain and France. In the nineteenth century, personalities like the British solicitor Abdullah William Quilliam, who converted to Islam after visiting Morocco and Algeria, opened the first mosques in Britain and promoted knowledge of Islam in the country (available at <http://www.history cooperative.org/proceedings/seascapes/dunn.html> last accessed 11 August 2011). In France Dr Philippe Grenier, who converted to Islam after visiting Algeria, was the first French Muslim to enter parliament and wear North African Muslim traditional clothes in the National Assembly (Sellam 2006: 48–9; Renard 2006: 585). Both of these important personalities made a significant early impact to give a new awareness and visibility to a community who from then on would be identified as the Muslims 'in' and 'of' Europe.[3]

The number of Muslims continued to grow steadily in Europe with the regular arrival of Muslim immigrant workers who were, after World War II, mainly of South Asian origin in Britain and of North African origin in France. The end of the British Empire and the establishment of the Commonwealth in the late 1940s, labour agreements made between France and its colonies and protectorates, and the labour shortage following World War II in Europe, made many Muslim single men come to Europe as temporary workers in the rebuilding of the European economy. These young Muslims did not intend to live the rest of their lives in Europe. They came to Europe primarily to save enough money to allow them to live a decent life in their home countries. Once established in Britain and France, chain migration started with immigrants calling for their fellows to come and work in the country. Solidarity between already established and new immigrants made these moves easier, with immigrants helping one another with housing and supporting each other in finding work (Lewis 2002: 17; Gallissot 1984: 1712).

Most of these immigrants arrived with a dream of Europe in mind. They aspired to a period of working in Europe in order to save enough money to go back to their home countries, buy an estate and live a 'perfect' life there with their families. But history turned out differently, as restrictive immigration measures were adopted in the 1960s and the 1970s in Britain and France (Mc Donald 1969: 65; Gokalp 1975: 889). Families had to quickly come and join these 'single men' and, later, the birth of their children in Europe came to put a definite end to their dream and what is known as 'the myth of return' – a possible return to their home countries. From this point on began the religious and political involvement of Muslim immigrants in their new home countries.

Whether in France or in the UK, voting goes hand in hand with citizenship. At the beginning of the mass immigration of Muslims, many elements – law, culture, history, religion, and other practical reasons – influenced Muslims' political involvement or detachment in their new host societies. Early Muslim immigrants in France, whether or not they planned to live the rest of their lives in the country, did not have the right to vote as they were not French citizens. However, at this early stage of immigration, the few who became naturalised French citizens could neither be appointed to any positions of public responsibility, achieve the right to vote for five years, or be elected for ten years (Weil 2002: 246). Moreover, later, in the words of a twenty-nine-year-old Moroccan educated woman talking about getting French citizenship: 'Nothing will change, according to me, the Arab remains the Arab. As far as work is concerned, we will always have an Arab face, I don't think that it is important to get the French nationality ...' (Kepel 1991: 49–50). Both these 'new French' and 'non French', deprived of recognition and any opportunity to play a social role, were therefore to remain in, and to be restricted to, a certain category of jobs. Institutional constraints and discrimination in their everyday lives credibly explain why the conviction that naturalisation allowed no active and positive role in society remained for a long time deeply entrenched among the French Muslim community.

In parallel, there were other historical and cultural factors at play within the Muslim community in France that may have prevented new immigrants from becoming naturalised and from voting. One obligation that went hand in hand with French naturalisation was the fulfillment of military service in the

French Army.[4] It is self-evident that to require Muslims in the 1980s in France to join an army that, just few years previously in the context of decolonisation, had violently repressed them and their fellows, was to ask them to betray their nation of origin. The price for French nationality was emotionally too high to pay for a people whose pride in having directly helped with or supported the independence of their country of origin before leaving it, was one of the only 'sacred' links that remained between them and their home countries.

In addition to representing betrayal towards their fellow countrymen and their country, naturalisation was in some cases felt even as a betrayal towards God and their religion. A key reason that may explain the almost non-active political role of the first generation of Muslims in France was the fact that some of them used to consider naturalisation as *haram*, a religious infidelity. This probably came from the fact that one condition, exclusively applied to Muslims in Algeria during French colonisation in order to get naturalisation and full French civil and political rights, was to give up the personal status of a Muslim and the practice of some Algerian Muslim religious habits (Weil 2006: 554). French naturalisation was thus associated in some way in Muslims' minds with the idea of a rejection of Islamic rights and duties. This idea was probably reinforced by some French colonial judges' special practices in favour of Algerian Muslim converts to Christianity, consisting of giving them, in some cases, the benefit of some French civil rights.[5] The granting of French rights therefore came to be associated, in the Algerian Muslim psyche, with the rejection of the Muslim faith as a whole.

The emergence at that time in Algeria of some theses pleading in favour of official recognition of full French civil rights and French naturalisation for Algerian Muslim converts to Christianity probably came to emphasise such ideas. For instance, André Bonnichon, in his law doctorate thesis of 1931, stated:

> ... two considerations usually retain the natives to apply for naturalisation: the need to abandon Muslim personal status, and the contempt often felt towards the *m'tourni*, that is to say towards the one who has accepted the law of the invaders. But Christians by their conversion are already *m'tournis*. The gap is already opened between them and their former co-religionists. As far as Muslim personal status is concerned, their new faith alone makes them a duty to give up almost all the institutions which are characterising it. It seems then that they [Algerian Muslim converts to Christianity] should all be naturalised ... (Bonnichon 1931: 13)[6]

Algerian Muslim converts to Christianity were here considered to have 'accepted the law of the invaders'. It is also worth noting the confusing analogy made here between the acceptance of French law, the acceptance of Christianity, and the suggestion made by the author that these Christian *m'tournis* 'should all be naturalised'. This could explain how, later, to Algerian

Muslim immigrants, becoming naturalised implied in some way acceptance and embracing of the Christian faith.

These elements explain the fact that later, in the context of mass Muslim immigration to Europe, many Muslim immigrants who settled in France believed that adopting the nationality of a non-Muslim country in which they were not born was a sin. Some of these Muslims agreed to ask for citizenship only for those of their children who were actually born in France.[7] It appears that it was only with the new generation of French-born Muslims that some Muslim parents started to realise that one can both be Muslim and a citizen of a non-Muslim country. The impact of all these factors was that only a relatively small number of North African Muslim immigrants acquired French nationality.[8] This played a significant role in the delayed, obstructed entry of Muslims onto the French political stage.

Moreover, it was reported that at the beginning of mass immigration in France, among the small group of Muslim citizens that existed, only a few of these 'potential electors' actually voted. The only French Muslim deputy, Mourad Kaouah, was a member of the Front National, which is the far-right French nationalist party (Kepel 1991: 323). So, despite the election of some other Muslim politicians, such as the *Harkis* (Algerians who fought on the side of the French Army during the Algerian War of independence) colonel Hocine Chabaga, who was standing for the Socialist Party, most Muslim immigrants in France did not find anyone on the political stage with whom they could really identify. In this post-colonial context, the *Harkis* could not claim to be representative of the majority of Muslim North-African immigrants in France. In the North African collective memory of the time, French naturalisation and voting was associated with the *Harkis*, who were still seen as 'traitors'.

Immigrants to Britain, as citizens of the new Commonwealth and Pakistan, had the right to vote, and therefore to take part in the political system of the country. Gilles Kepel emphasised the point that 'this juridical situation, unique in the world, meant that citizenship had no meaning as a criterion of national identity, since membership of the Commonwealth conferred automatic rights through nationality' (Kepel 1997: 97). This remark underlines that in such a system, it is possible to make a distinction between positive political participation through citizenship, and national identity.

However, to live in Britain as a religious minority was not a significant change for Muslims who had already been accustomed to living as a minority in India during the time of the British Empire. The British government was already acquainted with this issue as Britain ruled over India until 1947. Prior to any Muslim mass immigration in Britain therefore, the British government had been prepared to deal with the needs of its Muslim community in India. Such a notion was already present in India at the time of the British Empire within the Montague-Chelmsford Report of 1918, which led to the Government of India Act, 1919, which stated:

A *minority* which is given *special representation* owing to its weak and backward state is positively encouraged *to settle down into a feeling of satisfied security*; it is under no inducement to educate and qualify itself to make good the ground which it has lost compared with the stronger majority. (Philips 1962: 209)

It is interesting to note the concept of 'special representation' being mentioned at such an early stage of the community's formation in India. This idea is synonymous with the modern concept of 'special needs' intrinsic to the British model of diversity governance. It is interesting to note that, at the time of the British Empire, the British government showed a deep awareness that it needed to adapt its policy to make a place for its minorities in India. It achieved this via the Government of India Act, 1919, which granted special political representation to its Muslim minority so that they could live with a 'feeling of satisfied security' in India.

The granting of these political rights, whether exclusively applicable and valid within Indian borders, was still later to influence Muslim immigrants' attitude towards citizenship and voting in the UK. A study of the Rochdale council election showed that, as early as 1973, out of thirty-one candidates, two Pakistanis had been nominated to stand for the Liberal Party and one Pakistani to stand for the Labour Party (Anwar 1979: 146). This shows that it did not take long for Muslims to develop a presence, and appear and integrate into the British political arena through traditional parties. This process of Muslim immigrants' integration into the British political arena went on and developed through the 1980s. A study made at that time about Muslim Bangladeshi politicians in Tower Hamlets, reports that:

Formal political discourse presupposed a unitary constituency comprising a Bangladeshi community in solidarity as 'black' working class with the white working class. Bangladeshi electors, however were more interested in the 'Sylheti backgrounds and moral worth of the two young candidates' and were mobilized along kinship, village, and friendship networks. (Lewis 2002: 21)

In the early days of these Muslims' settlement in Britain, in which transmitting their cultural heritage to their now British-born children was a key challenge, it is clear that culture played a critical role in the formation of the community's identity. Moreover, as we have seen earlier, the community based on 'kinship, village and friendship networks' had been their first natural source of solidarity when they arrived in the country. So it is not surprising that when it came to politics, the community became their first political mobilisation asset as well.

Among other informal networks of this kind were also networks of mosques in which religious leaders were sometimes giving voting instructions to their congregations. Gilles Kepel reports that:

During the 1987 general election campaign, a leaflet entitled 'The Muslim Vote' was distributed in Britain, particularly in Birmingham. The leaflet, printed in English, Urdu, Gujerati and Bengali, asked Muslims to vote only for candidates who agreed that UK Muslims should be governed by Islamic behavioural codes and who supported the educational demands expressed by the Muslim Educational Trust. (Kepel 1997: 116)

The involvement of British Muslim religious leaders in politics seems here to mark their commitment to simultaneously preserve their religion and increase their visibility in the eyes of British society. Moreover, let also note here, that the political involvement of the first generation of Muslims in Britain was also influenced by practical reasons. The translation of political leaflets in different South-Asian dialects is an illustration of how political parties and Muslim leaders in Britain realised from an early stage the importance of informing and getting informed about political issues.

This contrasts starkly with a complete lack of information among French Muslims about the new French legislation such as the law of July 1978, and then the laws of the 8th and 20th December 1983, respectively repealing the incapacities of freshly French naturalised immigrants to be employed as civil servants, to vote during five years, and to seek an elective mandate before a deadline of ten years (Weil, 2005, 430). This was often due to language barriers, with the French language often badly spoken and understood by immigrants (http://www.ldh-toulon.net/spip.php?article2734, accessed 13 August 2011). But this was probably also due to a French government having little regard for this part of the potential electorate. The late development of French Muslim political awareness contrasts with the relatively early participation of British Muslims in the political life of the country they had settled in.

Finally, in France, as we would expect, these elements had a number of consequences for the Muslim community, most significantly, a certain detachment in the attitude of immigrants from the question of naturalisation, voting and political participation. This resulted in an invisibility in the political and social sphere of mainstream French society on the part of the first generation of Muslim immigrants. This was in stark contrast to their British peers who started to make a political impact relatively early, albeit initially a small one. Relatively soon after their arrival in the UK, Muslims could be seen represented on the political stage, which had consequences for the pace at which the community developed, the ability of Muslims to set up mosques and, generally, on their feeling of belonging in their new home country.

New patterns of Muslim political participation

Our analysis of the new patterns of European Muslim participation has been based on both quantitative and qualitative surveys.[9] This study provided us with some information on our young British and French Muslim respondents' present political participation. Our quantitative survey (not intended to constitute a representative sample) revealed that 83% and 76.47% of our French and British Muslim respondents respectively, said that they do vote. These figures cannot be said to be representative of the actual levels of political participation among these Muslim communities, but nevertheless they testify to a tendency towards the building of some kind of political awareness amongst these two communities. Both the French and British Muslim communities largely define voting as a way to participate in political and social life, even if our respondents also expressed that, in both communities, they do not really feel represented on the political stage.

What made British and French Muslims aware of the importance of voting? Our quantitative survey revealed that French Muslims put national social events as the first most important factor and, secondly, the influence of family and friends. Their British peers placed family and friends in first position and social events came second. There are no significant differences between the two main elements identified as their main sources of political mobilisation. We can, however, see in these answers the reflection of a traditional community, family, and friend-based approach to politics characterising British Muslim communities.[10]

As their third most significant influence French Muslims identified social networks, with their British peers naming local religious figures. In fourth position for French Muslims came media personalities, whereas for their British peers came social networks. Finally, in fifth and last position, French Muslims identified local religious figures whereas their British peers selected media personalities.[11] So, once again, the results were very similar except for the place and the role of religious figures: British Muslims place this factor in third position whereas French Muslims place it in fifth and last position. In light of what was discussed earlier regarding the historical background of the political participation of these communities, this may be seen as an inheritance and consequence of the political role that religious figures have (or have not) played among the first generation of Muslims. But this can also be seen as the internalisation of their respective national systems: in France, a separation of the state and the religious sphere occurs, whereas in Britain such a separation is rather more vague. Figure 6.1 below will provide a general view of the main features characteristising French and British Muslims present vote.

By internalisation I mean a multilateral, inclusive, dynamic process of appropriations and reformulations of norms and values that have been integrated. Our definition is based on two main elements. The first one is Olivier Roy's view that European Islam is '. . . not going towards the assimilation, but towards the interiorisation of the Western world' (Roy 1999: 99). Here the important distinction between assimilation and internalisation shows that as

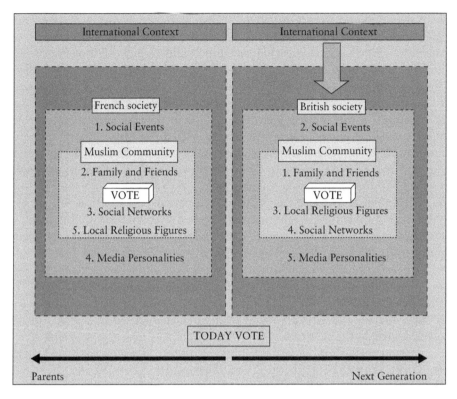

Figure 6.1 French and British Muslims present vote

far as European Muslims are concerned, the process of internalisation cannot be viewed as assimilation in the sense of a mere acceptance of values and norms.

The second element is the economist Gérard Kébabdjian's definition of internalisation as being composed of 'two aspects: one aspect of "integration" of external elements; one aspect of "disintegration" of the structure and regulations that were formerly prevailing inside' (Beaud 1999: 224).[12] What is interesting in the definition he proposes is that it emphasises the 'internal' disintegrating and opening process produced by the integration of what is seen as 'external' elements. Applied to European Muslims, this means that the elements that are integrated result in revealing the permeability of borders, whether they are national or community borders.

Moreover, our surveys also revealed that when it comes to gaining more political influence, both British and French Muslims stress the importance of getting rid of the image of terrorists. However, British Muslims show a particular concern about gaining political weight in order to be able to influence international issues and the foreign policy followed by its government. As an illustration of this, one of our British Muslim interviewees, of Irish and Egyptian origin, Yasmin, a twenty-one-year-old law student, told us about how she got involved in protests against what was happening abroad:

> We went to the British Council to get involved . . . it was just to bring a letter here to the local MP . . . Just the community . . . you know usually family and friends and you know you're talking about the same topics and things and then you get emails passed on from one to another telling you about what's happening you know you follow the news and things, and everybody knows that if you want to speak up about something Downing Street has a website you can actually post letters to them . . . Having origins from abroad, whether it's the Irish side or the Egyptian side, I do feel like, we are a global community it's not just about their problem, their country, their . . . you know they have to deal with it. As Britain is more developed, it has more resources, it can help out with more things, and they have more influence globally so it can try, you know if there is some war somewhere, it can try and get involved and you know minimise the disasters . . . I'm more interested by things abroad you know, what globally influences countries with one another especially with humanitarian aid things [. . .] So that's probably something that I changed over the years of study. Before I used to just think that, you know, there was Britain and that was it. But now I kind of think outside of that, and Britain is so small compared to all the rest so . . . . It's a very good country and I think masha Allah and what we do is. You have a lot going on here, but then you see what else . . . how much more need to be done outside of Britain. And that's probably what I find more interesting. Because I know Britain is kind of . . . it's safe, it's sorted, it can't really go that wrong really.

Here it is interesting to see how she uses well-internalised local and national legal rights, such as writing a letter to the 'local MP' and 'Downing Street', as a means to proper global action. The internalisation of these rights has led to 'open them up' to the global good. In the same dynamic we can observe in our interviewee's discourse the importance of the reinterpretation of frontiers, whether community or national borders. It is worth noting how her definition of the community extends from 'family and friends' networks (getting informal information, talking to each other, through emails and from the news), to 'origins from abroad', to a feeling of 'global community'.

Secondly, we can see how without rejecting the existence of national borders, the latter is put into a new global perspective as she now thinks 'outside of that, and Britain is so small compared to all the rest . . .'. Britain would actually continue to play its traditional role in terms of interventionism inside the 'global community', which does not appear to jeopardise the nation-state as such, since the interviewee thinks it is 'safe' and 'sorted' and 'can't really go that wrong'. On this point Vincent Latour argues that: 'Europeanization and globalization have not led (and certainly will not lead) to the erasure of national models' (Latour 2010).[13] So the internalisation at work among European Muslim communities is not about erasing the national model, but about putting it into a new perspective of global solidarity and transnational cooperation.

Here the community and national borders are no longer defined according to certain norms but according to a certain feeling of belonging to a 'global community'. On this feeling of belonging to the community and to the nation, Brigitte Maréchal observed that Muslims were showing flexibility and change '. . . in the ways of belonging to Islam' as they '. . . seem more changeable, and appear as part of a permanent process of restructuration' (Maréchal 2003: 11). The 'global community' here is not exclusively religious, ethnic or national, as illustrated by the respondent making reference to her 'Irish side'. In this way, the interviewee's discourse seems to tend towards a 'Cosmopolitan-autonomous integration: . . . orientated to the cultural global integration of Islam. Muslims are worried about an institutional integration of Islam and are developing a European Islamic discourse, all the while maintaining cultural and symbolic ties with worldwide Islam' (Dassetto and Nielsen 2003: 540).

For French Muslims and their quest to increase their political influence, the emphasis is on getting out of a kind of neo-colonial system in which they feel they are stuck.[14] In the words of twenty-year-old French Muslim high school student Abdel-Hakim, who feels that: '. . . I do not fit into the French model, the French Catholic who goes to Church on Sundays. We are put aside. My parents are of foreign origin and so am I. This is like in the suburbs, there are some young people who cannot integrate, and plus they are kept away from city centres . . .'. The normative and exclusive conception of the national model seems here to lead to a certain hierarchy inside society in which groups judged to be 'different' are relegated to certain parts of the city.

Political weight would also enable these French Muslims to fulfill the duty of memory that they feel they owe to their parents and grandparents, rewriting French national history by reintegrating its Muslim component.[15] On this point Stefano Allievi noted that '. . . it will not be possible to understand the history and the social evolution of Europe without taking into account its Muslim component' (Allievi 2003: 25). This idea was confirmed in our quantitative survey when respondents were asked if 'compared to their parents, they thought they had a particular political role to play'. French Muslims predominantly answered 'yes', citing a mix of negative ideas aimed at remembering and seeking revenge for the past, balanced with positive ideas of pride and validation of their parents' history and sacrifices. Half of our sample of British Muslim respondents answered 'yes', with their concerns more orientated towards the next generation.

Some people would be tempted to analyse these results as further proof of a so-called manipulation of the French Muslim community by an obscure past with its associated resentment from the community, or of the manipulation of the British Muslim community by some foreign leaders. But I think that it would be more accurate to see once again in these phenomena the internalisation of the society in which these European Muslim communities live and are part of. French Muslims show a tendency towards the same kind of attitudes, typically French pride, and sometimes even a 'cult' of the past. British Muslims express the same particular concern about foreign policy and British interventionism influenced by its 'special relationship' with the United States of America. In other words, the European Muslim vote is, at the end of the day, a reflection of the society they are part of, put in the context of globalisation.

Muslim women engaged in politics

The internalisation among Muslims of a diversity of norms and values has lent itself naturally to the emergence of Muslim women engaging in politics. A linear study of this phenomenon is quite impossible. The evolution of Muslim women engaged in national political movements since the beginning of mass immigration to the present day cannot be seen as a chronological succession of a new 'type' of women engaged in politics, implying the complete eradication of an older type. As new groups of women engaged in politics emerge on the political stage, older ones stay and retain their legitimacy.

Typology of European Muslim women engaged in politics

A typology of European Muslim women engaged in politics would identify three distinct types. Among these groups, the first one is composed of Muslim women fighting for values such as equality, rights and recognition. These women tend to define their movement within traditional political parties. An example of this is the participation of women in France in the famous '*marche des beurs*' in the 1980s (Lesselier 2008: 157), which resulted in Fadela Amara, traditionally associated with the Socialist Party, being nominated as minister for urban policies in the government run by the conservative Union for a Popular Movement (UMP) in 2007. In Britain, women such as Baroness Warsi would fall into the same category. Baroness Warsi was the first Muslim female co-chairman of the Conservative Party and minister without portfolio after the new government came to power in 2010.

The second group is composed of Muslim women fighting for the same values – equality, rights, recognition – and, in addition, the proper acceptance of their Muslim and ethnic identity. These women also define themselves within traditional parties. An example of this is Ilham Moosaid, the headscarf-clad NPA (New Anticapitalist Party) candidate, who made the headlines in 2010 during regional elections in France. In Britain, women in this category include Baroness Pola Uddin, a British Labour politician and community

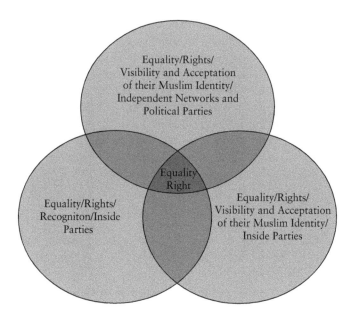

Figure 6.2 Typology of French and British Muslim women engaged in politics

activist who can sometimes be seen wearing a headscarf or traditional South Asian clothes.

Finally, the third group is composed of Muslim women fighting for the same values and acceptance of their Muslim identity, this time within independent networks and political parties. Among these women is Houria Bouteldja, leader of the new party of Les Indigènes de la République, created in 2010.[16] In Britain, Salma Yaqoob became leader of the Respect Party, created in 2004, a political candidate said to have been 'wooed' and 'courted' by the Conservative Party, the Labour Party and the Liberal Democrat Party.[17]

Despite their differences and peculiarities, instead of totally neutralising each other, these different groups of women engaged in politics appear to keep on nourishing each other around a common ground based on their democratic quest for equality and rights.[18] Figure 6.2 above will provide a typology of French and British Muslim women engaged in politics.

Obstacles encountered

Unsurprisingly, these women face many obstacles from wider society but also from the Muslim community itself. Indeed, in interview Kahina X, who claims to be a feminist, declares her belief that wider society only accepts Muslim women on the political stage because they seem to represent a certain 'political exoticism' (Kahina X 2008: 311). Instead of taking their political claims seriously, wider society is seen to perceive these atypical women as a source of amusement, putting on a show for their entertainment via their political involvement. Pola Uddin reports that when she started her career, instead of being evaluated on the work she had done:

> ... all the coverage centred on what value I could possibly add to the House as a woman who wore a sari and breast-fed her son in the female peers room. In fact, I was advised by my peers and so-called friends that I may wish to consider wearing a suit to be taken seriously.[19]

According to Houria Bouteldja, Muslim women engaged in politics were only tolerated by wider society because, contrary to their male peers, they appeared to be more 'civilisable'. She also highlighted the fact that women wearing the *hijab* (headscarf) encountered more difficulties because they appeared to clash directly with French republican ideals. This would explain the fact that sometimes the 'Muslim community' appears, according to her, to provide shelter to these women.[20]

Sometimes obstacles also originated from both wider society and the Muslim community itself as Salma Yaqoob, leader of the Respect Party testifies:

> When I stood as a *hijab*-wearing Muslim woman, one of the obstacles I had to overcome was the perception that I was a 'fundamentalist' interested only in 'Muslim issues'. In addition, I had to face male hostility: it was not 'my place' as a woman to contest politics.[21]

Such discontent from members of the Muslim community towards these women involved in politics is also to be found among their French peers. Saida Kada, president of the Femme Française Musulmane et Engagée (French Muslim and Engaged Women) reports that when she started her political movement, she 'had to face a certain disagreement. Not only on the part of brothers, because it was even harder on the part of sisters' (Boubeker and Hajjat 2008: 226).

Like other women engaged in politics, whether French or British, Muslim or not, these women have had to face many obstacles. By getting involved in politics, they are in an arena where they are not expected to be and, in addition, they have defied society's expectations of who they are in terms of their values, opinions and convictions. These women all have their particularities and their main converging point is not Islam, as one would expect, but the expression of modern society's pluralism and need for change and variety. The emergence of these women engaged in politics is challenging and redefining borders at both a national and a community level, which could in the future lead to the reinforcement of the convergence of European Muslims' civic participation.

The birth of European Muslim civic participation

As discussed in the preceding sections, managing the inclusion of plurality remains one of the key challenges for European societies. But does such a demand when expressed by Muslims on the political stage testify to the existence of a specific 'Muslim vote'? By 'Muslim vote' I mean an exclusive specific and uniform Muslim common agreement on voting issues predefining Muslim voters' vote orientation.

Both our quantitative and qualitative studies revealed that the great majority of our British and French Muslim respondents answered 'no' to this question. Our quantitative survey revealed that 80.39% and 69.23% of our French and British Muslims respondents respectively answered 'no' to this question. During our qualitative survey, most of our interviewees felt confused in the face of such a concept, which they considered irrelevant. Their answers placed the emphasis on Muslims as citizens, participating in the democratic process by voting.

Even if the idea of a 'Muslim vote' still tends to be associated in the common mind with the Labour Party in the UK and to the Socialist Party in France, the majority of our respondents seemed not to be aware of the existence of a specific 'Muslim vote'. It emerged from our studies that they may share a common view on problems they face as Muslims but there is no such a thing as a common Muslim agreement on voting and political issues. As for the minority of our interviewees who answered positively to the existence of or the need for a potential 'Muslim vote', their understanding of this concept was more in terms of the necessity of getting organised in terms of solidarity and of taking part as Muslim citizens in the public debate in order to express their opinions, especially in the current context of the stigmatisation of Islam worldwide and nationally.

How then to explain the extensive use in the media and by some politicians of the expression 'Muslim vote'? What is behind this expression? One of our anonymous French respondents who believed that such a vote does indeed exist, helps us to answer this question; his response was: 'if it doesn't exist, then how to justify the sudden interest for the quality of life in the suburbs just before elections . . . ?'. This answer is quite interesting as it emphasises the role of politicians in the creation, before election, of the idea of the existence of such a vote. The so-called 'Muslim vote' would therefore appear to represent a political strategy. Indeed, it may be easier for politicians, via the media, to either simply address, seduce or even despise Muslim electors as one bloc rather than to face the complex and diversified reality of European Muslims' growing involvement in politics.

In France, Gilles Kepel's summary report *Banlieue de la République*, based on a study carried out in the cities of Clichy and Montfermeil, has recently mentioned the 'birth of a "Muslim lobby"'. The latter would have the '. . . objective of mobilising the communitarian vote in order to have weight on candidates in local elections around Islamic issues'. This phenomenon could, according to the author, potentially end up in the '. . . emergence of a Muslim lobby on a national scale' (Kepel 2011: 23).[22] As my own study at a local level, in the city of Montbéliard in France, has revealed, the idea and prospect of a 'Muslim vote' is quite impossible. As far as a 'Muslim lobby' on a national level is concerned, some French studies underline that:

> Three essential factors counter the myth of a Muslim lobby. First, there is no unified Muslim community and as a consequence, no unique representative organization . . . In fact, there are many Muslim communities according to divisions along countries of origin, theological divisions and generational divisions. The second factor is related to the absence of an ethnic vote. Muslim voters' behaviour cannot be explained by the religious factor . . . Finally, foreign policy considerations only constitute a secondary concern for Muslims whose first worries relate to their place in society. (Ajala 2011: 91)

So, the idea of the potential emergence in France of a 'Muslim lobby' as defined by Gilles Kepel remains very low, if not impossible. The idea of this as a media-political tactic would probably help to explain the over-emphasis of this report in the media and the French President receiving the author just one month after he published his report. It is worth noting that this meeting happened as campaigning was heating up for the French presidential election in April 2012.

As far as Britain is concerned, the attempt at building a so-called uniform 'Muslim vote' was observed during the general elections of 2005 and 2010, during which some Muslim candidates such as Salma Yaqoob were accused of communitarianism[23] and, as discussed earlier, of being exclusively interested in Islamic issues. A form of Muslim 'lobbying', in terms of cooperation with the British government, embodied by Muslim organisations such as the Muslim Council of Britain (MCB) and the Forum Against Islamophobia (FAIR), does exist in Britain (Dilwar 2004: 392–3). Still, these organisations were rarely mentioned by our interviewees. This serves once again to underline the characteristic of Muslims' political participation as first being individualistic. With regards to Muslims' political participation in Britain, Dilwar Hussain emphasises that:

> The Qur'an exhorts believers to stand up for justice, even if it be against their own kin (4:135). Furthermore it asks people, especially people of faith, to find common ground and work together for good causes. The example of the Prophet Yusuf [. . .] shows how he took up a place in a non-Muslim government because in that was

scope for him to promote good and prevent harm, not just for himself but for the whole of that society. (Dilwar 2004: 399)

This contrasts starkly with the idea of a so-called exclusive 'Muslim vote' or exclusive 'Muslim lobby'. Some European political leaders trying to exploit such ideas may actually testify to their fear of losing their power in a changing political landscape. In our context of europeanisation and globalisation, such a political tactic may indeed testify to the 'political crisis' François Fourquet defined as not lying in the 'disappearance of politics' but in its 'displacement' on a global scale (Beaud 1999: 244).

Today, the religious community and the faith of politicised European Muslims does not represent an exclusive political end in itself, but a means as citizens to make their Muslim and non-Muslim peers aware of the importance of civic participation and social cohesion. During an interview with the French Muslim artist Médine, on French Muslims' political participation, he declared:

> Do we absolutely have to create a lobby which would put pressure on anything that moves, or would send in hordes of lawyers if even a comma is not in the right place in a sentence said about the Muslim community? No, on this point I'm not convinced, I'm in doubt. I think that Muslims are worth more than that . . . We will manage to get organised, maybe in a different way. Maybe in a non-confrontational way. . . . I don't really see a solution. This is why I come to the FEMYSO (Forum of European Muslim Youth and Student Organisations), this is why I'm going to a lot of conferences. This is precisely to try to get some answers in order to build up the beginning of an idea. . . . I'm not even thinking in the logic of telling myself that I have to make the balance sway in favour of the Muslim community. I really want to think that the Muslim community is actually in the balance, and on the right side of it. Let's think of ourselves as being on the right side of things. Let's not see politicians on one side, the community on another, young people from the suburbs on another, etc. . . . Let's think of ourselves as being part of a global dynamic. First, let's create some values, let's create jobs, let's create these kind of things, and then let's organise ourselves properly. . . . It's not exclusively about us, it is about working with other people. And then maybe without talking about 'lobbying', etc. . . . we will find the beginning of a solution in creating values.[24]

Here, the politically engaged artist stresses that the so-called idea of a 'Muslim lobby' could incorrectly pressure Muslims into positioning themselves in a relationship of power confrontation with politicians and therefore the government. He points out that his political engagement is not about giving weight to the Muslim community as such, since he considers it already to matter and to be positioned on the right side of the balance. Muslims should not consider themselves to be inherently in opposition to a surrounding environment, but to be part of a 'global dynamic' going beyond exclusive boundaries. His quest to find an answer to European Muslim citizens' real concerns and aspirations to take part in both the national and 'global dynamic' drove the artist to join the Forum of European Muslim Youth and Student Organisations (FEMYSO), a European organisation.

The artist was among the jury at the first European Muslim Youth Conference (EMYC), organised by the FEMYSO and held in Brussels last July (2011) on the theme: 'Wise up, Rise up: Get Active!'. The conference insisted on both: '. . . the importance of education and action in tackling common challenges, and the need for strong civic participation.'[25] The organisation of this conference was based on the fact that 'the European Muslim community is an integral and active part of Europe, particularly youth.' The panel discussions therefore focused on 'four main themes: Citizenship and Identity, Youth Participation and Leadership, Social Cohesion and Diversity (intercultural and inter-religious dialogue) as well as Human Rights and Islamophobia.' The EMYC was the first conference of its kind, but the FEMYSO as an organisation has existed since 1996. European Muslims are, in this way, laying the beginnings of participation in the European public space. In fifteen years, this non-governmental structure has worked to develop links with structures such as: 'the European Parliament, the European Commission, the Council of Europe, the Organization for Security and Co-operation in Europe (OSCE), the United Nations'.[26] Through this type of activity, European Muslims are providing a new dimension to issues of social cohesion.

In this way we can observe among European Muslims the premises of a transnational civic organisation and the birth of European civic participation as an alternative to the civically unproductive politicians' 'Muslim vote' and 'Muslim lobby' tactics. The expression of European Muslim plural identity in the public sphere should not be seen as the affirmation of an exclusive religious affiliation, but as a civic alternative to the exploitation of the ethnic and religious parts of their identity, and as a common action against any form of extremism whether intellectual, political or religious. Initiatives launched by some European artists and associations show how some of them have passed from reaction to proper action; and others from spontaneous action to more structured and organised activity. It appears that European Muslims, in line with their plural identity, are aware of the challenges that are still to be overcome, but are participating actively through civic actions to lay down the basis of a European union, identity and dynamism within the context of globalisation.[27]

Conclusion

To conclude, we can see that despite their very different histories and original relationships with voting, French and British Muslims show links between their voting participation, political engagement and Muslim identity. In the case of France these links are strongly influenced by the past, or in the case of the UK, by international issues, but overall they represent nothing more than the reflection among these Muslim communities of the national system they are part of. The relationship between these three components of the reality of citizenship among these Muslim communities is deeply linked to the internalisation of the national systems they are in, put in a European and global context. This has naturally led, as we have seen, to the visible emergence of Muslim women's political participation which, more than ever before, expresses our societies' pluralism and need for change. Their presence on the political stage is increasingly leading us to wonder what is really behind the expression of a 'Muslim vote' and 'Muslim lobby'. We have found out that, far from the idea of a uniform vote used to fulfill exclusively Islamic interests, it is the complex and diversified reality of European Muslims' growing political and civic participation that all this is actually about. As René Gallissot concluded more than twenty-five years ago, we may conclude here that: 'the secret of the second generation is maybe to be a political generation which is transnationalising' (Gallissot 1985: 64).

Notes

1. Report available at <http://www.ons.gov.uk/ons/rel/social-trends-rd/social-trends/no--35--2005-edition/index.html> (last accessed June 2011).
2. See Visram, R. (1986), *Ayahs, Lascars, and Princes: Indians in Britain, 1700–1947*, London: Pluto Press, pp. 25–35.
3. For more substantial information on the role of converts to Islam in the defintion of a European Islam, see also Allievi, S. (2000), *Nouveaux protagonistes de l'Islam européen: naissance d'une culture euro-islamique: le rôle des convertis*, Florence: EUI Working Papers Series, RSC no. 2000/18.
4. The obligation for every male French citizen to perform military service in the French Army was first suspended by Act no. 97–1019 of 28 October, 1997, and was finally abolished by Decree no. 2001–550 of 27 June, 2001. Available at <http://www.legifrance.gouv.fr/affichTexte.do?cidTexte=JORFTEXT000000368 950&dateTexte=> and <http://legifrance.gouv.fr/affichTexte.do;jsessionid=A574 DC3EB7B81D791299894BF8099473.tpdjo03v_2?cidTexte=JORFTEXT000000 224210&dateTexte=20090705> (last accessed September 2011).
5. For more information see Bonnichon, A. (1931), *La conversion au Christianisme de l'indigène Musulman Algérien et ses effets juridiques (un cas de conflit colonial)*, Paris: Sirey.
6. My clarification between brackets.
7. Informal interviews held with French Muslim immigrants aged between 50 and 70 years old.
8. For more information see Annexe III, table 1 'Actifs, chômeurs, salariés, actifs non salariés, suivant le sexe, le groupe d'âges et la nationalité actuelle ou anté-

rieure au recensement de 1982' in M. Tribalat, *Cent ans d'immigration, étrangers d'hier, Français d'aujourd'hui: apport démographique, dynamique familiale et économique de l'immigration étrangère*, 1991, Paris: P. U. F. Institut National d'Etudes Démographique (INED), p. 280. See also the official website of the National Institute for Statistics and Economic Studies (INSEE), table cd-ax-2 'Acquisitions réelles et enregistrées de la nationalité française (ensemble des résidences) selon la nationalité antérieure, de 1946 à 1999', *INSEE Résultats n°121 Société,* available at <http://www.insee.fr/fr/themes/detail.asp?reg_id=0&ref_id=ir-rp99pipe&page=irweb/rp99pipe/dd/rp99pipe_tabannexes.htm> (last accessed 4 September 2011).

9. Our research on the present political participation of European Muslims is based on a quantitative survey performed in the form of a questionnaire via the Internet, among 200 French and British Muslims on a national level, selected through an informal personal Muslim network. Respondents were aged between sixteen and sixty-eight years old, mainly of North African origin in France and of South Asian origin in Britain. Questionnaires were put online in February and March 2010. The second survey was based on twenty semi-structured interviews targeting French and British Muslims born in France and in Britain, aged between twenty and forty years old, in the city of Montbéliard in France and Birmingham in the United Kingdom. Interviews were carried out between April and September 2011.

10. Sometimes resulting in a form of family vote, which the British Muslim Politician Salma Yaqoob aimed at deconstructing, see: Salma Yaqoob, 'Doing it for ourselves', 15 February 2010, available at <http://www.newstatesman.com/religion/2010/02/muslim-women-woman-british> (last accessed 3 March 2011).

11. See Figure 6.1.

12. Gerard Kebabdjian gives this definition of the internalisation, and specifies that the 'disintegration' can be 'partial or not', page 224–5. For more information see the transcript of a debate between different specialists from different fields of study on the theme of globalisation 'Sept questions transversales sur la mondialisation' in Beaud M., *La Mondialisation: les mots et les choses,* 1999, Paris: Editions Karthala.

13. Vincent Latour, lecturer at the University of Toulouse specialising in Britain, France, multiculturalism and contemporary Europe, note in a paper (to be published) the same process of using transnational networks by both French and British governments for national interests. References of the paper: 'Europeanization, Globalization, Transnationalization. Reflections based on the British and French Models towards Diversity Governance', delivered at conference 'Européanisation et mondialisation/Europeanization and Globalization', UMR EEE 5222 CNRS, 2–3 December 2010, Maison des Sciences de l'Homme d'Aquitaine.

14. For more substantial information see Boubeker and Hajjat, (2008) *Histoire politique des immigrations (post) colonials France, 1920–2008,* Paris: Editions Amsterdam.

15. During the last election for the Socialist Party presidential candidate in October 2011, the two themes of getting out of a neo-colonial system and of integrating Muslim immigrants' history to the national history were mentioned by the politician Montebourg in favour of a 'reconciliation of France with Islam'. For more information see: 'Primaires socialiste: ce que les candidats proposent pour les banlieues et les zones urbaines', available at <http://www.lemonde.fr/poli tique/article/2011/09/26/primaire-socialiste-ce-que-les-candidats-proposent-pour-les-banlieues-et-les-zones-sensibles_1575788_823448.html> (last accessed 28 September 2011); 'Arnaud Montebourg: Mon Grand-Pere etait un arabe, pas un pied-noir, un arabe', available at <http://oumma.com/Arnaud-Montebourg-Mon-grand-pere> (last accessed 10 October 2011).

16. Houria Bouteldja, personal phone interview on French Muslims' political participation, August 2011: 'This is one dimension of our struggle with the Les Indigènes de la République (party); we consider that today, Islam is a European reality, that Muslims have the right to ask for equal citizenship. To be citizens like any others appears a self-evident basis to us, but we go a little bit further, we think that this is not necessarily about demanding to be citizens like any others, we think that we have to strongly require to participate in the building of the norm . . . To be French is also to be Muslim . . . Muslims are transforming France . . . That is to say that we are transforming the French norm, the French identity norm. What we add to this discourse is that we have to endorse this, that is to say that we have to claim this as such. . . . We have the right to transform the norm, to participate in the construction of the norm. In other words we do not simply ask for equality. . . . If we take a picture of France today, we would see that it is European, Christian, Jew, Muslim, Animist, it is atheist, it is West-Indian, it is African, it is black, it is Arab, it is Berber . . .'

17. See M. Bunting, 'Respect candidate spearheads quiet revolution to get Muslim women involved in politics', 23 April 2010, available at <http://www.guard ian.co.uk/politics/2010/apr/23/respect-candidate-muslim-women-politics> (last accessed 4 September 2011). See also Brett Gibbons, *Birmingham Post*, 7 July 2011, available at <http://www.birminghampost.net/news/politics-news/2011/07/07/salma-yaqoob-to-stand-down-as-birmingham-councillor-65233-29007875/2/#ixzz1irJBSQmf> (last accessed 13 July 2011). In July 2011 Salma Yaqoob announced on her official website: '. . . her decision to resign as the Councillor for Sparkbrook' for health reasons. See: 'Time to take a step back', 7 July 2011, available at <http://www.salmayaqoob.com/> (last accessed 13 July 2011).

18. See Figure 6.2.

19. See Pola Uddin, 'We need all kinds of women in Politics', 31 March 2009, available at <http://www.guardian.co.uk/commentisfree/2009/mar/31/local-government-women-representation> (last accessed 5 May 2010).

20. Houria Bouteldja, personal Internet interview on Muslim Women engaged in politics, March 2010

21. See Salma Yaqoob, 'Doing it for ourselves', 15 February 2010, available at <http://www.newstatesman.com/religion/2010/02/muslim-women-woman-british> (last accessed 4 March 2010).
22. Some French specialists like the political scientist Franck Fregosi reacted to this report. See: 'Islam et République: des specialistes réagissent au rapport Kepel', 16 October 2011, available at <http://religion.blog.lemonde.fr/2011/10/16/islam-et-republique-des-specialistes-reagissent-au-rapport-kepel-3/> (last accessed 20 October 2011).
23. See Naima Bouteldja, ' "Opération vote musulman", les réalités du "vote musulman" au Royaume-Uni', May 2005, available at <http://oumma.com/Operation-Vote-Musulman> (last accessed 6 June 2011).
24. Personal interview with the French Muslim artist Médine, Brussels, July 2011.
25. See FEMYSO facebook group document: 'FEMYSO Celebrates the European Muslim Youth conférence and its 15 years', 6 July 2011, available at <https://www.facebook.com/# !/groups/femyso/doc/10150254642823785/> (last accessed 10 August 2011).
26. All this information is available on the FEMYSO official website, <http://www.femyso.org> (last accessed November 2011).
27. Some elements of this section have been the subject of an article published on oumma.com: Salima Bouyarden, '11 Septembre 10 ans plus tard: la reponse des Européens de confession musulmane a l'extremisme?', 13 September 2011, available at <http://oumma.com/11-septembre-10-ans-plus-tard-La> (last accessed November 2011).

References

Ajala, I. (2011), 'The Muslim vote and Muslim lobby in France: myths and realities', *Journal of Islamic Law and Culture*, 12: 2, pp. 77–91.

Allievi, S. (2003), 'Islam in the Public Space: Social Networks, Media and Neo-Communities', in S. Allievi and J. Nielsen (eds), *Muslim Networks and Transnational Communities in and Across Europe*, Leiden and Boston: Brill, pp. 1–25.

Anwar, M. (1979), *The Myth of Return: Pakistanis in Britain*, London: Heinemann Educational Books.

Beaud, M. (1999), *La mondialisation: les mots et les choses*, Paris: Editions Karthala.

Bonnichon, A. (1931), *La conversion au Christianisme de l'indigène Musulman Algérien et ses effets juridiques (un cas de conflit colonial)*, Paris: Sirey.

Boubeker, A. and A. Hajjat (2008), 'Femmes musulmanes et engagées, entretien avec Saida Kada', in A. Boubeker and A. Hajjat (eds), *Histoire politique des immigrations (post) colonials France, 1920–2008*, Paris: Editions Amsterdam.

Bouteldja, H. (2010), personal Internet interview with the author on Muslim women engaged in politics, March.

Bouteldja, H. (2011), personal phone interview with the author on French Muslims' political participation, August.

Dassetto, F. and J. Nielsen (2003), 'Conclusions', in B. Maréchal, *Muslims in the Enlarged Europe, Religion and Society*, Leiden: Brill, pp. 531–42.

Dilwar, H. (2004), 'Muslim Political Participation in Britain and the "Europeanisation" of Fiqh', *Die Welt des Islams*, 44, pp. 376–401.

Gallissot, R. (1984), 'Le mixte Franco-Algérien', *Les temps modernes*, 452–453–454, pp. 1707–25.

Gallissot, R. (1985), 'Un regard sur l'histoire: les générations de l'entre-deux-guerres', *Revue européenne des migrations internationales*, 1, 2 (December), pp. 55–67.

Gokalp, C. (1975), 'Chronique de l'immigration', *Population*, 30, 4–5, pp. 889–96.

Kahina X (2008), 'Avridh d'avridh, el hak del hak, ce qui est juste est juste', in A. Boubeker and A. Hajjat (eds), *Histoire politique des immigrations (post) colonials France, 1920–2008*, Paris: Editions Amsterdam, pp. 301–12.

Kepel, G. (2011), *Banlieue de la République, résumé intégral*, available at <http://www.banlieue-de-la-republique.fr/sites/default/files/resume_integral_banlieue_republique.pdf> (last accessed 20 October 2011).

Kepel, G. (1991), *Les banlieues de l'islam: naissance d'une religion en France*, Paris: Le Seuil.

Kepel, G. (1997), *Allah in the West: Islamic movements in America and Europe*, Cambridge: Polity Press.

Latour, V. (to be published), 'Europeanization, Globalization, Transnationalization. Reflections based on the British and French Models towards Diversity Governance', conference 'Européanisation et mondialisation/Europeanization and Globalization', UMR EEE 5222 CNRS, 2– 3 December 2010, Maison des Sciences de l'Homme d'Aquitaine.

Lesselier, C. (2008), 'Mouvement et initiatives des femmes des années 1970 au milieu des années 1980', in A. Boubeker and A. Hajjat (eds), *Histoire politique des immigrations (post) colonials France 1920–2008*, Paris: Editions Amsterdam, pp. 157–66.

Lewis, P. (2002), *Islamic Britain: Religion, Politics, and Identity among British Muslims: Bradford in the 1990s*, London and New York: I. B. Tauris.

Maréchal, B. (2003), 'The Question of Belonging', in B. Maréchal, *Muslims in the Enlarged Europe, Religion and Society*, Leiden: Brill, pp. 5–18.

McDonald, I. A. (1969), *Race Relations and Immigration Law*, London: Butterworths.

McLoughlin, S. and T. Abbas (2010), 'United Kingdom', in J. Nielsen, *Yearbook of Muslims in Europe*, Leiden: Brill.

Médine, (2011), personal interview with the author on French Muslims' political participation, July.

Noiriel, G. (2008), 'L'immigration algérienne en France', 12 June, available at <http://www.ldh-toulon.net/spip.php?article2734> (last accessed 13 August 2011).

Philips, C. H. (1962), *The Evolution of India and Pakistan 1858 to 1947, Select Documents*, Oxford: Oxford University Press.

Renard, M. (2006), 'Séjour musulmans et rencontres avec l'islam', in M. Arkoun,

Histoire de l'islam et des musulmans en France du moyen-Age à nos jours, Paris: Albin Michel, pp. 564–86.

Robinson-Dunn, D. (2011), 'Lascar Sailors and English Converts: The Imperial Port and Islam in late 19th-Century England.' Paper presented at Seascapes, Littoral Cultures, and Trans-Oceanic Exchanges, Library of Congress, Washington DC, February 12–15, 2003, available at <http://www.historycooperative.org/proceedings/seascapes/dunn.html> (last accessed 11 August 2011).

Roy, O. (1999), *Vers un Islam Européen,* Paris: Editions Esprit.

Sellam, S. (2006), *La France et ses musulmans,* Paris: Editions Fayard.

Summerfield, C. and B. Gill (2005), *Social Trends,* 35, Office for National Statistics, London: Palgrave Macmillan.

Weil, P. (2002), *Qu'est-ce qu'un Français? Histoire de la nationalité française depuis la Révolution,* Paris: Grasset.

Weil, P. (2005), *La France et ses étrangers: l'aventure d'une politique de l'immigration de 1938 à nos jours,* Paris: Gallimard.

Weil, P. (2006), 'Le statut des musulmans en Algérie coloniale: une nationalité française dénaturée', in M. Arkoun, *Histoire de l'islam et des musulmans en France du moyen-Age à nos jours,* Paris: Albin Michel, pp. 548–61.

Zwilling, A.-L. (2010), 'France', in J. Nielsen *Yearbook of Muslims in Europe*, Leiden: Brill pp. 183–201.

PART TWO

◆ ◆ ◆

PARTICIPATION AS INTEGRATION

MUSLIM COLLECTIVE MOBILISATIONS IN CONTEMPORARY EUROPE: NEW ISSUES AND NEW TYPES OF INVOLVEMENT

Franck Frégosi

Muslims in the European Union have different visions of their religion, and often they are contradictory. Their attitudes towards the letter of the religion range from a strict adherence to practice to a critical attitude towards the rituals (Frégosi 2011). Indeed, a lot of Muslims do not use their faith as the only lens through which they interpret reality and are active within society.

It is important to discuss the different forms of mobilisation that these populations use, either one at a time or combined. We will use the ideal typical categories of mobilisation forms to study how they stage the complex relations between European Muslims and their religion, and how the fact of being a Muslim plays a part in the mobilisation process, at what level, under what form and to what end. In this chapter we will try to understand how the different ways of being Muslim (believing with or without belonging to an organised Muslim community, secular Muslims, Muslim cultural backgrounds only, etc.) are directly connected to different ways of involvement within the European societies. In another words, does Islam have any influence on the degree of integration and political commitment in French and other European societies?

1. Types of collective mobilisation of Muslims

Collective mobilisation refers in political science to the double conjunction of a deliberate acting together of social players intending to take action according to an explicit programme (Neveu 2002: 74). This acting together is used to claim the protection of precise material interests or to serve a cause that they believe to be socially legitimate. Among European Muslims (Dassetto 1996) we identify three major types of mobilisation: religious mobilisation, Islamic socio-political mobilisation and secular identity mobilisation. In reality, these mobilisations are combined and groups move across these boundaries in practice (Emerson 2009). Some Muslims can sometimes, for tactical reasons, use a certain type of mobilisation, but that does not mean they will not use other types.

1.1. Religious mobilisation

Religious mobilisations are based on a practising approach of Islam that focuses on defending and preserving the Muslim faith and/or its rituals. With this kind of voluntary action, the goal of the Muslim operators (imams, preachers, presidents of mosques . . .) is to remind the believers that faith is a major dimension of daily life, and that the ritual is central to the community. The objective of those actions is to get people with Muslim backgrounds to be more observant and to go to the mosque more regularly. This mobilisation has three complementary forms: ceremonial mobilisation, associative mobilisation and spiritual and sectarian mobilisation.

In Europe, Islam is a minority religion, which modifies the understanding that Muslims have of their religion. In a country where Islam is the religion of the majority, it is the social norm to have mosques or Islamic burial grounds, etc., but in Europe this requires special initiatives. In a delimited territory (local, regional or national) Muslims are going to mobilise in order to improve the conditions of the practice of their religion, asking, for example, to have places of worship built. The objective is to make the public practice of Islam work, to make sure that, for a certain percentage of Muslims living in a given society, there is a suitably corresponding number of religious facilities, especially of places of worship. The same perspective can make Muslims mobilise to have separate sections created in cemeteries, or to have certain dietary rules taken into account in the preparation of meals in institutions, etc.

These actions, led generally by male Muslim activists, cannot be reduced to simple mobilisations within the community. When the community needs authorisation for projects such as building permits, planning permission, or special help (public subsidies, loan guarantees, etc.) such initiatives are usually designed to convince local public authorities (elected representatives, state representatives, public agents). Such mobilisation can also seek support from conventional religious actors (Christian churches, Jewish communities). At state level, this religious mobilisation is more institutional, with initiatives that aim to provide Muslim communities with, for example, national representative bodies. Thus, the institutional interface between the European states and the different European Muslim communities seems to have become a concentrated space (Frégosi 2010). There are numerous official bodies, collegiate or centralised, which are partners to public authorities while representing the interests of Muslim believers. These bodies are directly legitimated by public authorities in order to have the voice of Islam heard at a national level. These measures reinforce the central role that the state plays in the process of institutionalisation over the other alternatives. Thus, in France as well as in Belgium, state authorities are the main actors in the organisation of the national Islamic scene; the situation is similar in Italy. These dynamics lead one to think that it is the states that are looking to be represented within the Muslim community, and not the other way round. These measures ultimately answer the desire to rationalise the Islamic scene, whose goal is to lay the foundations of social control, from above, of Islamic expression.

Muslims also resort to associative mobilisation. The goal is to structure and give substance to the idea of a Muslim community, and to create a Muslim community consciousness, using an organisational base that can be horizontal (neighbourhood communities) or vertical (federations). Religious associative mobilisation can take various forms. Thus ethnic-national belongings remain particularly important. It often leads Muslims to be part of representative organisations according to their geographical, sometimes even ethnic origins. Then, it becomes interesting to take into account the reality of Muslim community association networks that can be Maghrebi, Turkish, African, Bosnian, Indo-Pakistani, etc. These organisations represent well the immigrants of the first generation and of the 1970s and the 1980s; they are still relevant today, even if the generations born in Europe often contest this. Within the community associations of Muslim immigrants there is a political cleavage. This is how the opposition between the consular community associations promoting the official Islam of the state and the associations reflecting the point of view of oppositional Islam comes to expression. This was really important for a long time, especially regarding Turkish immigration in Europe. The fact that one of the avatars of Turkish oppositional Islam is today in office in Ankara (AKP) requires a re-think of the cleavages between official Islam and oppositional Islam; it does not mean that they have completely disappeared (Akgönül 2006). It is important to point out the fact that the young and politically committed Muslims born in Europe prefer developing their own community association networks, independent from the chanceries and national federations; and they rarely mobilise for strictly ceremonial issues or through negotiation with the state.

If Muslim religious mobilisation in Europe begins in mosques and uses community associations, it also deals with the various spiritual and sectarian expressions of Islam. These associations, formalised or not, are formed around rituals, canonical and supererogatory practices. This is the case with the various expressions of mystical Islam (Sufism). They echo internalised faith experiences, personal links to a spiritual master (*shaykh*) and the fact of belonging to an emotional community. There are also different sectarian groups such as pietistic streams, which are proselyte ritualistic movements. Primacy is given to preaching (*da'wa*), and to the ritual and ethical regulation of individual conduct. These are streams of orthopraxy, like the Indo-Pakistani *Tabligh,* focused on the strict observance of ritual techniques of worshipping.

They do not promote reflection or progressive comprehension (criticism) of the formulations of faith. There are also the various expressions of Islamic orthodoxy. These streams emphasise the importance of going back to the scriptures and refer to a uniform doctrine similar to the original Islam that was preached by the Prophet and his Companions. Today, various orthodox groups are strong religious opponents to each other. This is the case of the 'Salafist' (Amghar 2006) movement that seeks a puritan reformism that is strongly ritualistic and exclusive. The supporters of orthodox reformism defend another version of orthodoxy. Like the Muslim Brothers, they suggest going beyond the ethnic cleavages and schools of law, for the benefit of an Islam that would be at the same time purified and politically committed. Unlike the supporters of the Salafi stream, whose priority is the promotion of an Islamic countersociety in opposition to the surrounding societies (Adraoui 2008), the supporters of this neo-orthodoxy (e.g. Union of Islamic Organisations of France, Millî Görüs, Muslim Council of Britain) try to compromise with their societies by producing Islamic laws that are adapted to minority Muslim communities living in secularised societies. That is what is promoted by the European Council for Fatwa and Research, and it also is what Tareq Oubrou theorises in France (Oubrou 2004, 2009). A fourth alternative is the one offered by Al-Ahbash (the Association for Islamic Charitable Projects). Originally founded in Lebanon in the 1950s by Shaykh Abdallah al-Habashi, this movement was established in France and in Switzerland (Lausanne) in the 1990s. Their members call themselves the defenders of the traditional schools of law against the 'corrupted', that is to say the other forms of Islam (Muslim Brotherhood, Tablighi Jamaat, Salafi . . .) and refer to Sufism very often (they claim to be part of the Rifa'i *tariqa*).

Referring to recent studies, a link should be noted between strong religious belonging and weakness of classical political involvement such as voting or being active in a political party. This is clearly the case in France with sufi-oriented groups, Salafists and Tablighi Muslims. The withdrawal from all political commitment that characterises Sufi Muslims represents a general attitude of pragmatic warning to secular political authorities and worldly-oriented institutions in general. Political commitment is not at all a priority in their daily life. With Tablighis and more directly with Salafists the withdrawal from the world is grounded in their self-assurance of their personal sanctity and the feeling of belonging to a chosen people (*al-firqa al-najiyah*) among all the Muslims. Originally linked to Algerian revolutionary issues, French Salafi religiosity progressively moved (Amghar 2009), it became less revolutionary and is nowadays more an expression of social conservatism and more political abstinence. They intend to present themselves as guardians of the integral dogma of the Muslim religion. In their minds, policy is not a priority, so they don't participate as citizens in society. They prefer living beside the city and trying to organise their daily lives according to their strong vision of Islam centred on the religious opposition between *halal* and *haram*. These Muslims strive to create in the urban space a counter-society based on Islamic principles, *halal* food (pizza halal, doner kebab …), Islamic clothes, and bookstores. These sectarian groups set up a sort of 'safety barrier' between their militants and society, between an ideal community and a society seen as strongly corrupt.

The general tone of religious mobilisation is a tone of demand. The objective is to render public the demands of the believers, whether they be ceremonial only (devotional Islam), organisational (institutional Islam) or theological (competitive Islam). The goal is to ensure the future of Islam in Europe and its social rightfulness.

1.2. Islamic socio-political mobilisation

These groups take socio-political action strongly rooted in Islam, on theological foundations, at an international or national level or within European societies. Thus, being a Muslim means being committed both socially and politically. In a Muslim context, for those Muslim militants the social goal of Islam is to progressively establish Islamic states, and better to take into account Islamic law; in a non-Muslim context, it is to promote a fairer social order that would be in accordance with Islamic ethics. Those dynamics can lead to three types of mobilisation: civic mobilisation, nation-centred mobilisation, and radical mobilisation.

This type of mobilisation concerns usually young Muslims born in Europe, and to whom faith is not confined to the mosques and is not only a religiosity of the inner self. This mobilisation has been developed in France by active members in independent Muslim community associations like the Union de la Jeunesse Musulmane (Union of the Young Muslims). They are proud of being practising Muslims and are not afraid of showing it publicly (men grow a beard and women wear a headscarf). At the same time, they are equally proud to be French citizens. 'The goal is to integrate our religious values in our civic development', says a woman in charge of a Muslim women's association (Bouzar and Kada 2003). Being a Muslim means clearly being an active citizen, thus they engage in public debates and they promote a fairer Islamic perspective of social relations. These Muslims were, for example, very active in the demonstrations against the law of 15 March 2004 banning the *hijab* in schools and were active participants in the European Social Forum on anti-globalisation. On these occasions they joined forces with several movements (antiracist movements, human rights associations and green and leftist parties). Together with these groups (for example during the headscarf crisis) they organised joint actions (demonstrations in front of education offices, prefectures, etc.) and set up associations (Une école pour tous: A school for everyone). The conscience of being a Muslim conveys a theology of social commitment that prompts the believers to take a part in public action. In western societies, they have to bring a Muslim contribution to help resolve problems such as exclusion, unemployment and globalisation. 'There is no Islamic conscience without social conscience' says Tariq Ramadan '(. . .) no social conscience without political conscience' (Ramadan 2003: 128). Thus, Saïda Kada says: 'Being a Muslim also means that you have to be active in your neighborhood, to take part in big social debates, to feel concerned by all the problems, to be politically active, to fight for justice and democracy.' (Kada 2003). This type of mobilisation leads Muslims to be socially active in order to have an influence, globally or punctually, on the great issues of the society, defending Islamic ethics and democratic logic.

Nation-centred mobilisation is mainly used by the movements that have a political way of looking at Islam and that are structured by national parameters. They are the legalistic streams of islamo-nationalist organisations (such as Millî Görüs, Suleymanci). Defending Islam means defending the link with the home country, especially for expatriates. For those Muslims, who are closely linked to national political groups, the national frame is strong enough so that the actions they take regarding immigration follow the political evolutions of their home countries, the changes in the majority and national laws. It is a fact that Turkish organisations like Millî Görüs and MHP pay special attention to Turkish politics. Even if Millî Görüs has strong links with the Muslim Brotherhood, its story is linked to the story of Turkish immigration, and even if some of the members have taken European nationalities (French, Belgian, Dutch and others) the movement is mainly Turkish.

This mobilisation is typical of the radical Islamic movements in Europe: like the Kaplanci movement in Germany and in Belgium; the Hizb al-Tahrir al-islami (Party of Islamic Liberation) in Great Britain, Denmark, and the Netherlands (Mayer 2006); and the jihadist movement (Kepel 2004). In Europe, the Islamist militants are active within their organisations and inform their fellow countrymen of the political evolutions in their home countries, as well as supporting the national Islamic parties, symbolically and sometimes financially. But the most radical activists use the Internet (Guidère 2006) or publish leaflets and bulletins (*Al Ansar*) (Grignard 1997) that call for taking up arms to establish Islamic states. Nowadays, cyber activism is more efficient than preaching in mosques. If the use of violence is still possible (assassinations, bombings), making it global is difficult because it reflects badly on other European Muslims. It also reinforces the reigning skepticism towards Islam that strengthens those who make a living of Islamophobia (nationalist and extreme right movements) and it allows a more heterogeneous Islamophobic speech to emerge (Oriana Fallaci, Ayan Hirshi Ali and others). This radical mobilisation creates counter-mobilisations within organised communities, such as MINAB (Mosques and Imams National Advisory Board) in the United Kingdom. The double mission of MINAB, created in November 2007, is to develop a code of management for United Kingdom mosques and to play the role of adviser to the British Home Office when foreign imams want to enter British territory (Caruso 2007). MINAB was suggested by the task force created by Tony Blair after the London bombings in order to make the integration of Muslims in Great Britain more visible. Thus we can see the outlines of a real Muslim governance of the mosques emerge, which echoes the safety measures that the state asks for. Private Muslim players and public state players coordinate their actions towards a project that they establish together to fight radical Islamists and to prevent xenophobia against Muslims.

For Muslim activists living in Europe, most of the time the goal is to talk (press conferences, leaflets, websites) and to act (public demonstrations or more violent actions) against governments that have a certain dictatorial side to them, on the other side of the Mediterranean. The line of fracture between those socio-political mobilisations is in the choice of the means used to convey this speech (legally or not), in the desire to forge inter-confessional alliances and it also is geographically defined (Europe or home country). The Muslim activists that are involved in political mobilisation intend to resist (legally for the majority of them) socio-political processes whose effects could harm the way they see Islam. This is how the cultural process of assimilation in a European context works. It tends to even out cultural differences in the name of a neocolonial imperialism that is at the same time political and economic, the same way liberal globalisation does.

1.3. Identity and secular mobilisation

Finally, Muslims can take joint action to claim their identity in secular ways. These streams refer to Islam not to claim a specific religious identity but to claim a cultural identity, with its values and its historical landmarks that play a part in the definition of a person's identity together with ethnic, linguistic and cultural parameters. In France, that can be the Muslim association circle (Harkis) that represents and defends the interests and the memory of the Muslims repatriated from Algeria after the war of independence. Other groups share these ideas, such as the Parti des musulmans de France (Muslim Party of France) that was created in Strasbourg in 1997, or the Arab European League that was created in Antwerp[1] in 2000 by Dyab Abu Jahjah. The identity or secularised mobilisation has three very different forms: one is centered on republican ideology, another on memory, and the last one on radical secularism. They all use the same means (petitions, demonstrations, associations, cyber activism, etc.) but their ideas and goals are very different.

In Europe, a lot of people that were born Muslim do not always recognise themselves in the denominational approach of their identity. If they are sociologically seen as Muslims it is because their families come from societies where Islam is the predominant religion. For them, Islam is more linked to their family culture or inherited identity than it is to religious practices. Being a Muslim comes down to having an Arab-Muslim name and feeling slightly linked to Islam. Some of them are active in the struggle to defend the rights of immigrants, or they are institutional anti-racism activists or feminism activists, but in France they also work to denounce communitarianism, to defend the republican ideal of secular state. That is what is happening with, for example, a part of the feminist movement Ni putes ni soumises (Neither whores nor submissive). This group was created under the guidance of SOS Racisme (SOS Racism) with the support of the Socialist Party, but since then it has enlarged its political support. Its founder, Fadela Amara, became member of a conservative government. We can also talk about the so-called secular Muslim mobilisation. Born in France after the election of the French Council of the Muslim Faith in 2003, it focuses on the fact that it has a lot of representatives from the Union of Islamic Organisations of France. Just like the religious Muslim federations, the secular Muslim movement counts a lot of different groups like the Mouvement des Musulmans Laïques de France (Movement of French secular Muslims) or the Coordination des Musulmans Démocrates (Coordination of Democratic Muslims) whose president claims to belong to the republican *jihad*. Its main goal is to dispute the monopoly of religious representatives in representing Islam. This movement still claims to speak for the 'silent majority' of French Muslims. They also want to have an active part in the progressive modernisation of Islam by secularising it and by stopping so-called communitarian excesses (headscarf, schedule for Muslim women in public swimming-pools, public funding for mosques, etc).

The non-denominational and multiethnic movement called Le Parti di Indigènes de la République (Natives of the Republic Party) suggests a political alternative to the exclusion and the stigmatisation that touches immigrant populations descended from formerly colonised populations. Even if this movement does not directly identify with Islam, the issue of how Islam is dealt with in France by the public, the police and in the law has a special place in its discourse. Its priority is less the construction of an alternate Islamic identity than it is the deconstruction of the republican model and the logic of assimilation. They think that the creation of the French Council of the Muslim Faith is comparable to a neo-colonial management of Islam, and they denounce the fact that minorities (Maghrebis, black people and so on) are excluded from political life. Among those who wrote the famous manifesto '*Nous sommes les indigènes de la République!*' (We are the natives of the Republic!) of January 2005, which refers to the thoughts of Franz Fanon and Malcom X, there are Muslim intellectuals, Muslim associations or secular ones like the Mouvement Immigration Banlieues (Movement of the Immigration Suburbs). The Muslim signatories of this manifesto show another side of Muslim mobilisation: that of Muslims that refuse to be the prisoners of their religion and who fight against all forms of discrimination. They express a deep attachment to a human community that would go beyond religions, a community that includes those who were the victims of colonisation and slavery and who are today the victims of social exclusion and precariousness. By calling themselves the new 'natives' of a republic whose decolonisation would be yet to come, they want people to remember the dark side of the universalist republican ideal that has been violent with particular cultural, ethnic and religious identities and physical bodies (slavery, laws creating an inferior status for natives of French colonies, etc.). This movement, by exposing the colonial ideas that underlie the republican imagination, does not want to give up universalism. It works for the creation of internationalism, that of the oppressed, and to create real solidarity between all the anti-colonial struggles in the world (Palestine, Chechnya . . .).

This last type of mobilisation concerns activists and political exiles that were born Muslim and who publicly recommend leaving Islam. They use newspapers, colourful public conferences (T-shirts saying 'ex-Muslim') or websites (e.g. <http/www.ex-muslim.org.uk>, <www.ex-muslim.org.de> and www.ex-muslim.org.scan> last accessed 9 September 2012). They are also committed to defending an absolute freedom of conscience and openly criticise Islam. This leads them to denounce cultural relativism which ends up legitimating what they see as the progressive Islamisation of European societies. We count four representative structures, all of them called Central Committee for Ex-Muslims (Germany, Great Britain, Netherlands, Scandinavia). The most famous figurehead of this movement is Maryam Nazmieh. She is an activist close to the Worker Communist Party of Iran[2] and a former president of the International Federation of Iranian Refugees. She is one of the signatories of the manifesto *Ensemble contre le nouveau totalitarisme* (Together Facing the New Totalitarianism) of March 2006, published in the weekly newspaper *Charlie Hebdo* – other signatories include Ayaan Hirsi Ali, Irshad Manji, and Taslima Nasren. In the Netherlands, Ehsan Jami, a student of Iranian origin, former elected representative and member of the Dutch Labour Party, has created, choosing the symbolic date of 11 September 2007, a Central Committee for Ex-Muslims. He co-signed, with the populist deputy Geert Wilders, a caustic article that compares the supposed Islamisation of the Netherlands with the rise of Nazism, and the Prophet Muhammad with Adolf Hitler (Demetz 2007) in the newspaper *De Volkskrant*. In France, even if no group of this kind has been created yet, these analyses can be found, most of the time, in magazines like *Prochoix*, in the newspaper *Charlie Hebdo*, through the website of the association AIME (<http://www.assoaime.net> last accessed 24 July 2009) or via atheist websites. The actors of these mobilisations answer to the same logic of protesting and reacting to dynamics that could threaten certain models or values that are extremely important to them. For some of them it can be the republican secular model, for others it is the challenge of decolonisation, or it can also be the absolute freedom of consciousness including to leave religion. These protests are very dependent on the circumstances, and the effects of these actions cannot last very long. This is what happens with the strong republican-centred movement in France; it surfaces from time to time when something major happens (the headscarf issue, the cartoons controversy) and disappears afterwards.

2. Conclusion

Within Muslim mobilisation, there are two main cleavages. The first contrast consists of distinction between consensual forms of mobilisation and conflicting ones. In one case Muslims are looking to form partnerships, to gain social legitimacy from various political arenas (elected officials, local government) and private arenas (inter-religious circles, immigrants' associations) to find, for instance, arrangements to manage the local visibility of places of worship.

Other forms of mobilisation are based on more competitive confrontations (Arab police regimes, rival religious streams, Islamists) or are meant to stand up against social processes that would endanger certain values, or patterns of living, that are important to those Muslims.

There is another cleavage between the mobilisations that consider themselves to be the 'actions of the dominated' (Neveu 2002: 20) and those that refuse to give Muslims the status of a minority facing a majority because they choose to speak in terms of citizenship. Throughout their daily mobilisations, Muslims show that when it comes to coordinated collective actions heterogeneity is the norm, whereas uniformity is the exception.

Notes

1. This movement was created after the murder in Antwerp of a Muslim teacher from Morocco. It organised civil patrols in order to prevent police blunders towards Arab-Muslims.
2. This radical secularist party was founded in 1991 by former members of the Communist Party of Iran. It seeks the revolutionary overthrow of the Islamic Republic of Iran and the establishment of a Socialist Republic in its place.

References

Adraoui, M. A. (2008), 'Purist salafism in France', *Isimreview*, no. 21, pp. 12–13.

Ailleurs ou d'Ici Mais Ensemble (AIME), available at <http://www.assoaime.net> (last accessed 24 July 2009).

Akgönül, S. (2006), 'Millî Görus: Institution religieuse minoritaire et mouvement politique transnational (France et Allemagne)', *Maghreb-Machrek*, no. 188, pp. 63–85.

Amghar, S. (2009), 'Ideological and Theological Foundations of Muslim Radicalism in France', in M. Emerson (ed.), *Ethno-religious Conflict in Europe. Typologies of*

Radicalisation in Europe's Muslim Communities, Brussels: Centre for European Policy Studies, 2009, pp. 27–50.

Amghar, S. (2006), 'Le salafisme en Europe: la mouvance polymorphe d'une radicalisation', *Politique étrangère*, vol. 1, pp. 67–78.

Bouzar, D. and K. Sada (2003), (eds), *L'une voilée, l'autre pas. Le témoignage de deux femmes musulmanes françaises*, Paris: Albin Michel.

Caruso, G. (2007), *Au nom de l'islam . . . Quel dialogue avec les minorités musulmanes en Europe?*, Paris: Institut Montaigne.

Dassetto, F. (1996), *La construction de l'islam européen. Approche socio anthropologique*, Paris: L'Harmattan.

Demetz, J.-M. (2007), 'Pays-Bas. Tu n'abjureras pas l'islam!', *L'Express*, 15 November, 2007, p. 81.

Frégosi, F. (2010), 'From a Regulation of the Religious Landscape to the Preacher State: the French Situation', in *Muslim Organisations and the State-European Perspectives*, Nürnberg: Bundesamt für Migration und Flüchtlinge, pp. 111–22.

Frégosi, F. (2011), *L'islam dans la laïcité*, Paris: Fayard/Pluriel.

Grignard, A. (1997), 'La littérature politique du GIA Algérien. Des origines à Djamal Zitouni. Esquisse d'une analyse', in Dassetto (ed.), *Facettes de l'islam belge*, Bruxelles: Academia Bruylant, pp. 69–95.

Guidère, M. (2006), 'La toile islamiste dans tous ses états', *Maghreb-Machrek*, no. 188, pp. 45–62.

Kepel, G. (2004), *Fitna*, Paris: Gallimard.

Mayer, J.-F. (2006), 'Hizb ut-Tahrir: l'évolution d'un parti islamiste transnational en Occident (Grande Bretagne et Danemark)', *Maghreb-Machrek*, no. 188, pp. 87–103.

Neveu, E. (2002), *Sociologie des mouvements sociaux*, Paris: La découverte, Repères.

Oubrou, T. (2004), 'La sharî'a de minorité: réflexions pour une intégration légale de l'islam', in Frégosi (ed.), *Lectures contemporaines du droit islamique. Europe et Monde arabe*, Strasbourg: Presses Universitaires de Strasbourg, pp. 205–30.

Oubrou, T. (2009), *Profession imâm*, Paris: Albin Michel.

Ramadan, T. (2003), *Les Musulmans d'Occident et l'avenir de l'islam*, Lyon: Tawhid.

HOW POLITICALLY INTEGRATED ARE DANISH MUSLIMS? EVIDENCE FROM THE MUHAMMAD CARTOONS CONTROVERSY

Lasse Lindekilde

1. Introduction, questions and the limitations of the study

The degree of political integration of minorities in a society is a significant indicator of the 'health' of a democracy and social cohesion. Political integration is of great importance to feelings of belonging and shared identity. The inadequate political integration of minorities can potentially lead to social division, parallel societies, mutual distrust and conflict. In Denmark, the level of political participation and integration of Muslim minorities has been an issue of public debate for at least the last decade. In contrast to the debate in countries like France and Germany, the debate in Denmark has been less about formal voting rights for non-nationals or the establishment of a Muslim council with whom the government can discuss issues of special concern (although these issues have come up). Rather, the debate about political integration of Muslim minorities in Denmark has been driven by general concerns about the level of Muslim trust in and acceptance of Danish political institutions – their willingness to engage in democratic procedures and adhere to the fundamental values and principles of liberal democracy when doing so. An element of this debate has concerned the degree to which Danish society and majority institutions should accept and adapt to growing ethno-cultural diversity. In the context of the 'value struggle' launched by the right-of-centre government, which took office in 2001, the social and political integration of Danish Muslims has been questioned with reference to Muslim parallel institutions (schools, kindergartens, organisations, etc.), ghetto formation, and a lack of commitment to democratic principles and liberal values such as freedom of speech and gender equality. The government, and not least the Danish People's Party whose support the government has depended upon to form a majority, has argued and pushed for recognition of the need to spread and secure a Danish *leitkultur*, (meaning 'lead culture', the view that a certain culture should be dominant/given the lead in society) building on shared liberal-democratic (and Christian) values. The vision is manifested in a range of recent policies on, for example, citizenship education, citizenship tests, declarations of integration, citizenship acquisition rules, all of which share ambitions to make adherence to fundamental liberal-democratic principles and values a prerequisite for certain benefits and integration. Danish integration and immigration policies have thus followed what Christian Joppke has identified as the 'civic turn', where liberal-democratic states promise to protect newcomers from discrimination and provide equal opportunities in exchange for an explicit commitment to fundamental liberal-democratic principles (Joppke 2007; Joppke 2008). The highpoint in the public debate on the political integration of the Muslim minority in Denmark was the Muhammad cartoons controversy in 2005/6.

This chapter investigates the degree to which Danish Muslims can be said to be politically integrated as demonstrated by the public claims-making of Danish Muslims during the cartoon controversy. It does so by paying attention to the political integration of Danish Muslims in practice, i.e. in terms of public claims-making and participation, rather than in terms of formal rights and institutional arrangements. In line with the focus of the public debate on Muslim political participation and integration in Denmark, the chapter concentrates on the practical exercise of rights, and the values and frames accompanying actual Muslim claims-making in the public sphere during the intense debate on the cartoons. In line with Jean Tillie (2004), political integration is here understood as a multi-dimensional concept distinguishing three aspects: a) political trust in democratic institutions, b) political participation in public debates, and c) adherence to liberal-democratic values (for example freedom of speech and secularism). In this perspective, an individual or group can be said to be politically integrated into society when trust in mainstream political institutions can be observed, for example through interaction with these institutions and/or the acceptance of the legitimacy of their decisions; claims, viewpoints, or opinions are aired in public debates on issues of concern; and these claims, viewpoints or opinions are articulated in ways that respect fundamental liberal-democratic principles.

This conceptualisation clearly leaves ample room for interpretation in terms of how much trust must be displayed, how much participation must take place, and how closely political claims-making should follow liberal-democratic principles in order to be 'integrated'. In the context of Muslim minorities in the West, it is commonly demanded that Muslim citizens demonstrate the same kind of political trust, participation and adherence as the non-Muslim majority. However, no definitive or objective answer can be given to the 'how much' question. First, the answer appears to depend on who evaluates which actors' political participation. Displaying trust in national political institutions and adherence to liberal-democratic values seem to be virtues of political participation that especially the Muslim actors in the Danish context are expected to take very seriously, and actively engage with, in order to be considered truly Danish and integrated. Some see Islam as fundamentally undemocratic, which translates into heightened demands regarding the political integration of Muslims engaged in public claims-making. Secondly, the answer to the 'how much' question depends on situation and context. In times of political tension between a majority and a minority, the bar can be raised regarding the necessary political integration of the minority; conversely, during times of relative calm, less proof of political integration may be accepted from the same minority group. Thus, when we attempt to estimate the level of political integration of Danish Muslims during the cartoons controversy, we should be aware that this is a difficult endeavour, and the result is always debatable and of limited generalisability. Nevertheless, I believe that the actual political claims-making of Danish Muslims during the cartoons controversy constitutes an interesting – and in some respects critical – case for the assessment of Muslim political integration in Denmark.

There are several reasons for dwelling on the particular case of the Muhammad cartoons controversy when we discuss Muslim political integration six years later. First, the cartoons controversy sparked the largest Muslim mobilisation and political claims-making campaign in Denmark to date and therefore provides more material for a systematic analysis of the degree of political integration of Danish Muslims in practice than any other episode. Secondly, the cartoons controversy was essentially about adherence to an interpretation of fundamental liberal-democratic principles, such as freedom of speech, freedom of religion and tolerance. In fact, the publication of the cartoons was justified by a claim that Danish Muslims were not adhering to the principles of freedom of speech due to their inability to withstand 'scorn, mocking and ridicule'. Examining the subsequent debate provides a good opportunity to test the validity of this claim; and with it, an important aspect of the political integration of Danish Muslims. Thirdly, the debate emphasised and developed around issues of trust between Muslims and central political institutions and constitutes a natural laboratory for studying this trust and its limits in practice. Fourthly, the cartoons controversy was an episode of great tension between the majority and the Muslim minority in Denmark and therefore an interesting context in which to investigate the willingness and ability of Danish Muslims to play by the rules of the dominant political culture. Finally, it has often been claimed that the very nature of Danish Muslims' political participation during the controversy confirmed *Jyllands-Posten*'s initial claim regarding inadequate political integration. However, the pivotal question here is whether this claim can stand a systematic test.

The chapter builds methodologically on a political claims analysis approach that integrates elements of protest event analysis, discourse analysis and frame analysis (Koopmans and Statham 1999). A 'claim' is defined here as the expression of a political opinion by physical or verbal action in the public sphere. The chapter draws on an empirical database of claims-making during the Muhammad cartoons controversy.[1] The database contains the detailed coding of all of the newspaper chapters referring to the crisis published in the Danish daily *Berlingske Tidende* from 30 September 2005 when the cartoons were published until late March 2006 when demobilisation on the issue began. The choice of *Berlingske Tidende* is based on a pre-test which found that the newspaper occupied an intermediary position among the three largest Danish dailies in terms of blaming the Danish government and/or Danish Muslims for the escalation of the conflict.[2] Choosing to rely on a single newspaper can be justified by reference to research on newspapers as sources of data on protest cycles, which has shown that during intense public debates on a national scale, the same events and claims tend to be covered by all major newspapers (Strawn 2008). This also seems to have been the case during the Muhammad cartoons controversy in Denmark. Furthermore, from a pragmatic point of view, limiting the coding to one newspaper seemed necessary due to the extensive coverage of the controversy in the Danish press. *Berlingske Tidende* alone published 893 items about the controversy during the period under study.

A common criticism raised against this type of claims analysis approach is that the focus on newspaper data is bound to reproduce the selection bias inherent in newspaper coverage, which is based on certain newsworthiness criteria. Some actors and some types of claims-making (for example less audible or less visual forms of interest politics) will be underrepresented in the data. I try to compensate for this by including the coding of other types of material in my empirical database (internal newsletters, pamphlets, organisational documents, Friday sermons and recordings of internal debates and meetings) containing claims by Muslims who were active in the public debate about the cartoons. Another critique of the claims-making approach is that the complexity of the arguments and the dynamics of interaction involved in public claims-making are oversimplified by the focus on quantifying who said what, when, where and why. As a partial remedy to this objection, my analysis is further supported by interviews with representatives of the Muslim organisations that were active in the debate.

Obviously, this approach has important limitations in terms of estimating the level of political integration of Danish Muslims. First, the focus on public claims-making limits the results to the Muslim actors who were publicly engaged in the cartoons controversy. Many Danish Muslims did not participate in the debate, either directly nor indirectly. It can be argued that there is an element of selection bias in this approach, as the actors who did voice public claims can be suspected from the outset to be those most likely to display political integration, while those who remained silent might have done so for the very reason that they possessed limited trust in mainstream political institutions and little willingness to adhere to liberal-democratic principles. Unfortunately, the data analysed here does not allow a test of this claim. However, I believe that the starting point of any discussion about political integration must be actual political participation, and I choose to focus on the spectrum of actual claims-making during the controversy. In my view, the political integration of Muslim minorities in particular is far too often evaluated on the basis of isolated incidents and speculation concerning the lack of political integration of Muslims who keep to themselves. Secondly, it can be argued – as several actors did during the cartoons controversy – that if Danish Muslims displayed a high level of political integration during the controversy, they only did so for strategic reasons; for example if the Danish Muslim actors in the controversy adhered to liberal-democratic principles, they only did so because they desperately wanted an apology or because everybody's eyes were now upon them. During the controversy, several claims regarding such strategic political integration were heard, often suggesting that Danish Muslims were duplicitous; saying one thing in the public sphere and something else – supposedly less politically integrated – within the confines of the Muslim community. However, by including codings of Muslim materials in the database that were not intended for the public sphere, it becomes possible to compare external and internal Muslim claims-making, and thereby empirically test the 'double-tongue' hypothesis. Finally, the focus on public claims-making during the Muhammad cartoons controversy sets aside more formal forms of political integration of Danish Muslims, such as voting (for a Danish study, see Togeby 1999). But the approach used here allows for a discussion of other procedural forms of political participation, for example litigation and administrative complaints, in as much as Danish Muslims did so and it was mentioned in the analysed media content.

The remainder of the chapter discusses the level of Muslim political integration, as conceptualised using Tillie's three-level definition, against the empirical claims-making database described above. Section two investigates the degree of trust in political institutions displayed by Danish Muslims during the controversy. 'Political trust' is operationalised here as the degree to which Danish Muslims were addressing claims to mainstream political institutions and using the established channels to make their political views heard. A central issue will, thus, also be the use of less official forms of claims-making, not least the element of transnational campaigning of Danish Muslims, for example the so-called 'imam delegations' that travelled the Middle East in December 2005. Section three examines the level of Muslim political participation during the controversy, operationalised as the Muslim share of total claims-making compared to non-Muslim claims-making, and the variety of Muslim actors involved in the public debate. Section four analyses the degree to which Muslims were adhering to and drawing upon fundamental liberal-democratic principles in the content and justification of the claims raised. It compares the proposed solutions and justifications of Muslim claims across the different phases of the controversy in an attempt to trace developments in adherence. Moreover, the justifications of Muslim external (newspaper material) and internal (organisational material) claims-making are compared to test the 'two tongues' hypothesis. The final section uses the empirical results as background for a broader discussion of the long-term effects of the cartoons controversy on the political integration of Danish Muslims.

2.   Trust in political institutions

As mentioned, the claims analysis approach may overestimate the degree of trust in political institutions among Danish Muslims, as it excludes actors who did not engage in public claims-making, potentially because they distrust mainstream political institutions and view interaction as forbidden or simply not worthwhile. Although such distrust is problematic from a democratic perspective, it is not fundamentally different from the kind of political apathy and disgust which has been identified and is said to be increasing among non-Muslim Danes in recent years (Adelberth Hansen and Jensen 2009). We cannot expect everybody in a liberal-democratic setting to display trust in and respect for political institutions; only that nobody will work actively to dismantle democratic institutions as such.

Despite these limitations, I will argue that the public claims-making of Danish Muslims during the cartoons controversy says something important about generalised trust in political and legal institutions. The publication of the Muhammad cartoons was experienced as a severe blow by many Muslims, who felt outraged and hurt by this seemingly gratuitous offence. The subsequent Muslim protests took many forms. Outside Denmark, some Muslims reacted by boycotting Danish products, burning flags, attacking Danish diplomatic representations, offering bounties for killing the illustrators and issuing religious *fatwas*. In contrast to the violence that the publication led to abroad, Danish Muslims reacted peacefully and demanded an apology from *Jyllands-Posten* and/or some kind of intervention by political or legal institutions in order to restore Muslim feelings of justice. Within Denmark, the tactics ranged from issuing press releases, giving interviews and writing chapters to contacting ministers and diplomats, holding demonstrations, taking legal action, petitioning and sending delegations to the Middle East. Common to the actions – or 'contentious performances'[3] – undertaken in Denmark were the relatively familiar ways of raising collective claims aimed at political actors, be they *Jyllands-Posten*, the Danish government or the legal system. Thus, it was fundamental to Muslim reactions that they expected action from political or legal institutions, thereby signalling that Muslim actors had sufficient prior trust in these institutions to address their claims to them.

To substantiate this claim, we can examine the total Muslim claims raised in the debate, addressees and types of contentious performances. Looking first at

the addressees, 25% of all Muslim claims were directed towards official political institutions, primarily the Danish government, and the legal system. About
35% of the claims were addressed to media institutions, more than half to
Jyllands-Posten. The bulk of the remaining claims, about 25%, were directed
at other Muslim actors, one third of these at foreign Muslim actors. Thus, a
little less than 33% of all Muslim claims were addressed to official political
and legal institutions requesting that some sort of action be taken. Considering
that the cartoons controversy was triggered by an independent newspaper and
that the Danish government was very reluctant to make it a political issue, this
share of claims targeted at the political and legal establishment is considerable
and can be read as a sign of a relatively high level of political trust among the
involved Muslim actors. Some would probably object that the fact that Danish
Muslims even addressed political authorities on these matters proves that they
do not fully comprehend 'our' democratic traditions and culture of the free
press. Why involve political institutions in a conflict between an independent
newspaper and a religious community? However, this objection seems uncon-
vincing for several reasons. First, although *Jyllands-Posten* is an independent
newspaper, it had strong historical ties to the political parties of the Danish
government at the time. Many Danish Muslims therefore found it natural to
ask whether the government shared *Jyllands-Posten*'s views. Secondly, most
Danish Muslims did not ask the government or other political institutions to
punish *Jyllands-Posten* or limit the freedom of press. They simply asked for
support and recognition and for politicians to condemn the message expressed
by the caricatures. Finally, the argument put forward by leading politicians at
the time, including then-Prime Minister Anders Fogh Rasmussen, that the caricatures were a legal rather than a political issue and thus something he would
not comment upon, sounded slightly hollow given that the same politicians
had no problem commenting on or criticising concrete priorities of the press
on many other occasions.

Some Muslim claims addressed political or legal institutions directly – via
official letters, complaints or litigation, others used 'mediatised' claims, for
example press interviews – to indirectly pose demands on political or legal
institutions. Other claims were raised via direct action, for example by shout-
ing at demonstrations. Table 8.1 divides the types of contentious Muslim
performances into three fundamental categories: procedural, mediatised and
direct.

'Procedural performances' cover strategies that directly target official
institutions in a formal manner. 'Mediatised performances' are conventional
techniques for dealing with and 'using' the media as an arena for making one's
claims visible in the broader public sphere. 'Direct performances' target the
public at large or limited audiences directly, following non-formalised scripts.
Direct performances are often designed to attract media attention and can turn
into mediatised performances, for example when a demonstration leader is

Table 8.1 Three major types of contentious performances used by Danish Muslims

	Procedural performances	Mediatised performances	Direct performances
Relevant contentious performances	• legal action • official letters • official complaints • diplomatic contacts • contacting councils or boards	• press conferences and releases • interviews in the media • articles • open letters • advertisements • PR	• demonstrations • petitioning • public meetings • IT activism • delegations • religious rituals
Percentages of all Muslim claims (N=226)	8.8	64.6	26.5

interviewed or a Friday sermon is broadcast live. Considering how much the three types of contentious performances make up the total Muslim claims-making, we see that it was dominated by mediatised performances – by almost two-thirds. Given the media-driven nature of the cartoons controversy and the fact that, following the publication of the caricatures, the Danish media were more than willing to lend themselves to Muslim reactions, this is hardly surprising. The fact that 26.5% of Muslim claims used direct performances, primarily demonstrations and Friday sermons, to air viewpoints in the debate while only 8.8% used official procedural forms of protest could be interpreted as Danish Muslims not having so much trust after all in the established political system and its willingness to do something about Muslim grievances. Why else would they rely so heavily on the media to air their viewpoints or deploy the 'weapon of the weak': direct political action?

The answer to this question can be found by examining the developments in Muslims' use of the three main types of contentious performances over time. Table 8.2 shows this development over four phases of the controversy.[4]

Table 8.2 illustrates two clear trends: 1) procedural performances were carried out by Muslim actors, particularly in the two first phases of the controversy; and 2) the share of mediatised performances drops sharply in phase 3 of the controversy and is replaced by a large increase in direct performances. This pattern can be explained by first considering the response that Danish Muslims received when they tried to activate the official procedures to protest against the cartoons. In brief, they met with closed doors and cold shoulders. The official letters that the ad hoc coalition of Muslim organisations that spearheaded the initial protests sent to the Prime Minister and several other ministers soon after the publication of the cartoons were never answered. Requests for a

Table 8.2 Developments in Muslim use of main types of contentious performances (column percentages)

		Phase 1	Phase 2	Phase 3	Phase 4	Total
Mediatised	Frequency	23	54	38	31	146
	Percentage	63.9	72.0	51.4	75.6	64.6
Direct	Frequency	8	11	33	8	60
	Percentage	22.2	14.7	44.6	19.5	26.5
Procedural	Frequency	5	10	3	2	20
	Percentage	13.9	13.3	4.1	4.9	8.8
Total	Frequency	36	75	74	41	226
	Percentage	100.0	100.0	100.0	100.0	100.0

meeting with the Prime Minister by Muslim ambassadors in Denmark were turned down. Even the large petition against the cartoons sent to the Minister of Integration was never officially processed. Moreover, the litigation against *Jyllands-Posten* involving charges of racism and blasphemy was rejected by the state prosecutor and never tried in the courts. Thus, Danish Muslims soon came to feel that the willingness of political and legal institutions to help them recover a sense of justice was quite limited. In this way, their initial trust in political and legal institutions was put to shame. It is worth noting that it was only after these experiences of 'closed political opportunity structures' in Denmark that Danish Muslims decided to internationalise the issue and sent the so-called 'imam delegations' to the Middle East (late December 2005) in an attempt to raise support there. This interpretation is supported by the interviews. Ahmed Akkari, spokesman for the protest coalition, put it this way:

> After two months of trying to explain our viewpoints in Denmark without anybody listening or responding to them, we saw no other way than to contact influential people abroad in the hope that they could make our voice heard. (Ahmed Akkari interviewed on 10 August 2006)

Thus, what motivated Danish Muslims to internationalise the cartoons issue was a fading trust in the willingness of political and legal institutions to take Muslim claims seriously. Nevertheless, the actors behind the imam delegations were heavily criticised, especially after the violent escalation of the controversy abroad in early February 2006 (phase 3), for escalating the conflict and involving regimes with less impressive records of human rights observance to put pressure on the Danish authorities. In this way, the imam delegations had important consequences for the subsequent claims-making of Danish Muslims (see also Lindekilde 2008; Lindekilde 2010). The actors behind the imam delegations, most importantly the ad hoc protest coalition and the most influential Muslim organisation in Denmark prior to the cartoons, The Islamic

Faith Community, were forced onto the defensive after the imam delegations had returned, corresponding to less public claims-making from these actors from phase 3 onwards. A parallel development is the sudden drop in media-tised claims-making and a corresponding increase in direct action in the third phase of the controversy, as noted in Table 8.2. As the controversy intensi-fied and turned violent abroad, the media became less willing to air Danish Muslims' claims, and they were left with direct action as the only way of making their claims heard.

Summing up my argument so far: If we take the addressees and type of contentious performances of Muslim claims-making during the cartoons con-troversy as indicators of Muslim trust in mainstream political and legal institu-tions, there is evidence that Danish Muslims initially exhibited a good deal of political trust. Danish Muslims addressed almost one-third of all their claims to official political and legal institutions, making use of formal, institutional-ised procedures for protesting and raising claims with authorities. As the con-troversy developed, however, there were signs of this initial trust diminishing, triggered by rejections from political and legal institutions and leading to shifts in the addressees and types of performances used by Muslim claims-makers.

3. Political participation

The Muslim minority in Denmark has repeatedly been subjected to exces-sive criticism, accusations and mockery and has usually reacted with relative silence. However, the publication of the twelve Muhammad cartoons led to large, sustained mobilisation and protest from Danish Muslims. The key Muslim actors in Denmark initially considered once again following a strategy of silence. The late imam and spokesman of the Islamic Faith Community, Ahmed Abu Laban, argued at an internal meeting a few days after the car-toons were published that if Danish Muslims protested, these shameful images would spread and receive more attention than necessary (Interview with Kasem Ahmed: 12 March 2007). His prediction proved correct. Nevertheless, just two weeks after the publication of the cartoons, Denmark witnessed its largest 'Muslim demonstration' ever. Then came petitions, formal letters to ministers, a storm of letters to *Jyllands-Posten*'s editors, followed by the mass mobilisation of Danish Muslims on the issue, including the creation of new organisations, debate forums, dialogue initiatives, etc.

Below, I will substantiate this image of a high level of Muslim mobilisa-tion and claims-making during the cartoons controversy, arguing that Tillie's second criterion of political integration – actual political participation – was most certainly met by Danish Muslims during the controversy. In fact, I will go a step further and argue that the controversy set new standards for Muslim political participation and, thus, for political integration.

If we first examine the percentage of the total amount of claims-making

Table 8.3 Danish claimants in the Muhammad caricatures controversy: percentage of total claims-making

	Frequency	%
Muslim actors	147	22.7
Government	84	13.0
Scientific institutions/scholars	73	11.3
Legislative	61	9.4
Media and journalists	49	7.6
Employers' organisations and firms	43	6.6
Artists and artistic organisations	43	6.6
Public commentators	41	6.3
State departments/agencies	28	4.3
Political parties	21	3.2
Churches	18	2.8
Solidarity and welfare organisations	8	1.2
Judiciary	7	1.1
Radical right organisations/groups	6	0.9
Professional organisations	5	0.8
Ethnic minority organisations	5	0.8
Other	9	1.4
TOTAL	648	100

during the controversy by different Danish actors, we get a sense of a massive mobilisation of Danish Muslims. As shown in Table 8.3, Muslims account for 22.7% of the total number of claims presented by Danish actors, rendering them by far the most active group of actors in the debate considering that Muslims in Denmark make up roughly 4% of the total population.

One could argue that it is hardly surprising that Danish Muslims are the most active in a controversy in which central Muslim interests are at stake. In the Danish context, however, Muslims have long played the thematic lead role in debates about integration and immigration, and Muslim interests are frequently bypassed, but Danish Muslims had never previously been prominent actors in the debates, nor had they mobilised and engaged in continued claims-making (Bæk Simonsen 2000; Hussain 2003; Rytter 2003). Another objection might be that the data merely reproduces the fact that the Muhammad cartoons were a media-driven initiative, that one major point of the project was exactly to investigate the reactions of Danish Muslims and consequently they were naturally contacted and given space in the media to explain themselves. While this is somewhat true for the initial mediated claims-making by Danish Muslims, it cannot explain the continued high level of Muslim claims-making throughout the controversy. Figure 8.1 shows how the share of Muslim claims of the total claims-making is especially high at the beginning of the contro-

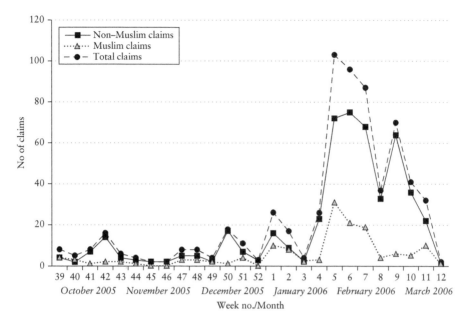

Figure 8.1 Muslim and non-Muslim claims by week of the Muhammad caricatures controversy, N=648

versy, while non-Muslim claims-making increases more than Muslim claims-making when the controversy intensifies in late January 2006. Generally speaking, however, Muslim claims-making fluctuates with the total amount of claims by all actors.

A third objection, which was often heard throughout the controversy, is that the high level of political participation by Danish Muslims as indicated by the data on claims-making represents the excessive protests of a small group of Muslim actors who did not have much support among ordinary Danish Muslims. In this perspective, the high level of political participation of Danish Muslims is seen as a sign of inadequate political integration rather than the contrary. The high degree of protest, mobilisation and claims-making led by a small group of 'dark' religious authorities proved that *Jyllands-Posten* was correct in accusing Muslims of having a problem with liberal-democratic principles, it is argued. However, while it is true that the initial protests were orchestrated by a few leading imams spearheading the ad hoc protest coalition, this picture changed over the course of the controversy. As the controversy dragged on, many different Muslim actors raised claims in the debate, some in line with the initial protests, but many others actually spent more time criticising how the group of imams had handled the affair. Thus, in the database on claims-making, seventeen different Danish Muslim organisations were found to be the direct senders of claims. There were also a couple of dozen individual

Muslim claims-makers who did not directly represent any collective entity. Furthermore, it is worth noticing that although the initial protests were led by a few imams, the protest coalition that they built counted twenty-seven, predominantly local Muslim, organisations, which attests to some support. The members of the protest coalition might not have agreed on all the steering committee's decisions. In line with the principles of representative democracy, however, they vested authority in their community leaders to speak on their behalf in the controversy. As mentioned, however, this protest drive also resulted in substantial counter-mobilisation and claims-making by other Muslim actors, most prominently in the establishment, in the midst of the cartoons controversy, of Democratic Muslims. This new organisation aimed at mobilising the 'moderate and silent majority' of Danish Muslims against what they saw as the misrepresentation of their views by the leading imams in the protest coalition. Democratic Muslims positioned themselves against the publication of the cartoons, but in explicit adherence to democracy, freedom of speech and the separation of religion and politics.

In summary, I have argued that the cartoons controversy fostered unprecedented massive and diversified political participation among Danish Muslims. The controversy set new standards for the political participation of Danish Muslims in terms of diverse actors participating, intensity of internal discussions/divisions, and magnitude of claims raised in the public sphere. In keeping with Tillie's conceptualisation, I interpret this as signs of maturing political participation and political integration among Danish Muslims rather than 'cultural backlash' or an outburst of 'ethnic politics'. In this perspective, the cartoons controversy is the catalyst of Muslim political integration in the long term. I will return to this in the last part of the chapter.

4.   Adherence to democratic values

Tillie's last criterion of political integration is adherence to fundamental liberal-democratic values. As mentioned, the suspicion of a widespread lack of such adherence among Danish Muslims was initially used to justify the publication of the cartoons. The basic argument put forward by Flemming Rose, who wrote the article accompanying the twelve cartoons, was that many Muslims want to limit freedom of speech when it comes to criticising Islam and demand special treatment, 'insisting on special consideration for their own religious feelings' (Rose 2005). However, if we consider the actual content of Danish Muslim reactions to the publication of the cartoons, what evidence supports this claim? I investigate this by first looking at the 'prognostic framing' of Muslim claims, i.e. the substantial demand or solutions proposed by Muslim actors (Snow 2004). Secondly, I examine the 'justificational framing' of Muslim claims – the kind of argumentation that is given in support of the substantial claim. Central here is the question of whether or not Danish

Muslims were drawing upon liberal-democratic arguments or using religious reasoning as 'conversation stoppers' in the debate (Rorty 1994). Finally, I will compare the Muslim justifications in the public sphere (newspaper material) to the justifications used in more internal claims-making (organisational material). The aim here is to discuss whether there is any proof of the 'two tongues' hypothesis, which suggests that Muslims, for strategic reasons, were using a moderate, adapted argumentation in the public sphere while arguing in less 'integrated' terms when addressing the issue internally.

Table 8.4 shows the prognostic framing of Muslim claims in the cartoons controversy. A look at the overall distribution of prognostic frames gives us a sense of which issues and solutions Danish Muslims typically focused on in the debate.

In contrast to the initial framing of the cartoons in *Jyllands-Posten* and later by the Danish government, Danish Muslims were much less inclined to frame the cartoons as an issue of freedom of speech and argued to a limited extent that the solution to the conflict had to be found in the reformed regulation of the limits on freedom of speech. Only 7.3% of Muslim prognostic frames went in that direction, of which most actually did not call for further restrictions on freedom of speech in the form of outlawing blasphemy or hate speech, but rather for furthering freedom of speech in a manner so that Muslim perspectives were also heard in the public debate. The main argument made by Danish Muslims in the debate was that while *Jyllands-Posten* had, and should have, the right to publish the cartoons, this did not mean that they should have done so. The right to say everything does not mean that everything should be said, it was argued. A major part of the Muslim prognostic framing therefore called for greater tolerance of diversity and the need to engage in dialogue with the Muslim minority in order to build mutual understanding and respect (20.7% of Muslim prognostic frames). Following this line of reasoning, Danish Muslims especially called upon *Jyllands-Posten* to apologise for deliberately offending Muslim religious sentiments (5.7%), and for the government to engage in dialogue with Muslim representatives (4.7%). Likewise, Danish Muslims called upon both the media and the government to treat Muslims and non-Muslims alike (5.7%), and, thus, for equal treatment rather than special treatment. However, the largest part of Danish Muslim prognostic frames called for action by fellow Muslims (33.7%), particularly in two ways: defend the Prophet's honour (10.4%) and respond to the cartoons by democratic means instead of violence (9.8%). A diachronic view at Table 8.1 reveals that Muslim calls for action in the first phase of the controversy were largely about either raising awareness of the caricatures (calls for protest/defence of the Prophet and for spreading the word abroad) or about receiving symbolic reparation (an apology from *Jyllands-Posten* or a diplomatic meeting with the government). As the focus of the debate shifted, so did the solutions preferred by Danish Muslims. From phase 2 onwards, the calls for dialogue became

Table 8.4 Prognostic frames of Muslim claims by phases of the controversy[a]

	Phase 1		Phase 2		Phase 3		Phase 4		Total	
	N	%	N	%	N	%	N	%	N	%
Calls on Muslims for action	15	44.1	21	31.3	23	36.5	6	20.7	65	33.7
– *Defence of Prophet/raising awareness abroad*	9	26.5	6	9.0	5	7.9	0	0.0	20	10.4
– *Calls for Muslim non-violence*	1	2.9	2	3.0	14	22.2	2	6.9	19	9.8
– *Calls for other Muslim actions*	5	14.7	13	19.3	4	6.4	4	13.8	26	13.5
Calls for tolerance/dialogue	5	14.7	14	20.9	15	23.8	6	20.7	40	20.7
– *Calls for tolerance/respect of difference*	2	5.9	0	0.0	4	6.3	2	6.9	8	4.1
– *Calls for further dialogue*	3	8.8	14	20.9	11	17.5	4	13.8	32	16.6
Calls for action by media actors	9	26.5	8	12.0	1	1.6	0	0.0	18	9.3
– *Jyllands-Posten should apologise*	6	17.6	4	6.0	1	1.6	0	0.0	11	5.7
– *Calls for other media action*	3	8.9	4	6.0	0	0.0	0	0.0	7	3.6
Calls for action by the Danish Government	2	5.9	8	12.0	3	4.8	2	6.9	15	7.8
– *Take meeting with Muslim representatives*	1	2.9	4	6.0	2	3.2	2	6.9	9	4.7
– *Calls for other Government action*	1	2.9	4	6.0	1	1.6	0	0.0	6	3.1
Calls for furthering/limiting freedom of speech	2	5.8	7	10.4	2	3.2	3	10.3	14	7.3
Calls for equal treatment	1	2.9	4	6.0	3	4.8	3	10.3	11	5.7
Calls for restoring the Caliphate	0	0.0	2	3.0	5	7.9	2	6.9	9	4.7
Calls for better Muslim integration	0	0.0	1	1.5	2	3.2	3	10.3	6	3.1
Calls for anti-discrimination measures	0	0.0	1	1.5	3	4.8	0	0.0	4	2.4
Other	0	0.0	1	1.5	6	9.5	4	13.8	11	5.7
Total	34	17.6	67	34.7	63	32.6	29	15.0	193	100

a. The percentages in each cell show the percentage of a specific prognostic frame relative to all of the prognoses made within a given phase.

central to Muslim prognostic framing. Likewise, following the embassy attacks in the Middle East, Muslim calls for non-violence boomed in phase 3 (22.2% of prognostic frames in this phase). My interpretation here is that the linking of the imam delegations and the escalation of the conflict abroad in the public debate placed heavy pressure on Muslim claimants in Denmark to officially distance themselves from the use of violence and actively embrace dialogue and calls for tolerance. Doing so became a condition for further participation and claims-making in the debate.

My argument regarding the substantial arguments and calls for action taken by Danish Muslims is that, on average, they generally adhere to fundamental liberal-democratic values such as freedom of speech, dialogue, tolerance, respect, equal treatment, anti-discrimination and non-violence. Rather than calling the fundamental principles into question, as suggested by, for example, Flemming Rose, Danish Muslims were questioning how these principles were put to use in practice. The only prognostic frame in Table 8.4 that is clearly at odds with liberal-democratic values is the call to 'restore the Caliphate' (4.7%) and, thus, for a theocracy. Rather than holding such claims against all Danish Muslims, however, it is important to realise that this claim was limited to the marginal, but very active and outspoken, Danish branch of Hizb ut-Tahrir.

At the level of the justification of Muslim claims (Table 8.5), we see a shift away from 'blaming' *Jyllands-Posten* and the Danish government through 'injustice/victimisation' frames towards more 'neutral', especially rights-based justifications stressing free speech, anti-discrimination and human rights, which sets in from phase 2, but really materialises in phase 3 of the controversy.

Parallel to this development, religious justifications, although prominent throughout the controversy, were increasingly used by Muslims in phase 3. One interpretation is that Danish Muslims, under increased pressure, were returning to familiar and internally resonant – but externally dissonant – justifications of claims. If we look at the details of the Muslim justifications, however, we realise that the increase in religious frames is due to the increased use of religious affirmations of values stressed by many non-Muslim actors in the debate, such as tolerance, non-violence, freedom of speech and democracy. The authoritative sources of Islam (Qur'an and the *Sunna* of the Prophet Muhammad) are used to highlight certain aspects, norms and values of Islam. My argument here is that when Danish Muslims (re-) emphasise how freedom of speech, democracy, tolerance, and non-violence are fundamentally Islamic values at exactly this point in the debate, it can be a way of turning external pressures for affirmation of certain values into an internal obligation of being a good and virtuous Muslim. An example is the following quote by Sherin Khankan, spokeswoman for Critical Muslims, a relatively small group of well-educated Muslims advocating a kind of 'European Islam':

> Some Muslims have forgotten the words of the Prophet: Islam is exemplary behaviour. The example given by the Prophet demands forgiveness, indulgence, and tolerance. Besides, it demands of us to meet our opponents with the best and most beautiful arguments. (Press release, Critical Muslims, 14 February 2006)

Table 8.5 Justificational frames of Muslim claims by phases of the controversy[a]

	Phase 1		Phase 2		Phase 3		Phase 4		Total	
	N	%	N	%	N	%	N	%	N	%
Injustice/victimisation	13	41.9	14	26.9	7	14.0	16	41.0	50	29.1
– *Gratuitous offence by Jyllands-Posten*	6	19.4	10	19.2	3	6.0	6	15.4	28	16.2
– *Unjust treatment by Danish Government*	7	22.5	4	7.7	4	8.0	5	12.8	22	12.8
Rights-based justification	5	16.1	12	23.1	10	20.0	6	15.4	33	19.2
– *Freedom of speech*	3	9.6	7	27.5	6	12.0	2	5.1	18	10.5
– *Anti-discrimination/human rights*	2	6.5	5	9.2	4	8.0	4	10.3	15	8.7
Religious justification	10	32.3	13	25.0	25	50.0	10	25.6	58	33.7
– *Referring to the religious status of the Prophet*	7	22.6	11	21.2	10	20.0	6	15.4	34	19.8
– *Religious affirmation of 'liberal' values*	3	9.7	2	3.8	15	30.0	4	10.2	24	13.9
Cultural justification	0	0.0	4	7.7	3	6.0	0	0.0	7	4.1
Historical justification	2	6.5	2	3.8	1	2.0	3	7.7	8	4.7
Consequentialist justification	1	3.2	5	9.6	3	6.0	2	5.1	11	2.9
Other	0	0.0	2	3.8	1	2.0	2	5.1	5	2.9
Total	31	20.9	52	30.2	50	29.1	34	19.8	172	100

a. The percentages in each cell show the percentage of a specific justificational frame of all of the justifications given by Muslim actors within a given phase.

Here, rational dialogue and non-violence become religious imperatives. In a situation in which some Danish Muslims were accused of being at least partially responsible for the violent escalation of the conflict, this increasingly defensive version of religious justification made good sense. Rather than using religious justifications as 'conversation stoppers', Danish Muslims were trying to bridge religious rhetoric and secular modes of justifying claims.

The remaining question is whether these adaptive expressions of adherence to fundamental liberal-democratic principles were not merely the product of strategic calculations by 'duplicitous' Muslim actors; that they were not really 'sincere'. In order to 'test' this, we can compare the justifications of Muslim claims within different arenas of claims-making – the public sphere at large (claims in the newspaper material) and the internal sphere of Muslim communities (claims in internal organisational material), respectively.

Table 8.6 shows considerable differences (statistically significant correlation). For example, injustice frames are by far the most used justifications of claims in the newspaper material (35.6% vs 25.7%), while religious justifica-

Table 8.6 Justifications of Muslim claims within different arenas of claims-making (column percentages)[a]

		Public claims-making	Internal claims-making	Total
Religious justification	Frequency	17	41	58
	Percentage	28.8	36.3	33.7
Injustice/victimisation	Frequency	21	29	50
	Percentage	35.6	25.7	29.1
Rights-based justification	Frequency	8	25	33
	Percentage	13.6	22.1	19.2
Consequentialist justification	Frequency	7	4	11
	Percentage	11.9	3.5	6.4
Historical justification	Frequency	0	8	8
	Percentage	0.0	7.1	4.7
Cultural justification	Frequency	4	3	7
	Percentage	6.8	2.7	4.1
Moral/ethical justification	Frequency	2	3	5
	Percentage	3.4	2.7	2.9
Total	Frequency	59	113	172
	Percentage	100.0	100.0	100.0

a. $x^2=13.51$, P=0.03, V=0.28.

tions heavily dominate internal Muslim claims-making (36.3% vs 28.8%). Muslims on average used 'secular arguments' more when raising claims in the public sphere at large than when airing claims internally. Rather than seeing this as proof of the 'duplicity' hypothesis, however, I see this as the natural result of adapting one's message to the audience – of trying to ensure resonance (Benford and Snow 2000). Danish Muslims seemed able to translate their religious despair into a discourse of injustice/victimisation when entering the public sphere. In other words, Danish Muslims were translating particular religious motives into generalisable principles (Ungureanu 2008). The translation was somewhat strategic, aimed at maximising the chances of invoking sympathy with potential non-Muslim allies. This strategic adaptation can also be detected in the use of religious justifications. In the public sphere, it was affirming and defensive, while religious justifications in mosques stressed the holiness of the prophet and cited the holy texts in a more assertive manner. However, reading this adaptation as a sign of Danish Muslims lying about their genuine intentions or manipulating the Danish non-Muslim population would be erroneous. The references to the central liberal-democratic values, rights and duties inherent in the injustice frames, rights-based justifications and affirmative religious justifications in public Muslim claims-making were more than a ploy, more than strategic rhetoric. In fact, Danish Muslims used rights-based justifications more in internal claims-making than in external claims-making (22.1% vs 13.6%).

In summary, then, while the results presented above provide some evidence that Muslims adjusted the justification of claims according to the arena of claims-making and potential listeners, there is little to suggest that they were duplicitous – saying fundamentally different things in different contexts. To situate a message in different ways depending on your audience is not the same as being duplicitous. Everybody who wants to get a message across does this to some extent.

5.   Conclusions and long-term perspectives

The empirical analysis argues that if we apply Tillie's definition of 'political integration' to the Danish Muslims' claims-making during the cartoons controversy, there is good reason to say that the Danish Muslims who were active in the public debate were, on average, well integrated into secular politics. This stands in sharp contrast to the widespread public perception of what happened. In fact, Danish Muslim actors displayed considerable trust in democratic and legal institutions, relying mainly on procedural forms of claims-making, and addressing their claims to established mainstream political and legal institutions. As the controversy developed, however, indications of this initial trust diminishing began to emerge, triggered by rejections from political and legal institutions and leading to shifts in the addressees and types of performances used among Muslim claims-makers, including transnational claims-making. The cartoons controversy also revealed unprecedentedly large and diversified political participation among Danish Muslims. The controversy thus set new standards for the political participation of Danish Muslims in terms of the diversity of the participating actors, the intensity of the internal discussions/ divisions, and the magnitude of the claims raised in the public sphere. Finally, Danish Muslims displayed a large degree of adherence to liberal-democratic values in the substantial content and justifications of claims. Rather than questioning fundamental liberal-democratic principles, Danish Muslims questioned how these principles, primarily freedom of speech, were put to use in practice. Likewise, rather than using religious justifications as 'conversation stoppers', as often suggested, Danish Muslims were trying to bridge religious rhetoric and secular modes of justifying claims. This was also visible in how Danish Muslims attempted to achieve resonance depending on the context of their claims-making. I have argued that this contextual adaptation of claims-making, using references to central liberal-democratic values, rights and duties (especially in public Muslim claims-making), was more than a mere ploy, more than strategic rhetoric. Adherence to the principles was genuinely sincere and not an example of 'duplicitous talk'.

To put the results of the empirical analysis into perspective, I will briefly examine the long-term consequences of the cartoons controversy on the political integration of Danish Muslims six years later. Obviously this discussion can only be sketchy but I would like to share a few observations. First, among some Muslims, the controversy undoubtedly reduced their trust in legal and political institutions in Denmark, particularly the Muslim actors who advocated charges against or an apology from *Jyllands-Posten* or a symbolic meeting with the government on the issue. It so happens that the strongest advocates of such measures were the same actors who took the initiative to the imam delegations, i.e. the Muslim organisations involved in the protest coalition led by the Islamic Faith Community. For these actors, the cartoons controversy meant a loss of political trust, but also a loss of political credibility in the eyes of political authorities as well as many Muslims. The cartoons controversy thus led to a political derailing of Muslim actors who, before the crisis, were influential and involved in, for example, negotiations with political authorities regarding integration.

Secondly, the debate about the Muhammad cartoons initiated a reconfiguration and diversification of the public representation of Danish Muslims, which seems to have continued during the years since the original publication of the cartoons. The re-publication of the cartoons in 2008, following the exposure of a plot to kill cartoonist Kurt Westergaard, can serve as an example. As in 2005/06, the Islamic Faith Community was the strongest Muslim opponent of the re-publication but its protests were immediately questioned and denounced by other Muslim organisations in Denmark. Most notable were the critical comments from some of the numerically large Turkish Muslim organisations, for example The Association of Turkish Muslims in Copenhagen and The Union of Muslim Immigrants, two organisations that had remained relatively quiet in public debates concerning Islam in Denmark, including during the 2005/6 controversy. Spokesperson Erfan Kurtulos explained: 'We share a common religion, but they do not represent us, and we oppose the way the imams of the Islamic Faith Community are participating in public debates. Fanatics cannot patent Islam and the work for integration in Denmark' (quoted in Lumby 2008). Similarly, the status of the Islamic Faith Community as representing 'Danish Muslims' has been challenged by two new Muslim umbrella organisations established after the 2005/06 cartoons controversy in attempts to unite the majority of Danish Muslims and give them a common voice: The Muslim Federal Council (Muslimernes Fællesråd), an initiative driven by Muslims in Dialogue, with more than 40,000 members, and The Danish Muslim Union (Dansk Muslimsk Union), an initiative of the Union of Muslim Immigrant Associations. It seems as though the failure to unite Danish Muslims during the first cartoons controversy has renewed interest in building a common organisational platform, which can work as the centre of claims-making in future debates.

Finally, although the representation and participation of Danish Muslim interests in public debates has diversified since the cartoons controversy, there are also signs of a homogenisation of the mode of public claims-making by Danish Muslims. In a political context in which numerous terrorist plots have been exposed, all referring to the Muhammad cartoons as a justifying cause and where fears of the radicalisation of young Danish Muslims has been high on the political agenda, the pressure to explicitly adhere to liberal-democratic principles when raising claims in public has increased for Danish Muslim actors. The limits of tolerance regarding 'deviant' (religious) practices and political opinions/views seem to be shrinking, making the public room for manoeuvre smaller among neo-orthodox Muslim groups who, for example, are passive vis-à-vis participation in Danish politics and democratic elections. The relative balance of power among Muslim actors pushing different interpretations of Islam seems to have shifted – at least in public debates – in favour of actors who unconditionally embrace integration as their goal. I will argue that this development and the danger of being labelled as 'extremist' or 'radical' prevents more Muslim actors today from presenting their views in public debates (see also Lindekilde 2012).

Looking at these trends as a whole, the cartoons controversy seems to have had mixed long-term consequences for the political integration of Danish Muslims; some positive, others more negative. Considering the degree of political integration in practice among Danish Muslim actors during the cartoons controversy and in the years after, however, I believe there is good reason to question the oft-heard criticism regarding the 'inadequate political integration of Danish Muslims'.

Notes

1. The database was developed as the basis for my PhD dissertation: 'Contested Caricatures: Dynamic of Muslim Claims-Making during the Caricatures Controversy' (2008).

2. In the newspaper landscape *Berlingske Tidende* locates itself between the poles of *Jyllands-Posten*, which insisted on the subordination of other values/rights to freedom of speech, and *Politiken*, the main voice criticising the cartoons and the Danish government's handling of the crisis. *Berlingske Tidende* chose not to publish the cartoons out of respect for Muslim sentiments, but supported both *Jyllands-Posten*'s right to publish them and the government's 'non-intervention' strategy.

3. I borrow this term from Tarrow and Tilly (2006: 202), who themselves are in debt regarding the use of the term 'performance' in the anthropological work of, for example, Erving Goffman, where it refers to the activities of an individual before a set of observers. Performances, in contrast to everyday life activities, are thus meant for an audience (Goffman 1986).

4. The periodisation builds on the application of two criteria of demarcation: 1) scope of contention and 2) intensity of contention. In simple terms, phase 1 is character-

ised by being local/national in scope and by a relatively low intensity of contention; phase 2 by an international scope and medium level of intensity; phase 3 by an international/global scope and high level of intensity; and phase 4 by a national scope and low-to-medium level of intensity. The precise dates of the phases are: Phase 1: 30 September 2005 to 25 December 2005; Phase 2: 26 December 2005 to 3 February 2006; Phase 3: 4 February 2006 to 25 February 2006; Phase 4: 26 February 2006 to 20 March 2006.

References

Adelberth Hansen, K. and H. Nygaard Jensen (2009), 'Undergraver tv-nyheder den politiske tillid?', *Politica*, 39: 1, pp. 14–30.

Benford, R. D. and D. A. Snow (2000), 'Framing Processes and Social Movements: An Overview and Assessment', *Annual Review of Sociology*, 26, pp. 611–39.

Bæk Simonsen, J. (2000), 'From Defensive Silence to Creative Participation: Muslim Discourses in Denmark' in Dassetto (ed.), *Paroles d'islam*, Paris: Masionneuve et Larose.

Goffman, E. (1986), *Frame analysis: An essay on the organization of experience*, New York: Harper & Row.

Hussain, M. (2003), 'Diskurs om Islam i medier of politik' in Sheikh et al. (eds), *Islam i bevægelse*, Copenhagen: Akademisk Forlag.

Joppke, C. (2007), 'Beyond national models: Civic integration policies for immigrants in Western Europe', *West European Politics*, vol. 30, pp. 1–22.

Joppke, C. (2008), 'Immigration and the identity of citizenship: the paradox of universalism', *Citizenship Studies*, vol. 12, pp. 533–46.

Koopmans, R. and P. Statham (1999), 'Political claims analysis: integration protest event end political discourse approaches', *Mobilization: The International Journal of Research on Social Movements, Protest and Collective Behavior,* vol. 4, pp. 597–626.

Lindekilde, L. (2008), 'Mobilizing in the Name of the Prophet? Danish Muslim Mobilization during the Muhammad Caricatures Controversy', *Mobilization: An International Journal*, vol. 13, no. 2, pp. 219–38.

Lindekilde, L. (2010), 'Soft Repression and Mobilization: The Case of Transnational Activism of Danish Muslims during the Cartoons Controversy', *International Journal of Middle East Studies*, vol. 42, no. 3, pp. 451–69.

Lindekilde, L. (2012), 'Neo-liberal Governing of "Radicals": Danish Radicalization Prevention Policies and Potential Iatrogenic Effects', forthcoming in *International Journal of Conflict and Violence*, 5(2).

Lumby, E. (2008), 'Muslimer i oprør over Islamisk Trossamfund', *Berlingske Tidende*, 21 February 2008.

Rorty, R. (1994), 'Religion as a conversation-stopper', *Common Knowledge*, vol. 3, no. 1, pp. 1–6.

Rose, F. (2005), 'Muhammeds Ansigt', *Jyllands-Posten*, 30 September.

Rytter, M. (2003), 'Islam i bevægelser' in Sheikh et al. (eds), *Islam i bevægelse*, Copenhagen: Akademisk Forlag.

Snow, D. A. (2004), 'Framing Processes, Ideology, and Discursive Fields', in D. A. Snow, S. A. Soule and H. Kriesi (eds), *The Blackwell Companion to Social Movement Studies*, Malden, MA: Blackwell Publishing.

Strawn, K. D. (2008), 'Validity and Media-derived Protest Event Data: Examining Relative Coverage Tendencies in Mexican News Data', *Mobilization: The International Journal of Research on Social Movements, Protest and Collective Behavior*, vol. 13, pp. 147–64.

Tarrow, S. and C. Tilly (2006), *Contentious Politics*, Boulder: Paradigme Publishers.

Tillie, J. (2004), 'Social capital of organisations and their members: explaining the political integration of immigrants in Amsterdam', *Journal of Ethnic and Migration Studies*, vol. 30, pp. 529–41.

Togeby, L. (1999), 'Migrants at the polls: an analysis of immigrant and refugee particpation in Danish local elections', *Journal of Ethnic and Migration Studies*, vol. 25, pp. 665–84.

Ungureanu, C. (2008). 'The Contested Relations Between Democracy and Religion: Towards a Dialogical Perspective', *European Journal of Political Theory*, vol. 7, no. 4, pp. 405–29.

LIMITS AND POTENTIALITIES OF THE ITALIAN AND BRITISH POLITICAL SYSTEMS THROUGH THE LENS OF MUSLIM WOMEN IN POLITICS

Alessia Belli

1. Introduction

This chapter examines the debate on the supposed crisis and even death of multiculturalism in Europe. It aims, in particular, at analysing the limits and potentialities of the Italian (Allievi 2010: 147–80; Triadafyllidou 2006: 117–42; Zincone 1994) and UK (Malik 2010: 11–64; Modood 2006: 37–56; Parekh 2006; Phillips 2007) political systems, two interesting and contrasting case studies. To address this issue, a strategic point of view has been chosen, namely the participation of Muslim women[1] in the traditional spaces of politics, both at the local and at the national level. It should be recognised at this juncture that for women in general this kind of involvement is the most difficult to gain access to, even within contemporary Western settings. The additional merit of choosing the perspective of minority women stems from the fact that, in their case, participation not only implies the achievement of citizenship rights, a precondition that, for instance, in Italy has not yet been fulfilled, but also mastery of the material and symbolic tools of the political and cultural setting of the country; not to mention the capacity to clear the traditional social and cultural obstacles that keep women away from political representation in the first place. Adopting the lens of Muslim women's experiences, therefore, offers an insightful diagnosis of the Italian and British approach to cultural and religious pluralism and of the influence of gender on mainstream notions of citizenship and national identity. At a time of high polarisation and of a general trend toward assimilationist positions (Phillips 2007), the new visibility and active engagement of Muslim women not only works as a litmus test of the status quo but also as a sensor of the complex social dynamics under way. Beyond the descriptive level, then, it can also orientate political pathways that avoid the looming scenario of a clash of civilisations.

1.a.   The strengths of a comparative study

While the specific characteristics of Italy and the UK make it impossible to produce a univocal and universally valid recipe for managing multicultural societies, the comparative analysis that will be developed in this chapter can nonetheless give insightful suggestions. In this sense, the fact that the UK is assumed as the model does not mean that the relative success of certain multicultural policies undertaken by British governments should be applied sic et simpliciter to the Italian context. What it actually means, is that the theoretical background that has informed specific British policymaking initiatives can represent a stimulus also for Italy, where a coherent and thorough debate on these issues is urgently required. The objective is to underline the ways in which the Italian and British political systems face and react to the growing visibility of differences and how Muslim women, the symbol of difference par excellence, engage, challenge and even alter respective socio-cultural and political attitudes. More specifically, this chapter aims to understand whether or not the participation of minority women can make any difference in terms of bringing gender issues and gender equality into the mainstream of society. Exploring these questions seems of the utmost importance when one considers the obstacles that still prevent all women from gaining access to political participation in the West. In the case of Italy such debate is even more essential in light of the patriarchal backlash, evident also at the political level, that risks further delaying the achievement of women's emancipation and gender equality (Zanardo 2010).

2.   Methodologies and methods: a feminist perspective[2]

Before embarking on the journey into Muslim women's manifold experiences, I consider it not only appropriate but also essential to devote some space to clarifying the methodology and methods that underpin my research. First of all, the choice of method, which is based on interviews, stems from the feminist credo of the need to listen to women's voices. For this reason, the interviews were semi-structured, in order for both interviewer and interviewees to follow the flux of conversation without being constrained in an inflexible prescribed questionnaire. A semi-structured interaction, in fact, represents a more contextual-sensitive tool that allows research to be conducted on the participants' terms as much as possible while enabling the interviewer to observe what is relevant to her interlocutors. Through such an approach, the theoretical categories are exposed to a continual process of questioning, broadening and clarification, according to the concrete ways in which these concepts are translated into people's everyday lives. Nine interviews were conducted in the UK[3] with Muslim women who were appointed or nominated at the local and at the national level (political elections 2010). In Italy, I only conducted three[4] interviews, one working at the national (parliamentary) level and the others at local level (one elected in the municipality of Rovereto in 2009; the other rallied in local elections in Perugia in 2009 without being elected). While in Britain the interviewees represent a huge variety of ethnic origins, age, cultural background, political orientation and dress code, in Italy variety is limited due to the small number of women involved: I interviewed two Moroccans and one Jordanian (two were veiled). The reasons for this difference need to be sought in the two states' approach towards immigration: compared to the UK, immigration in Italy is relatively recent and the state is still struggling to find its own model for accommodating newcomers. It is as if Italy, with its long history of emigration, has found it difficult to recognise the change in its status to a multicultural country. Moreover, the ethnic connotation of Italian national identity represents an additional barrier to the naturalisation process and the assignment of political rights to immigrants. I will focus on these aspects in more detail in the following paragraphs, where a more detailed analysis will test the concrete capacity of the two states to address and integrate cultural and religious diversities and to understand whether multiculturalism as a state policy can still represent a viable tool for tackling pluralism. In reporting the visions of the interviewees, I am aware of drawing only one of many possible paths within such a diverse panorama. For this reason, the research does not claim to be scientific in the sense of representing the experience of all Muslim women politicians, let alone Muslim women in general. Any research, in fact, pays the price of being only a glimpse, a specific selected route. When analysing the data, what emerges is a broad variety of positions: differences and contradictions are the real fabric of the study. My aim is to bring out precisely this heterogeneity, fluidity and blended margins. Despite the recognition of these limits, my research represents nevertheless a 'true' trajectory in the sense of reflecting and retracing the life-paths of some women who have found themselves enmeshed in pressing and constraining circumstances. The points of view of the participants, in other words, reflect their specific backgrounds: gender, age, class, ethnicity, are all interacting elements that contribute to forge unique stories. Far from conceiving this sort of contextuality as a fatal limit, according to the feminist credo, I rather value it as a conditio sine qua non in order to render and interpret the complexity of real life and each and every person's manifold responses.

3. The UK

3.a. *What does Muslim identity have to do with politics? Being Muslim between ordinariness and strategic positioning*

The women interviewed reflect a huge variety of positions in terms of living out their Muslimness in the political sphere. Some of them firmly identified themselves as Muslim while others presented religion as a private issue. Between these poles there is an array of less defined positions. Identifying oneself in the political sphere as a Muslim is regarded, for some, as a duty, especially at a time of growing Islamophobic sentiments: their voice becomes a badge of honour that enables them to break pervasive stereotypes (Afshar 2005: 262–83), and to bring in and defend those whose voices and interests often remain hidden in the public and political arenas. 'I took my identity as a campaigning identity' says Haleh Afshar,[5] British academic and member of the House of Lords, 'because we need Muslim women who are proud to be so and from this stance speak on behalf of all Muslim women'. Since an effective empowerment can only originate from within, being engaged, vocal and outspoken is, for her, pivotal to emancipation. With 9/11 and 7/7 Islam has crept into the political arena making a natural way of expressing cultural and religious affiliations a visible marker of identity for society at large. In the case of Pola Uddin[6] (Labour Party), the first Muslim woman to be appointed to the House of Lords, it is only with the bombing attacks of 7 July 2005 (7/7) that, increasingly associated with Islam by non-Muslims, she has become more assertive: ethno-religious symbols have proved useful in legitimising and encouraging the expression of people's identity at a time of general suspicion. Far from nurturing communal identities, being visibly Muslim enables a struggle for the rights of all human beings and the construction of a more just and equal society for everybody. This universal commitment is evident in the words of Salma Yaqoob, a young Muslim woman, formerly a leader of the Respect Party and Birmingham City Councillor. Concerning her Muslim identity, she says:

> For me it's just OK; I'm a person and I have my own values, my principles, my culture. I wouldn't enforce that when discussing with anybody, because for me it's natural. But if there's an injustice like the *hijab*, or the *burqa* ban I take a position to defend freedom of choice. This is something that I do not only for women, or for Asians or for Muslims but for humanity as a whole. (Yaqoob 2010)

While Salma Yaqoob is convinced that being a Muslim woman in politics can be helpful in reaching out to minorities and in motivating and empowering women who are materially and symbolically disadvantaged, others regard the use of the label 'Muslim' as a source of isolation and regression. Liberal Democrat Baroness Kishwar Falkner[7] explains this point when she says:

> I entered politics as a human being who cares about justice and injustice, and not as a Muslim. Muslim identity is not my full identity: it is relevant only in so far as there is a group that needs a voice. And I'm prepared to give my voice if the argument has merit. But there are times when I actually take a divergent position from Muslim groups. Identity is for me a political identity, I fight for civil liberties and my liberal identity comes before my Muslim identity. (Falkner 2010)

Although speaking as a Muslim, as she admits, can on specific occasions infuse a level of authenticity to the debate in a way that a white non-Muslim feminist could not, she nonetheless highlights that assuming the Muslim badge prevents the achievement of rights that are universal and cannot be differentiated along cultural or religious lines. Working for the emancipation of Muslim women requires, in her opinion, the language of human rights rather than that of identity politics. Despite the differences, there is one element that plays a unifying role: after 7/7, religion increasingly impinged on their political function and made their Muslim identity public. The many ways in which they mediate and bargain internal and external instances are de facto pressing the political domain to adjust itself to present circumstances. Muslim women are the agents of a profound transformation in which the traditional liberal-democratic frontiers between culture, religion and politics are opened to question. The forms of their mutual accommodation will decide the physiognomy of the spaces of coexistence in multicultural environments.

3.b.   *Dress code: a badge of identity or an obstacle?*

In what ways do Muslim women who are in politics engage with the Islamic headscarf[8] at a time when it is regarded as the ostensible sign of a supposedly provocative Muslim difference (Afshar 2005)? Between those who do not wear the *hijab* and those who do, there is a wide array of more nuanced attitudes that are based on pragmatic reasons. All the interviewees recognise that the obsession surrounding the practice of veiling, assumed as the sole identifier of Muslim women, ends up ignoring the complexity and fluidity of their personality. It is to break the stereotype of the ones who cover themselves as the only acceptable model of Muslim femininity that Salma Yaqoob encourages the presence of different kinds of women within the Respect Party: in politics ideas and morals should be regarded and respected more than one's dress code. Using the knowledge of their groups' cultural milieu, by dressing modestly or by wearing a loose scarf when addressing religious audiences or attending traditional meetings and spaces, many show a practical wisdom that allows them to push their ideas of equality and justice forward while establishing good relationships with communities. Rana Naseer,[9] a Muslim candidate for the Respect Party in Birmingham, tells of her pioneering experience of speaking in the mosque (the audience was exclusively male) after Friday prayer:

> I worn the headscarf as a sign of respect within the mosque, but when I was outside leafleting and speaking with people I wasn't covered . . . although I was worried that they could judge me, they openly engaged and accepted me without questioning the fact that I didn't wear the *hijab*. (Naseer 2010)

It is through mediation, compromise and small adjustments that these women gain respect and power and work as catalysts for cultural change and for women's emancipation. They also break stereotypes in wider society, where the veil is still the universal marker of Muslim women's passivity and/or menacing presence. In this sense, they try to restore the pristine meaning of the veil as a personal journey that nobody has the right to question or judge (Bullock 2002). Some women wear it naturally, with pride and confidence in the public sphere while others choose not to wear it, as in the case of Haleh Afshar for whom the Qur'an does not demand to cover; or Shahida Akhmed,[10] artist and Labour town councillor in Nelson, Lancashire, who positions herself at a stage in her faith where wearing the veil is still not a priority. On the opposite front, veiling is seen, especially in the form of the burqa and the *niqab*, as a way of further isolating minority women as Baroness Kishwar Falkner explains: ' . . . like they said "already I'm considered weird in this culture, so let me become more weird, let me wear a big black tent!"'.

However, even when veiling is contested, priority is always given to respect for the liberal principles of freedom of choice and dress. While they remark that every Muslim woman should be free to manifest her identity as she wishes, many agreed on the potentially hampering role of the veil in the political realm. Haleh Afshar makes this point clear when she recognises that in Parliament, if a Muslim woman respects the dress code and looks a bit like the others, she is perceived as less threatening even when standing up and saying all kinds of controversial things.

Pola Uddin remarks that while faith (expressed in visible symbols) is not going to assist a Muslim woman when gaining high office, the fact that a growing number of women, even veiled, obtain political success is a relevant phenomenon. Once accepted in the political realm, in fact, the veil can also release positive effects: firstly, being a role model for all those who are still minoritised and who lack the inspiration and confidence to make their own way in the public sphere; secondly, reassuring society generally with their commitment to human rights, justice and equality, thus building mutual trust between communities. The common expectation is that in the very near future the headscarf will be considered a natural expression of identity, and a non-issue: people will not have to hide or change who they are because they are judged for their ideas and values rather than for their dress code.

3.c.   Overcoming the sharp divide between communal and universalist politics: the pragmatic alternative of Muslim women

When asked about specific issues concerning Muslim women compared to the broader category 'women', the interviewees adopted divergent positions. Although all of them pointed out the importance of achieving equality within society, they pursue it differently: some by adopting a form of universalism that is skeptical toward differences and some by addressing those differences as the only way to make equality effective. The former tend to deny the specificity of Muslim women and to read their experiences in terms of universal needs and rights. Working through civil liberties that apply to all would be the best solution for also empowering vulnerable subjects. Since the majority of Muslim women are unemployed or have no personal pensions nor life insurance, making them economically active rather than 'bringing them up in silos' (Falkner) is the only way to mainstream them. Accordingly, there are not specific Muslim preoccupations, what every woman wants – Sikh or Buddhist, Hindu, white working class or posh – is an opportunity to improve their lives in terms of economic security, the rule of law, decent schools and medical care. Specific instances should not be presented as religious claims since this would exclude a lot of people. It would be better if Muslim women presented certain issues in more universalistic terms and followed a common course with other women who have the same needs. In this sense, all the interviewees agree that there are general issues that affect the broader category 'women' regardless of their ethnic, cultural or religious background, which revolve around education, unemployment, domestic violence, and health care. Many of them, however, highlight the importance of tackling specific problems in a clear, decisive and even controversial manner, even at the risk of being accused of threatening the universal values of the country by using their Muslim identity to claim specific rights.

As Salma Yaqoob explains, 'although I deal with questions concerning all communities, I won't apologise for taking an issue about Muslims because I think there is a need for it; I don't want to be afraid of being seen too close to Muslims'. Since equality does not mean sameness, the main issue is tackling problems that are naturally related to differences without playing into the hands of communal politics. The specific needs of Muslim women, as Haleh Afshar remarks, need to be pointed out in the appropriate political venues. If the government fails to take into consideration the specific necessities of its citizens this will have discriminating effects on those subjects whose voice goes unheard. Polygamy and informal marriages, for instance, are issues deeply ingrained in the Muslim community that heavily affect women. Polygamy, in particular, creates a category of citizens that have neither rights nor entitlements: wives in polygamous marriages are particularly vulnerable in cases of divorce or violence. British law, instead of turning a blind eye, should ban informal marriages. As Afshar suggests, the best strategy is on the one hand to enforce the same laws about marriage and divorce, which should be secular and apply to all religions, and, on the other hand, to give people the option of having both a religious and a civil marriage. This form of accommodation is not only compatible with the universalist ethos of politics but is also the precondition to fulfilling its egalitarian goal. Listening to and bringing up grassroots voices will work as an antidote to communal vagaries and lead to informed political responses that reflect the dynamics on the ground and the real needs of different citizens.

The attention to Muslim women, however, neither exhausts the political mandate of my interviewees nor absorbs all their energies. The fact of using their Muslim identity to empower a particularly disadvantaged group of women does not prevent them from taking a position on a wide variety of issues that are not necessarily related to Islam, both at a local, national and international level. Far from threatening the liberal democratic fabric of Western contexts, the different ways in which these women act in the political sphere represent an insightful response to the new challenges posed by cultural and religious pluralism. They are, at the same time, the measure and the source of a significant political change.

3.d.   *Judging the political system by living multiculturalism from within*

Secularism, equality, justice, and freedom of expression are the principles that all the interviewees support. Some identify them as pillars of multiculturalism while others are of a more integrationist platform. In general, multiculturalism is presented as a good political strategy for tackling pluralism: it establishes the superiority of the British system in comparison with other European approaches.

i.   Multiculturalism as synonymous with ghettoisation

There was only one woman who expressed an overall dissatisfaction with multiculturalism and multifaithism (Patel 2010, 2011). During the meeting, Baroness Falkner criticised the UK response to cultural and religious differences accusing it of ghettoising people instead of encouraging them to abide by the cultural laws available. According to her, young British Muslim women have plenty of opportunities to exercise their rights and freedoms: they have good education, good access to information, and they know what equality means. Instead of giving up their independent thought and claiming a regressive Muslim identity, they should defend their freedom of choice against the oppressive and manipulative dynamics within their faith communities. Multicultural policies are creating a silo and diverting attention from education and employment, the real issues that prevent Muslim women's emancipation. Multiculturalism also stumbles on the issue of legitimate representation: the lack of representativeness of so-called community leaders, a phenomenon that is common in Islam, impinges on the government that, failing to acknowledge the differences that inhabit faith groups, ends up ignoring internal dissenting voices. For this reason, according to Baroness Falkner, the Western liberal modes of election should be given priority to groups that present themselves as credible interlocutors. However, she appreciated certain Labour measures that facilitated the liberation of Muslim women from cultural and religious dictates and protect them from physical violence, emotional blackmail and unwanted marriages, such as the Forced Marriage Unit and the age restrictions (twenty-one years of age) for marrying a foreign citizen.[11] The growing visibility of Muslim women in the political sphere is not a sign, according to Baroness Falkner, of the success of multiculturalism in achieving integration. Apart from those appointed, the majority of women were elected in deprived areas where Muslims and other minorities make up a majority. The only exception in such a panorama is Sayeeda Warsi, Cabinet Minister and Conservative Party Chairman:

> She came from a modest background, in a ghettoised town, she went to a modest university, she got a modest degree, she wasn't part of the elite in any sense, yet she decided that she was ideologically a conservative; she talked the talk, she walked the walk in a party that had never seen someone like her. And she is in cabinet: it's quite remarkable. (Falkner 2010)

ii.   The strength of multiculturalism
A different position is expressed by other interviewees who regard multiculturalism as a culture of equality and of anti-racism that allows people to be accepted for who they are. In this sense, the growing visibility of Muslim women in the political sphere is seen as the natural outcome of the multicultural idea that people's cultural, religious and ethnic background deserves respect and should not remain hidden. Multiculturalism builds on the struggles of anti-racist movements, community activism and also the Labour Party's commitment to justice. In this sense, it neither creates ghettoisation nor terrorism. The latter depends on a detrimental foreign policy (war in Iraq and invasion of Afghanistan) and on the failure of the Western model of economic development that has broadened the gulf between a small wealthy elite and the vast majority of poor people (Salma Yaqoob). 'Communities', Haleh Afshar says

> live together, not only because of creed, but also because of class. Whatever you do, you're going to have the Irish going to the same pubs: it's what people do and that for me is fine. Provided that communities are permeable, provided that people from one community don't fear going into another, it's OK. So, you need an acceptance that clustering together could also be empowering as well as useful as in the case of newcomers. (Afshar 2010)

iii.   Multiculturalism between theory and practice
While appreciating multiculturalism, women are nonetheless aware of weaknesses that stem from specific governments' attitudes. Despite the great expectations of the years between 1997 and 2001, the era of New Labour, in 2001 the situation changed dramatically. For the first time the Muslim

community was regarded as a threatening presence and therefore made the target of a series of initiatives tackling extremism and terrorism: especially after 7/7, the Prevent Violent Extremism Agenda (PVE), and the Cohesion Agenda (Cantle 2008) saw the active involvement of Muslim communities as pivotal to the eradication of extremism. According to them, however, after 9/11 multiculturalism became a security agenda for tackling the problematic presence of Muslims in the UK: focusing on Muslims and blaming them for the bombing attacks worked as a diversion for the government to avoid its responsibilities both in domestic and foreign policy. Although the kind of identity asserted by the Muslim community in response to the growing attacks was quite aggressive, it is nonetheless presented as an important step towards becoming aware, for the first time, of being on a par within British society. Many expressed a sincere appreciation for the capacity of the host community to accept this new Muslim visibility. The recognition accorded to cultural and religious identities has nurtured a climate of respect and peaceful accommodation of differences that makes Britain a better environment compared to other European countries. The fact that the government embraced a more assimilationist approach does not deny the positivity of the multicultural project per se: reframing certain practices, therefore, is crucial to restoring the multicultural vocation to justice and equality (Parekh 2000; Eade 2008). In this sense the Cohesion Agenda promoted under the Labour government is criticised 'because cohesion is "like me, the English person"' says Haleh Afshar,

> but we don't want to be like you; and you're lucky for that because you eat a lot better than before, you have a huge variety of festivals. We enrich society by bringing in differences. Celebrate that! You know? Curry and chips has become the standard eating in Yorkshire. But if Community Cohesion means that all of us have to change colour, creed, practices to become like the British, then there's no room for London. How to explain London? It is vibrant, diverse, all kind of religions, languages, foods. This is what multiculturalism should be. (Afshar 2010)

Another criticism concerns the way the Labour government engaged with Muslim groups: it strengthened the worst forms of patriarchy by giving power to men who by being connected to large families could deliver the block vote. Moreover, very often these men did not speak English well and used emotional blackmail to orient the electorate's preferences. This practice, therefore, disenfranchises young people and women within communities because it relies on keeping people uneducated. As Salma Yaqoob points out, this is the antithesis of what multiculturalism should aim at, namely fighting communal politics. Pola Uddin denounces the lack of willingness by the Labour government to listen to the voices of minority women. These have often been exploited to serve a different agenda, well illustrated by the PVE or by the Forced Marriage

Unit. While the former shows the instrumental role assigned to Muslim women as pivotal agents in eradicating terrorism within their communities, the latter, by focusing exclusively on violence rather than on education and employment, reveals the government's failure to remove the real obstacles that hamper the participation of Muslim women in British society. Despite this, all the interviewees appreciate the results achieved and look with great expectation at the growing presence of Muslim women in the political sphere. Although the risk of becoming a token is real, 'if you have an opportunity don't care what they call it, take it and run with it and make it happen', says Haleh Afshar who provocatively continues: 'I'm a token? OK, fine, I get on with it. If tokenism is empowering, then I'm all for it!'. The possibility of changing the political system and of setting multiculturalism on a different course against an assimilationist backlash also depends on these women's capacity to transform their visibility into effective courses of actions. In this sense, the fact that the Prime Minister, David Cameron, has made Sayeeda Warsi so public in the newly elected executive is generally seen as a positive sign in the direction indicated above.

3.e.   The potential of Muslim women's activism

When trying to make sense of the advantages of having Muslim women nominated or elected in politics, different levels of discourse emerge. The first merit is at the community level: all my interviewees speak of the harsh battle that they fight against male leaders who still regard women's activism as inconvenient. By using their power, they are changing traditional patriarchal attitudes like being allowed to speak after Friday prayer in the mosque, a place usually forbidden to women (Salma Yaqoob), or obtaining the building of a place of worship for women. Although it will take time to erode ancient patriarchal attitudes, things are changing and women are increasingly accepted as legitimate and respectable interlocutors. Moreover, a Muslim woman politician can be a point of reference for all those women who need support but who, for a variety of reasons (language, cultural taboos, etc.) remain hidden. Knowing the Muslim community, she can ensure that relevant issues are communicated centrally and therefore included in the government agenda. All the interviewees are aware of the importance of being a role model: by looking at their example, other women can find the motivation and self-confidence necessary to fill the gap and gain access to the political system. Their political involvement has positive effects also on broader society. More visibility helps break the stereotypes of the Muslim terrorist, unreliable and threatening. Their involvement in national parties and their ideas of universal justice and equality reassure the public about the respect and defence of common values. At the same time, by bringing their cultural, ethnic and religious differences they make people more aware and familiar with the internal pluralism of the country. By engendering a virtuous circle that works both ways, the acceptance of differences at the grassroots level also makes their acceptance in the political system more likely: this, in turn, can legitimise the recognition of those differences and further contribute to making them a normal component of the socio-political fabric of the UK.

3.f. Winds of change

In contrast with widespread stereotypes, the women who have been appointed or elected come with a huge variety of experiences and ways of expressing their Muslim identity. This, in particular, is always one part (more or less relevant) of their overall identity in which cultural and religious backgrounds always interact with national belonging, commitment to liberal principles, to human rights and women's equality. In other words, they are not enclosed in silos imbued with tradition; rather, they are deeply engrained in the British context and are proud of being active citizens of that country. After all, 'the Muslims are the most British that you get: fans of *EastEnders*, *X Factor*, fish and chips, black beans . . . there is actually more than we can realise' (Yasmin Qureshi[12]). The growing presence of Muslim women in politics, then, reflects a vibrant pluralism where the interaction of differences is so much more natural and ordinary than is normally portrayed by the media and by certain political forces. Their presence and activity represent an opportunity for liberal democracies to overcome certain resistances and to find new balances for accommodating cultural and religious pluralism. Far from throwing Western political systems into the tangle of communal politics, they show a universalist commitment to equality and justice. By raising issues that are controversial both within the Muslim community (promoting different images of Muslim women, defending the rights of gay and lesbian people, defending the choice of abortion, denouncing pedophilia within mosques, etc.) and within the overall society (attacking the internal, economic and foreign policy of the government, tokenism by political parties) they fight 'dirty politics': 'Isn't it ironical? Politics is usually short-term, with numbers, elections, so it would be easier to foment hate, division, being cynical, prejudiced. It would be easier' (Salma Yaqoob). They work, instead, to build trust and cohesion both within and between communities. It is a long-term strategy that is based on a systematic approach. Changing political attitudes is a fundamental prerequisite to overcoming injustice and to achieving an effective equality. If Parliament is going to represent the composition of the country, the fact that a growing number of Muslim women have recently entered it is a positive sign that reflects the dynamics under way and for this reason is more likely to nurture a healthy pluralism.

4. Italy

4.a. *The beginning of a phenomenon*

Although in Italy the interviews were limited in number (three) compared to the UK, since very few Muslim women have gained access to the political realm so far, those encountered represent nonetheless a heterogeneous and interesting panorama.[13] Among these women Suad Sbai,[14] a politician of Moroccan origin, is the only one who serves in the Chamber of Deputies. More specifically, she was part of the Berlusconi-led coalition government, Popolo della Libertà (PDL). Aisha Mesrar,[15] originally from Morocco, became town councillor in Rovereto (Trentino Alto Adige) within the Partito Democratico's list (PD) during the last local elections (May 2010). Although Maymuna Abdel Qader,[16] of Jordanian origin, participated in the same elections as a candidate of 'Sinistra, Ecologia e Libertà' (a left-wing party led by Niki Vendola) in Perugia (Umbria), she was not elected. Like Maymuna, Rasha Rashea El Nakhouri is a young Muslim woman who has tried, unsuccessfully, to pass the last town election in Milan with Radicali Italiani. Even though I was unable to interview Rasha, I have used some of her articles and videos available on the Internet to give further depth to the experiences of female Muslim activists in Italy. Many of them did not express a rooted sense of political affiliation; they rather pointed out the main limits of the country's party system with specific reference to Muslims. Especially those who were not elected did not exclude the possibility of passing to the opposite political faction, generally from left-to right-wing formations, in order to find an effective space in which to express their ideas. The following paragraphs are an attempt at understanding the complexity of this 'primordial' scenario.

4.b. *Political identity and Muslim identity*

All the interviewees highlighted the private character of their Muslim identity. As in the UK, the arguments brought forward reflect an internal fluidity. Maymuna Abdel Qader, for instance, justified her political engagement as the natural outcome of her inner desire to participate and make a contribution to the town where she grew up. She entered politics as an Italian citizen, Perugian, who wanted to do good for the community at large, 'and religion does not stop you caring about health, education, the environment'. Interestingly, she defined her inner religiosity as not entirely detached from her political commitment:

> I don't need to specify my religion because I manifest it through my behaviour. Exactly in this way I show that Muslims are good, that they have principles. I wanted to show my Muslimness in order to counter the widespread stereotype of the Muslim as terrorist. I wanted to demonstrate, without stressing my religious belong-

ing too much, that in politics Muslims can make a difference and make a substantial contribution. (Abdel Qader 2010)

If Maymuna refrains from using her identity in an assertive way, she is also careful not to neglect her religion or those in the Muslim community who supported her political adventure. Also for Aisha Mesrar politics present a fundamental chance to make a contribution to the town where she has lived for a large part of her life (twenty years) and to her fellow citizens. Her political activity, as she explains, crosses all issues and all communities. In this sense, her visible Muslim identity neither makes her the champion of immigrants' rights nor the natural representative of Muslim women in the town council. While she does not publicly identify herself in religious terms, and acts in the political sphere as an Italian citizen, people outside do not seem to miss the opportunity of making her feel different, of continually labeling her as nothing more than 'a Muslim woman'. In opposing their attempts at tailoring narrow and artificial definitions, Aisha describes her natural and spontaneous way of living her religious identity.

The ascribed nature of the label 'Muslim' is denounced also by Suad Sbai who laments the fact that only Muslim women are asked about their religious identity. Manifesting this unease, she repeated throughout the interview that she rather considers herself a free woman, a politician and a journalist: religion was the last of her preoccupations and did not play any role in her political career, where capacities and ideas were fundamental, instead. She presents herself as a laywoman who has never used her Muslim background as a strategic tool to obtain favours: 'the rights of equality are my only religion', she says. As a politician, Suad Sbai refuses to be associated with the Muslim community. According to her, the use and display of Muslim identity is a form of undue exploitation and self-limitation that runs counter to women and to freedom; it represents a step backwards with reference to the goals achieved, not only by Western women but also by a conspicuous part of Eastern ones as well. Compared to the UK, Muslim women politicians in Italy tend not to deliberately use their religious identity. They are less assertive in terms of making their Muslimness a privileged position that could enable the empowerment not only of Muslim women, but women and men in general.

4.c.   A free choice or a matter of coercion? The veil in the political debate

i.   A secular approach
Following the example of France and Belgium, the bill on the ban of the burqa and the *niqab* proposed by Suad Sbai has spurred the debate over the Islamic dress code in Italy as well. According to her, this initiative embodies a universal commitment to freedom and to the rights of women. The shift from the *hijab*

to the *niqab*, is a sign of the worrying advance of Islamic fundamentalism from North Africa. The advance of religious radicalism, in other words, explains the increasing number of women wearing the partial or full veil in the West. These women, for Suad, are exploited by Islamist leaders who try to gain access and take control of Western institutions, or are abused and coerced by their fathers, brothers and husbands. Drawing from the battles that secular women have fought in recent history in many North African countries, Suad associates women's liberation with the removal of the headscarf that for her represents a fundamental lack of freedom. Accordingly, wearing the veil in the West especially by Italian converts, is considered an identity pathology which has detrimental effects on all Muslim women. Those who are in the public eye, in particular, are accused of exploiting the veil to pursue agendas that often conceal men's interests: 'What is the difference', she asks 'between them and those who use their body to advance in their political career?'

The real battle, for Suad, does not revolve around the veil, but around rights and freedom: 'I don't want to fight for the veil, to show men that we are inferior! We have to use our faces, not our veils. I don't want to start my battle with the veil, because I'm free'. Hence, the battle for liberty cannot be fought with those who use and display their religious identity because they represent an opposing front with irreconcilable agendas and priorities. Finding common platforms is therefore a waste of time since the simple presence of visibly religious women slows the overall group down. In this sense, Sbai distinguishes between Muslim and Arab women to stress the gulf between the two categories: the growing visibility of veiled Muslim women means that the secular, 'moderate Muslim' is increasingly discriminated against in society. The question is then, whether wearing a headscarf actually prejudices a commitment to women's rights; whether using the veil means playing into the hands of Islamist and misogynist men, thus translating it at best into a form of adaptive preference or at worst into a deliberate plan to subvert the tenets of Western democracy.

ii. Ordinariness and potentials of the veil
Beyond this scenario that reflects Sbai's personal experience and the history of feminism in North Africa, the other interviewees interpreted the use of the veil in Western countries in different ways. The headscarf, according to them, can be a normal, ordinary expression of inner religious convictions. It can also have positive effects on different fronts: first, in the Muslim community, whose patriarchal attitudes are still an obstacle to the public presence of women; and second, in the wider society, whose prejudices against supposed female Muslim oppression are overwhelming. They condemn the political exploitation of the veil that conveys the idea of voiceless and subjugated women as if this were the norm in Muslim settings. The ordinariness of wearing the veil is deliberately ignored by some Italian politicians who prefer using certain Arab-Muslim

women to pursue their own agendas. Aisha Mesrar criticises the distorting voices that falsely depict Muslim contexts as supposedly inhabited by ghosts wearing the burqa. This kind of strategy, far from helping those women who really need support, creates and fuels an unrealistic scenario that prevents the objective analysis of what is actually happening and the distinction of effective problems from the natural and positive dynamics of integration that are already underway (Silvestri 2010a, 2010b). Irreducible to the experiences of North African, Middle and Far Eastern, and Asian countries, the use of the veil in the West is a complex phenomenon that stems from the unique encounter of different cultures and traditions. The case of second generation Muslim women is emblematic in this respect. Opposing the misuse of women's bodies lies at the core of Rasha Rashea el Nakouri's choice of wearing the *hijab*. The veil, in her case, is an important tool for challenging the Western myth of beauty and to reassert her unique and dissenting identity. The needs of a twenty-nine-year-old Italian woman of Egyptian origin, in other words, are very different from those of a Pakistani, Tunisian or Saudi Arabian one. The voices of these women could help the policy makers develop initiatives that are more effective because they would be attentive and related to the real dynamics underway. If this opportunity fails to be grasped, as they suggest, the pressure from Western societies not to veil risks threatening Muslim women's freedom as much as the imposition of it by their men.

4.d.   *Muslim women and the political agenda*

Acting for the general interest, and not only for one part, be it immigrants, the Muslim community or Muslim women, is a shared commitment among all the interviewees. Apart from issues like the elderly, unemployment, etc., they insist on the need to promote citizenship rights in order to avoid separated compartments that divide people along religious, gender, cultural and ethnic lines. 'Giving the entitlement to vote', explains Aisha, 'is the first step to become a full citizen and to feel a legitimate and active part of the wider society. Knowing that one is protected is important for taking a stand on different issues and making a contribution'. Each woman, however, gave a different interpretation of this universal commitment. Maymuna, for instance, often mentioned her willingness to give voice to the second generation and to young people: 'I really hoped to be elected because I have so many ideas; I wanted to represent the youth, the young person that could be multicultural, Italian, religiously different, differently able: different in all the existing meanings. I wanted to be an example'. Second generation is a relevant topic also for Aisha who has always worked in the field of immigration and participates in organisations that deal with Italian and foreign youth. Moreover, all of them expressed an interest in women's rights. In particular, they recognised the urgency of tackling certain issues that affect Muslim women, and that revolve mainly around domestic violence and other forms of discrimination.

Different and interesting visions emerged from Maymuna and Suad. The latter concentrates on supporting and rescuing especially Muslim women from violence and abuse suffered within families and communities. The former encourages and stimulates Muslim women to become an active part of society through their involvement at the local level. Suad Sbai describes second generation women as pivotal in the emancipation of Muslim women, in fighting the oppression of the veil and the power of radical and misogynist Islamist leaders. Supporting them is fundamental since 'they are living in hell in this country: they suffer from the first generation that does not accept their Western attitudes and from the wider social and political system that ignores them'. While for Sbai young Muslim women are crucial because they represent a breaking point from all those cultural and traditional ties that discriminate against women, for Maymuna the great potential of the second generation resides in their bridging role between different worlds: as such, they are in communication with the first generation and can help their emancipation. As a veiled Muslim, Maymuna presents herself as a modern Italian who has neither renounced her cultural and religious background, nor severed the dialogue with older people within the community. In her account, relationships between different generations end up being more fluid and changing than in Suad's picture. Maymuna focuses more on the ordinariness of being a young woman who practises and tries to balance, with all the related difficulties, her Muslim and Italian sense of belonging; Suad concentrates more on the anomaly of being a victim of violence enmeshed within hostile and misogynist communities. For Suad Sbai, working on rights and equality helps uncover the abuses and the aberrations that Muslim women suffer; for Maymuna it helps uncover the positive dynamics that are underway, and to take advantage of the potential embodied in young Muslims. Through their energy and strategic positioning they can be a cohesive force that helps overcome the barriers and prejudices separating people along cultural, ethnic, gender and religious lines. They can favour, in other words, a virtuous circle of mutual dialogue and respect. Beyond the differences, all my interviewees agree that a Muslim woman should be more than a victim of violence, and a housewife 'who cooks chicken': Muslim women should be supported but, at the same time, they must help themselves in order to make sense of their own lives according to their specific character and aspirations.

4.e. Limits and potentialities of the Italian political system

The fact that Suad, Aisha and Maymuna stood for different parties is a useful lens for obtaining a wider picture of the Italian political system and for identifying its limits and potentialities.

i. A Muslim voice from the centre-right

Among the interviewees Suad is the only one who has a long history of
political militancy: having started as a socialist in Morocco, she has found the
space to carry forward her personal battles in Gianfranco Fini led Alleanza
Nazionale. This shift, as she explained, was motivated by the fact that while
the left has constantly stressed her ethnic and religious background, her party
colleagues have always treated her as an equal, as a normal person. The left
in general, according to Suad, is guilty of laxity and is affected by a fear of
criticising different cultures. Worried of being accused of racism, the left
condones abhorrent practices against women that take place within minorities. Harsh is also her critique against the PD's choice to appoint Khaled
Chouki (the former president of GMI: Giovani Musulmani d'Italia, Young
Italian Muslims) as president of the Young Democrats. A tokenistic choice,
as she calls it, that should offend the intelligence and competences of many
worthy young Italians who are militant within the PD. Throughout the interview, however, the picture of the right wing coalition does not emerge as a
harmonious one either and is characterised by divergent positions. Spurred
by my questions, Sbai expressed her disappointment toward a certain part
of the Northern League and against Daniela Santanchè, whose recent comments on Muslims (Muhammad as a paedophile) reveal, according to her,
ignorance, imprudence and political shortsightedness. What Sbai accuses
Italian women politicians of, across all parties, is the inability to converge
and create a lobby that can challenge men's power: that the problem resides
in their frivolity (more interested in fashion and cosmetic surgery than in politics) or in their subservience to the Church (referring mainly to PD's women,
described as 'resembling nuns'), they de facto remain unable to break isolation. For Sbai, this phenomenon is particularly detrimental, considering the
advance of fundamentalism that requires standing as a united front, especially
by women.

ii. The critical stance of Aisha and Maymuna

Before being co-opted by the PD for the 2010 elections in the municipality of Rovereto, Aisha Mesrar was an activist in civil society working in the
field of immigration for public institutions and for various organisations.
After her initial uncertainty due to the risk of becoming a token Muslim, she
finally decided to make a more significant contribution to her city. Although
exploiting Muslims is a widespread attitude that crosses all political forces,
she accuses the right of using only those voices that are instrumental to con-
solidating a logic of fear. Instead of taking 9/11 as an opportunity to conduct
a serious analysis of what is actually going on within Italian society and of the
reasons that caused that event, the government seems to have taken revenge on
Muslims by engaging personalities that tend to overemphasise the most negative aspects related to Muslim culture. According to Aisha, this approach is

at the base of immigrants' disillusionment and dissatisfaction toward politics. Only by giving them rights can a sincere willingness to participate and make a contribution be triggered.

Also Maymuna shares the idea that enfranchising immigrants is a fundamental precondition to making them part of the country. Maymuna's perspective is of particular interest for a number of reasons: her disillusionment toward politics is emblematic of Italian youth in general, and in this sense it proves that the second generation is already part of the fabric of society. On the other hand, when she says that she does not follow any specific political ideology since her priority is working in the interest of her city and fellow citizens, she reveals a desire to open up new forms of political activism, be it the creation of a civic list or a cross-party group that works on common ideas. This manifests an urgency to overcome the structures of a political system that is stuck in the dichotomy of right/left and that is unable to express the attitudes and new ideas of young people. According to Maymuna, the problem is that Italian politics is not ready to recognise the existence of differences. Far from nurturing victimhood, she does not exempt the Muslim community from criticism either. In particular, she points to the difficulty of finding a form of representation that gathers all Muslims and that could facilitate dialogue with the government. Older men, who created the first organisations, tend to maintain their power and to exclude those coming from different Muslim countries and cultures. After all, as Maymuna points out 'Islam is one but Muslims are many and all different'. This is a relevant obstacle that makes it very difficult for the government to find legitimate interlocutors. While a credible Muslim voice is still lacking, the second generation is testing new pathways for overcoming internal ethnic, geographical and cultural gulfs. The experience of GMI is emblematic in this respect because its members are working on the common denominator of being all young Italians. In this sense, they can represent a pioneering model of representation that the government could (and should) look at.

iii. *What ways forward?*

Asked about a possible Italian way of coping with cultural and religious differences, almost all women showed an initial skepticism toward multiculturalism, regarded as synonymous with ghettoisation and a potential source of further racism. However, when explained in more detail through concrete examples drawn from the UK, they generally ended up admitting that Italy is lagging behind and is still delving confusingly into its own history and culture. Their skepticism, in other words, reflects more a lack of familiarity with the multicultural language than a deep knowledge of it. Suad was the only interviewee who explicitly rejected the multicultural credo, opting for an integrationist paradigm. All of them, however, tended to favour a model based on individual rather than collective rights. Where integration is the best solution for Suad, Aisha, however, expressed her concerns toward a concept that implies assimilation and homogenisation. She rather promotes a model of 'civil coexistence' where every person represents herself. By and large, their fluctuation between the refusal of multicultural measures and assimilationist policies reflects the specificity of the Italian system: the fact of not yet having developed a specific model makes it also potentially more malleable because it is less burdened by ideological assumptions.

4.f.   Muslim women in politics: a glimmer of hope?

i.   Overcoming the traditional political chaste

The first aspect that stands out when trying to draw a picture of Muslim women's political activism in Italy is that it is still at a very early stage. All the limits that have been highlighted throughout this chapter contribute to relegating Muslim women's presence to a niche phenomenon. At an embryonic level, however, it is producing effects that could become relevant in the near future. First of all, the growing activism, especially of young people, could trigger a new interest in politics by Italian youth thus challenging widespread sentiments of disillusionment and dissatisfaction. Embodied by new generations, this visibility can also erode the idea, which is deeply rooted in Italy, that politics is the prerogative of old men. The fact that women stand for election makes a huge impact in that it introduces a female presence into a traditionally male bastion. In this regard, the crucial question is whether the presence of women will make gender equality more relevant in a political setting that at the moment is not exactly renowned for its gender-sensitive orientation.

ii.   Renewing the feminist debate

Moreover, Muslim women's activism could represent a catalyst for renewing the debate on the role of Italian feminism as a whole and, in this case, could open up new pathways for women's emancipation. The willingness expressed by the interviewees to overcome cultural, religious and ethnic differences and to find common denominators for working together may prove to be a more effective strategy for achieving unity among women than feminism. At another level, the recognition and legitimisation of Muslim women in politics represents a precious tool for empowering them within their own communities, thus hindering patriarchal and misogynist attitudes that are still influential. Here, women are already negotiating their role with their partners and the image of the man as being 'waited on hand and foot' is significantly on the decline. Looking at them as role models, then, other Muslim women can find the courage to emerge and to turn a disadvantaged position into a platform for pursuing their rights and expressing their skills and capacities. They drive forward, in other words, a virtuous circle that gradually redresses unequal power relations and can lead to new forms of representation that are more gender-sensitive and democratic.

iii.   *Toward a more inclusive concept of citizenship*

If the system opens up to them, Muslims can feel part of the country and therefore more relaxed and favourably disposed. If the highly polarised tones of the debate are turned down, they may develop a peaceful self-confidence, which is able to transform a reactive and defensive identity into a dialogical and proactive one. This shift would also be fundamental for the government so as to set up a model that accommodates cultural and religious differences and which proves to be effective because it is non-ideological. Far from adopting the strategy of the 'securitisation of Islam', politics should listen to the emerging voices of Muslim women because they embody a fundamental pass key to a reality that, despite widespread assumptions, is already an active part of Western settings.

4.g.   *Multicultural pathways*

i.   *Bargaining with the context: the advantages of a flexible approach*

Having acknowledged that listening to Muslim women's voices is the most viable recipe for tackling issues related to cultural and religious pluralism in an effective way, this section explores some indicative pathways that could be politically useful. As mentioned above, these are only a few ideas that do not claim to be exhaustive in any way. Above all, although these refer to forms of group representation, they must not be thought of as an alternative to the traditional mechanisms of democratic representation but rather as an integration of them. In other words, they do not discard the fundamental role of the individual but are intended as a further implementation of the individual's rights and equality. The balance between these measures always relies on a process of compromise and bargain that draws from each specific context and cannot be decided a priori and once and for all. The first reflection, then, draws from the murder of two young women, Hina Saleem (Pakistani origin) and Sanaa Dafani (Moroccan origin), respectively in 2006 and 2009 by their fathers. These events focused attention on honour killings, a phenomenon that Italy thought had been definitively abandoned decades ago. Public and political debates focused on attacking the Muslim community, which they depicted as misogynous and backward. Ideological and confrontational tones, in other words, were overwhelming and prevented any objective analysis of the problem and thereby the discovery of effective measures to deal with it. As in the UK with the Forced Marriage Unit, the creation by the government of an analogous ad hoc group to study and elaborate solutions to tackle honour killing would have been a significant step forward in the pursuit of gender equality and women's rights. This working group would have comprised minority women and Muslim women, who are already active within civil society in particular, since the incidence of honour killing seems more rooted in Muslim contexts. These women, in fact, have a wider knowledge of the situation within their community and know what tools are best to eradicate this practice. While helping the government to address the problem more effectively, the active involvement of Muslim women would make them credible voices thus empowering them from within their communities. This would lead to the gradual but inescapable erosion of patriarchal powers. In turn, the engagement of Muslim women would make them more aware of their role in improving the situation inside Muslim settings and in bridging different realities together. The main outcome of such a move would be that the implementation of equality and justice would go hand in hand with a focus on the gender dimension that at this particular moment in Italian history should not be underestimated.

ii.   What role for the government? When politics faces Muslim women's activism

At another level of analysis, the government could support the setting up of local focus groups around the country in which Muslim women can speak of their difficulties and suggest possible solutions. The creation and coordination of such groups would involve Muslim women who are already active at the grassroots level and are therefore facilitated in gaining access to minority women. Despite Suad Sbai's criticism, in fact, in Italy there are many Muslim women's organisations: the government should look at local efforts and initiate a direct line of communication with them based on a series of constant consultations and dialogue-oriented initiatives, in order to get to know the real situation and problems. The outcome of the focus groups could be gathered into specific studies and be used as a frame of reference for policymaking.[17] As already mentioned, it would not be a top-down and artificial action by the government, but would only require support for something that already exists but that still faces severe difficulties in being heard. These kinds of measures have the merit of stimulating dynamics of active participation, thus nurturing and strengthening the democratic fabric of society.

Another initiative that could be beneficial is the re-establishment of the National Commission for Equal Opportunities (CNPO). This, in particular, could address issues and problems concerning minority women, and Muslim women in particular, more thoroughly. Joint committees and round tables where associations and NGOs participate and give their contributions would be important tools to be employed and implemented. This would also contribute to re-establishing gender mainstreaming at the centre of the government agenda after a prolonged break.[18]

iii.   Recognising pluralism

As mentioned at the beginning of this section, these forms of representation must be considered neither exclusive nor fixed, but rather as a malleable and fluid tool that works as an expansion and strengthening of democracy. This goal can be fulfilled by triggering internal dynamism and the processes of political representation within minority communities by empowering so-called minorities within minorities, first and foremost women. At a time of growing xenophobic and anti-Islamic sentiments such a dialogue and active engagement could be a fundamental antidote to self-enclosure and radicalisation. Having said that, however, the first step to be made remains modification of the current law on citizenship to enfranchise those people who, despite already playing an active part in Italian society, are still not considered Italian citizens.

5.   Conclusion

5.a.   *The British case: a promising kind of multiculturalism?*

In the UK the growing participation of Muslim women within the political system is representative of its multicultural tradition. The variety of their positions reflects a vibrant climate where different religious and cultural identities interact quite naturally within the public sphere. Although their relationship with the political realm is not always a harmonious one, the dialogue is nonetheless established and ongoing. The fact that Muslim women have been elected or appointed manifests the relative flexibility of a political system that despite all its limitations recognises differences. Thanks to their example, Muslim women promote an idea of multiculturalism that counters the accusations of reinforcing minorities' ghettoisation and radicalisation. Drawing from their voices, it emerges that they successfully use and combine different languages: that of human rights, of anti-racism, of feminism, and of religion as well. The content they introduce to the political debate, although challenging, is not contrary to the tenets of Western political theory; quite the opposite, they are gradually reshaping certain categories and concrete approaches that are no longer adequate, in their traditional formulation, for confronting contemporary scenarios. Whether their visibility translates into effectiveness will depend on the interplay of many factors that operate at the national and the international level, most obvious of which being the global economic recession and the growth of right-wing, xenophobic and nationalist parties that are fuelling an assimilationist reassertion throughout Europe. Beyond these risks, the kind of multiculturalism that British Muslim women are supporting represents a way of tackling contemporary pluralism that is more promising than the strategies experimented with so far at least in terms of allowing recognition and participation to members of minorities. Certain versions of multiculturalism, in other words, seem more adequate than assimilation and integration in assuring equality within Western political systems.

5.b.   *Italy: present situation and future developments*

As far as Italy is concerned, the low number of Muslim women politicians reveals the emergence of a phenomenon that is quite recent. That their silent but nonetheless growing political engagement is a result of the anti-Muslim sentiments that inhabit the Italian public and political spheres, or of the fact that the country is relatively new to the Muslim presence, is not preventing these voices from opening an important debate on the accommodation of cultural and religious differences. Instead of adopting apocalyptic tones, it is more useful to look at the ways in which these women approach the political sphere. It emerges, in fact, that far from promoting religious radicalism and anti-democratic values, they subscribe to the tenets of Western political thought, namely individual rights, secularism, equality and justice. They know and appreciate Italian culture and abide by the constitution. In their political activity, they do not live out their Muslim identity as assertively as British Muslims do. Except for Suad Sbai, they are generally approaching a world that is still unfamiliar to them, for the first time. For this reason, they move with caution and gauge the activities within politics and the reactions of politicians. If the Italian political system engages with them in a non-prejudiced way, Muslim women can make an important contribution on various fronts. If, on the other hand, it embraces an ideological attitude, closure and reciprocal hostility will be the natural outcome and Italy, at large, will pay the price of a division that perpetuates inequality and injustice. This preliminary moment, in which the two parts get to know each other, is fundamental to the future because it will either orientate the political course towards a collaborative or towards an antagonistic coexistence.

Notes

1. The term Muslim, in this expression, refers to women's awareness of being at the crossroads of different and even conflicting definitions. While in other contexts, I have deliberately used the expression 'Muslim women', here I rather prefer speaking of women from Muslim backgrounds. The former, in fact, highlights the decision of assuming publicly their religious identification whilst the latter does not necessarily imply this deliberate stance. By and large, as will emerge throughout the chapter, their faith may become, but not necessarily, a political move at a time when the label 'Muslim' assumes a negative connotation. For the purposes of my research, I decided to leave out the distinction between the different strands of Islam that these women follow. It would be interesting, however, to analyse how those same differences influence their activism.

2. Although in this chapter I cannot deepen certain aspects related to the choice of adopting a feminist perspective, I just refer to the fundamental role of reflexivity and of the related categories of positionality and power as well as the ethical concerns implied in the research process. These are all aspects that I have taken into due consideration in my PhD dissertation of which this chapter is a part. Sandra Harding, 'Introduction: Is There a Feminist Method?', in S. Harding (ed.), *Feminism and Methodology: Social Science Issues*, Indiana University Press, Bloomington 1987; D. Haraway, *Simians, Cyborgs, and Women*, Routledge, New York, 1991, but also C. Sandoval, 'U.S. Third Feminism: The Theory and Method of Oppositional Consciousness in the Postmodern World', *Genders* 10: 2–24; see also P. Hill Collins, *Black Feminist Thought: Knowledge, Consciousness, and the Politics of Empowerment*, Routledge, New York, 2000; S. Gorelick, 'Contradictions of Feminist Methodology', *Gender & Society*, vol.5, no. 4, 1991; M. M. Fonow and J. A. Cook (eds), *Beyond Methodology. Feminist Scholarship as Lived Research*, Indiana University Press, Bloomington and Indianapolis, 1991, p. 142; A. Coffey, 'Ethnography and Self: Reflections and Representations', in T. May (ed.), *Qualitative Research in Action*, Sage Publications, London, 2002, pp. 327–8; L. Haney, 'Negotiating Power and Expertise in the Field', in T. May (ed.), *Qualitative Research in Action*, cit., pp. 286–99.
3. The interviews were conducted mostly in 2010.
4. In Italy interviews were conducted between 2010 and 2011.
5. Since Haleh Afshar has been my PhD co-supervisor and I have spent two visiting periods at the University of York, where she teaches, I have had the chance of speaking to her several times (between 2009 and 2011) both in York and in London, at the House of Lords, where she has been nominated Baroness.
6. The meeting with Pola Uddin was held in London, at a women's centre in Whitechapel in October 2010.
7. The meeting was held in London, in a cafeteria at the House of Lords in November 2010. Since Baroness Falkner works with Haleh Afshar in the Lords, it was quite easy to contact her, and she accorded the interview in a very short time. During our encounter, she spoke quietly and clearly so that I could follow her arguments without problems. Although she expressed a different position to the majority of other women, the atmosphere was very familiar and she listened carefully to my arguments.
8. A variety of head-dresses worn by Muslim women and girls in accordance with *hijab* (the principle of dressing modestly) are sometimes referred to as veils. Many of these garments cover the hair, ears and throat, but do not cover the face. The *khimar* is a type of headscarf. The *niqab* and *burqa* (Afghanistan) are two kinds of veils that cover most of the face except for a slit or hole for the eyes. When I use the term 'headscarf', I refer to the piece of clothing that covers only a woman's head.
9. I was invited to Salma Yaqoob's home outside Birmingham to conduct the interview: it was November 2010. I spoke to Salma and Rana Naseer on the same occasion and the meeting was one of the friendliest ever. The warm attitudes and body

language (hugs and kisses) that especially Rana employed, made me feel at ease and transformed the interview into a long, free and informal chat. This behaviour is representative of a different idea of politics that the Respect party claims and promotes, based on face-to-face interactions and on building trust through solidarity and empathy.

10. After having tried to contact her several times, we fixed a meeting (October 2010) at the Global Peace and Unity Event, an annual two-day conference held at the ExCeL Exhibition Centre in Royal Victoria Dock, London, organised by the Islam Channel, where she was exhibiting her art.

11. This law was struck down by the Supreme Court last year (2011).

12. The interview took place in the House of Common in October 2010.

13. The interview with Aisha Mesrar (in Rovereto) and Maymuna Abdel Qader (in Perugia) took place in December and November 2010 respectively. I met Suad Sbai (in Rome) in September 2011.

14. The meeting took place on 16 October 2011 in Montecitorio, where the Italian Chamber of Deputes is based, in Rome.

15. I interviewed Aisha in Rovereto in December 2010. She is the first Muslim woman to be elected in Trentino Alto Adige.

16. We met in Perugia and had a long and confidential chat in a cafe.

17. As in the case of the booklet *She Who Disputes,* cit., in the UK.

18. The Commission was abolished in 2003 by Stefania Prestigiacomo, minister of the Berlusconi-led coalition.

References

Afshar, Haleh, R. Aitken and M. Franks (2005), 'Feminisms, Islamophobia and Identities', *Political Studies,* vol. 53, pp. 262–83.

Allievi, S. (2010), 'Multiculturalism in Italy: the Missing Model', in A. Silj (ed.), *European Multiculturalism Revisited*, London: Zed Books, pp. 147–80.

Bullock, C. (2002), *Rethinking Muslim women and the veil: challenging historical & modern stereotypes,* Richmond: The International Institute of Islamic Thought.

Cantle, T. (2008), *Community Cohesion. A New Framework for Race and Diversity*, Basingstoke: Palgrave Macmillan.

Coffey, A. 'Ethnography and Self: Reflections and Representations', in Tim May (ed.), *Qualitative Research in Action*, London: Sage Publications, 2002.

Eade, J., M. Barrett, C. Flood and R. Race (eds) (2008), *Advancing Multiculturalism, Post 7/7*, Newcastle: Cambridge Scholars Publishers.

Fonow, M. M. and J. A. Cook (eds), *Beyond Methodology. Feminist Scholarship as Lived Research*, Bloomington and Indianapolis: Indiana University Press, 1991.

Gorelick, S., 'Contradictions of Feminist Methodology', *Gender & Society*, vol. 5, no. 4, 1991.

Haney, L., 'Negotiating Power and Expertise in the Field', in T. May (ed.), *Qualitative Research in Action*, cit., pp. 286–99.

Haraway, D. (1991), *Simians, Cyborgs, and Women*, New York: Routledge.

Harding, S. (ed.), *Feminism and Methodology: Social Science Issues*, Bloomington: Indiana University Press, 1987.

Hill, P. C. (2000), *Black Feminist Thought: Knowledge, Consciousness, and the Politics of Empowerment*, New York: Routledge.

May, T. (ed.), *Qualitative Research in Action*, London: Sage Publications, 2002.

Malik, M. (2010), 'Progressive Multiculturalism: the British Experience', in A. Silj (ed), *European Multiculturalism Revisited*, London: Zed Books, pp. 11–64.

Modood, T. (2006), 'British Muslims and the Politics of Multiculturalism', in T. Modood, A. Triadafyllidou and R. Zapata-Barrero, *Multiculturalism, Muslims and Citizenship. A European Approach*, London and New York: Routledge, pp. 37–56.

Parekh, B. (2006), *Rethinking Multiculturalism. Cultural Diversity and Political Theory*, London: Palgrave Macmillan.

Patel Pragna, 'Cohesion, Multi-Faithism and the Erosion of Secular Spaces in the UK: Implications for the human rights of minority women', in *The Struggle or Secularism in Europe and North America*, WLUM Dossier 30-1, July 2011, available at <http://www.wluml.org/sites/wluml.org/files/WLUML%20dossier%20 30-31%20v2.pdf> (last accessed October 2011), pp. 127–48.

Patel Pragna, 'From Multiculturalism to Multifaithism? A Panel Debate', *Studies in Ethnicity and Nationalism*, vol. 10, issue 2, pp. 310–14, October 2010.

Phillips, A. (2007), *Multiculturalism Without Culture*, Princeton and Oxford: Princeton University Press.

Runnymede Trust (2000), *The Future of Multi-Ethnic Britain. The Parekh Report*, London: Runnymede Trust.

Sandoval, C., 'U.S. Third Feminism: 'The Theory and Method of Oppositional Consciousness in the Postmodern World', *Genders* 10: 2–24.

Silvestri, S. (2010a), 'La questione del burqa in Europa', available at <http://www. ispionline.it/it/documents/Commentary_Silvestri_13.5.10.pdf> (last accessed November 2011).

Silvestri, S. (2010b), 'Europe's Muslims: burqa laws, women's lives', available at <http:// www.opendemocracy.net/sara-silvestri/french-burqa-and-%E2%80%9Cmuslim-integration%E2%80%9D-in-europe> (last accessed November 2011).

Triandafyllidou, A. (2006), 'Religious Diversity and Multiculturalism in Southern Europe: the Italian Mosque Debate', in T. Modood (ed.), cit., pp. 117–42.

Zanardo, L. (2010), *Il Corpo delle Donne*, Serie Bianca Feltrinelli.

Zincone, G. (1994), *Uno Schermo Contro il Razzismo*, Donzelli Editore, Rome.

10

REPRESENTING 'ISLAM OF THE *BANLIEUES*': CLASS AND POLITICAL PARTICIPATION AMONG MUSLIMS IN FRANCE

Z. Fareen Parvez

1. Introduction

The issue of the political representation of Maghrebi (North African) immigrants and their descendants in France, now redefined as a question of representation of Muslims, has been a long-standing debate in the French policy arena. The importance of representation in the French case is perhaps more heightened than in other EU countries because of France's particular model of secularism (*laïcité*) and statist political ideology. More so than other countries, the French state has raised numerous obstacles to Islamic practice, thus making political participation among Muslims a high-stakes endeavour. In order to make claims on the state and demand religious rights and recognition – in an era of anti-Islam discourse and in political and cultural fields that seek the elimination of religion from public space – French Muslims critically require means of political participation. But the question of who can represent the diversity of French Islamic practices and religious needs looms large, especially when the state demands Muslim interlocutors. It is commonly thought and argued that representation is difficult because Muslims in France are divided by ethnic background. While there are important ethnic differences among Algerians, Moroccans, Turks, and black Africans, I suggest that these are not nearly as salient as they are usually made out to be. For the younger generation of Muslims, they are even less consequential. The question of who represents the Muslim population is fraught not because of ethnic divisions but because of differences in political beliefs that stem largely from class location.

The research supporting the arguments in this chapter is based on participant observation among Muslim communities in the city of Lyon, France's third major metropolitan area. I argue in this chapter that Muslim class position and class relations are central to the dynamics of Islam and politics in France.

Political participation among Muslims varies by class location and for those in the working-class *banlieues* (suburbs, typically lower-class), participation is affected by the strength or weakness of their ties to the Muslim middle-class. As these ties have severely declined in the last decade, the Muslim political field is bifurcated by class and the urban-periphery divide. These divisions also underlie an increasing cultural separation between 'mainstream' Muslims and sectarian, Salafist Muslims in *les quartiers* (vulnerable neighbourhoods) who practise strict veiling and gender segregation.[1]

After presenting some relevant indicators and background on Maghrebis in France, I present first political participation among middle-class Muslims in Lyon. I show their predominant politics of recognition, or activities to support Muslim identity and claims of the state for religious rights and respect. This middle-class field, however, includes many activists and some associations that are critical of state control and of the marginalisation of an economic redistribution agenda. As a whole these associations are regretfully removed from Muslims and Salafist Muslims in the stigmatised urban periphery of Lyon. In the periphery Salafists in particular have not only withdrawn from state-directed politics but also from political participation as members of civil society. Further, their vulnerability and fears of state surveillance have blocked the mere recovery or building of Islamic civil societies. The precariousness of everyday life for working-class Salafist women and men has made collective projects and political participation an elusive desire and possibility. Neither their form of religious practice nor their daily economic concerns are represented by mainstream Islamic associations. Political participation among Muslims in France must therefore be considered not simply through the dominant frames of cultural identities or electoral possibilities but also through a lens of class variation and class relations.

2. From conflicted identities to political opportunities

The literature on Maghrebi political participation in France is vast, as it spans earlier studies conducted through the lens of immigrant incorporation (Noiriel 1996 [1988]; Sayad 1991; de Wenden 1988; Grillo 1985; Sayad 1984) to more recent work conducted through the lens of Islam. To a large extent this reflects transitions in French political discourse, which in the 1990s began to conflate immigrant dispossession, urban unrest, Islam, and terrorism (Noiriel 2007; Tissot 2006). In this respect the question of 'Muslim political participation' is new.

While there exist different approaches to Muslims and politics in France, two principle themes in the literature are cultural identity and political opportunity structures. The complex formation of identity among French Muslims is a long-standing and ubiquitous theme in the pursuit of understanding to what extent Muslims feel themselves to be citizens of the republic (Roy 2006,

2004). The assumption is that only when French Muslims identify as being French may they participate in politics, whether electoral or through civil society associations. In the quest for political 'integration' Muslims navigate multiple terrains of experience: their faith in Islam, their beliefs in republican values, the daily rejections they encounter, and their claims to French citizenship (Fernando 2010; Killian 2006). On the other hand, many argue that they cannot easily navigate such conflicted terrains. Feelings of alienation from both majority and minority (foreign) cultures and hence, inability to reconcile conflicting identities, leave some individuals susceptible to the appeal of radical versions of Islam and, ultimately, terrorism (Awan 2008; Kepel 2006 [2002]).

The second strain in the literature moves beyond explorations of Muslim subjectivities and looks instead at the political opportunities and obstacles in national political landscapes. Here *laïcité* and the formal refusal of ethnic categorisation in France in favour of minority assimilation define the political opportunities for minorities. Specifically, minority identity is an illegitimate basis for making claims on the state (Maxwell 2010; Peace 2008). This not only hinders Muslims from organising within French civil society but facilitates the claims of political neglect made by Muslim communities. Politicians can easily ignore them, especially when Muslims cannot legitimately form a voting bloc (Richard 1999, 2004).

In examining political opportunity structures and electoral politics in France, the conclusions about Muslim participation are somewhat unclear. While survey research shows that Maghrebi voter turnout is relatively lower, this is largely due to their living in the stigmatised and disadvantaged urban periphery – rather than due to socio-economic status or political attitudes per se (Maxwell 2010). While Muslims do indicate low levels of trust in France's political institutions, the rates are similar to non-Muslim working-class respondents (At Home in Europe Project 2011: 240). Because Maghrebis are more likely to live in *les quartiers sensibles* (officially designated 'sensitive neighbourhoods'), they are less likely to vote and thus, more at risk of being depoliticised by the system (Pan Ké Shon 2004).[2] According to a survey by the Open Society Institute, the voting gap between Maghrebis and non-Maghrebi citizens is more than 30%. Others have argued, in contrast, that immigrant associations of the 1990s led to significantly greater voter registration among Muslim youth, including those in the *banlieues* (Laurence and Vaisse 2006). Moreover, it is argued, French politicians imagine the existence of a 'Muslim vote' that both the UMP and Socialists pursue – despite the absence of such a vote in reality (Laurence and Vaisse 2006; Kelfaoui 1996).

In some cities, such as Marseille, the deception of *laïcité* is that there exists a politics of communal clientelism, whereby ethnic communities have been constructed for political and electoral purposes (At Home in Europe Project 2011: 228). Ethnic 'mediators' manage relations between Muslims and municipal administration (Moore 2004). Although this has not translated into systematised power for the city's Muslims, these are indicators that ethnic clientelism is becoming a national trend in France. The implications for Muslim political participation remain to be seen. Thus far, clientelism has had only a placating effect. According to one study of Lille:

> These [ethnic minority] groups . . . have failed to engage with the local authority since the 1980s. This has kept them in a double bind between clientelism and division and exclusion, giving them just enough resources to keep them contented and to preserve law and order, while consistently marginalising them from any real influence or visibility. On the surface, then, the local authority can conveniently ignore the issue of ethnic minorities. (Garbaye 2004: 48)

Above all, however, many Muslims are excluded from French electoral politics because of their status as foreigners. In the same Open Society Institute survey cited above, only 41% of Parisian Muslim respondents were eligible to vote (2010: 187). Clearly, the political opportunities to mobilise or vote along lines of religious identity are seriously restricted in France for various reasons.

The arguments I present in this chapter are informed by the central role of the state in shaping the political possibilities for Muslim minorities. However, I acknowledge the theoretical critiques of the political opportunity structures approach, namely the neglect of strategic decisions made by ethnic minority groups themselves. Bousetta (2000), for example, argues for the importance of examining 'infra-political mobilisation' – or, informal mobilisation within ethnic communities apart from the larger political system. While emphasising the centrality of the state, I present here the political and anti-political dynamics of Muslim communities, specifically in the city and periphery of Lyon. In doing so, this chapter contributes to the literature in two primary ways. First, it presents ethnographic research on Muslim worshippers, including poor and working-class women in *les quartiers*. Most of the literature on Muslims in France looks only at middle-class Maghrebi populations. Second, it shifts the focus away from questions of integration and identity and instead toward the role of the state and class position and class relations among Muslims. Political participation among Muslims in Lyon differs across class but is further complicated by important ideological divisions within the middle class that have largely to do with differing attitudes towards the state. The result is a hegemonic middle-class politics of recognition that is estranged from the religious practice and antipolitics of Salafist Muslims in Lyon's *banlieues*.

3. Integrating Maghrebis and institutionalising Islam

With its approximately six million Muslim citizens and migrants, France is home to the largest Muslim population in Europe. Yet France hinders Islamic

Table 10.1 Comparison of living conditions between Maghrebi and European immigrants

Living conditions	Region of origin	
	Maghreb	Europe
Residing in 'sensitive urban zones'	25%	6%
Residing in public housing with many immigrants*	19%	5%
Residing in 'uncomfortable lodging'†	42%	17%
Renting 'dilapidated housing'*	26%	10%
Below poverty line	43%‡	24%

Sources: Observatoire national des zones urbaines sensibles, Rapport (2011); INSEE, Jauneau and Vanovermeir (2008); INSEE, Lombardo and Pujol (2007); and Simon (1998).

Notes:
Figures for Turkish and sub-Saharan African immigrants are generally higher than for those of Maghrebi immigrants. None of these figures include the descendants of Maghrebi immigrants, though they appear to live in ZUS at roughly the same percentage
*   Includes only Algerian, Moroccan, Portuguese and Spanish immigrants.
†   Uncomfortable housing was defined either by overpopulation or by a number of indicators from plumbing and heating conditions to square footage.
‡   The 43% figure includes all African immigrants. The estimated probabilities of being poor for Maghrebis versus Black Africans are the same (Lombardo and Pujol 2007: 42–4).

practice to a much greater degree than its neighbours, Britain and Germany, despite high levels of Islamic organisation (Fetzer and Soper 2005: 90–2). Islam in France has gone through two distinct phases, according to Jonathan Laurence (2005). From the 1970s to 1989 there was minimal accommodation of Islamic practice. This was followed by a period, from 1990 to the 2004 creation of CFCM (Le Conseil Féderal du Culte Musulman), marked by government efforts to incorporate Muslims as a permanent part of the French political landscape.

As France reluctantly accepted the permanence of Islam and Muslim religious requirements, middle-class Muslim activists have had little choice but to expend their political effort in securing state recognition of Islam rather than anti-poverty or employment measures. This is despite disproportionate poverty and poor living conditions among Maghrebis. Housing segregation and unemployment have partly defined the trajectory of colonial and post-colonial immigrants in France, although the majority of Maghrebi immigrants and their descendants do not today live in precarious neighbourhoods. Table 10.1 summarises some of the salient features of the living conditions and poverty rate among Maghrebi immigrants, using figures for European immigrants as comparison.

Notwithstanding these figures of poverty and poor housing, there did develop an educated, French-Maghrebi middle class. However, middle-class activists and elites remained disconnected from those in the *banlieues* and especially from Islamic practice and Muslim community leaders (Geisser 1997: 151–63). Activists in *les quartiers* in turn have tended to view the few elites as 'Arabes de service' who are co-opted by political parties and legitimate the notion of an Islamist threat in the *banlieues*.[3]

Indeed, the history of French statism (*étatism*) reveals the tight control the state exerts over immigrants and their representation. The city and periphery of Lyon have been no strangers to such state control (Grillo 1985). The apex of state regulation was by many accounts the creation of CFCM, the culmination of fifteen years of political debate and consultation with Muslim leaders. The government had been seeking an official interlocutor for all Muslim communities, surely with the intention of controlling the future of Islam in France. But as then-Interior Minister Jean-Pierre Chevènement stated in 1997, it wanted an interlocutor that the majority of Muslims would consider legitimate (Billon 2005: 24). As it turned out, the state invited a handful of associations, necessarily excluding many individuals and places of worship (Kepel 2005). In my research, CFCM was commonly accused of not adequately representing French Muslims. Although its regional councils are active in securing religious recognition at the local level, the association is considered not only a weak appendage of the state but also disconnected from concerns among Muslims in the *banlieues*. Further, its original conception was precisely a depoliticised one, as CFCM was to be concerned only with matters of religious practice (Alaoui 2005).

Thus, for activists and those intensely critical of the state, CFCM is unable to represent their interests or economic concerns. For Muslims in the *quartiers* who practise Salafist Islam, the official representative of *le culte* (religion) is removed from their material concerns but is also at ideological odds with their religious practice. Moreover, for many Salafists, engagement with politics and the state is merely a profanation of Islam (Amghar 2009). In this sense, the Islam of the dispossessed urban periphery differs from the officially institutionalised Islam that is fundamentally republican (Wieviorka 2002).

4. Method

The following discussions present the middle-class field of Islamic associations and their politics, the relationship of this field to Islam in the working-class *quartiers*, and the anti-political stance of Salafists in the urban periphery of Lyon. My arguments are based on ten months of participant observation conducted in Lyon and its suburbs, primarily the neighbourhood of Les

Minguettes in the suburb of Vénissieux. Les Minguettes has a foreign population of 31% (INSEE 2009) and was the site of the first major immigrant rights demonstration in the 1980s. I attended two mosques in the neighbourhood, one of which was inside a housing project. Les Minguettes and the Salafist community there do not necessarily represent life in other working-class *banlieues* but it was the neighbourhood that most frequently arose in reference to the growth of Islam in the region and indeed, became the epicentre in many ways of the recent controversy over the burqa. Apart from my research there, I also attended Mosquée Hijra in Villeurbanne, adjacent to Lyon, where I met most of my middle-class informants. (All proper names for individuals and mosques have been changed to protect confidentiality.)

My participant observation in mosques and study circles consisted of prayers in congregation, listening to *khutbas* (sermons), attending classes, listening to explications of the Qur'an and *hadith*, and participating in discussions. In the women-only religious spaces, I also was privy to numerous conversations about everyday life, politics, and family issues. Additionally, I attended several events at the city's Grand Mosque, iftar dinners (for the breaking of the Ramadan fast) at people's homes, social gatherings, and the communal Eid prayer in 2007. I also attended three days of the annual UOIF (l'Union des Organisations Islamiques de France) convention at Le Bourget, outside Paris, in 2006. As part of the research I conducted fifteen semi-structured interviews with association members, leaders, and activists.

Informed by the extended case method (Burawoy 1998), this study was not directed toward the ideal of representativeness. The arguments I present do not represent all religious Muslim practices and politics in Lyon. However, in time I did gather a broad picture of the activist Islamic network and the major debates with which many Muslims were grappling, and the study did capture significant trends and neighbourhoods that have defined debates about Islam in France.

5.   Middle-class politics of recognition

Lyon's field of middle-class Islamic associations is a vibrant mix of religious and cultural events, mosque activities, and political engagement. Central to this field is a politics of recognition that encompasses middle-class relationships to the state, to each other, and to Muslims in the working-class *banlieues*. Middle-class activists make recognition claims on the state, struggle amongst each other for recognition as legitimate representatives of French Muslims and, finally, conflict with Salafist Muslims in the working-class *banlieues* over the legitimacy of their religious practice. I distinguish these associations and activists broadly, by those who invite and accommodate the state in the struggle to achieve recognition and those who take a more militant approach in their opposition to the state. The former category is further divided between state-created institutions and those that are independent. Taken as a whole, however, the field is estranged from Muslims in the *quartiers* and unable to effectively incorporate a politics of economic redistribution. This was not always the case, as I will discuss. During the last three decades there was a rise and eventual fall in the bonds connecting middle-class Muslim activists with those in the *quartiers*.

I present here a brief profile of mainstream and middle-class Islamic associations in the city. While these are not intended to represent the entire field, they include regional branches of well-known organisations and a prominent mosque that enlists many local Muslim leaders and activists. The field also includes Lyon's Grand Mosque (La Grande Mosquée de Lyon), which in addition to housing daily prayers, offers children's and adult classes, children's performances, special lectures, Ramadan prayers and Eid festivals, as well as a recently created social service section that manages requests for emergency assistance from Muslim families. The mosque also collects donations for Palestinian children, orphans, and victims of natural disasters.

Generally, mainstream associations have tended to engage the language of integration, insist on the peaceful and law-abiding nature of the vast majority of Muslims, and accept the idea that Muslims must conform to the requirements of *laïcité*. The first of such organisations in this category is the state-created CRCM (Le Conseil Régional du culte musulman-Rhône Alps), the regional branch of CFCM. CRCM is by mandate and necessity engaged in a politics of recognition that includes negotiations with municipal administrators toward mosque and Islamic school approval. During my research, CRCM's president had just completed negotiations with the Vénissieux municipality to obtain final approval for the construction of a mosque for the Turkish community. The project had been obstructed by the municipality in some form or another for twelve years. CRCM and major mosques are always in a delicate dance with mayoral authorities to assuage public fears of Islam and ensure cooperation with public events.

CRCM is closely connected to Mosquée Hijra, one of the mosques I regularly attended. Located in a lower middle-class and working-class area adjacent to Lyon, the mosque tends to be managed by a relatively young group of educated Muslim worshippers who are politically engaged and proud of their simultaneously Muslim and French belongings. Mosquée Hijra, like other larger mosques, hosts monthly conferences with academics and religious scholars or imams that address practical and spiritual religious issues but also political debates such as voting and the civic obligations of Muslims. It has also on occasion encouraged demonstrations against anti-Muslim gestures such as those of the Front National. Protests and demonstrations were not, however, always over religious recognition. Many Friday *khutbas* at Mosquée Hijra were outspoken against the war in Iraq and sometimes urged attendees to go to street demonstrations. Political and humanitarian activism around Palestine was very prominent in Lyon, close to the hearts of many in the Hijra mosque community, and *khutbas* sometimes addressed these issues. During the 2007 siege of Gaza, for example, the *khutbas* and atmosphere at the mosque were particularly emotionally charged.

Political activity among members of the mosque also included the work of *Le comité 15 mars*, a group that formed after the 2004 banning of the head-scarf. A number of people at Mosquée Hijra took part in *Le comité*, trying to offer support to the schoolgirls dealing with the consequences of the law and engaging in public protest. More recently, the mosque is forming a committee to better organise opposition to anti-Islam rhetoric and violence (such as the vandalising of Islamic sites) and to speak out against the UMP's exploitation of Islam for political gain.

Several of Lyon's associations are connected to UOIF, a national umbrella organisation founded in 1983 and comprising over 200 religio-cultural associations (Bowen 2007). Many of the Islamic activists I knew were at some point involved with UOIF, though some were also very critical of it. One long-time activist referred to UOIF as his 'first love' and felt very strongly and optimistically that it would facilitate the integration and creation of French Islam. Indeed, UOIF had facilitated or overlapped with the work of many youth activists, for example. JMF (Jeunes Musulmans de France) is a part of UOIF and holds numerous cultural and sporting events, usually promoted through the mosque. When I was there UOIF leaders were starting a programme to choose twenty-five students (boys and girls) that they would groom to become JMF leaders. They would receive two years of training in prayer, Arabic, and Islamic law. EMF (Étudiants Musulmans de France), a national student group, conducts activities to support Muslim identity as well as to help Muslim students manage discrimination in their universities.

Among Lyon's more popular associations is UJM (l'Union des Jeunes Musulmans de France), a twenty-year-old association that has undergone many changes throughout its existence. Like other Islamic organisations, it operates entirely though donations. UJM holds cultural events, religious activities, and also numerous conferences and lectures around political issues. Themes range from the compatibility of Islam and democracy, to how to live in a *laïque* society, to the role of women in the Palestinian struggle. UJM also facilitates all-night religious sessions that include prayers, discussions, and Qur'anic explications. Most prominently, it created a publishing house and bookstore in 1999. The bookstore, Tawhid, is not far from downtown Lyon and attracts several passersby every day. Tawhid is a peaceful respite for those involved with the organisation. While Tawhid has held Islamic classes since 1999, it began housing a formal educational programme in 2006 known as Le Centre Shâtibî. The Centre consults with some well-known imams in the area as well as with Tariq Ramadan and Hani Ramadan, who taught a series of courses there despite some local opposition.

Tawhid, in fact, is among the organisations that are generally more critical of the state and skeptical of discourses centred on Muslim responsibilities to 'integrate.' As Kamal, a dedicated activist in one of the youth organisations, stated matter-of-factly: 'They don't want to integrate Islam – they just want to control it.' Farid, who gradually withdrew from a number of Islamic associations, was most vocal and pessimistic in his beliefs about the state. While he remains active around specific political and international causes, his hopes for recognition and respect for Islam have dissipated:

> Alright, I'm going to be a little mean in saying this. But the French state, maybe even all European states, have never wanted to really integrate Islam and Muslims. Even if there are some humanitarian [humanist] politicians who want Islam to be integrated, the majority aren't interested. Quite simply, they don't want us. So what does [the state] do? It just passes laws that are increasingly repressive. . . . Forget about 'integration' – even just respecting Muslims is a problem, to stop considering them as terrorists, Islamists, fundamentalists and instead as normal people that just want to live their lives. But politicians and journalists insult us morning, afternoon, and night.

Farid's political opinions were perhaps the more extreme version of the deeply negative view of the state I so frequently encountered. Many activists and mosque participants I knew were suspicious of state involvement in Islam and lamented the obstacles local government often posed. Although it is increasingly the case that mosques and Islamic schools obtain municipal approval, they continue to face delaying tactics and local hostility. Around the time of my research, France's third private Islamic high school, Al-Kindi, was constructed in one of Lyon's *banlieues*. Just before its anticipated opening, the education department claimed the building violated hygiene and safety codes, and the school opening was delayed by several months. Further, Alain Morvan, the head of the Academy of Lyon, admitted his opposition to the school for its *communautarisme* (communalism). (He was later dismissed by President Sarkozy.)

For exactly such reasons, some activists strive for diplomatic relations with the state in order to prevent these incidents. For Hakim, attaining cooperative relations with local government is the primary solution for enabling Islamic practice. 'In France, Muslims are victims of the law,' he said to me. Hakim was a long-time leader with UOIF and had worked for several years towards the opening of a new Islamic centre in a small town near Lyon. His great excitement for the centre and its future potential was endearing, and he was very personally invested in the project, having campaigned for donations and literally laying down tiles and painting walls with the help of his wife. Hakim summoned all his diplomatic skills to maintain good relations with the municipality, asking his colleagues to let him control the negotiations himself. Without government allies, he remarked, they might have faced the same last-minute bureaucratic obstacles as did Al-Kindi. With his enthusiastic optimism for a uniquely French Islam, Hakim's long-term goal is to be involved in local politics. 'Muslims aren't politically informed or involved. And they don't vote in high numbers, which is why politicians don't care about them.'

6. Political divisions and class abandonment

As I have argued, these activities and forms of political participation by middle-class Muslim associations have generally been oriented towards religious recognition as opposed to issues of economic redistribution. This is predictable, I suggest, because the French model of *laïcité* has sought to remove religion from the public sphere and has, in turn, left Muslim communities struggling to attain forms of recognition that were secured in earlier decades by Catholic and Jewish communities. Moreover, the post-9/11 context of securitisation and intrusive state monitoring, which all of the Islamic associations I knew had encountered, has further pushed religious rights and recognition to the top of Muslim middle-class agendas. Episodes of 'Islamophobia', coexisting with racial profiling and surveillance of mosques, have lent urgency to ethno-religious recognition.

But I argue that the overshadowing of redistribution concerns is also part of the disconnect from poor and working-class Muslims in the *banlieues*, where problems of poor schooling, poverty, and unemployment are rampant. This class disconnect has obvious effects on Muslims in the *quartiers* but it has also been a source of conflict and division within the field of middle-class associations. Apart from some of the associations I presented above, Lyon also has a network of groups and activists that are more critical of mainstream associations and decry their willingness to work with the state as well as their abandonment of redistributive concerns. This network includes Tawhid, which according to one member is 'not interested in trying to compromise with the state, shake the hands of politicians, bow down to politicians.' Groups like Tawhid are sometimes allied broadly with anti-globalisation movements and include secular and non-Muslim allies. Moreover, there is some overlap with members of the Mosquée Hijra community and UOIF members, as individuals have gone back and forth in their trajectories.

I include in the category of critical social justice associations, secular groups like Forum Social des Quartiers Populaires (FSQP) and DiverCité, because their members overlap considerably with current or former Muslim Islamic activists. Abbas, for example, is a longtime activist in the Lyon region with both Muslim associations and groups like DiverCité. His primary focus has been socio-economic problems in the *quartiers*, police violence, and anti-Muslim hate crimes and discrimination. He has been stigmatised and blacklisted as a fundamentalist for several years. He told me that he had made it to the top three of a list of candidates for a teaching post in Lyon but was dropped at the last minute following accusations of being a fundamentalist (*intégriste*). He diligently rummaged through the piles of papers on his desk to show me the complaint of discrimination he filed. Abbas is a leader among activists who are highly critical of the mainstream and media-savvy Islamic field, specifically for being so removed from life in the *quartiers*:

> We call them [this new class of *bourgeois* Muslims] '*bobos*'. They've been run over by individualistic values and just want to work for themselves. It's not Islamic. Getting food in everyone's stomachs is the foremost duty of Muslims. The Prophet said 'He who sleeps on a full stomach while his neighbour goes hungry is not one of us.'[4]

Abbas recounted a story (that I had also heard from others later) about the Interior Minister some years back inviting a group of Muslim leaders to dinner. The meat that was served was not halal, and no one spoke up about it. Some ate the dinner, while others put aside the meat. Apparently, he argued, it was a deliberately manipulative attempt to see just how pliable these leaders would be.

In the 2007 national elections Abbas supported the candidacy of José Bové, a radical syndicalist and anti-globalisation activist. He travelled to Château-Chinon, to the training institute for imams, for electoral discussion and campaigning. He wound up arguing with one of the instructors when he claimed that all political parties were the same and bad for Muslims. Students and instructors castigated him and insisted on voting mainstream. This was a classic example of Abbas's alienation from the mainstream Islamic community. Abbas faces the harsh challenge of balancing his loyalties to Muslim communities and Islam and his overall commitment to social justice that transcends the need for religious recognition. In other words, in my observation, he was disappointed both with the lack of redistribution politics among middle-class Muslims and the lack of recognition politics among the secular social justice organisations he supports (Peace 2008).

Although there is conflict and criticism within the field, there is also a striking sentiment of lamentation over the abandonment of the *quartiers*. UJM, for example, is a principle association that had a social base in the *quartiers* in the 1990s and now, according to current and former volunteers, has lost that base. In the mid-1990s the apparent strength of UJM was precisely that it was anchored in places like Vénissieux and had the respect of local residents. According to a former volunteer, UJM had a real audience back then and it prevented many young people from sectarian practices, drugs, and '*delinquence*,' while also encouraging them to be political and embrace a Muslim identity. With social activities and events, families in the *quartiers* developed trust in UJM leaders. 'And so the state detested us,' claimed Farid. Many members of UJM themselves, had come from the *quartiers* in the early years. This provided the organisation with a great *richesse* that also diminished over time, as the older generation left and/or became preoccupied with its own families. Bilal, now a volunteer with Tawhid, expressed great regret over this disconnect. 'We've become detached from the very base of the community,' he said. 'It's one of our main preoccupations but it's just too difficult. We're far from the *banlieues* for one thing, and we don't feel welcome there anymore.' Farid, in a separate set of conversations with me, concurred. 'At some point all the Islamic groups lost their weight to Salafism. We just no longer correspond to their [residents'] reality on the ground.' So UJM has focused now only on youth education, teaching Arabic, and Islam. According to Farid, UJM and UOIF are only equipped to handle their own structures and activities, and there aren't enough people today to take the lead in expanding their mission to once again include redistribution.

Even secular-left organisations like DiverCité have had trouble maintaining a base in working-class neighbourhoods. The role of Islamic practice in the *quartiers* and the organisation's uncertainty in engaging religious residents is very much part of these concerns. According to one volunteer, DiverCité is not nearly as active as it was in the 1990s because of these varied crises it has faced. Ilyas, a long-time member of DiverCité, admitted that the association already had had its 'hour of glory,' and that the *banlieues* now (at least of Lyon) were a 'no man's land,' stating:

> It's difficult now to mobilise people in the *banlieues*. When we go to discuss things with them, we realise that it's the same discourse as before, the same reports! [We have nothing new to offer them.] And nothing's changed for them! For everyone, not just for Muslims, for the first time we don't know what's going to happen tomorrow or what's going on right now. We do know that people have moved more toward Islam, and this has become predominant.

Ilyas reflected a great deal on this state of disillusion, telling me (as did several others) that many Maghrebis were increasingly seeking ways to leave France. As for his own activism and the future, he was pragmatic and thoughtful:

> Today's generation isn't interested in politics and associations. But there are other means now, like blogs. There are countless blogs coming out of the *banlieues*, and that's not a coincidence. It's up to us now to see how we can connect with them through these different means.

In this context of regret and political division, the Muslims I knew in Les Minguettes, for example, questioned the legitimacy of associations like CFCM to represent them. Middle-class Islamic associations have been accused of failing to justly represent the issues of non-practising and working-class Maghrebi youth or those of Salafist Muslims. For example, during the 2005 urban riots, the major middle-class associations denounced the riots instead of making any statement about the validity of the grievances that led to the rioting. UOIF went so far as to issue a fatwa against the riots. When it came to debates about the banning of the burqa, CFCM and the Paris Mosque (La Grande Mosquée de Paris) had announced their support for the National Assembly debate and made clear their stance that the burqa was not part of Islam. (Note, however, that neither CRCM nor the Grand Mosque of Lyon took such a position.) As Sara, a woman who lived near Les Minguettes and wore the burqa, complained, 'they don't represent us at all.'

Although rioting youth and Salafist worshippers may appear diametrically opposed, they often inhabit the same families and living conditions. So that Sumaiya, a highly religious worshipper and mosque teacher, expressed sympathy for Maghrebi youth in the *quartiers*: 'I understand why they riot!', she exclaimed. In other words the social and economic realities of life in a place like Les Minguettes are beyond the full comprehension of today's generation of middle-class Muslim activists. Although many are aware of this disconnect, it remains unclear as to how they can represent Muslims residents of the *quartiers* in the political field, especially when they have had little choice but to neglect issues of redistribution.

Embedded in this political class disconnect is an important cultural dimension. As activists Farid and Ilyas discussed, the growth of Salafist Islam in the *banlieues* has posed a serious obstacle to 'mainstream' Muslim associations. Indeed, the middle-class activists I knew nearly universally held strong disdain for the Salafist movement. Several people considered Salafist practice 'superficial' and 'narrow-minded,' while others went as far as to consider practices like the burqa as *bid'a* (unwanted innovations or corruptions of Islam) or grave misinterpretations of Islam. Another common contention with Salafist Muslims was their relative isolation and refusal to engage the state or wider French society politically. Nadia, a thirty-year-old woman of Algerian origin, active in Lyon's mosque communities, found Muslim isolation in the *banlieues* very troubling: 'They don't care about the future of Islam in France. They just turn their backs and then make their wives stay inside.' According to Maryam, also a dedicated activist in one of the city's mosque communities:

[Salafists] don't see themselves as French. They don't call themselves French. But it takes a strength of character, a certain maturity, to be able to say 'you can close your door on me, but I will struggle so that you understand me and understand that I *am* French.'

Whether it was their political dispositions, gendered practices, or vesture, Salafists were accused of missing the true spirit of Islam and undermining its future through political disengagement.

7.   Precarity and antipolitics in the *banlieues*

While it was indeed the case that Salafist Muslims in the *banlieues* are politically disengaged, the reasons are multiple and complex and, I argue, extend
beyond ideological beliefs about politics. First is the fact that Muslims in the
banlieues more broadly do not constitute a voting bloc or formally politically
mobilise. One marginal exception to this is the Parti des Musulmans en France
(PMF), a political party that enlists candidates in a handful of local elections.

PMF, though not well known, has a negative reputation. Its platform is
'anti-*laïcité*' and anti-Zionism, and it seeks the overturn of the anti-headscarf
law among other things. One of the few towns where a PMF candidate con-
tended in local elections is Vénissieux. I met Nadir Ben-Abbes the same year he
had received just over 1% of the vote in that year's election after a low turnout
and minimal campaigning. Ben-Abbes has lived in France since infancy after
his parents left Algeria and he now lives in Lyon, working as a bus driver and
tramway operator. 'My parents, my grandparents – they *died* for this country!'
he turned red and became increasingly upset as he spoke:

> I say to my kids, 'you are *home*, this is *your* country.' I don't ever want them to feel
> ashamed [the way we did]. I'm with PMF because Muslims shouldn't feel ashamed
> to practise their religion or stand up for their rights, to organise politically on the
> basis of this identity.

Ben-Abbes had been politically active for over twenty years. Having
avoided the Communist Party for their staunch atheism, he worked for many
years with the Socialists. However, he always felt marginalised and felt that
their anti-religious stance was excessive.

Ben-Abbes did not exactly come across as professional. He himself complained that other politicians have entire teams of assistants writing their
agendas and feeding them lines, something he could never afford. André
Gérin, Vénissieux's mayor at the time, made insulting comments about Ben-
Abbes' candidacy, and other candidates also did not take him seriously. But
he believed that there could be a day when his platform would resonate with
people. He deliberately chose to run in Vénissieux because of the high concentration of Muslims. It's difficult to say what the real electoral potential would
be of a more professional and affluent Muslim political party, but a party
focused so heavily on religious recognition is surely overlooking the majority
of issues that are critical to residents of areas like Vénissieux's *quartiers*.

What, then, is the political participation among working-class Muslims in a
quartier like Les Minguettes? In the mosque communities I observed there was
no desire to engage the state or make political claims. This withdrawal from
political life emerges out of a context of the collapse of civil societies, heavy
police surveillance, and public and official hostility toward veiling practices.

The severe retreat of Islamic civil societies has occurred largely because of the demoralisation of activist groups in the last decade caused by surveillance and police harassment. The raiding of mosques, arrests of young men, and deportation of imams have all occurred in Les Minguettes. As a consequence, the working-class Muslims I knew rejected politics, finding it both profane and dangerous.

I have argued that the women of the mosque communities I joined are not engaged in politics but rather, a form of antipolitics (Parvez 2011). Their antipolitics is a withdrawal from the state and a substitute for democratic political participation – but it is not the equivalent of being apolitical. It is instead foremost a valorisation, defence, and reconfiguration of their private spheres, whereby they defend their right to wear the burqa (for example) as something constitutive of their private selves. Second, antipolitics is a retreat into a moral community where Salafist women provide mutual spiritual support for each other to cope with their difficult family relations and social stigma. Despite their moral community, however, there is a fundamental lack of social trust – which in turn prevents these spaces from developing into civil societies. Because of the intrusion of surveillance activity in the neighbourhood and inside the mosque, women's mosque communities are prevented from forming bonds and the norms of social trust that constitute the basis of a strong civil society. Finally, antipolitics emphasises the achievement of serenity over material or political considerations and desires. Acceptance of suffering and trust in God was a regular theme in mosque teachings. Given this, political participation to alter one's conditions had no place in the religious spaces of Les Minguettes.

The antipolitics I saw in Les Minguettes came not only from the recent history of surveillance and state hostility but also from the precariousness of people's lives, work, and in many cases, relationships. References to such precariousness appeared routinely in Islamic teachings and discourses and everyday conversations at the mosque. Mosquée Ennour, one of the mosques I attended in the neighbourhood, provided a small space where several women I knew could talk, complain, and laugh about their worries. These discussions were often interjected in the middle of Qur'anic teaching sessions. They frequently involved anxieties over immigration status, frustrations with various French bureaucracies, and complaints about their struggles to find work or self-employment activities. In general there was a certain degree of instability to the religious community because of the precarious nature of immigration status and work. Saara, who had been teaching Arabic over a short period had to end the class when her legal stay in France expired. I didn't realise the class was over until the very last day when she embarrassedly and abruptly confessed to me that she had to return to Algeria. Sumaiya, a migrant from Syria, also had a very hesitant approach to the future, even in mundane greetings. Whenever I would say 'see you next week,' she would reply 'maybe, but who knows. I don't know. I always say *insha Allah* [God willing].'

Sumaiya was one of the teachers at Mosquée Ennour. She taught Arabic literacy and Qur'anic memorisation and explication. After several months of knowing her, she broke down in front of me one day at her apartment in Minguettes, much to her embarrassment. Her two-year-old daughter was crying, as Sumaiya complained to me about her numerous errands that week: going to the pediatrician, the pharmacist, her daughter's nursery, her own job-training in Lyon, job-searching, dealing with the bureaucracy of receiving her family assistance checks, taking the bus to buy groceries, and applying and reapplying for citizenship. She had enormous anxiety over her inability to acquire French citizenship. She had submitted several dossiers for citizenship, each time getting rejected due to some bureaucratic requirement.

Sumaiya survived on approximately 300 euros a month. She had worked on and off in Lyon, was recently laid off from a job as a telephone operator, and was receiving training to be a licensed babysitter. But like other women I knew, she was having difficulty completing the state-required training for a babysitter's license, as the multiple, all-day training took place in different locations throughout Lyon. She argued that it was too difficult to get hired by companies while she wears the veil and was fed up and exhausted with looking for work. (She was willing to take off the veil in order to find a job.) Her mosque persona was cheerful and confident. But as I saw her that day, she wasn't able to hide her anxiety. On top of everything, she was considering divorcing her husband, a Tunisian man who'd been living abroad and rarely visited her and their daughter. It was her second marriage. 'Please,' she said. 'Don't tell anyone at the mosque.' Sumaiya's solitude, her desire to hide the reality of her life from the others at Mosquée Ennour, reflected the overall desolation I found unique to Les Minguettes.

What I have described so far of Les Minguettes applies predominantly to the Muslim women I knew. While I had some exposure to Salafist men in working-class neighbourhoods, I have only a broad sense of the teachings and issues at stake. There were elements of antipolitics among Salafist men, however, there was also a more public orientation at the neighbourhood level. Salafist men do meet in available public spaces in the *banlieues*. Muslim-owned 'McSnack shops' in the *banlieues* have become important spaces for Salafist men to meet, discuss ideas, and watch soccer matches.

Yassin, a young man of Algerian origin, spent a good deal of time at these shops, though he did not himself identify as Salafist. Yassin grew up in a nearby *banlieue*. His father worked in a factory, producing elevator cables, and his mother worked briefly cleaning houses. Yassin had gone to local university and had employment – but it was occasional and precarious. He was the only one among his several siblings who performed daily prayers and actively strove toward greater piety. He acknowledged that Salafist men had had a social impact in his neighbourhood, where they had campaigned against drugs, alcohol, and gangs. But he disliked certain elements of the movement and viewed it entirely as a result of economic dislocation. 'In a way, since society has excluded them, they've dug in their heels and said, "we don't need society." This is why there's an attraction to this movement.'

I met Yassin through his close childhood friend, Mounir. Both Yassin and he grew up in *les quartiers*. Mounir was deeply disaffected with his life in France and the potential for political participation and 'integration.' This was coloured entirely by the state's hostility toward Islam. For example, a small mosque that he and his father had attended for many years was forcibly closed at the mayor's direction in 2004 with vague promises of the construction of a new mosque. Mounir and Yassin complained also about a Tablighi prayer space in their *banlieue* that had been rented from a Catholic church association. When the Church's lease expired, the association wished to move forward and sell it to the Tablighi group. The mayor tried desperately to obstruct the purchase but eventually legal assistance from the international Tablighi movement enabled the purchase to proceed.

Mounir's particular housing project complex, similar to those in Minguettes, was among those notorious for crime and drug activity. According to him, it was the proselytising of Tablighi and Salafist Muslims in his complex that led to dramatic declines in alcohol abuse and street fights. 'Islam has cleaned up all these problems,' he exclaimed. 'It's a totally different place now, and it's safe.' At the time when I met Mounir, he was not actively involved in any Islamic group, though he had many Salafist friends. A year later, during a conversation with Yassin, I learned that Mounir had actually begun to identify himself as Salafist, even though he was very ambiguous about it with me. The ambiguity with which many like Mounir identify as Salafist, I found, was an easily observed phenomenon, true to the loosely defined and individualist orientation of Salafism in the *banlieues*. Mounir never directly told me he considered himself Salafist, though he spoke often about the movement and his Salafi friends. This was likely because he knew the degree to which Salafism was stigmatised and despised by middle-class Muslims.

Thus, Mounir and Yassin engaged the Salafist movement in the *banlieues* from different perspectives but both acknowledged its social impact. In this respect Salafism among men in the *quartiers* may have a more public orientation in contrast to the women's antipolitics that I regularly observed. Men are certainly stigmatised and harassed, but their practices are not the centre of national attention as is the case for Muslim women. Nonetheless, they all face great uncertainty in their lives and consequently focus on individual salvation rather than a collective political project. In sum, Salafist Muslims in Les Minguettes remain withdrawn from the state, politically alienated, and estranged from the field of Muslim middle-class recognition politics.

8. Conclusion

In December 2011 a mosque in Lyon's *banlieue* of Décines was desecrated with swastikas. CRCM condemned this act of Islamophobic violence, while the local, newly formed Enfants de la Patrie called for stronger denunciation and mobilisation. There have been multiple incidents of desecration in the Lyon area in recent years. Although there have been great strides in local approval of Islamic institutions and mosques, episodes like that in Décines show how much political work remains to be done. Because of such incidents and because of the rigidity of *laïcité*, collective projects and state-directed political participation are primarily about religious recognition. But this is not without contestation and serious political fractures within the field of Muslim middle-class politics.

In this atmosphere the marginalisation of a class-based imaginary partly explains the separation of middle-class Muslim activists and worshippers from the socio-economic concerns of those in the working-class *banlieues* and the political withdrawal and antipolitics among Salafists in *les quartiers*. Religious and cultural judgment of Salafism, I argue, only masks this class divide. Again, state surveillance and control largely created this class dynamic.

The complexity of 'Muslim political participation' in Lyon thus points to the importance of moving beyond explorations of European Muslim subjectivities and cultural identity. There are numerous factors in state structures and the public arena that define the boundaries of political participation. I have tried to point out the strategic choices and agendas pursued by Muslim minorities across classes but these are made, of course, within existing structures of opportunities. For example, Muslims in a few French cities may exploit religious identity but typically to the benefit of municipal politicians or machines. Many Muslims are excluded from all voting rights because of foreign nationality, making it even more difficult to form a coherent voting bloc. As the hopes for the representative potential of CFCM and national associations are tenuous, political potential may lie primarily at the municipal level and within Islamic civil societies. As I have argued, this potentiality will be directed in significant part by the future of class relations.

Notes

1. A movement originating 100–200 years ago that sought to modernise Sunni Islam. Salafism transformed eventually into a movement intended to restore the original teachings and practices of Islam. It is often discussed interchangeably with *Wahhabism*. Salafism has historically been a pietist and apolitical movement, after some involvement in state politics in the late nineteenth and early twentieth centuries (Stemmann 2006). See Euben and Zaman 2009; and Hourani 1983.
2. Pan Ké Shon (2004) shows that living in an officially-classified sensitive urban zone

increases the probability of non-registration. However, he argues that what appears to be a neighbourhood effect is most likely covering up other individual variables.

3. 'Arabes de service' is a slang term that connotes token minority individuals, who are patronised and exoticised. When I heard the term in conversation, it sometimes also referred to one who would enact the stereotype in exchange for status or position.

4. The term *bobos* is French slang for a lie or propaganda. Abbas is applying it here to Maghrebis who seek their own advancement over community justice.

References

Alaoui, F. (2005), 'Le CFCM, réalité et conditions de réussite,' *French Politics, Culture & Society*, vol. 23, no.1 (Spring), pp. 115–17.

At Home in Europe Project (2010), *Muslims in Europe*, New York: Open Society Institute.

At Home in Europe Project (2011), *Muslims in Marseille*, New York: Open Society Foundations.

Amghar, S. (2009), *Ideological and Theological Foundations of Muslim Radicalism in France*, MICROCON Policy Working Paper 4, Brighton: MICROCON.

Awan, A. (2008), 'Antecedents of Islamic Political Radicalism Among Muslim Communities in Europe,' *Political Science & Politics*, vol. 41, no. 1 (January), pp. 13–17.

Billon, A. (2005), 'Les fondements idéologiques et les choix de la consultation,' *French Politics, Culture & Society*, vol. 23, no. 1 (Spring), pp. 23–36.

Bousetta, H. (2000), 'Institutional theories of immigrant ethnic mobilisation: Relevance and limitations,' *Journal of Ethnic and Migration Studies*, vol. 26, no. 2 (April), pp. 229–45.

Bowen, J. (2007), *Why the French don't like headscarves*, Princeton: Princeton University Press.

Burawoy, M. (1998), 'The Extended Case Method,' *Sociological Theory*, vol. 16, no. 1 (March), pp. 4–33.

De Wenden, C. W. (1988), *Les immigrés et la politique: Cent-cinquante ans d'évolution*, Paris: Presses de la FNSP.

Euben, R. and M. Zaman (2009), 'Introduction', in R. Euben and M. Zaman (eds), *Princeton readings in Islamist thought: Texts and contexts from al-Banna to Bin Laden*, Princeton: Princeton University Press.

Fernando, M. (2010). 'Reconfiguring freedom: Muslim piety and the limits of secular law and public discourse in France,' *American Ethnologist*, vol. 37, no. 1, pp. 19–35.

Fetzer, J. and C. Soper (2005), *Muslims and the State in Britain, France, and Germany*, Cambridge: Cambridge University Press.

Garbaye, R. (2004), 'Ethnic Minority Local Councillors in French and British Cities: Social Determinants and Political Opportunity Structures', in R. Penninx, K. Kraal, M. Martiniello and S. Vertovec (eds), *Citizenship in European Cities*, Burlington: Ashgate.

Geisser, V. (1997), *Ethnicité républicaine: les élites d'origine maghrébine dans le système politique français*, Paris: Presses de Sciences Po.

Grillo, R. (1985), *Ideologies and Institutions in Urban France*, Cambridge: Cambridge University Press.

Hourani, A. (1983 [1962]). *Arabic thought in the liberal age*, Cambridge: Cambridge University Press.

Janeau, Y. and S. Vanovermeir (2008), *Les jeunes et les ménages modesties surestiment plus souvent le confort de leur logement*, no. 1209, INSEE.

Kelfaoui, S. (1996), 'Un 'vote maghrébin' en France?', *Hérodote*, no. 80 (January–March), pp. 130–55.

Kepel, G. (2008 [2002]), *Jihad: the trail of political Islam*, London: I. B. Tauris.

Kepel, G. et al. (2005), 'Réussir les objectifs de l'État et de la religion organisée: les limites de la représentation,' *French Politics, Culture & Society*, vol. 23, no. 1 (Spring), pp. 122–9.

Killian, C. (2006), *North African Women in France: Gender, culture, and identity*, Stanford: Stanford University Press.

Laurence, J. and J. Vaisse (2006), *Integrating Islam: Political and Religious Challenges in Contemporary France*, Washington, DC: Brookings Institution Press.

Laurence, J. (2005), 'From the Elysée Salon to the Table of the Republic: State-Islam Relations and the Integration of Muslims in France,' *French Politics, Culture & Society*, vol. 23, no. 1 (Spring), pp. 37–64.

Lombardo, P. and J. Pujol (2010), *Niveau de vie et pauvreté des immigrés en 2007*, INSEE.

Maxwell, R. (2010), 'Political Participation in France among Non-European-Origin Migrants: Segregation or Integration?', *Journal of Ethnic and Migration Studies*, vol. 36, no. 3 (March), pp. 425–43.

Moore, D. (2004), 'Migrants as Mediators in a Comparative Perspective', in R. Penninx, K. Kraal, M. Martiniello, S. Vertovec (eds), *Citizenship in European Cities*, Burlington: Ashgate.

Noiriel, G. (1996 [1988]). *The French Melting Pot: Immigration, Citizenship, and National Identity*, Minneapolis, MN: University of Minnesota Press.

Noiriel, G. (2007), *A qoui sert 'l'identite national?'*, Marseille: Agone.

Observatoire national des zones urbaines sensibles (2011), *Rapport 2011*.

Pan Ké Shon, J.-L. (2004), 'Determinants of Electoral Non-Registration and Sensitive Neighbourhoods in France,' *Population-E*, vol. 59, no. 1, pp. 143–56.

Parvez, Z. F. (2011), 'Debating the Burqa in France: the Antipolitics of Islamic Revival,' *Qualitative Sociology*, vol. 34, no. 2, pp. 287–312.

Peace, T. (2008), 'L'impact de la 'participation musulmane' sur le mouvement alter-mondialiste,' *Cultures & Conflits*, no. 70 (Summer), pp. 109–28.

Richard, J.-L. (1999), 'Comment votent les jeunes français issus de l'immigration?', *Ville-École-Intégration*, vol. 118, no. 3 (September), pp. 119–34.

Richard, J.-L. (2004), *Partir ou Rester? Destinées des jeunes issus de l'immigration*, Paris: Presses Universitaires de France.

Roy, O. (2004), *Globalized Islam: The Search for a New Ummah*, New York: Columbia University Press.

Roy, O. (2006), 'Islam in Europe: Clash of religions or convergence of religiosities?', in K. Michalski (ed.), *Conditions of European solidarity, vol II: Religion in the new Europe*, New York: Central European Press.

Sayad, A. (1984), *L'immigration Algérienne en France*, Paris: Editions Entente.

Sayad, A. (1991), *L'immigration, ou, Les paradoxes de l'altérité*, Bruxelles: Editions Universitaires.

Simon, P. (1998), 'Ghettos, immigrants, and integration: the French Dilemma,' *Netherlands Journal of Housing and the Built Environment*, vol. 13, no. 1, pp. 41–61.

Situation des demandeurs d'emploi inscrits (2009). INSEE and Pôle emploi.

Stemmann, J. (2006), 'Middle East Salafism's influence and radicalization of Muslim communities in Europe,' *Middle East Review of International Affairs*, vol. 10, no. 3, pp. 1–14.

Tissot, S. (2006), 'Y a-t-il un 'problème des quartiers sensibles'? Retour sur une catégorie d'action publique,' *French Politics, Culture & Society*, vol. 24, no. 3 (Winter), pp. 42–57.

Wieviorka, M. (2002), 'Race, Culture and Society: the French Experience with Muslims', in N. AlQayyad and M. Castells (eds), *Muslim Europe or Euro-Islam. Politics, Culture, and Citizenship in the Age of Globalization*, Lanham: Lexington Books.

PART THREE

• • •

INSTITUTIONS AS GATEWAYS

CREATING THE IMAGE OF EUROPEAN ISLAM: THE EUROPEAN COUNCIL FOR FATWA AND RESEARCH AND IRELAND[1]

Adil Hussain Khan

The recent focus on European Islam has sparked an interest in establishing representative Muslim networks that seemingly span the continent of Europe. However, unifying European Muslims onto a single political platform has largely been an elusive process for Europe's Muslim communities. The image of Muslim representation in Europe has been aided by international organisations, such as the European Council for Fatwa and Research, whose prestigious network of esteemed scholars purportedly address the concerns of western Muslims, while acting as one of the few representative voices of European Islam. Although this image of a unified 'European Islam' would indeed, at first glance, appear to be an impressive accomplishment for Europe's Muslim communities, it is not the outcome of local efforts by European Muslims at the grassroots level. Rather, organisations like the European Council for Fatwa and Research are the result of a top-down approach intended to project an image of European Islam. This has shaped the development of Muslim communities in countries, like Ireland, where transnational influences have promoted the vision of a globalised Islam. Efforts to fabricate this image of European Islam have remarkably transformed Dublin into the seat of the European Council for Fatwa and Research, despite Ireland having one of the smallest Muslim populations in Western Europe. This chapter will explore the role of external influences on the construction of the image of European Islam and on the notion of Muslim representation in Europe, with particular reference to the historical development of Ireland's Muslim community.

1. Introduction

The increased focus on the Muslim presence in Western European countries has broadened the ongoing debate about the relationship between religion and politics. Whereas secularisation, as it has traditionally been conceived, has evolved as a question of church-state relations, the discourse has long since been expanded to include a more generalised notion of religion itself, as a means to accommodate the various other religious traditions in contemporary European societies. With regards to Islam, this discourse has initiated a re-evaluation of the boundaries between religious authority and political authority, which Muslims have openly contested since at least the crisis of succession that emerged following the death of the Prophet Muhammad. In this respect, the European context has provided a unique framework for the development of the Islamic discourse on religion and politics, which is being furthered through discussions on Islamic law and Muslim polity by contemporary *'ulamā'* and activists alike. However, successfully negotiating religious concerns within a European framework has proved to be a challenge for those who desire to see normative Islamic legal practices included in European postulations of diversity in a way that enables Islamic ideals to be presented as acceptable alternatives to traditional European moral values. This has been made difficult for various reasons, not least of all by the sheer variety of religious and political views throughout the Muslim world, as well as the diverse array of religious outlooks and political perspectives throughout contemporary European societies.

With this in mind, one can see why conflating Muslim voices onto a single political platform might seem like an appealing concept to struggling (or indeed restricted) Islamist organisations in Muslim majority countries, where linguistic, ethnic, and socio-economic differences as well as divergent religious interpretations cloud the political arena each election year. For this reason, Muslim unity in the name of religion may have appeared to be far more attainable in a European setting, where the religious aspects of European Muslims' multifaceted identities have come to dominate outsider-imposed categorisations of Islam, since unassuming outsiders tend to overlook the subtleties and diversity of immigrant communities, as if all were monolithic. In this regard, political activists with pan-Islamic visions of the Muslim world might have had an easier time convincing immigrant Muslim communities who live as minorities in foreign settings, such as in Western Europe, that uniting under the banner of Islam is worthwhile, irrespective of other differences. This is not to say that political Islam has been successful in Western Europe or that it has flourished unopposed, but only that it appears to have been easier to convince Muslims that a unified representation of Islam at the European level is more productive for the Muslims of Europe than asserting divergent aspects of one's idiosyncratic identities to outsiders, who are largely unfamiliar with internal debates and are, at times, unaware of the cultural depth of the Islamic tradition. This has led to fierce competition amongst aspiring representatives of European Islam with regards to determining who ought to have the privilege of representing 'Islam' to government officials at the local level, since doing so is accompanied by a sense of authority, insofar that it furnishes the group in question with the right to sift through the broader Islamic discourse and portray its own opinions as if they were representative of all Muslims.

Considering the increased desire of European governments to firmly establish Muslim representatives who embody the voice of 'moderate' Islam (Birt 2006: 687–705), Islam in Europe has undergone a process of institutionalisation that was unnecessary in classical times. Likewise, within the Muslim world, the notion of having authoritative representatives who speak for all Muslims is vacuous, since it contradicts the development of the broader Islamic tradition, which is well known to have evolved without a hierarchical clergy (Zeghal 2007: 122–3; Gaborieau and Zeghal 2004). Even Shi'i Islam, with its ostensibly hierarchical framework, has historically remained remarkably non-institutionalised in comparison to Christian traditions. For this reason, authoritative Muslim organisational structures have tended to represent, inter alia, the views of particular governments, sectarian movements, or administrative bodies, but not Islam in its entirety as a religion.

In Europe, however, this process has developed rather differently. Government pressure on Muslim communities has certainly accelerated the institutionalisation of Islam in the post-9/11 era. This has opened the door for political opportunists to take advantage of an uninformed public discourse on Islam in Europe by presenting themselves as the sole representatives of global Islam (Roy 2004; Mandaville 2007, for more comprehensive definitions of globalised Islam). Nevertheless, Muslims and Muslim organisations in Europe have adapted themselves to fit the European mould of special interest groups in hope of establishing themselves as expert religious authorities, which often take the shape of umbrella organisations with a corporate structure.

2. The rise of Muslim umbrella organisations at the European level

It is important to recognise that European Muslims have been organising themselves in various capacities ever since the first waves of Muslim immigrants established viable Muslim communities on European soil. However, the pan-Islamic ideal of establishing a Muslim umbrella organisation appears initially to have originated with the demise of the Ottoman caliphate, in conjunction with the rise of nationalism, when the decentralisation of authority gave way to new political leaders in the Muslim world (Hardy 1972: 175–8). Early pan-Islamic movements, such as the Khilafat Movement, founded in 1919 in colonial India, were short-lived but regionally influential. Others, such as the Muslim World Congress (Mu'tamar al-ʿĀlam al-Islāmī), founded in 1926, might have experienced a similar fate had it not been revived in 1949 with Pakistani support (see www.motamaralalamalislami.org, last accessed February 2012). These undertakings were expanded within the framework of

Islamic non-governmental organisations (NGOs), such as the Muslim World League in 1962, which made an overt effort to canvass European nations in support of Muslims worldwide (Van Bommel 1992: 129).

The notion of establishing an umbrella organisation to serve as a representative of European Muslims first began to take shape in the early 1970s when Islamist activists from political movements in the Muslim world began setting up overarching organisations consistent with their globalised vision of Islam. Amongst Arabic speaking communities, this process was spearheaded by figures who articulated their views in a way that shared the sentiments expressed by popular political parties such as the Muslim Brotherhood (al-Ikhwān al-Muslimūn). Within South Asian communities in Europe, the rhetoric was appropriately adapted to convey familiar notions of accepted themes from prominent Islamist organisations such as Jama'at-i Islami. It may be worth mentioning that a number of recent publications dealing with the Muslim Brotherhood seem to exaggerate the role of Islamist groups in Europe or otherwise blur the distinctions between the numerous variations of Islamism in the West by effectively treating popular outlets of Islamism, like the Muslim Brotherhood and Jama'at-i Islami, as if they were the same organisation (for examples see Rubin 2010; see also Vidino 2010). This has led to a number of debatable conclusions, regarding the Brotherhood's role in Europe and North America, which ought to be highlighted further but are simply beyond the scope of this chapter. However, one of the most balanced treatments of the Muslim Brotherhood's recent activities in the European context may be found in Brigitte Maréchal's *The Muslim Brothers of Europe* (2008). The most relevant aspects of Maréchal's analysis, for our purposes, include her assertion that the Muslim Brotherhood is attempting 'to impose their presence' in Europe as representatives of Islam (Maréchal 2008: 34). Insofar as this specifically relates to the creation of the European Council for Fatwa and Research, which shall be discussed later, Maréchal highlights the Brotherhood's growing desire to establish recognisable reference points capable of functioning as religious authorities for European Muslims (Maréchal 2008: 237–9). Overall, Maréchal's work provides the most comprehensive source of information regarding the attitudes of individual Brothers in Europe. This includes both Brothers and non-Brothers who were (often jointly) involved in establishing some of the umbrella organisations discussed below from various Islamist platforms, which subsequently have influenced the contemporary Brotherhood's ideology (Maréchal 2008: 73).[2]

One such organisation, the Islamic Council of Europe, was founded in 1973 in London by Saudi diplomat Salem Azzam (1924–2008). Azzam was from an influential Egyptian family with political ties to the Muslim Brotherhood's founder, Hassan al-Banna, through his uncle (Vidino 2010: 33, 234, and note 54), 'Abd al-Rahman 'Azzam (Mitchell 1993: 56), who notably served as the first secretary-general of the Arab League from 1945 to 1952 (see Coury 1998). The Islamic Council of Europe remained reasonably active, particularly in London and Paris, through the early 1980s and published a number of booklets, including the *Universal Islamic Declaration of Human Rights* in 1981, which was widely distributed as a delayed response to the United Nations Universal Declaration of Human Rights of 1948 (Azzam 1981; Azzam 1998: 102–12). This was followed by the drafting of a model constitution in 1983 for would-be Islamic states (Azzam 1983), perhaps in hope that the recent revolution in Iran would spread to other parts of the Muslim world.

Although the success of the Islamic Council of Europe was limited, it paved the way for future umbrella organisations to emerge in later years at the European level (Khan 2011: 493–4). The ultimate failure of the Islamic Council of Europe may have been due, in some part, to the lack of influential representative organisations at the national level, since the process of institutionalising Muslim organisations at the national level did not gain adequate momentum in Europe until the late 1980s. Nevertheless, the creation of the Islamic Council of Europe represents an early attempt at forming a Muslim umbrella organisation at the European level. It also illustrates the desire of Islamist counterparts, such as those who represented ideological strands of the Muslim Brotherhood and those associated with Jama'at-i Islami, to coordinate their efforts on the European front. In one Islamic Council of Europe publication, Salem Azzam collaborated with Khurshid Ahmad, a leading figure of Jama'at-i Islami (Esposito and Voll 2001: 39–53), to produce literature that would appeal to European Muslims from both Arab and South Asian backgrounds (Ahmad 1976, with foreword by Salem Azzam), effectively broadening their respective audiences beyond the scope of their own Islamist platforms.

By 1989 many of these organisational endeavours were consolidated through the formation of the Federation of Islamic Organisations in Europe (FIOE). Although the FIOE remained centred in Britain, it included other influential organisations in Western Europe, such as France's Union des Organisations Islamiques de France (UOIF) (Maréchal 2008: 61; Khosrokhavar 2010: 137), as well as Germany's Islamische Gemeinschaft Milli Gorus (IGMG) and Islamische Gemeinschaft in Deutschland (IGD) (Steinberg 2010: 149–51; Vidino 2010: 30). At present, the FIOE claims to be 'the largest Islamic organisation on the European level' representing the voice of European Islam, which consists of 'hundreds of member organisations spread across 28 European States' (www.euro-muslim.com, under the 'About Us' link, last accessed February 2012). In its approach towards establishing a representative umbrella of Europe's Muslim communities, the Islamist ideologies of previous decades were not altogether abandoned despite shifts in Islamist thought, in the sense that political interpretations of Islam have remained a key feature of the FIOE's mission (Maréchal 2008: 174; Caeiro and Saify 2009: 111). The FIOE presents itself as the culmination of previous attempts to mobilise European Muslims, which thereby has succeeded in 'unifying the political discourse' with respect to European Islam. This has purportedly been achieved through the FIOE's 'ceaseless [efforts] in seeking to remove the barrier built on fear of the Islamic presence in the West; a fear fed by biased media, and some political forces that advocate hostile language and attitudes against the Muslim minorities' (www.euro-muslim.com, under the 'About Us' link, last accessed February 2012).

3. The European Council for Fatwa and Research

Although the FIOE appeared to represent a political force in European society, it still needed to formalise its agency at the European level to secure its long-term future. To do this, the FIOE established a number of 'specialised institutions' that were capable of representing different strands of the public discourse on Islam at the European level (www.euro-muslim.com, last accessed February 2011). This included the formation of the European Media Association, the European Forum of Muslim Women, and the Forum of European Muslim Youth and Student Organisations. However, to demonstrate the backing of European Muslims and bolster its political platform, the FIOE needed to incorporate an authoritative body exclusively within the religious sphere of European Islam. As a result, the FIOE assembled the European Council for Fatwa and Research (ECFR). In this respect, the ECFR may perhaps be seen as an attempt to establish a religious authority capable of complementing the FIOE's ambitions of establishing political authority. Thus far, the most extensive accounts of the European Council for Fatwa and Research have been provided by Alexandre Caeiro, whose illuminating expositions have helped shape the course of research for this study (Caeiro 2011: 121–41; Caeiro and Saify 2009: 109–48; Caeiro 2010: 435–49; Caeiro 2006: 661–85).

The first meeting of the European Council for Fatwa and Research took place in London over the last weekend of March 1997 (ECFR 2003: 1; see also www.e-cfr.org, last accessed February 2012). Over fifteen scholars, primarily from the Middle East, comprised the council as an authoritative assembly of *'ulamā'* for European Muslims. A constitution was drafted in the first meeting, which specified five conditions for membership. Although the fourth condition stipulated European residency for each member, a concession was made for additional scholars approved by the majority of existing members. Moreover, the council's bylaws state that the total number of ECFR members who are not in European residence may not exceed 25% (ECFR 2003: 4–5). This was an important step in creating a sense of legitimacy for the council's rulings, since a mufti's familiarity with local customs and practices is imperative in the establishment an authoritative fatwa within the classical framework of Sunni *usūl al-fiqh* (Kamali 2003: 369–83). As such, the ECFR's constitution deliberately attempts to distinguish itself from other authoritative fatwa councils in the Muslim world by adopting a distinctly European flavour. However, the extent of the European orientations of the ECFR's members may be called into question, as discussed below.

At present, the most notable figure in the ECFR's executive is its president, Sheikh Yusuf al-Qaradawi, an Egyptian national who was educated at al-Azhar and is now living in Qatar (Skovgaard and Gräf: 2009). Despite distancing himself from certain aspects of the movement, Qaradawi is widely regarded as the spiritual figurehead for the Muslim Brotherhood's religious ideology (Maréchal 2008: 147–50). Qaradawi enlisted the services of several colleagues with mutual concerns and similar ideals from various parts of the Muslim world in order to establish the core of the ECFR's roster. Other prominent members who shared this spiritual outlook included the ECFR's Lebanese vice-president, Faisal Mawlawi, who passed away in 2011. Although Mawlawi had French ties, he was best known for his central role in a different Islamist organisation, al-Jama'a al-Islamiyya, which remains active in his native Lebanon (Mawlawi 2008; Maréchal 2008: 150–1). There was also Rachid Ghannouchi, a Tunisian national who until the revolution of January 2011 was living in exile in Britain (Tammimi 2001; Esposito and Voll 2001: 91–117). Ghannouchi has since returned to Tunis to assist the next generation of supporters of his al-Nahda movement in carrying out transitional political reforms (see www.bbc.co.uk/news/world-africa-12318824, last accessed February 2012; see also www.bbc.co.uk/news/world-africa-12320950, last accessed February 2012). Another important figure was 'Isam Bashir, who held a prominent position in the Sudanese government under Hasan Turabi, prior to Turabi's fallout with the Brotherhood. The ECFR also includes Ahmed al-Rawi, an Iraqi immigrant to the UK who headed the FIOE throughout 2006 (Maréchal 2008: 251; Vidino 2010: 51–2), as well as Ahmad Jaballah, who took over the FIOE's leadership after al-Rawi (Maréchal 2008: 155). On a national level, Jaballah has also played an active role in the Union des Organisations Islamiques de France (UOIF) (Maréchal 2008: 69, 158; Vidino 2010: 48).

The council's clear preference for scholars with similar worldviews and shared political affiliations necessitated a diversification of the membership roster in order to establish a greater sense of legitimacy. To accomplish its goals, the ECFR needed to devise a way to obtain the backing of European Muslims who did not affiliate with the major organs of the FIOE and hence were less likely to share its ideological persuasions. For this reason, a number of eminent figures in the Muslim world were recruited to give the ECFR a more balanced look and ultimately a greater sense of religious authority. These alternative voices in the ECFR have been represented by various figures since the council's inception. However, three prominent non-Islamist scholars stand out at present. They are: Sheikh Abdullah bin Bayyah, a Mauritanian scholar who currently resides in Saudi Arabia; Mufti Muhammad Taqi Usmani, who served as Pakistan's former Supreme Court Justice; and Mustafa Cerić, who was till recently the Grand Mufti of Bosnia. This move was seemingly appreciated by Europe's less political Muslims who could now look to scholars recognised independently for their contributions to Islamic scholarship.

Despite fluctuations in membership, the council's members in European residence have always been underrepresented, with the exception of those in Britain, France, and Germany (see also Caeiro 2011: 125). The geographic asymmetry in the ECFR's European representation was reinforced by a decision made in the council's second session, which determined that two subcommittees for fatwa would be established in Britain and France to provide relief from the excessive workload accumulated during the ECFR's ordinary sessions (ECFR 2003: 7). Together, these moves undermined the input of significant numbers of European Muslims living beyond the confines of Western Europe's most populous countries. It is clear from its earliest endeavours that the ECFR needed to provide a more equitable representation of Europe in order to achieve ascendency amongst Europeans. At first glance, resolving the issue was a simple matter. With some manoeuvring, the ECFR could expand its scope of influence by involving Muslims from other European countries.

The ECFR subsequently relocated its headquarters to the Republic of Ireland in accordance with its European objectives.[3] From there, the ECFR enlisted as its general secretary Hussein Halawa, the recently arrived Egyptian imam of Dublin's newly opened mosque. Although this certainly broadened the scope of the ECFR's European image, the move left some Irish Muslims confounded, which is an understandable reaction, considering the preceding historical development of Islam in Ireland. For other European countries, like Britain and France, their colonial history has shaped their involvement with the Muslim world for several centuries. However, for a country such as Ireland, which was itself colonised by Britain, the public discourse on Islam has developed rather differently.

4.   Historical background of Muslim organisations in Ireland

For the latter part of the twentieth century, Ireland had primarily been home to a transient population of Muslim medical students of South Asian descent, who first came to Dublin from South Africa to escape the educational restrictions of the newly enacted apartheid legislation. As a result, the first viable Irish Muslim community seems to have crystallised in the 1950s, when Muslim students from South Africa began arriving at the campus of the Royal College of Surgeons in Ireland in 1952.[4] The Royal College of Surgeons agreed to admit a regular quorum of South Africa's 'Indian' students each year in direct opposition to the apartheid legislation. Although the arrangement was not an official accord between the two countries, it initiated a steady stream of Muslim migration, which enabled an early Irish Muslim community to take shape in the Dublin area (Khan 2010: 44–5).

In the earliest days, the religious activities of the medical students revolved around organised prayer meetings, charity collections, and *'īd* celebrations. Interestingly, most Muslim gatherings took place at a Protestant sponsored halls of residence called Koinonia House where the bulk of incoming international students stayed. However, as mature medical students began branching out into private accommodation around the city, the members of Dublin's Muslim community began making use of alternative facilities beyond the university setting. By January 1959, a few students headed by Yousuf Jhavary managed to form the Dublin Islamic Society, the first formal organisation for Muslims in Irish residence (Khan 2011: 487–8). However, discussions about the construction of permanent mosque facilities did not take place until much later.[5]

In the summer break of 1970, the Muslim medical students of the Royal College of Surgeons decided to solicit donations from friends and family members upon their return home to South Africa for the holidays in the interest of acquiring a mosque site. Although they managed to raise considerable funds from personal contacts, it was still not quite enough to purchase a suitable property for Dublin's first mosque. In 1972, an early Irish Muslim community leader, Tajmmul Hussain Hayat, initiated a major fundraising campaign in which he began to seek donations from various governments abroad. In the same year another early Irish Muslim community leader, Dr Yusuf Vaizie, invited diplomatic representatives from Middle Eastern countries, whose Irish embassies were then based in London, to visit Dublin in connection with student recruitment for the Royal College of Surgeons.[6] Between 1972 and 1973, Vaizie accompanied four RCSI professors to London for additional meetings with diplomatic dignitaries from the Egyptian, Kuwaiti and Saudi Arabian embassies regarding these objectives (Khan 2011: 492). These meetings provided embassy officials with an opportunity to acquaint themselves with the mosque project through someone who was directly involved. A breakthrough came in March 1974 when the Dublin Islamic Society procured a sizeable donation of nearly £18,000 from King Faisal of Saudi Arabia. Interestingly, the donation was arranged through Salem Azzam, the Saudi diplomat in London who, as mentioned above, founded the Islamic Council of Europe the same year (Khan 2011: 492). In this respect, the Dublin mosque project coincided with Azzam's broader efforts to establish multiple Islamic institutions throughout Europe, including his own Islamic Council of Europe, whose funding was assured through his affluent contacts worldwide (Khan 2011: 493–4).

In 1976, just three years after Azzam founded the Islamic Council of Europe, the Dublin Islamic Society purchased its first mosque property in Dublin city centre. Some months prior to the opening of the mosque, the members appointed a new board of trustees to oversee the administrative affairs of the society. As one might expect, four of the five newly appointed trustees were South African in origin, which was consistent with the ethnic composition of the Irish Muslim community of the time. However, the fifth trustee selected was Salem Azzam, in appreciation of his role in helping to secure King Faisal's financial contributions towards Dublin's first mosque.[7] Although Azzam was not expected to participate in the daily affairs of ordinary Irish Muslims, he nonetheless acquired an influential role in the direction of Ireland's only Muslim organisation. As a trustee of the mosque with influential connections in London and the Middle East, Salem Azzam was given an authoritative position within the Dublin Islamic Society, despite his lack of involvement with local Irish Muslims at the grassroots level.

The steady increase of Arabic speaking Muslims through the 1980s altered the internal dynamics of the Irish Muslim community once again, since even a small boost in Muslim population figures had a relatively large impact on a congregation of this size. The changing circumstances made it easier for Muslims in permanent Irish residence to reconsider their roles in a globalised context, since the prospering Irish Muslim community remained modest in size yet fluid with continual changes in its student membership. By then, the Dublin Islamic Society consisted of a diverse conglomeration of Muslim medical students and migrant workers with mixed ethnic backgrounds from Africa, the Middle East, and Malaysia. By the early 1990s, however, Dublin's Gulf students were in a much better position to solicit funds for a new mosque project, as the Irish Muslim population continued to grow in accordance with the arrival of refugees from the wars in Bosnia and Iraq (see Bradley and Humphries, 1999, for background information). Shared business ventures between the United Arab Emirates and Ireland made the Maktoum family of Dubai a prime candidate for potential donations (Khan 2011: 502, note 59). Local Muslims had been aware of the Maktoum family's investments in the international horse racing industry, including in Ireland. In addition, it was known that the Maktoum family kept and trained several race horses at family-owned stables situated primarily around County Kildare, prior to the construction of their current facilities in Britain and Dubai (www.godolphin.com, last accessed February 2012; Butler 1997: 101).[8] With this in mind, the rationale is understandable behind the Maktoum family's willingness to fully sponsor Dublin's most recent mosque in Clonskeagh, Dublin 14, after being approached by an Emirati student from the Royal College of Surgeons in 1992. Nevertheless, local Irish Muslims involved in the process contend that the student's influential family background and personal sympathies shaped the subsequent trajectory of the project in way that has proven favourable to the proponents of global political Islam.

A decision was made to build a large mosque in Dublin equipped with full facilities for the future notwithstanding the report of Irish census figures indicating that only 3,875 Muslims were living throughout the Republic of Ireland in 1991 (Government of Ireland 1995: 22). These figures suggest that upon construction, the vast majority of Ireland's Muslim population could potentially have fit into the mosque at Clonskeagh at the same time. Nevertheless, the mosque project continued as planned and was completed in anticipation of Dublin's growing Muslim population. The Islamic Cultural Centre of Ireland (ICCI) in Clonskeagh was inaugurated by Irish President Mary Robinson and Deputy Ruler of Dubai Sheikh Hamdan bin Rashid al-Maktoum on 16 November 1996. In addition to the restaurant, mortuary, and residential quarters, the new mosque complex incorporated the site of Ireland's first Muslim National School. Remarkably, the full cost of the mosque's construction and its subsequent maintenance to date, including its extensive administrative staff, has generously been provided in its entirety by the Maktoum foundation.

5.   Dublin as the centre of *fiqh al-aqalliyyāt*

Only months after the opening of the ICCI in Clonskeagh, the inaugural meeting of the European Council for Fatwa and Research took place in London. Within the next five months, the first official session of the ECFR had taken place in Sarajevo in August 1997, which was hosted by the then Grand Mufti of Bosnia, Mustafa Cerić. By the second meeting in October 1998, the ECFR had conveniently relocated its headquarters to the newly built facilities of the ICCI in Clonskeagh, Dublin 14 (ECFR 2003: 6). The motivation for the move may also have involved financial considerations, since the regular meetings of the ECFR have been fully funded by the Maktoum foundation since at least 1998. Coincidentally, the ICCI's recently appointed imam from abroad, Sheikh Hussein Halawa, was in an ideal position to take over as the ECFR's general secretary, representing the voice of Islam in Ireland. Much to the dismay of local Irish Muslims, imam Halawa lacks conversational fluency in the English language. Nevertheless, imam Halawa has remained an influential figure in the ECFR's secretariat since his timely arrival in Dublin corresponding with the ICCI's opening. This is certainly not to say that Halawa or any other members of the ECFR are incompetent, inept of scholarly ability, or somehow unversed in the traditional Islamic sciences. However, cultural differences and communication issues in particular have drawn considerable attention to the European orientation of the European Council for Fatwa and Research's membership at the local level. These issues have also given rise to internal debates within the Irish Muslim community regarding the suitability of such imams, who were privately selected from abroad and brought in to countries, such as Ireland, with small Muslim populations and limited mosque space.

In a recent posting on the FIOE's website, Halawa elaborated the objectives of the ECFR with regard to the dissemination of *fiqh al-aqalliyyāt*, the jurisprudence of Muslims living in a minority status in the West (Wasatiyya online interview with Hussein Halawa, n.d., available through the FIOE's website, www.euro-muslim.com, last accessed February 2012). The basic premise of *fiqh al-aqalliyyāt* suggests that the minority status of Muslims in Western countries necessitates certain legal provisions, which would otherwise be forbidden in a majority situation. It has been suggested that Taha Jabir al-Alwani, a former ECFR member and the founder of the Fiqh Council of North America, was the first person to use the term in relation to Muslim political participation in America (Masud 2002: 17). However, Halawa has suggested in personal conversation that the development of *fiqh al-aqalliyyāt*, as it is currently understood, was a joint effort by ECFR members under the direction of Qaradawi's intellectual guidance, despite Alwani's usage of the term prior to the formation of the ECFR.[9] The notion of *fiqh al-aqalliyyāt* has since been both praised and heavily criticised by Muslim scholars worldwide. Notable critics include Swiss academic Tariq Ramadan (Ramadan 2004: 191), who himself claims to have been offered membership to the ECFR on four separate occasions, which he has consistently declined (Ramadan 2005: available at www.tariqramadan.com/Responses-to-the-Muslim-scholars,311.html, last accessed February 2012). Another outspoken critic has been the prominent Syrian scholar, Sheikh Muhammad Sa'id Ramadan al-Bouti, who maintains that the ECFR was set up to fulfil the political aspirations of its members by appeasing Western authorities (ECFR 2008: 3). Such statements are antithetical to the council's purported agenda and have damaged the council's reputation beyond its Islamist base.

The controversial nature of the ECFR's methodology involves a reinterpretation of the traditional legal concept of *darūra* (necessity) in a way that seems to broaden its scope beyond a pressing need by equating it to a *hāja* (lesser need) (ECFR 2003: 162). This has raised numerous questions regarding the validity of the ECFR's rulings, particularly from the scholars of *usūl al-fiqh*, which has further led to a profound sense of scepticism surrounding the council's fatwas throughout the Muslim world. These fatwas have made it permissible for Muslims residing in Europe to take out mortgages in certain situations, which would otherwise have been forbidden (ECFR 2003: 160–8, or fatwa 26 from the second collection of fatwas). It has also made concessions for Muslims inheriting from deceased non-Muslim relatives (ECFR 2003: 148–9, or fatwa 19 from the second collection of fatwas), for Muslim women converts in the West to remain married to their non-Muslim husbands (ECFR 2008: 4; Caeiro 2011: 134–6), and for Muslim women to remove their hijabs (headscarves) under the right circumstances (ECFR 2003: 34–6, or fatwa 6 from the first collection of fatwas). However, it is interesting to note that within an Irish context at the local level, the council's less controversial fatwas seem to have caused the greatest stir.

6. Regulating Ramadan in Europe

In an effort to promote Muslim unity, the ECFR passed a resolution during its third ordinary session, which declared that it would begin appointing in advance the dates for the months of Ramadan and Shawwal based on astronomical calculations (ECFR 2003: 15–16, 123–4, or fatwa 8 from the second collection of fatwas). Considering the nature of lunar observation, determining the precise dates for the months of the Islamic calendar as well as the dates for Islamic festivals like *'īd al-fitr* (the holiday following the month of fasting during Ramadan) in particular, has become a precarious exercise subject to geographic location and atmospheric conditions. In these regards, the ECFR's decision to use scientific data to calculate the appearance of the new crescent moon for a specific location, which could then be extended for use by the rest of the world, initially appeared to be a simple administrative matter. In Muslim majority countries, questions concerning timekeeping, dates, and calendars are officially addressed by the religious authorities of the state to ensure uniformity in mainstream religious practice across each country. For Muslims in the West however, designating common dates for the observance of Ramadan and *'īd al-fitr* (i.e. the first day of Shawwal) has notoriously posed a problem, due to the lack of recognised Muslim political authorities.

The ECFR's desire to impose a unique date for the beginning of the months of Ramadan and Shawwal for European Muslims was consistent with Qaradawi's claim that 'the objective of this Council is to promote a uniform Fatwa in Europe and to prevent controversy and intellectual conflicts regarding the respective issues wherever possible' (ECFR 2003: ix). Accordingly, the ECFR issued a statement affirming that Ramadan 2010 would end after twenty-nine days of fasting on Wednesday, 8 September, instead of after thirty days of fasting, which remained the only other possibility for any particular lunar month. Therefore, the first day of Shawwal, and hence *'īd al-fitr*, was determined in advance to take place on Thursday, 9 September 2010 through careful lunar calculations, as opposed to its establishment through direct observation (ECFR n.d.).

In anticipation of local compliance with the ECFR's fatwa, the ICCI in Dublin issued Ramadan timetables to its Muslim members, detailing the appropriate timings for daily prayers and fasting throughout the month of Ramadan. To simplify matters further and to prevent any causes for confusion, the ICCI only printed timings for twenty-nine days, effectively eliminating the possibility of a thirty-day month of Ramadan in 2010. This was done in contrast to most other mosques in Europe, whose local administrators typically print timetables for the full thirty-day period, since the length of a lunar month in Islam has traditionally been determined retroactively by the actual sighting of the new crescent moon. In this respect, the moon may or may not be visible on the twenty-ninth night of any given lunar month depending on multiple factors. For example, moon sightings may be further complicated by local atmospheric conditions, such as cloudiness or haze, even though sighting the moon would have otherwise been possible on a clear night. Moreover, in many European countries like Britain, the new crescent moon might be visible in southern cities, like London, a day or two prior to becoming visible in northern cities, like Glasgow, due to the angling of the Earth in relation to the lunar orbit, which, once again, makes geographic location rather important in predicting the visibility of the new crescent moon. These issues amongst British Muslims apparently captured the attention of astronomers at the Royal Observatory in Greenwich, who for a number of years have listed information pertaining to the visibility of the new crescent moon in major British Muslim centres like London, Manchester, Leeds, and Glasgow.[10] As such, the distribution of a limited Ramadan timetable in Dublin was a clear attempt by the ICCI to address the challenges facing ordinary Irish Muslims at the local level.

For some unknown reason, the ICCI officially refused to acknowledge in advance that *'īd al-fitr* would be celebrated on Thursday, 9 September 2010 as the pre-printed timetables suggested. Perhaps this was an attempt to avoid confrontations with rival Muslims who disapproved of the ECFR's use of astronomical calculations for determining the date of *'īd* before the twenty-ninth evening of Ramadan. However, the Irish Council of Imams, Ireland's national umbrella organisation, which is also chaired by Halawa, held a private meeting in which it concurred with the ECFR's fatwa. As a result of the meeting, participating Irish imams resolved that *'īd al-fitr* 2010 shall be celebrated on Thursday, 9 September in every mosque across Ireland without exception.[11] At approximately 3:00 in the afternoon on Wednesday, 8 September 2010, on the supposed eve of *'īd al-fitr*, the Muslim Association of Ireland (MAI), whose mosque in Tallaght, Dublin 24, is officially listed as the FIOE's headquarters in Ireland, sent out text messages *en masse* declaring that the *'īd* prayers would be held on the following morning in all Irish mosques based on the fatwa issued by the ECFR.[12] The text messages included full citations of the ECFR's website for further confirmation, which seemingly conveyed a greater sense of credibility for the premature decision.

Despite the efforts to coordinate the Muslims of Ireland, it was decided at the ECFR's headquarters in Clonskeagh, Dublin 14, shortly after sunset (*maghrib* prayer) on Wednesday, 8 September 2010 on the night before the declared date for *'īd al-fitr* that Irish Muslims should indeed fast the next morning for the thirtieth day of Ramadan, despite the ECFR's fatwa. Consequently, it was announced that *'īd al-fitr* would now be celebrated on Friday, 10 September 2010 in all mosques across Ireland. In response to the sudden change, a second text message was sent out by the Muslim Association of Ireland shortly after midnight, reiterating that *'īd al-fitr* was conclusively determined by the ECFR to fall on Thursday, 9 September 2010. However, due to a 'lack of commitment' of certain mosques to the ECFR's fatwa, *'īd* would now be delayed by one day to Friday, 10 September throughout Ireland in an act of solidarity.[13] The last minute decision of ECFR members to ignore their own fatwa created an even greater sense of disorder amongst ordinary worshipers, which consequently has invigorated a new debate amongst Irish Muslims at the local level.

Considering the logistical problems of overturning the ECFR's decision once the initial text message had been sent, several confused members of the Irish Muslim community experienced great difficulty in determining whether they ought to fast for the extra day on such short notice, since fasting is usually initiated before sunrise, and once again, the second text message was sent after midnight. To make matters worse, a number of Irish Muslims had already refused to celebrate *'īd* on Thursday, prior to receiving the Muslim Association of Ireland's second text message stating that *'īd* celebrations would be moved to Friday. These Muslims were apparently compelled by the fact that they had watched the live broadcast of the voluntary *tarāwīh* prayers being offered in Mecca (on Islam channel) via satellite TV, which rightly indicated that *'īd al-fitr* would not take place until Friday in the holy city. With this in mind, a number of dissenting Muslims must have voiced their objections to the ECFR's fatwa prior to sunset on Wednesday, 8 September 2010.

Although the example of Ramadan 2010 might seem inconsequential, it draws attention to the scope of the ECFR's authority and the extent of its credibility amongst ordinary Irish Muslims at the grassroots level. The fact that the ICCI itself did not adhere to the ECFR's fatwa is an important contradiction, since the ICCI doubles as the international headquarters of the ECFR, in the sense that both organisations are run from the same offices by the same administrative staff. This illuminates the obscured tension between ordinary Muslims and their institutional representatives at various levels. The example also demonstrates how the ECFR, as an external organisation, has attempted to assert itself as a religious authority upon the Muslim population of Ireland, and perhaps upon Muslim communities throughout Europe. Moreover, the Ramadan example raises concerns about the validity of other organisations such as the FIOE and its affiliates. These issues ultimately call into question the very basis of *fiqh al-aqalliyyāt*, which is marketed throughout the world as a legal theory for western Muslims, whereas its western orientations are regarded with a sense of suspicion by local Muslims in Ireland. In this sense, the example of Ramadan 2010 illustrates the process by which transnational organisations have attempted to impose Islamic ideologies upon European Muslim communities.

7. Reconciling additional ECFR fatwas in an Irish setting

Although the case of Ramadan 2010 only constitutes a single example, there are a number of other fatwas which outwardly conflict with the interests of local Irish Muslims and perhaps with the interests of other European Muslims as well. In a different fatwa issued by the ECFR, the council authorised the combining of certain daily prayers under special circumstances (ECFR 2003: 115, or fatwa 4 from the second collection of fatwas). Based on similar concerns, the ECFR declared it permissible for Muslims to perform the Friday (*jum'a*) prayer before its usual time when *zuhr* (the noon prayer) begins, as the sun crosses its zenith (ECFR 2003: 18). The reasoning behind the issuance of the fatwa revolves around the unusually long summer days of northern European countries in conjunction with the customary working hours for European employees. Whereas Fridays have typically been regarded as holidays throughout the Muslim world, European Muslims are often obliged to attend the Friday prayers irregularly during their lunch breaks whenever possible.

Depending on the season, the window for initiating the Friday prayer in northern cities like Dublin might either be significantly larger or smaller than in southern European locations like Sicily, such that the variations may constitute hours. Most mosques, including those located in regions where the discrepancy is great, such as in Scotland, would correlate the Friday services with the arrival of the prayer time, irrespective of the season. The drastic seasonal changes make it inconvenient for working Irish Muslims to attend the Friday prayer regularly, since many would require special arrangements to attend the service on a weekly basis throughout the year. As with the fatwa intended to coordinate the observance of Ramadan, the ruling concerning the Friday prayer was intended to provide European Muslims with an opportunity to develop a sense of consistency in weekly religious practices without interfering with professional responsibilities. As a result, the timing of the Friday prayer at the ICCI's mosque in Clonskeagh did not vary for more than 15 minutes each way throughout 2010, despite the seasonal fluctuations in the length of day. The ICCI's decision to implement the ECFR's fatwa appears to have been a genuine attempt to make it easier for working Muslims to participate in the weekly services with minimal disruption to their work schedules. However, the fatwa was not implemented by Dublin mosques, that cater predominantly to non-Arab Muslims, which is an indication that the non-Arabic speaking Muslims of Ireland are less influenced by the Middle Eastern scholars who dominate the ECFR's roster. Overall, the ECFR's fatwas have largely been ignored by mosques that neither collaborate with the FIOE nor support its religious ideology.

Although the ECFR has perhaps received the most attention for its fatwa permitting the use of mortgages under special circumstances (ECFR 2003: 160–8, or fatwa 26 from the second collection of fatwas), the ruling has not been widely accepted by other legal authorities. The administration of the ICCI mosque at Clonskeagh itself continues to issue statements against interest-based loans in accordance with normative Islamic legal interpretations regarding such measures. For example, a stack of fliers for distribution inside the administrative entrance to the ICCI warns of the dangers of interest-bearing transactions (ICCI n.d.). Although these warnings may not necessarily conflict with the fatwa permitting the use of mortgages, which even within the ECFR's own framework is presented as a special case, they demonstrate the challenges facing the ECFR as it attempts to balance tradition with the realities of contemporary Western societies.

These issues raise questions about the impact of the fatwas beyond the ECFR's target audience of European Muslims. Although it would be difficult to document, it appears as though the ECFR, at least initially, is having less influence in Europe than amongst more conventional audiences in the Arabic-speaking Middle East where Muslims have closer ties to the ECFR's most prominent members. If this is indeed the case, then there is a sense of irony in the fact that the *fiqh* for western Muslims is being realised in the East, where Muslims appear to be more eager to implement the ECFR's dispensations. This is perhaps due in part to the social pressures associated with the type of independent legal reasoning that responds to changing circumstances with fresh, creative, and perhaps what might be considered within Muslim major-ity societies as dangerously innovative ideas. Instead, European Muslims seem less interested in having formal religious authorities sanction pre-existing behaviour, which might be a result of the way in which Islam in the West has developed, since normative religious practices of western Muslims have typi-cally been made to evolve in isolation from local religious authorities. This has meant that western Muslims have not been afforded the luxury of waiting idly for the appearance of fatwas that address the dynamic circumstances or the pressing needs of daily life in non-Muslim lands. This would entail to some extent that the ECFR rulings are not necessarily ahead of their time, as most proponents seem to infer, but rather that the ECFR is too late in its attempt to sanction practices such as mortgages, mixed marriages, and headscarf concessions, which are already becoming increasingly widespread amongst western Muslims who have had no recourse to official Islamic authorities. Furthermore, this is not to say that these trends have somehow circumvented Middle Eastern Muslim practices, but only that religious authorities have had little involvement in their development in the West until relatively recently.

It seems clear that most Muslim intellectuals who express serious interest in the ECFR's rulings are considered to fall within Qaradawi's scope of influence, which is problematic from a legalist perspective. Although some members of the ECFR are certainly well versed in the rulings of multiple *madhhab*s (legal schools of thought), the council's reformist outlook is clear from mul-tiple statements that condemn the 'fanatic allegiance to one opinion and the total rejection of others' (ECFR 2003: 13). On its own, this statement might seem quite reasonable. However, within a legalist context its likely function is to dissuade readers from adopting a rigid form of *taqlīd* (adherence to a particular *madhhab*), which would effectively counter the underlying premises that validate the council's existence and undermine its religious authority. In this sense, there seems to have been a conscious effort by the ECFR to avoid any methodological favouritism towards any one of the four Sunni *madhhabs*, perhaps as a means of promoting this reformist approach. In an introductory statement about the purpose of *fiqh*, Qaradawi has chosen to cite a quotation from Sufyan al-Thawri (d. 778), an early scholar whose own *madhhab* has long since fallen into disuse, despite its subsequent influence on the development of Sunni Islam (ECFR 2003: *xi*). Within this context, his choice could be interpreted as a rather subtle indication of the ECFR's commitment to taking a broader multi-*madhhab* approach, which remains implicit throughout the council's self-descriptions.

8. Conclusion

In conclusion, we see that the struggle for religious authority in Islam has pervaded Muslim communities in Europe, not only through the formation of transnational Muslim networks, but also through the sharpening of notions of European Islam. Within the context of Irish Islam, this struggle has exposed an underlying tension between the practised Islam of ordinary Muslims and the Islamic legal rulings being instituted by authoritative umbrellas at national and international levels. This includes the European Council for Fatwa and Research with its headquarters in Dublin's main mosque. Interestingly, the greatest testament to this tension in Ireland is found not in the most controversial fatwas of the European Council for Fatwa and Research as one might suspect, but rather in the uncontroversial rulings which attempt to facilitate the practices of European Muslims through creative means, such as the coordination of Ramadan observances or convenient dispensations in the Friday prayer. The contradictions between the Islamic legal rulings being promoted and disseminated by transnational umbrellas, such as the FIOE and the ECFR, and the daily religious practices of the Irish Muslims who they claim to represent raises doubts about the commercialised notion of European Islam, which is currently being propagated through the public discourse both within and beyond the Muslim communities of Europe. This begs the question of why so much effort has been exerted to establish and publically promote these umbrellas, particularly in European countries with relatively obscure Muslim populations such as Ireland, when Irish Muslims appear to be content pursuing a less grandiose role in contemporary Islam.

The suggestion that the prospect of Muslim representation in Europe has captured the attention of Muslims with political orientations should perhaps have been self-evident in light of the objectives of political Islam. However, the repercussions in terms of establishing authoritative bodies in this way, which have at times been in conflict with local Muslim opinion, are reflected in the resulting notion of European Islam. By forming umbrella organisations, such as the Federation of Islamic Organisations in Europe, which portray the image of Muslim unity, the proponents of political Islam have transformed 'European Islam' into a political platform. However, this notion of European Islam relies heavily upon the hierarchical imposition upon local Muslim communities in European countries, such as Ireland, of authoritative structures, including the FIOE, the ECFR, and even the Irish Council of Imams. This, once again, is visible through the disregard of religious authorities, who serve as self-proclaimed representatives of Europe's Muslim communities, by Irish Muslims who directly and decisively repudiate officially sanctioned legal rulings, as seen in the Ramadan fiasco of 2010.

Within the broader context of contemporary Islam, the function of self-declared representative organs like the European Council for Fatwa and Research is more indicative of a special interest group attempting to create a viable Muslim lobby. By deliberately arranging mosques in an even distribution across the continent and by attaching to them official spokespersons in residence, who indirectly represent little more than corporate employees, a concerted effort has been made to create a visible network of influential figures, which extends well beyond European borders. The names of a few prominent *'ulamā'* and the proliferation of vogue terms, like *fiqh al-aqalliyyāt*, have been used to substantiate the lobby and to direct its administrators to engage with the European mainstream through a form of political activism. In this regard, the ECFR's inclinations towards establishing a successful lobby in Europe may be found in its fourth declaration of 'Means and Methods' for achieving its broader goals. Here, the ECFR explicitly defends its desire to make 'relentless efforts with the official authorities in European countries to acknowledge and officially recognise the Council, and to refer to the Council in reference to Islamic judgements' (ECFR 2003: 2). This seems remarkably similar to the council's numerous calls in other locations to seek recognition for Islam in Europe, as if the two were the same (ECFR 2003: 11). This implies a strong connection between the ECFR's self-image and its assumed role as symbolic bearer of the voice of Islam, even though this voice may involve a rather focused religio-political orientation, which operates at the expense of Muslims with dissimilar views. This sort of self-image is typical of political Islamist movements whose ambitions involve establishing combined religious and political authorities that represent an idealised notion of Islamic authenticity, not only in Ireland or Europe, but throughout the world. The long term consequences of arbitrarily assuming the role of religious authority over a population may not yet be clear, even though the apparent contradiction in the methodology employed by contemporary political Islamist movements is already evident, as we have seen. By attempting in earnest to enfranchise the Muslim populations of Europe, the Islamists have ultimately left European Muslims disenfranchised.

For outsiders witnessing this process from afar, there have been two notice-able outcomes, namely the creation of the image of European Islam and the creation of transnational networks that endorse it. It is worth noting once again that the emergence of both phenomena has taken place under the aus-pices of highly respected scholars and major Middle Eastern funders, which is significant considering that Muslims in European countries, such as Ireland, initially lacked access to both. Nevertheless, this exchange has facilitated the development of a religious infrastructure for Irish Islam in return for tacit network support. In addition, the leverage applied through the presence of private funders who require elitist access has markedly shaped the resulting organisational structures of the gradually developing Muslim communities of Ireland, as well as the landscape of European Islam.

As seen above, there is clear evidence that external influences have targeted Ireland as the hub of a European network, despite the relative insignificance of Ireland's Muslim population. The fact that there has been an attempt to displace local Muslim opinion with rulings endorsed by hierarchical institutions, which view Ireland in terms of its strategic value as an integral component in the crea-tion of a romanticised construct of European Islam, illustrates the nature of political Islam today. The ongoing challenges facing the ECFR in establishing authoritative fatwas in Ireland may be indicative of the discrepancy between the image and reality of contemporary European Islam. However, one should not mistakenly presume that organisations like the ECFR are not influential. In fact, it is this influence itself that has somewhat successfully aided in creating the false perception of European Muslim unity, which subsequently has led to the creation of the false image of European Islam.

9. Epilogue

I would like to note that this paper was written during autumn 2010, and it therefore reflects the situation at the time of writing. Since then, the most prominent members of the ECFR's membership roster appear, at least for the time being, to have gone into some sort of hiatus, even though their names are still associated with the council and are listed in current council publica-tions. I was somewhat surprised to see that virtually none of the ECFR's most prominent members attended the ECFR's Dublin meeting during summer 2011. It was made clear to me while in attendance that various developments have since affected the stability of the ECFR's executive in recent months. However, the absence of key figures at the summer 2011 meeting may be attributed to a number of factors which need not represent a trend, at least for the time being, including Qaradawi's advanced age, his health concerns, and his inability to travel as freely as in previous years. In addition, the ongoing upheaval resulting from the Arab Spring since January 2011 has momentarily distracted several members from their ECFR responsibilities in favour of more urgent engagements. In this sense, the future of the ECFR's membership roster appears to be unclear. Nevertheless, these developments only underscore the discrepancy between the ECFR's public image and the reality on the ground, which altogether only strengthens the overall argument expressed above.

Notes

1. I would like to thank the participants of the conference on 'Muslims and Political Participation in Europe' at the University of Copenhagen in October 2010 for their input on the direction of my research. I would also like to thank Dr Yusuf Vaizie, Abderrazak Zeroug, and Oliver Scharbrodt for their critique of earlier drafts of this paper. This research was funded by the Irish Research Council for the Humanities and Social Sciences (IRCHSS) and the Department of *An Taoiseach* through a postdoctoral fellowship at University College Cork from 2009 to 2011.

2. In this section, Maréchal provides an interesting discussion on the relationship between the Muslim Brotherhood and certain institutions in Britain, such as the Islamic Foundation and the Markfield Institute, which have primarily been associated with Jama'at-i Islami.

3. A similar step was taken by the FIOE itself in 2007 when it relocated its head-quarters to Brussels.

4. Although Muslims, and indeed Muslim students, had certainly been present in Ireland prior to 1952, the incoming students at the Royal College of Surgeons were largely responsible for organising fellow Muslims into a viable community.

5. The subsequent information is based largely on entries in the unpublished *Logbook* of the Dublin Islamic Society and personal communication with Dr Yusuf Vaizie.

6. Until recently, most of Ireland's diplomatic affairs were conducted through existing embassies in nearby Britain.

7. A donation of nearly £18,000 was made from King Faisal's personal finances, instead of the standard procedure of allocating funds through the Saudi Ministry of *Awqāf*.

8. The Maktoum family has since expanded its operations significantly and owns at least eight premier stables with outstanding facilities throughout the Republic of Ireland. These include Kildangan Stud, Ragusa Stud, Old Connell Stud, Ballymany Stud, and Derrinstown Stud in County Kildare; Blackhall Stud in County Wexford; Ballysheehan Stud in County Tipperary; and Woodpark Stud in County Meath. For more information, see the website of Sheikh Mohammed bin Rashid Al Maktoum's global breeding operations at www.darley.co.uk, last accessed February 2012.

9. Personal conversation with Sheikh Hussein Halawa at his Dublin office at the ICCI (October 2010).

10. For Ramadan 2011, see <www.rmg.co.uk/blogs/rog/2011/07/start_and_end_dates_of_ramadan.html> last accessed February 2012. Although this particular webpage is not stable, the Royal Observatory typically updates its website with

a similar timetable for each current year, which should adequately illustrate this example once the webpage expires. In addition, it may be worth mentioning that the website has at least for the last few years supplemented its data with a disclaimer warning that the timings 'may not correspond exactly with the official (religious) sighting of the crescent moon.'

11. Personal conversations with members of the Irish Council of Imams (September 2010), who prefer to remain anonymous.
12. The Muslim Association of Ireland's role as the FIOE's Irish representative further illustrates how multiple mosques are used to create the image of a European network, whereas the Muslim Association of Ireland relies on financial support arranged through the ICCI, Clonskeagh.
13. Generic text messages sent out to the Irish Muslim community by the Muslim Association of Ireland.

References

Ahmad, K. (1976), *Islam: Its Meaning and Message*, London: Islamic Council of Europe.

Azzam, S. (1981), *Universal Islamic Declaration of Human Rights*, Paris: Islamic Council of Europe.

Azzam, S. (1983), *A Model of an Islamic Constitution*, London: Islamic Council of Europe.

Azzam, S. (1998), 'Universal Islamic Declaration of Human Rights', *The International Journal of Human Rights*, vol. 2, no. 3, pp. 102–12.

Birt, J. (2006), 'Good Imam, Bad Imam: Civic Religion and National Religion in Britain post-9/11', *The Muslim World*, vol. 96, no. 4 (October), pp. 687–705.

Bradley, S. and N. Humphries (1999), *From Bosnia to Ireland's Private Rented Sector*, Clann Housing Association.

Butler, K. (1997), 'People of the Crescent in Dublin', *Dublin Historical Record*, vol. 50, no. 2 (Autumn), pp. 94–104.

Caeiro, A. (2006), 'The Shifting Moral Universes of the Islamic Tradition of *Iftā'*: A Diachronic Study of Four *Adab al-Fatwā* Manuals', *The Muslim World*, vol. 96, (October), pp. 661–85.

Caeiro, A. (2010), 'The Power of European Fatwas: The Minority *Fiqh* Project and the Making of an Islamic Counterpublic', *International Journal of Middle East Studies*, vol. 42, pp. 435–49.

Caeiro, A. (2011), 'Transnational ulama, European fatwas, and Islamic authority: a case study of the European Council for Fatwa and Research', in M. van Bruinessen and S. Allevi (eds), *Producing Islamic Knowledge*, London: Routledge, pp. 121–41.

Caeiro, A. and M. Saify (2009), 'Qaradawi in Europe, Europe in Qaradawi?', in J. Skovgaard-Petersen and B. Gräf (eds), *Global Mufti: The Phenomenon of Yusuf al-Qaradawi*, London: Hurst, pp. 109–48.

Coury, R. M. (1998), *The Making of an Egyptian Arab Nationalist: The Early Years of Azzam Pasha, 1893–1936*, Reading: Ithaca Press.

Esposito, J. L. and J. Voll (2001), *Makers of Contemporary Islam*, Oxford: Oxford University Press.

European Council for Fatwa and Research (2003), *Fatwas of the European Council for Fatwa and Research*, Cairo: al-Falah Foundation.

European Council for Fatwa and Research (2008), 'Scientific Review of the European Council for Fatwa and Research', no. 12–13.

European Council for Fatwa and Research (n.d.), 'Statement on Determining the Start of the Month of Shawal the year 1431 Hijri'.

Gaborieau, M. and M. Zeghal (2004), 'Autorités Religieuses en Islam', *Archives de Sciences Sociales des Religions*, vol. 49, no. 125, (January–March), pp. 5–21.

Government of Ireland (1995), *Census 1991: Volume 5 – Religion*, Dublin: Central Statistics Office.

Hardy, P. (1972), *The Muslims of British India*, Cambridge: Cambridge University Press.

Islamic Cultural Centre of Ireland (n.d.), *The Facts about Usury*, Islamic Cultural Centre of Ireland.

Kamali, M. H. (2003), *Principles of Islamic Jurisprudence*, Cambridge: The Islamic Texts Society.

Khan, A. H. (2010), 'Muslim Students in 1950s Dublin', *History Ireland*, vol. 18, no. 4, (July–August).

Khan, A. H. (2011), 'Transnational Influences on Irish Muslim Networks: From Local to Global Perspectives', *Journal of Muslim Minority Affairs*, vol. 31, no. 4, (December), pp. 486–502.

Khosrokhavar, F. (2010), 'The Muslim Brotherhood in France', in Barry Rubin (ed.), *The Muslim Brotherhood*, New York: Palgrave Macmillan.

Mitchell, R. P. (1993), *The Society of the Muslim Brothers*, Oxford: Oxford University Press.

Maréchal, B. (2008), *The Muslim Brothers in Europe: Roots and Discourse*, Leiden: Brill.

Masud, M. K. (2002), 'Islamic Law and Muslim Minorities', *ISIM Newsletter 11* (December).

Mawlawi, F. (2008), *al-Muslim Muwātinā fī Ūrūbā* [Muslim Citizenship in Europe], al Itahād al-ʻāmiyya al-ʻulamā al-Muslimīn.

Ramadan, T. (2004), *Western Muslims and the Future of Islam*, Oxford: Oxford University Press.

Ramadan, T. (2005), 'Responses to the Muslim Scholars and the Leaders', (29 April 2005).

Roy, O. (2004), '*Globalized Islam: The Search for a New Ummah*', New York: Columbia University Press.

Rubin, B. (ed.) (2010), *The Muslim Brotherhood: The Organization and Policies of a Global Islamist Movement*, New York: Palgrave Macmillan.

Skovgaard-Petersen, J. and B. Gräf (eds) (2009), *Global Mufti: The Phenomenon of Yusuf al-Qaradawi*, London: Hurst.

Steinberg, G. (2010), 'The Muslim Brotherhood in Germany', in B. Rubin (ed.), *The Muslim Brotherhood*, New York: Palgrave Macmillan.

Tammimi, A. S. (2001), *Rachid Ghannouchi: A Democrat within Islamism*, Oxford: Oxford University Press.

Vidino, L. (2010), *The New Muslim Brotherhood in the West*, New York: Columbia University Press.

Van Bommel, A. (1992), 'The History of Muslim Umbrella Organizations', in W. A. R. Shadid and P. S. van Koningsveld (eds), *Islam in Dutch Society: Current Developments and Future Prospects*, Kampen: Kok Pharos.

Wasatiyya online interview with Hussein Halawa (n.d.), 'The European Council for Fatwa and Research are More Capable of Understanding the Status of Muslims in the West'.

<www.bbc.co.uk/news/world-africa-12318824> (last accessed February 2012).

<www.bbc.co.uk/news/world-africa-12320950> (last accessed February 2012).

<www.darley.co.uk> (last accessed February 2012).

<www.e-cfr.org>(last accessed February 2012).

<www.euro-muslim.com> (last accessed February 2012).

<www.godolphin.com> (last accessed February 2012).

<www.motamaralalamalislami.org> (last accessed February 2012).

<www.rmg.co.uk/blogs/rog/2011/07/start_and_end_dates_of_ramadan.html> (last accessed February 2012).

<www.tariqramadan.com/Responses-to-the-Muslim-scholars,311.html> (last accessed February 2012).

Zeghal, M. (2007), 'The "Recentering" of Religious Knowledge and Discourse: The Case of al-Azhar in Twentieth-Century Egypt', in R. W. Hefner and M. Q. Zaman (eds), *Schooling Islam*, Princeton: Princeton University Press.

12

THE POLITICAL PARTICIPATION OF POLISH MUSLIM TATARS – THE RESULT OF OR THE REASON FOR INTEGRATION? FROM TEUTONIC WARS TO THE DANISH CARTOONS AFFAIR

Agata S. Nalborczyk

Polish Muslim Tatars constitute a religious minority with an interesting status. They were settled in the Polish-Lithuanian territories at the beginning of the fourteenth century, above all because of their military service. The tradition of military service was continued by their descendants in subsequent centuries, even when military service was no longer compulsory. This kind of involvement in the political life of the Republic of Poland resulted in Muslim Tatars being granted social and religious privileges – this will be discussed later in this chapter. Recognition of the Tatars' service to the country has remained in the consciousness of Polish society to the present day and is visible in the approach to public matters concerning this minority.

1. History: the participation of Muslim Tatars in the Polish-Lithuanian and Polish armed forces

The first Muslims emerged within the borders of the Polish-Lithuanian state in the fourteenth century (Tyszkiewicz 1989: 146f); Poland[1] and the Grand Duchy of Lithuania had at that time been connected through the person of the ruler since 1385. These Muslims were Tatars who originated from the Mongol Khanate of the Golden Horde, a state nominally Islamic since the thirteenth century (Borawski and Dubiński 1986: 13–14).[2] They were prisoners of war and political refugees and, later, in the fifteenth century, mercenaries invited by the Grand Duke of Lithuania, Vytautas the Great (1401–40),[3] to fight the enemies of his country; Lithuania at that time shared its borders with the Golden Horde.

The Grand Duke of Lithuania began to settle Tatars, refugees[4] or invited mercenaries, in his lands in the fifteenth century (Tyszkiewicz 1989: 147f). In return for military service under his command and for fighting the enemies of

Lithuania, Vytautas granted Tatars principal fiefs (Pol. *ziemia hospodarska*, that is granted by a prince), which gave them a social status similar to that of the local Lithuanian nobility called *boyars* (Pol. *bojarstwo*) (Tyszkiewicz 2002: 16–17).[5] The number of Tatar settlers increased in subsequent centuries,[6] and it is estimated that during the course of the sixteenth and seventeenth centuries their number reached as many as 25,000 (Sobczak 1984: 43f). They were settled on the same terms as those before them who were settled by Vytautas, and land was given to them together with a duty to serve in the armed forces (Borawski 1983: 56–7; Konopacki 2010: 40–1). They continued to serve in their own units of cavalry called banners (Pol. *chorągiew*) (Sobczak 1984: 49f),[7] basic administrative units of soldiers in both the Crown and Lithuanian army, which consisted on average of 100 to 200 horsemen or infantrymen. There were different kinds of banners, for example district banners (*chorągiew ziemska*) formed by knights of the district or clan banners (*chorągiew rodowa*) formed by clans or families, etc. Tatar banners (*chorągiew tatarska*) were special among them: although they belonged to district banners, they were organised separately from the main banners' territorial structure (Zakrzewski 2004: 129).[8] Each of them was commanded by a *Chorąży* ('standard-bearer'), who was directly subordinate to a prince or king and during war performed the duties of a local military commander (Borawski 1994), but in peace performed the duties of a civil and judicial superior on the piece of land on which the unit was settled (Sobczak 1984: 66f; Konopacki 2010: 39). Tatars were mobilised at the command of a prince or king (or later the commander-in-chief; Pol. *hetman*), unlike other district banners, who mobilised only during the common mobilisation of armed forces (Pol. *pospolite ruszenie*) (Zakrzewski 2004: 67–8). Tatars also served in police squads, supervised the execution of decrees, suppressed revolts and served in patrols in times of unrest (Zakrzewski 2004: 137).

Some researchers claim that military service in the Polish and Lithuanian armies was the main reason for the Tatars' loss of their language in the sixteenth century (Zakrzewski 1989: 92–3) and their ongoing assimilation in subsequent centuries. Many Tatars were army officers and in order to perform the duties of an officer one had to be fluent in Polish – both spoken and written (Borawski 1991: 168f, 178).

Commanders and monarchs often expressed flattering opinions of Tatars' military service and praised them for their bravery, training and commitment (Zakrzewski 2004: 136). For instance, Hetman Krzysztof Radziwiłł, in a letter to King Sigismund III Vasa, wrote that local officials 'gave testimony that Tatars acted bravely and valiantly when necessary' (AKAD AR: IV).

Tatar units participated in all significant battles and military campaigns of the Polish-Lithuanian armies, for instance in the great victory over the Order of Teutonic Knights in the Battle of Grunwald (the First Battle of Tannenberg) in 1410 (Konopacki 2010: 28); or in the Polish-Teutonic War of 1519–21

(Tyszkiewicz 1989: 170f). In the fifteenth and sixteenth centuries, fulfilling their duty to defend the Polish crown and the Lithuanian borders, Muslim Tatars fought against their own kinsmen, Tatars who were attacking from the south (Miśkiewicz and Kamocki 2004: 22–3).

One of the most important campaigns in which Tatars took part were the wars with the Order of the Teutonic Knights of St. Mary's Hospital in Jerusalem, known in Polish as *Krzyżacy* ('the Teutonic Knights'). They were the most dangerous among the enemies of Lithuania because in Western Europe they claimed to fight pagans – Lithuania was the last country in Europe to be Christianised (in 1385). The power of the Teutonic Knights was broken at the great Battle of Grunwald on 15 July 1410, where they were defeated by joint Polish-Lithuanian forces.[9] About 1,000–2,000 Tatars fought in the Lithuanian army. Some of them were mercenaries already settled in Lithuania, and some 300 were the troops of Jalal ad-Din, a refugee from the Golden Horde. He was the son of Tokhtamysh Khan and, along with other supporters of his defeated father, took refuge in the Grand Duchy of Lithuania and formed a military alliance with the Grand Duke of Lithuania, Vytautas the Great (Konopacki 2010: 25–6). Before the battle Tatars conducted reconnaissance and delivered reports and orders, and during the battle they formed the advance guard of the Polish-Lithuanian armies.

However, the Teutonic Knights were not completely defeated and military campaigns continued, especially during the reign of King Sigismund I of Poland in the years 1519–21. In this military campaign there were, in different periods, 200–300 Tatars among 2,500–3,000 soldiers of light cavalry (Tyszkiewicz 1988: 90f).[10] A registry has survived of 306 Tatars, mentioned by name, who enlisted in 1520 (Tyszkiewicz 1989: 190–1). At that time most Tatars fought in the reserves (the main army was at war with the Teutonic Knights in the North) against the attacks of their fellow believers from the Crimea whom they treated as invaders of their homeland. Earlier they told them: 'Neither God nor the Prophet tells you to plunder, therefore we take you for plunderers'. Tatars wrote to the Polish king about Vytautas the Great and the freedom of religion he gave them, and they assured the king of their devotion to the Polish-Lithuanian nation: 'We swore on our sabres that we love Lithuanians, when we were their prisoners during war, and when we entered this land they told us that this sand, this water and these trees belong to all of us . . . We are not aliens in your country' (Tyszkiewicz 1989: 189).

In the next centuries Tatars fought, among others, in the war against Russia (1660–3), in the war with the Ottoman Empire (1669–99), during which the life of the Polish king, Jan III Sobieski, the commander of the united troops, is said to have been saved by one of his Tatar soldiers.[11] Tatars were granted land by King John III Sobieski in 1679 in Podlachia, which started their settlement in the territories of modern-day Poland (Kryczyński 2000 [1938]: 27).[12]

In addition to land, from the very beginning Tatars were granted the right to enjoy freedom of religion, to practise Islam, to erect mosques on royal privileges, and there were no serious attempts to convert them to Christianity (Konopacki 2010: 71f; Borawski and Dubiński 1986: 74). Their military service is regarded by researchers as the reason for this tolerance (Tyszkiewicz 2008: 151; Konopacki 2010: 71–2).

Local Tatar communities were concentrated around mosques and were presided over by a local Tatar *chorąży* (standard-bearer). Mullahs (Pol. *mołła* or *mułła*), elected by the communities imams (Tyszkiewicz 2008: 155), were not only mosque leaders, but also acted as community representatives before courts and in offices, kept register books of births and deaths (Konopacki 2010: 92–4), and administered oaths (Sobczak 1984: 77).

Until the sixteenth century the social status of Tatars who served in the army in return for land was comparable to that of Lithuanian *szlachta* (the Polish name for the nobility) (Zakrzewski 1988: 573), and in the seventeenth century they officially received all the civil rights of this social class (Borawski and Dubiński 1986: 85–7; Zakrzewski 1988: 579). In the second half of the eighteenth century the legal status of their land ownership was changed from fief to hereditary property (Kryczyński 2000 [1938]: 31f; Borawski 1983: 66), and the Constitution of 3 May 1791 finally granted them full political rights (Bohdanowicz, Chazbijewicz and Tyszkiewicz 1997: 14).

In 1795 due to the third partition carried out by Russia, Prussia and Habsburg Austria, Poland lost its independence. The lands inhabited by Tatars were incorporated into the Russian Empire and Polish Muslims came under Russian authority (Tyszkiewicz 2002: 77). Many Tatars participated in armed resistance before the partitions and throughout the period of the partitions, for instance the 4th Regiment of the Advance Guard of the Army of the Grand Duchy of Lithuania commanded by General Józef Bielak, who was of Tatar origin, fought in the Kościuszko Insurrection in the 1790s (Tyszkiewicz 2002: 33–47). This regiment consisted of eight squadrons and each was commanded by officers of Tatar origin. Tatars also fought in subsequent uprisings directed against Russia (Kryczyński 2000 [1938]: 38) – in the November Uprising of 1830–1 and in the January Uprising of 1863–4 – including a woman, Rozalia Buczacka, who served in the National Gendarmerie (Miśkiewicz and Kamocki 2004: 45f).

2.   Official recognition of Islam as a religion in Poland

Another privilege Tatars received from the Polish state was the official recognition of Islam as a religion. The recognition was preceded by talks and negotiations with representatives of the Polish government, the relevant ministries and offices.

After Poland attained independent statehood in 1918, the population of Polish-Lithuanian Tatars in its lands numbered about 5,500, and there were nineteen Muslim religious communities registered. Before 1918 they lived within the borders of the Russian Empire and matters concerning religion were under the authority of the Mufti of Simferopol (the Crimea) (Tyszkiewicz 2002: 82).

In the Republic of Poland at that time Polish Muslims enjoyed full freedom of worship[13] but they did not have an all-Polish organisation. In 1925, with the support of the Ministry of Interior and the Ministry of Denominations and Public Enlightenment, the All-Polish Convention of Delegates from Muslim Communities (Wszechpolski Zjazd Delegatów Gmin Muzułmańskich) established Muzułmański Związek Religijny (the Muslim Religious Union, henceforward the MZR) (Sobczak 2004: 188f) and elected the mufti Jakub Szynkiewicz (1884–1966).[14] After several years of negotiations between the Polish government and the MZR, Islam was officially recognised by the Polish Parliament in the Act of 21 April 1936 on the relations between the state and the MZR in the Republic of Poland.[15]

Apart from defining in detail the relationship between the State and Muslims represented by the MZR, the Act described the functions and principles of the MZR. The Union was independent from clerical and secular authorities, it gained legal entity and so did all local Muslim communities (Article 35). They were granted tax allowances or tax exemptions, which were enjoyed by other denominational organisations, whereas the head offices of the clergy and the MZR authorities were to be treated on equal terms as the offices of public servants (Article 41).

According to this Act, Muslim religious officials were entitled to special rights guaranteed by the state legislature to the clergy of officially recognised denominations (Article 24), including the right to receive state-funded salaries paid by the Ministry of Religious Denominations and Public Enlightenment (Article 38).[16] Islamic religious instruction in primary and secondary schools was introduced on generally accepted terms. All historical buildings belonging to Muslim communities were taken care of by the state (Article 39), and *waqfs*, i.e. religious foundations, were exempt from taxation and other payments (Articles 43–45). Muslims were also given the right to spiritual care in hospitals and the army (Article 22).

As a testimony to the tradition of Tatar military service, there was also the Tatar squadron of the 13th Regiment of Wilno Uhlans in the Polish army, with an imam, slightly different uniforms, to which Muslims were recruited. Tatars were also appointed by the Ministry of Foreign Affairs to diplomatic service in Muslim countries (Miśkiewicz and Kamocki 2004: 76). Tatars held important positions in the army and public administration, for example Olgierd Najman Mirza Kryczyński, prosecutor of the Supreme Court in Warsaw from 1933–8 and vice president of the Appellate Court from 1938 to the beginning of the Second World War in 1939 (Tyszkiewicz 2002: 146), and Leon Najma Mirza Kryczyński, who was the vice president of the Regional

Court in Gdynia (Tyszkiewicz 2002: 131f). Tatars who were high-ranking officers included General Aleksander Romanowicz (the commander of the Tatar Uhlan Regiment), his successor, Podpolkovnik (Lieutenant Colonel) Zenon Kryczyński, Podpolkovnik (Lieutenant Colonel) Bahaeddin-Bej Emir Hassan Chursz (the commander of Mahometan Squadron, 1920–2), and Rittmeister Aleksander Jeliasiewicz (the commander of Tatar Squadron). Lieutenant Colonel Leon Mirza Huźman Sulkiewicz served in the artillery and was awarded the highest military decoration in Poland, the Order of Virtuti Militari, and Lieutenant Colonel Fuad Aleksandrowicz (Konopacki 2006: 33).

During the Second World War, Tatars served in all units of the Polish Army on almost every front in the world; in the II Corps of the Polish Armed Forces in the West and in the Polish 1st Tadeusz Kościuszko Infantry Division under Soviet command. Interestingly, even Tatar women shared a similar focus on military service – nine women served in the Women's Auxiliary Service in the II Corps of the Polish Armed Forces in the West (Konopacki 2006: 33). The most well-known of them is Dżennet Dżabagi-Skibniewska (1915–91), a women's military training instructor; in 1939 she took part in the defence of Gdynia, for which she was given the rank of lieutenant. During the war, she fought in the Home Army (Pol. *Armia Krajowa*) in Cracow, and subsequently had to flee the country. In 1942 she became an educational officer and a war correspondent in the II Corps of the Polish Armed Forces in the West. She sustained two serious wounds, one during the Battle of Monte Cassino in 1944 (Miśkiewicz and Kamocki 2004: 136–7).

Tatars are exceptionally proud of their past and the military service of their ancestors. Contemporary magazines, books, and poetry volumes published by Tatars often feature mentions of officers of Tatar origin serving in the Polish army.

3.   The present day

After World War II, only a small part of the territories inhabited by Polish Tatars remained within Polish borders. The largest Muslim settlements located around Vilnius fell to the USSR, mainly the Lithuanian and Belarusian SSR's. Only two mosques, in Kruszyniany and Bohoniki, and three pre-war religious communities (in the two villages named above and in Warsaw) remained in post-war Poland. Being Polish citizens, Tatars were forced to leave the USSR and were mostly relocated to the so-called Recovered Territories, i.e. parts of pre-war Germany granted to Poland after the war by the three superpowers (Miśkiewicz and Kamocki 2004: 81f). This land had belonged to Poland since the tenth century, before the war it was a part of the Third Reich. As a result the Tatar community was dispersed. Many educated Tatars lost their lives in the war. The number of imams and places of worship was grossly insufficient.

Post-war Poland was politically dependent on the USSR, the prevailing ideology being socialism. The state was organised according to socialist ideas and the country changed its name to the People's Republic of Poland in 1952. Religion as such was by no means regarded as a positive phenomenon by the communists and even though the year 1947 saw the reactivation of the Muslim Religious Union (known as the Muslim Religious Union in the People's Republic of Poland) and although the Sejm (parliament) did not revoke the Act of 1936, the religious life of Polish Muslims (Tatars) did not enjoy favourable conditions. Religious instruction was banned from schools and it was only provided in private houses (Nalborczyk 2011: 185). The role of imams was assumed by people educated before the war (Bohdanowicz, Chazbijewicz and Tyszkiewicz 1997: 81) as there was nowhere to train new imams and travelling abroad to get religious education (even to Yugoslavia) did not meet with the approval of the authorities, who had the right to grant or retain citizens' passports. What is more, the financial burden of such a journey was too great for the impoverished Tatar community, which was further deprived of income from the *waqfs,* which had been nationalised by the socialist government.

After the war, the number of chaplains was reduced in the Polish Army and a separate unit for Muslim soldiers was not revived. This meant there was no field imam.

Until 1989, Poland was not a democratic country and freedom of speech and the political activity of citizens were very much limited. This was true also for Polish Tatars, although sometimes the authorities tried to use them to build relations with Arab countries, for example by organising the Lebanese Mufti's visit to Poland and to Tatar communities in 1984 (Bohdanowicz, Chazbijewicz and Tyszkiewicz 1997: 84).

After the political transition of 1989 Polish citizens regained their rights and freedoms, including freedom of association and freedom of speech.

There are no precise data available concerning the number of Polish Muslims, but there is no doubt that nowadays Muslims in Poland constitute only a small religious minority. Official statistics provide only the number of members of the MZR (the Muslim Religious Union in the Republic of Poland) – in 2002 there were 5,123 members (GUS 2003: 135–7).[17] The Muslim population consists of two groups: Tatars, whose number is estimated at 5,000,[18] and immigrant Muslims – estimated at 20,000–25,000 – and these two groups together amount to 0.06–0.08% of the total population of the country.

3.1.   The Danish cartoons affair

A more recent example of Muslim Tatars' involvement in political and public life in Poland is the Danish cartoon affair.

On 30 September 2005 a Danish newspaper, *Jyllands-Posten,* in an article entitled *Muhammad Ansigt* (The Face of Muhammad), published twelve cartoons of the Prophet. By the beginning of 2006 Muslims all over the world had protested against the cartoons. Some Western newspapers reprinted all of the cartoons or selected cartoons to show their support for freedom of the press.[19]

In Poland two cartoons were printed in the *Rzeczpospolita* daily newspaper on 4 February 2006. The Polish article was titled *Wolność słowa nie jest prowokacją* (Freedom of Speech is not a Provocation) (<http://new-arch.rp.pl/artykul/597105.html> last accessed 23 November 2010). The editor-in-chief of the newspaper, Grzegorz Gauden, in his comments in an editorial (Pol. *Od redakcji*) explained why his newspaper had published the cartoons, writing that 'Freedom of speech has to be defended. Even if we do not agree with the contents' (Gauden 2006b). It is important to state that 49% of *Rzeczpospolita*, one of Poland's best-selling newspapers (subscribed to by all public offices), belongs to the state treasury through the owner, Państwowe Przedsiębiorstwo Wydawnicze 'Rzeczpospolita' SA.

Polish Muslims raised protests against the publication of the cartoons and the Muslim Religious Union demanded an apology from the editors of the newspaper for insulting Muslim religious feelings.[20] The Mufti, Tomasz Miśkiewicz, the president of the Highest Muslim Board of the Muslim Religious Union, expressed this protest in a letter to the editor-in-chief of *Rzeczpospolita* in which he wrote that freedom of speech cannot lead to insulting religious feelings and that the publication of the cartoons in *Rzeczpospolita* is 'an arrogance'. He also stated that Polish society is raised 'in the spirit of tolerance and respect for others' and this cannot be 'destroyed and trampled upon' (available at <http://www.arabia.pl/content/view/282349/161/> last accessed 23 November 2010).[21]

The Muslim Religious Union is a traditional and the oldest organisation of Polish Muslims and therefore it is associated by the Polish public with Tatars. The Polish government quickly and firmly reacted to the protest of the Muslim Religious Union and other important public institutions supported it. The Polish Prime Minister at that time, Kazimierz Marcinkiewicz, issued a statement on the day of the publication of the cartoons (http://wiadomosci.gazeta.pl/wiadomosci/1,55670,3147589.html, last accessed 23 November 2010) in which he wrote that 'the publication of the cartoons crosses the boundaries of the well-understood freedom to express one's opinions' and that he shares 'the feelings of those who may feel offended by the publications in the newspaper.' Moreover, he emphasised that 'Poland was and still remains a country of tolerance. This fact is confirmed by the 600-year presence of the Muslim Tatar community in the territory of the Republic of Poland.'[22] The Deputy Prime Minister, Ludwik Dorn, stated that the government attempted to dissuade the newspaper from reprinting the cartoons (Gauden 2006a).

On the same day, the Minister of Foreign Affairs, Stefan Meller, reacted to the publication:

On behalf of the Ministry of Foreign Affairs and the government of the Republic of Poland, I would like to ask Muslim worshippers of Muhammad[23] for forgiveness. At the same time I would like to ask especially the ambassadors of Muslim countries accredited in Poland that they explain to the public opinions of their countries that this is indeed a misunderstanding, because the cartoons are somewhat quoted from the European press. (Strybel 2006)

The Media Ethics Council also reacted quickly and issued a statement on 5 February 2006 in which it criticised the publication: 'One cannot ridicule images and symbols of any religion, regardless of circumstances' (available at <http://www.radaetykimediow.pl/index.php?option=com_content&view= article&id=83:w-sprawie-przedruku-w-rzeczpospolitej-z-0302-br-karykatur-proroka-mahometa-&catid=20:rok-2006&Itemid=27> last accessed 29 August 2012).

The representatives of the Roman Catholic Church, the largest Christian Church in Poland, also expressed their opinion. The Commission of the Polish Episcopate for Dialogue with Non-Christian Religions issued a statement on 4 February 2006 in which the President of the Commission, Bishop Tadeusz Pikus, expressed disapproval of the lack of respect 'from the supporters of unlimited freedom of speech towards people of faith and religious images, symbols and values' (Pikus 2006). Priest Adam Boniecki, the editor-in-chief of the opinion-forming *Tygodnik Powszechny* weekly newspaper, Archbishop Sławoj Leszek Głódź, and Priest Professor Piotr Mazurkiewicz from the University of Cardinal Stefan Wyszyński, expressed their opinion against the abuse of freedom of religion and insulting religious feelings (http://www.znak. org.pl/index.php?t=wydarzenia&id=3749, last accessed 23 November 2010).

On 7 February 2006 the editors of *Rzeczpospolita* apologised for the publication of the cartoons. The editor-in-chief, Grzegorz Gauden, wrote:

The Saturday publication in *Rzeczpospolita* hurt the feelings of a large group of people, Muslims, but also Christians and non-believers. We know it today. We assure you that this was not our intention, and we are very sorry about it. (Gauden 2006b)

What is significant about the events connected with the publication of the cartoons in Poland is that it was the representatives of Tatars, the traditional Polish Muslim community, who expressed their opinions about the issue, and that the publication was immediately condemned by the Polish authorities. Members of parliament from different political parties also expressed their disapproval of the publication. On 10 February 2006 representatives of the Muslim Religious Union, with Mufti Tomasz Miśkiewicz, were guests of Marek Jurek, the Marshal of the Sejm (parliament) of the Republic of Poland. The Marshal expressed his sympathy concerning the publication, but he also emphasised that the families of Polish Tatars 'have the greatest tradition of freedom fighting' (http://www.wirtualnemedia.pl/artykul/marszalek-sejmu-jest-mi-przykro, last accessed 23 March 2010). On 8 June 2006 the exhibition 'Tatars – Muslims in the territories of the Republic of Poland' was opened in the Sejm by Marshal Jurek.

Therefore, the public statements reflect the awareness of the history and tradition of Muslim Tatar presence in the Polish territories. It allows us to assume that it was partly due to the pride of many Tatar families and involvement in the fight for the independence of Poland, that the protests of Polish Muslims were met with such good will from the authorities.

3.2. *The tradition of military service amongst Tatars in the twenty-first century*

The great tradition of military service by Muslim Tatars in the Polish Army is still visible in their relationship with the highest Polish authorities, e.g. with the President of Poland.

On 25 November 2010 in Gdańsk, President Bronisław Komorowski unveiled a monument to the Polish Tatars. The statue depicts a Tatar horseman in the uniform of the Tatar Squadron of the 13th Regiment of Vilnius Uhlans in the Polish army. During the ceremony, President Komorowski expressed his profound gratitude to the Tatars for their patriotism, love and loyalty to their motherland Poland, which they have served for over 600 years (http://www. prezydent. pl / aktualnosci / wizyty - krajowe / art , 29 , nie - ma - jednego - wzorca - patriotyzmu.html, last accessed 15 September 2011). President Komorowski stressed that Tatars have fought for Poland from the battle of Grunwald in 1410 through to the Second World War:

> There was no enemy of Poland against whom they did not draw their weapons for the good of their motherland. They fought and forced out Russians, Swedes and even Turks despite their common religion – Islam. Without them the memorable victory in the Battle of Vienna would not have been possible and for this reason King John III Sobieski took them to his heart.

At the end of the ceremony, a division of soldiers saluted the Tatars who died in service to their country.

On 17 February 2011, representatives of Polish Muslim communities and imams (about one hundred people) were invited to the Presidential Palace to celebrate the 85th anniversary of the establishment of the Muslim Religious Union. During this meeting President Komorowski decorated Muslim Tatars for their contribution to Poland, the Muslim community and interreligious and intercultural dialogue. In his speech, the President stressed once again the significance of Tatars in Polish history, serving in the Polish army against the country's enemies. He recognised this meeting as an opportunity to thank the Polish Muslim Tatars for their fine and commendable service to the Republic of Poland (http://www.prezydent.pl/aktualnosci/wydarzenia/ art,1663,prezydent-dziekuje-tatarom-polskim-i-polskim-muzulmanom.html, last accessed 15 September 2011).

The President decorated 100-year-old imam Stefan Mustafa Jasiński from Białystok with the Knight's Cross of the Order of Polonia Restituta[24] and the Mufti and president of the Muslim Religious Union Tomasz Miśkiewicz with the Gold Cross of Merit. The following representatives of other Tatars were posthumously awarded: imam Aleksander Chalecki, awarded the Officer's Cross of the Order of Polonia Restituta, Bekir Jakubowski – major in the Polish Army, veteran of the Second World War – decorated with the Order Virtuti Militari[25] and the Cross of Valour, imam Ali Ismail Woronowicz – a military chaplain in the Tatar squadron of the 13th Regiment of Vilnius Uhlans in the Polish army[26] – awarded the Knight's Cross of the Order of Polonia Restituta (http://www.prezydent.pl/aktualnosci/ordery-i-odznaczenia/ art,901,prezydent-odznaczyl-osoby-zasluzone-na-rzecz-muzulmanow-w-polsce.html, last accessed 15 September 2011).

3.3. Protest against a new mosque in Warsaw

Another event which in a somewhat specific way shows the attitude of Polish society towards Muslim Tatars was the protest against the construction of a mosque in Warsaw, organised by an unknown association called Europe of the Future (Europa Przyszłości) on 27 March 2010. The mosque is being built by the Muslim League, a new religious association, which was registered in 2004 and brings together mostly immigrants and their families (Nalborczyk 2011: 189–91). After initial protests directed against Muslims in general, and after subsequent arguments from researchers and experts in the field that Tatars have been present in Poland for over 300 years and not only have they never been a threat but they have also been faithful citizens and soldiers, Europe of the Future had to change their action so that it did not look like a protest against Tatars.[27]

4. Conclusions

Tatars have taken an active part in political life since the very beginning of their presence in Polish and Lithuanian territories. This has manifested itself in the armed fighting waged by the Polish-Lithuanian Commonwealth, as Tatars were brought to the territories of the Commonwealth predominantly as mercenaries. They fought in all major battles and military campaigns, often against Muslim fellow believers. In return for military service they were granted numerous privileges in Poland and Lithuania – principally land, which later changed from fief to hereditary; their social status was equal to that of the local nobility (*szlachta*) and they were granted freedom of religion and permitted to construct sacred buildings.

In the first half of the twentieth century Poland officially recognised Islam as a religion and Muslims were granted numerous religious privileges.

The awareness of the history of the Tatar minority is present in Polish society to this day and is evident not only in the published opinions of Tatars themselves, but also in how Tatars are treated in the public sphere, for instance in the reaction of the Polish authorities to the Muslim protests raised against the publication of cartoons of Muhammad in the Polish press. Tatar participation in the military in the past has contributed to the fact that, despite their present small population, Tatars feel that they are fully-fledged Polish citizens, with all the rights that citizenship accords.

Notes

1. Poland was known then as the Crown of the Polish Kingdom (Pol. *Korona Królestwa Polskiego*).
2. Tatars coming to Polish territories were a mixture of local Turkic tribes, mainly Kipchak, and Mongol invaders (Borawski and Dubiński 1986: 12–13). For the origins of the name 'Tatar', see Tyszkiewicz (1989: 59f).
3. However the first settlements come from the time of another duke, Olgierd (1345–77) (Konopacki 2010: 24–5).
4. For more details see J. Tyszkiewicz, *Z historii Tatarów polskich 1794–1944*, Pułtusk 2002, p. 17f.
5. There were also Tatars settled in cities whose occupation was handicraft – they did not have the privileges of Tatar-fiefholders (Kryczyński 2000 [1938]: 17).
6. For the history of Tatar settlements in Lithuania and Lithuanian–Tatar relations, see Tyszkiewicz (2002: 14f.).
7. Since the seventeenth century military units called 'banners' had their own imams – military chaplains; for more details see Tyszkiewicz (1989: 298–9).
8. Especially starting from the seventeenth century.
9. It was a huge battle: Polish-Lithuanian forces were estimated at 34,000–39,000 men and Teutonic forces, which were much better equipped and trained, at 21,000–27,000 men.
10. Cavalry and infantry from the Czech state and Moravia also served in the Polish-Lithuanian army, while in the Teutonic army there were volunteers from Western Europe – the role of Tatars in the enemy forces was exaggerated to encourage fighting with pagans (Tyszkiewicz 2008: 71f).

    A part of a song of praise for the Grand Master of the Teutonic Knights, Albrecht Hohenzollern, goes as follows: 'Die Thattern dorneben seint nicht gutt, Sie han vergossen vil christlich blut' ['Besides the Tatars are not good, they have spilled/shed a lot of Christian blood.']; the song also mentioned 30,000 Poles and

Tatars ('Polen und tatthern ein grosse schar XXX M unser feinde' ['The Poles and Tatars (were) a big troop(s)/detachment – 30,000 (of) our enemies. ']), which was certainly an overestimated figure (Voigt 1819: 388–9).

11. As one of the historical transmissions reports (Boghdanowicz, Chazbijewicz and Tyszkiewicz 1997: 23). This was Rittmeister Samuel Mur Krzeszowski, who commanded his own small banner of sixty horsemen.

12. In two of the granted villages, Bohoniki and Kruszyniany, there are still Muslim communities, mosques and *mizars* (cemeteries). There are also Tatars living in Krynki and Sokółka to this day.

13. For more details about state-church relations in the Republic of Poland at that time see Nalborczyk and Borecki (2011: 346).

14. For more information about Szynkiewicz see Tyszkiewicz (2002: 149–51).

15. For the circumstances surrounding the passing of the bill see Sobczak (2004: 173f).

16. Furthermore, the Act quoted oaths on the Koran, which were to be sworn by MZR officials and in which they pledged to remain loyal citizens of the Republic of Poland, contribute to her wellbeing and obey the Constitution (Article 9, 11, 19).

17. *Mały rocznik statystyczny 2004* does not quote any data concerning members of the MZR in Poland.

18. In the 2001 census around 3,000 people declared Tatar nationality, *Rocznik Demograficzny* (GUS 2002–2003). However, Tatars consider themselves Muslim Poles, so the number may be lower than the actual number of people of Tatar origin (some Tatars are Christian).

19. For more details see Modood, Hansen, Bleich, O'Leary, Carens (2006).

20. The Muslim League in the Republic of Poland is a new Muslim religious organisation, which gathers mostly immigrants and their families and was registered by the Ministry of Interior and Administration in 2004. It did not take an official stance on this matter; for the differences between the MZR and the Muslim League see Nalborczyk and Borecki (2011: 350–1).

21. The Muslim Religious Union also filed notification of a crime at the Public Prosecutor's Office, who on 19 July 2006 stated that according to the opinion of the experts who were appointed to investigate the case, the cartoons may have been insulting to Muslims; 'The cartoons may have been insulting', Jews-Christians-Muslims Forum (http://www.znak.org.pl/index.php?lang1=pl&page1=news&subpage1=news00&infopassid1=4365, last accessed 23 November 2010).

22. The Prime Minister explained in his statement that the Polish government does not regulate the content of media releases, but that he understands the consequences of unconsidered publications, and that is why he expressed his sympathy towards those who felt offended by the publication in *Rzeczpospolita* (Piątek 2006).

23. The press noticed the unsuitable phrase 'the worshipper of Muhammad' and considered it to be a faux pas.

24. Order of Rebirth of Poland.

25. Virtuti Militari – the highest Polish military decoration.

26. Ali Ismail Woronowicz also performed the duties of imam in the local

community in Warsaw and was a member of the Muslim Highest Board of the Muslim Religious Union. He was killed by the Soviets in 1941 (Tyszkiewicz 2002: 148–9).

27. For instance, through banners saying 'Tatars yes, Arab radicals – no!' Only a small group of people (around seventy) took part in the protest and it did not make much sense because the mosque had been constructed for over a year and permission for construction had been granted two-and-a-half years before and there was no legal basis to revoke it; for more details see Nalborczyk (2011: 191).

References

AKAD, Archiwum Główne Akt Dawnych, AR IV, t. 22., kop. 294. nr 156.

Bohdanowicz, L., S. Chazbijewicz and J. Tyszkiewicz (1997), *Tatarzy muzułmanie w Polsce*, Gdańsk: Rocznik Tatarów Polskich.

Borawski, P. (1991), 'Asymilacja kulturowa Tatarów w Wielkim Księstwie Litewskim', *Odrodzenie i Reformacja w Polsce*, vol. 36, pp. 163–91.

Borawski, P. (1983), 'Sytuacja prawna ludności tatarskiej Wielkim Księstwie Litewskim (XVI–XVIII w.)', *Acta Baltico-Slavica*, vol. 15, pp. 55–76.

Borawski, P. (1994), 'Zwierzchnicy wojskowi Tatarów w Wielkim Księstwie Litewskim', *Acta Baltico-Slavica*, vol. 22, pp. 59–83.

Borawski, P. and A. Dubiński (1986), *Tatarzy polscy, Dzieje, obrzędy, tradycje*, Warszawa: Iskry.

Gauden, G. (2006a), 'Co i skąd wie rząd', *Rzeczpospolita*, 9 February 2006, <http://new-arch.rp.pl/artykul/598021.html> (last accessed 23 November 2010).

Gauden, G. (2006b), 'Od redakcji', *Rzeczpospolita*, 4 February 2006, <http://new-arch.rp.pl/artykul/597111.html> (last accessed 23 November 2010).

GUS (2003), *Niektóre wyznania religijne w Polsce w 2002 r.*, *Mały rocznik statystyczny 2003*, Warszawa: GUS.

Karykatury Mahometa mogły byćobraźliwe (2006), Forum Żydzi-Chrześcijanie-Muzułmanie, 19 July 2006, <http://www.znak.org.pl/index.php?lang1=pl&page1=news&subpage1=news00&infopassid1=4365> (last accessed 23 November 2010).

Konopacki, Artur (2010). *Życie religijne Tatarów na ziemiach Wielkiego Księstwa Litewskiego w XVI–XIX w.*, Warszawa: Wyd. UW.

Konopacki, A. (2006), *Muzułmanie na ziemiach Rzeczypospolitej*, Białystok: Elkam.

Kryczyński, S. (2000 [1938]), *Tatarzy litewscy. Próba monografii historyczno-etnograficznej*, Gdańsk: Rocznik Tatarów Polskich.

Marszałek Sejmu: Jest mi przykro (2006), Portal Wirtualnemedia.pl, 10 February 2006, <http://www.wirtualnemedia.pl/artykul/marszalek-sejmu-jest-mi-przykro> (last accessed 23 November 2010).

Miśkiewicz, A. A. and J. Kamocki (2004), *Tatarzy Słowiańszczyzną obłaskawieni.* Kraków: Universitas.

Miśkiewicz, T. (2006), *List Muzułmańskiego Związku Religijnego do 'Rzeczpospolitej'*, portal Arabia.pl, <http://www.arabia.pl/content/view/282349/161> (last accessed 23 November 2010).

Modood, T., R. Hansen, E. Bleich, B. O'Leary and J. H. Carens (2006), 'The Danish cartoon affair: free speech, racism, Islamism, and integration', *International Migration*, vol. 44 (5), pp. 4–62.

Nalborczyk, A. S. (2011), 'Mosques in Poland. Past and present', in K. Górak-Sosnowska (ed.) *Muslims in Eastern Europe. Widening the European discourse on Islam*, Warszawa: University of Warsaw.

Nalborczyk, A. S. and P. Borecki (2011), 'Relations between Islam and the state in Poland: the legal position of Polish Muslims', *Islam and Christian-Muslim Relations*, vol. 22 (3), pp. 343–59.

'Nie ma jednego wzorca patriotyzmu', 25 November 2011, Oficjalna strona Prezydenta Rzeczypospolitej Polskiej, <http://www.prezydent.pl/aktualnosci/wizyty-krajowe/art,29,nie-ma-jednego-wzorca-patriotyzmu.html> (last accessed 15 September 2011).

Oświadczenie Rady Etyki Mediów w sprawie przedruku karykatur Proroka Mahometa, 5 February 2006, <http://www.radaetykimediow.pl/dwn/rem_newsletter_2.doc> (last accessed 12 November 2010).

Piątek, J. (2006), *Karykatura Mahometa dzieli Polskę*, 6 February 2006, <http://wiadomosci.polska.pl/specdlapolski/article,Karykatura,id,210738.htm> (last accessed 23 November 2010).

Pikus, T. (2006), *Oświadczenie Komitetu ds. Dialogu z Religiami Niechrześcijańskimi*, 4 February 2006, <http://www.episkopat.pl/?a=dokumentyKEP&doc=200624_0> (last accessed 23 November 2010).

Polski rząd przeprasza za karykatury Mahometa w 'Rzeczpospolitej' (2006), Portal Gazeta.pl, 4 February 2006, <http://wiadomosci.gazeta.pl/wiadomosci/1,55670,3147589.html> (last accessed 23 March 2010).

Polskie echa publikacji karykatur Mahometa (2006), <http://www.znak.org.pl/index.php?t=wydarzenia&id=3749, http://www.znak.org.pl/index.php?lang1=pl&page1=news&subpage1=news00&infopassid1=3749> (last accessed 23 November 2010).

Prezydent: Dziękuję Tatarom polskim i polskim muzułmanom, 17 February 2011, Oficjalna strona Prezydenta Rzeczypospolitej Polskiej, <http://www.prezydent.pl/aktualnosci/wydarzenia/art,1663,prezydent-dziekuje-tatarom-polskim-i-polskim-muzulmanom.html> (last accessed 15 September 2011).

Prezydent odznaczył osoby zasłuz.one na rzecz muzułmanów w Polsce, 17 February 2011, Oficjalna strona Prezydenta Rzeczypospolitej Polskiej, <http://www.prezydent.pl/aktualnosci/ordery-i-odznaczenia/art,901,prezydent-odznaczyl-osoby-zasluzone-na-rzecz-muzulmanow-w-polsce.html> (last accessed 15 September 2011).

Sobczak, J. (2004), 'Położenie prawne polskich wyznawców islamu', in R. Baecker and Sh. Kitab (eds.) *Islam a świat*, Toruń: Mado.

Sobczak, J. (1984), *Położenie prawne ludności tatarskiej w Wielkim Księstwie Litewskim*, Warszawa-Poznań: PWN.

Strybel, Robert (2006), 'Wolnośćsłowa a obraza świętości', *Polish Daily News*, 13 February 2006, <http://www.dziennikzwiazkowy.com/index.php/komentarze/2549.html> (last accessed 23 November 2010).

Tyszkiewicz, J. (2008), *Tatarzy w Polsce i Europie. Fragmenty dziejów*, Pułtusk: Akademia Humanistyczna.

Tyszkiewicz, J. (2002), *Z historii Tatarów polskich 1794–1944*, Pułtusk: Wyższa Szkoła Humanistyczna.

Tyszkiewicz, J. (1989), *Tatarzy na Litwie i w Polsce. Studia z dziejów XIII–XVIII w.* Warszawa: PWN.

Tyszkiewicz, J. (1988), 'Rejestr chorągwi tatarskich walczących w wojne polsko-krzyż ackiej 1519–1521', *Zapiski historyczne*, vol. 53 (1–2), pp. 85–99.

Voigt, J. (1819), 'Franz von Sickingen und der deutsche Orden von Herrn Professor Voigt', in *Beiträge zur Kunde Preußens*, vol. 2, Köningsberg: Universitätsbuchhandlung.

Zakrzewski, A. B. (1988), 'Czy Tatarzy litewscy rzeczywiście nie byli szlachtą?', *Przegląd Historyczny* 79: 3: pp. 118–29.

Wolność słowa nie jest prowokacją, 'Rzeczpospolita', 4 February 2006, <http://new-arch.rp.pl/artykul/597105.html> (last accessed 23 March 2010).

Zakrzewski, A. B. (2004), 'Służba wojskowa Tatarów w Wielkim Księstwie Litewskim (XVI–XVIII w.). Chorągwie ziemskie', in A. Dubonis, Z. Kiaupa and E. Rimša (eds), *Istorijo akiračiai*, Vilnius: Leidykla.

Zakrzewski, A. B. (1989), 'O asymilacji Tatarów w Rzeczpospolitej', in M. Bogducka (ed.) *Tryumfy i porażki. Studia z dziejów kultury polskiej XVI–XVIII*, Warszawa: PWN.

THE ALEVI QUEST IN EUROPE THROUGH THE REDEFINITION OF THE ALEVI MOVEMENT: RECOGNITION AND POLITICAL PARTICIPATION, A CASE STUDY OF THE FUAF IN FRANCE

Deniz Koşulu

1. Introduction

The Alevis are one of the lesser-known Muslim immigrant communities in Europe; on a political front they constitute an organised movement at a European level. The word 'Alevi' refers simultaneously to Ali, Mohammed's cousin, and to *Ahl al Bayt*, the family of the Islamic prophet. In this context, Alevism is defined as 'to adore Ali and his family' and to follow in his footsteps (Yaman 2006: 101). Due to the origin of the word, Alevism is frequently confused with Shi'ism. Today, although they have certain beliefs in common with the Twelver Shiites, Alevi rites of worship[1] are wholly different from other Shia practices (Zarcone 2007). During the period of conversion to Islam in Anatolia, the Turcomans who were nomadic and semi nomadic Turkic tribes, did not completely abandon all of their previously held religious beliefs such as Shamanism, Animism, and Buddhism, which subsequently became the cultural and confessional framework within which the newly adopted religion evolved (Melikoff 1998). The origin of the Alevi religion is therefore a syncretic type of Islam generated by the superposition of the previous belief systems that the Turcomans practised between the tenth and fourteenth centuries (Zarcone 2004). Thus Alevism can be defined as a result of religious and cultural interactions between nomad groups from Central Asia to the Middle East and to the Balkans during this period.

We should also not forget to make a brief mention of Bektashism, the Sufi order founded by Haci Bektas Veli in the thirteenth century in Anatolia, which had very close connections with the Janissary corps, an important force of the Ottoman military down to the nineteenth century. Alevism and Bektashism represent two distinct but closely related phenomena. They share almost all the same syncretic belief sources and they both perform secret ceremonies

(Zarcone 2004: 298). On the other hand, Alevism is not structured as a *tariqa*.[2] Affiliation to the Bektashi order can be established through an initiation ritual, whereas an individual is born into the Alevi religion. Some scholars consider Alevism to be a popular version of the Bektashi networks (Birge 1937), for instance the Bektashism of village; or the Bektashis as the urban Alevis (Mélikoff 1993). Today Alevi actors assimilate Bektashism to Alevism by using the term 'Alevi-Bektasi' in order to highlight their common cultural and religious background.

The emergence of the term *Kizilbas*,[3] in the late fifteenth century marked the beginning of Alevi politicisation in history. *Kizilbas* were supporters of the Safavid brotherhood composed mainly of a majority of rural, nomad Turcoman warriors, a power-base enabling their leader Ismail to become the Persian Shah in 1501 (Massicard 2005). The outcome of the political conflict between the Sunni Ottoman Empire and the Twelver Shia Savafid Empire was to be the marginalisation of the *Kizilbas* Alevis by the Ottomans. *Kizilbas* became a pejorative term (Bozarslan 2003) and it was supplanted by 'Alevi' only after the end of the nineteenth century (Kehl-Bodrogi 2003). Today the Alevis tend to consider that particular passage of history as a period of repression by the despotic Sunni Ottoman State (Bozarslan 2000). As of the early sixteenth century *Kizilbas* Alevis were deported, arrested and massacred en masse. They were defined as 'atheists' and 'heretics' by the theologians of the Ottoman era. The *Kizilbas* phenomenon highlights one of the central instances of intransigent Ottoman orthodoxy (Massicard 2005). It is important to include this brief historical background of the first moment of politicisation of Alevi identity and, although not entirely satisfactory to fully understand contemporary Alevi mobilisation and political participation, it is nevertheless useful as a reminder that, even today, many traces of this early politicisation of Alevi religious identity against the Ottoman Sunni orthodoxy in the reformulations of the political claims among Alevis in Turkey and in Europe, are still to be found.

Furthermore, it can be argued that Alevis developed a defensive reflex against the politicisation of Sunni Islam (Camurouglu 1998). It is a commonly held impression that with the foundation of the modern Republic of Turkey, the Alevis entered into an alliance with the secular Kemalist regime; however they were not shielded from the law banning *tekkes*[4] and *zaviyes*[5] in 1925. With the ban on Muslim confraternities and *tarikas* in Turkey, the functions of *dedes*[6] and Alevi places of worship were abolished. Thus the Alevis no longer officially existed on the Turkish religious map, administered by the Directorate of Religious Affairs (DIB: Diyanet Isleri Baskanligi).[7] In the intensely politicised atmosphere of the late 1970s, organised pogroms by the Turkish nationalist movement against several Anatolian Alevi villages in Turkey were recorded. Alevi migration to Europe, which had started in the early 1960s, became an important phenomenon after the 1980 military coup.

A rise in the political movements with identity-based religious and ethnic discourses was to be observed in Turkey by the mid-1980s, in parallel with the international context of an identity revival (Ayata 1997). In this context, it was argued that the Kurdish conflict also constitutes a source of ethno-religious renewal among Kurdish Alevis (Camuroglu 1997). Through these politicising elements, the political claims regarding the formulation of different dimensions of Alevi identity began. Due to the fact that there is no single Alevi people with a single identity, discussing a unique Alevi social movement is a complex operation (Erman, Goker 2000). To define any single form of Alevism as an identity-based political movement is nigh impossible due to the sociological diversity of the Alevis and their cultural, political and religious claims, especially in the Turkish political field, though at the European level Alevi mobilisation represents a more homogenised structure. Therefore in this chapter, I will use Alevism and the Alevi identity movement in a generic sense in order to illustrate different Alevi movements.

Alevism, which is the mobilisation of Alevi religious, cultural, political and symbolic resources, concerns a non-violent movement which appeared in the 1960s but which was more fully present in the political arena in the late 1980s, with modern-type organisations, such as foundations and associations. Today at the international level the Alevi movement, which has a transnational character (Massicard 2005), is mobilised under the single umbrella organisation of the European Confederation of Alevi Communities (AABK: Avrupa Alevi Birlikleri Konfederasyonu). In this article, which explores some of the results of my extensive field research on Alevi claims and movement,[8] I will examine Alevi mobilisation and political participation in Europe especially through the example of the Federation of Alevi Communities of France (FUAF: Fédération des Unions des Alévis en France), whose organisational model is today shaping the institutionalisation of European Alevism. I will argue that, at a European level, Alevi political claims are still structured in accordance with Turkish political life. I will also demonstrate that although we can talk about a relatively homogenised European Alevism, different European Alevi communities had to go through diverse political strategies in order to partake in the political arena of European countries. Finally I will discuss the shifting dynamics of the European Alevi movement.

2. The plural structure of Alevi claims

The plural character of Alevi claims, which is directly related to the multiple and divergent Alevi self-definitions, confers a multifaceted nature onto the Alevi movement. Turkish-speaking, Kurdish-speaking and Arabic-speaking Alevis[9] constitute the Alevi community of Turkey, whose number is estimated to be between 12 and 20 million by the European Commission.[10] This sociolinguistic diversity and the syncretic roots of Alevi Islam are occasionally pointed to as the reasons underpinning Alevi 'inability' to find a compromise formula that defines their identity and their main claims in an indivisibleway. On the other hand, the analyses adopting this kind of approach, tending to understand Alevism and the Alevi movement as a stable and decontextualised concept, can be seen as 'essentialising', just like analyses which link, for example, the 'democratic and secularist' nature of Alevism to their alliance with the Turkish left (Bozarslan 2003). Subsequently, I examine Alevi plurality by examining the conditions under which it evolved and became concrete rather than through the 'nature' of Alevism. During my research in France and in Turkey, when we asked Alevis how they identify themselves and their 'Alevism', the variety of their definitions was remarkable. Despite this diversity, three main groups emerged:

- 75% of interviewed Alevis define their Alevism as a way of life, a philosophy of life or as cultural heritage
- 40% of the sample identify Alevism as a religion
- 20% of those interviewed define Alevism as a political attitude.

The Alevis also illustrate their identity in a more entangled structure by attributing it, on occasion, to two of these dimensions; however there is some regularity to definitions, which emerge in a more distinct pattern. The second group, for whom being an Alevi chiefly means belonging to a religion, can mention the definition of the first group, but the first group, which identifies Alevism primarily as a philosophy of life, only attributes this in part to religion and most often not at all. In this first group who identify Alevism as a philosophy of life above all, we find atheists who consider themselves also to be Alevis. The Alevi atheists tend to emphasise how they are closely tied to their Alevi identity. Alevi actors of the second group, who identify Alevism first and foremost as a religion, are equally divided into two parts, 68% of which consider Alevism to be aligned to Islam and 32% of which assert that Alevism is a separate religion. These actors, who conceive of Alevism as a religion outside Islam, mention their adherence to Ali's path and to *Ehlibeyt*[11] whilst simultaneously rejecting the link with Shia Islam.

These self-definitions may be interpreted as identity confusion (Massicard 2005). Even so, if such is the case, Alevi actors generate these definitions, which embody the general framework of their claims through particular historical and political contexts. Referring to human perception and responses which show that humans may identify, evaluate and engage with identical perceptual 'inputs' in quite different ways depending on the meanings that we associate with these inputs (Kruzman 2008). The commonality of these self-definitions reflects the fact that the Alevi meaning-making process is mostly dependent on their perceptions and self-understandings according to the Sunni interpretation of Islam. On one hand the Alevis disqualify the religiosity of

Alevism or identify it as a totally different religion from Islam by defining themselves as victims, the righteous, the good and the humanist, standing against the unjust, the repressive, the cruel, the evil whose religion is also Islam, thus the two cannot coincide. On the other hand the believer Alevis who consider that Alevism exists inside Islam also define along the same lines or on the same pattern by always highlighting that 'Alevism is the real Islam' and thus that Sunnism is not. This Alevi self-positioning in relation to Sunnis shows up regularly in actors' discourses. As discussed by Vorhoff, this kind of a 'We vs Them' dichotomy runs through the whole depiction of Alevi history and Alevi authors tend to illustrate the stereotypical contrast between Alevis and Sunnis as two distinct moral communities. It can be argued that if we consider this dualism from the point of view of the new literature on Alevism, such a perspective seems to be seeking to contribute to the construction of a collective Alevi identity. (2003: 103).

Today, the objective of the Alevi leaders at the European level is to transform these meaning-making processes which frame their claims and the movement and which are pointed out by the leaders as one of the main raisons for the political failure of the movement. Before discussing this strategy at the European level, we will explore the primarily political and cultural claims of the Turkish and European Alevis.

3. Political claims

It is difficult to analyse Alevi claims in Europe without reference to the Turkish political field. Despite the plural nature of the Alevi movement, it is appropriate to determine two main streams in Turkey: the Pir Sultan Abdal Association (PSAD: the Pir Sultan Abdal Dernegi)[12] Movement and the Cem Fondation (Cem Vakfi) movement. These two main streams represent the two different Alevi ways of perceiving the Turkish political field. While Cem Vakfi try to negotiate with the government and to mobilise political opportunities via the Alevi opening launched by the Justice and Development Party (AKP: Adalet ve Kalkinma Partisi) in order to be officially integrated into the Turkish religious field, the PSAD questions the credibility of the opportunity for integration, interpreted as an another assimilation policy against the Alevis similar to earlier policies. According to the PSAD, it is neither possible, nor desirable to be integrated in order to ensure that one be considered an independent actor in the Turkish religious field. We can observe some commonality between the PSAD and the Cem Vakfi in that they both claim the official recognition[13] of the *Cemevis*,[14] however, even on this point they differ in defining the general terms of recognition. The PSAD's posture on the *Cemevi* recognition issue can be considered ambiguous: some members of the PSAD movement may request a sort of social and cultural recognition, a degree of acceptation of their religion in society and perhaps also in order to benefit from public subsidies like the Sunni mosques, however they do not want *dedes* to be trained and financed by DIB (Diyanet Isleri Baskanligi: Directorate of Religious Affairs), which is another of the points of disagreement between the two streams. While the PSAD would like to see the closure of the DIB, the Cem Vakfi demands representation within the DIB by their own Alevi religious leaders and *dedes* independently and on an equal footing with Sunnites. We may observe the same situation on the issue of mandatory religious lessons: Cem Vakfi tends to demand an Alevi adjunct to these lessons monopolised by the Sunni interpretation of Islam, whereas the PSAD demands their absolute abolishment.

At the Turkish level, political lassitude dominates Alevi claims, constantly reconstructed according to Alevi-Sunni political experiences. Up till the present day, none of these claims have been satisfied except an Alevi addition, in September 2011, to the textbook regarding the compulsory Religious Culture and Moral Studies lesson. While Alevi associations are losing their reliability and credibility in the Turkish political field as actors, the Alevis have therefore created a system of claims-transferal to the Alevi movement in Europe.

Even if the politicisation of Alevism in Europe was/is still in relation to Turkey, Alevi political claims acquire a slightly different character at the European level. The European confederation of Alevi communities (AABK) and the Federation of Alevi communities of France (FUAF), by emphasising in priority the convergence between Alevi and European values and their contentment at being a part of the European community, have divided their political claims into two parts. The first is social and seeks to facilitate the integration of Alevis into the host countries by contributing to the vision of a society underpinned by equality, democratic laws, solidarity and social justice, total freedom of thought and faith and the fight against religious fundamentalism, racism and terrorism. These claims display a convergence between Alevi claims and a broader context of European rights and values. The second is constituted by claims that are still European Union oriented but concern the field of Turkish politics more directly. Here we meet claims such as: the Recognition of the Alevis and the halting of discrimination against them; the abrogation of mandatory Sunni religious lessons and DIB and that of Alevi assimilation policies at schools; the official recognition of the *Cemevi*s as the institutions necessary to maintain Alevi belief and culture in the same way as mosques, churches, temples, synagogues do for their own congregations; the cessation of the construction of mosques in Alevi villages and the removal of religious affiliation from identity cards.

When we discussed these political claims with the leaders and members of the FUAF, they regularly highlighted that as Alevi immigrants the acquisition of the right to vote and be elected in France is also one of their main claims. As a matter of fact, during our research the claims regarding DIB and obligatory Sunni religious lessons played second fiddle to the purportedly more important political claim. Alevi claims are firstly structured around ignorance of the Alevi religion and culture, prejudices and discrimination against Alevis, not only at state level but in everyday life in society. The main Alevi claim is 'recognition' however neither in Turkey, nor in Europe are the contours of this recognition very clear. We can also observe in Alevi discourse that recognition can be synonymous with an acceptance of Alevi religion and culture by Sunni people in society.

Recent occurrences in Austria constitute an example through which we can observe the crystallisation of the two main characteristics of Alevi political claims: the relationship to the Turkish religious and political fields; the plurality of Alevi self-definitions affecting the formulation of the recognition claim. In 2009 the Federation of Alevi Communities of Austria (AABF: Avusturya Alevi Birlikleri Federasyonu) applied to the Bureau of Religion (Kultusamt) of the Austrian Ministry of Education for the recognition of Alevism as a separate religion. At the same moment, Austrian Alevi Culture Unity (VAKVB: Viyana Alevi Kultur Birligi), a sub-organisation of the federation, applied for the same recognition but demanded the recognition of Alevism not as a religion apart, but as existing inside Islam. The demand of the second group was accepted and the Austrian Alevi Islamic Community (IAGO: Islamische Alevitische Glaubengemeinschaft in Österreich) was officially recognised.

The decision, which was applauded by the Turkish government, divided the Austrian Alevi movement. VAKVB, which has close relations with the Cem Vakfi movement in Turkey, is accused of being an instrument of the Turkish government and of abetting the assimilation of Alevis by Sunni Islam. As may be observed, in fact plural Alevi self-definitions also tend to blur the framework of their claim for recognition. While DIB constantly and definitely specify that the recognition of the *Cemevi*s, thus the recognition of Alevism by the Turkish State, will place the Alevi religion outside Islam because according to the DIB, for all Muslims, there is only one place of worship, which is the mosque. The undertone of this discourse prescribes to Alevis in fact the one and only way of being a Muslim and practising Islam in Turkey. So the Alevi definition of Alevism and its recognition even in Europe is profoundly related to this Sunni point of view in Turkey. On this account, even the Alevi actors who define Alevism as a 'popular Anatolian Islam', avoid positioning it inside Islam when formulating their recognition claims, thus perceiving 'Islam' as a 'Turkish Sunni Islam' defined by the regulator of the Turkish religious field, the DIB.

On the other hand those Alevis who contradict the Austrian government's decision, qualify it as a 'political decision', whose motivation is to use the Alevis in order to create a docile and well-domesticated image of Islam in view of the other existing Muslim minorities in the country. However, in other European countries the Alevi movement strategically emphasises some of their differences compared to other Muslim minorities, such as mixed religious practice, no headscarves for Alevi women, etc. Furthermore,

262] *Muslim political participation in Europe*

another question that the Austrian case raises is: when one part of a religious minority doesn't identify itself in the same way as the European State does, through recognition, can this recognition be held to correspond to the whole societal reality of this minority group? In Germany, we see that the Alevis are recognised as a religious and cultural community, not bracketed within Islam, but as a separate religion. So the question which ensues is: can a double recognition formula in Europe be envisaged, both for the Alevis defining Alevism as included within Islam, and for the Alevis who identify it as a religion apart?

4. Cultural claims based on fear of loss of identity and political mistrust

As numerous Alevi actors state that their claims are primarily angled towards religious, cultural, and societal recognition, and not political claims at the state level, they have realised nonetheless that their 'objectives may only be reached by inscribing their purely cultural and religious demands in the agendas of political institutions' (Lagroye 2003: 263). This post-republican period politicisation of Alevism also operates in reverse: today, Alevi mistrust of the Turkish political field, which results from the frustration of their claims; and the fear of losing their cultural and religious identity as a minority group after emigration to Europe and migration to the big cities in Turkey, have simultaneously had a depoliticising effect on the Turkish, but a politicising effect, on the European Alevi movement.

Alevi self-criticism regarding the decline in the transmission of Alevi religion and culture to future generations and the fear of identity loss are two prominent fixtures in Alevi life history narratives in both Turkey and France. An Alevi actor states that:

> Alevism is not only a religious phenomenon. Today, Alevis don't know what they want. Some of them are talking about Cemevis; even though they are very few, some of them want to found a political party, but a political party can't solve any problems. We must learn first our Alevism and live it in our everyday life. Alevism is an identity, if you can't feel your own Alevism, you just can't keep it alive.[15]

Observable here is the fact that the loss of Alevism identity also constitutes a concern for Alevis who do not identify Alevism principally as a religion. The same actor adds that:

> Family is very important. Mobilisation of civil society should begin in the family. Nobody asks you which religion you have chosen: if you were born in a Sunni family, you become Sunni, if you were born in an Alevi one then you become Alevi. Above all, you learn in it in your family. The Alevi culture should be passed on through families.[16]

We can find many examples of this discourse, which places the issue of cultural and religious transmission at the very core of the Alevi claim and in order to deal with this identity-loss problem actors attribute the main role to the family, but not to the institutions of the movement. As in other European countries, in France the Alevis constitute a Muslim minority group within a socio-historically Christian society, but also a heterodox Muslim minority according to the views of Sunni immigrants from Turkey and all the other Maghrebin and African Muslims. This triple dimension of being a minority also greatly increases the level of fear of loss of identity – one of the main activities of Alevi associations in Europe is regularly organising seminars, conferences and workshops, especially for Alevi youth, in order to transmit Alevi culture and religious doctrines. Even the majority of those associations do not define Alevism first and foremost as a religious phenomenon. Alevi political despair, generated through previous Alevi-Sunni experiments in the Turkish political arena, is articulated by mistrust in the institutions of the movement. Furthermore there has been a more recent and progressive return to discourses that revolve around the family, which is regarded more and more as the main bearer of Alevi religion and culture. No doubt these factors have a depoliticising effect on Alevism, though there is no total refusal towards affiliation with Alevi institutions nor has there been a complete retraction from political positions corresponding to Alevi political claims. This element of despair can be interpreted rather as a result of the transfer from the Turkish to the European Alevi movement, entailing the politicisation of Alevism in Europe permanently, in relation to the field of Turkish politics.

5. Evolution of the Alevi movement

Alevi rural migration from Anatolia to Istanbul and other major cities of Turkey and migration to Europe, primarily Germany, started nearly at the same time, early in the 1960s. Owing to the labour recruitment agreement between Turkey and Germany, which ended officially in 1973, Germany was one of the first European countries to which Alevi labour migration was oriented in large proportions. Germany therefore constitutes the first country where the Alevi movement settled in Europe. Our aim here is not to re-illustrate each detail of the historical evolution of Alevi immigration and movement in Germany; there has already been a lot of research done, especially after 2000, on these issues. After briefly highlighting the principal framework of Alevi immigration to Europe, I will now discuss the French Alevi movement, which today is reorienting European Alevism, mainly at an institutional level.

Even though the first Alevi organisation was founded in 1960 in the south of Germany as a workers' association (Massicard 2005: 281), Alevis were not very visible in German society until the late 1980s. Alevis continued to practice *takiya*, a strategy they had used in Turkey, namely that of dissimulating their religious identity and rituals in order to protect themselves from discrimination and accusations voiced by Sunnis (Sokefeld 2008a: 271). Turkey entered into a highly politicised and polarised period of history in the 1970s, which ended with the military coup of 12 September 1980. The Turkish army voided and then monopolised the Turkish political field after the military coup through the abolition of all political parties, unions and a multiplicity of organisations that comprised civil society. Thus Alevi immigration to Europe, which had already started in view of the pogroms organised by the Turkish nationalist movement against several Anatolian Alevi villages in the late 1970s, accelerated, while imprisonment and persecution of radical left-oriented Alevis was ramped up by the military. From the late 1970s onwards, Alevi immigration, initially for political motives, to other European countries like the Netherlands, Austria, France and Switzerland increased. Then, from the early to mid-1980s, the Alevis gradually stopped dissimulating their religious identity and *Cem*[17] started being performed publicly in Europe. Towards the end of the 1980s Haci Bektas Veli associations led by *dedes* emerged in Germany. These associations were founded for religious objectives; they were even in favour of the separation of Alevism from politics. However, they also claimed for Alevi representation at the DIB. Besides the Haci Bektas Veli associations, Alevi cultural centres began to defend a more social and political Alevi organisation (Massicard 2005: 286).

In parallel with the rise of identity politics in the international arena, the left-oriented Alevis who had migrated to Germany after the 1980 coup no doubt played a capital role in politicising Alevi organisations, which had originally been essentially religious in Europe. Furthermore, during the post-coup period, the Turkish political field was reformatted according to a Turkish-Islamic synthesis, which was adopted as the official ideology by the Turkish State, so that the marginalisation of the Alevis was increasingly heightened by the penetration of Sunni Islam into political life as an important player. During the 1990s, an Alevi literature emerged, explaining 'Alevism' as a just and revolutionary rebellion against Sunni oppression.

Towards the mid-1990s, not only the Alevis in Turkey, but the European Alevi movement, were profoundly affected by two events that occurred in Turkey: the Sivas massacre in 1993 and the Gazi event in 1995. The former resulted in thirty-five Alevi and two non-Alevi deaths, people burned alive by a radical Islamic group in a hotel during an Alevi cultural festival in Sivas; the latter event happened in 1995 in Gazi, which is one of the suburban districts of Istanbul where Alevis have migrated in large numbers. In Gazi, fifteen people were wounded and one person was killed by a group who opened fire on local coffeehouses from a taxi they had stolen after having murdered the driver. After these tragedies, hundreds of people flocked to Gazi to protest against the attack. The Alevis in the district had deduced that the police had ignored the attack on purpose and might even have helped the assailants, who have never been captured. The Alevi protestors pelted the police with stones and the tense situation quickly escalated, ending with the police opening fire on the crowd. Two more people were killed but the situation only got worse. Alevi demonstrations spread to other parts of Istanbul and to Ankara. Seventeen people died at the end of the events in Gazi and according to the official reports seven of them were killed by police bullets. These two events occupy a capital place in Alevi life history narratives. It has been argued that the Sivas and Gazi events had a decisive effect on the mobilisation of Alevis (Sokefeld 2008b: 70). These events reawakened bitter memories of the pogroms organised in 1978 and 1980 and they enabled the articulation of the founding myths of Alevi identity, which have been constantly constructed and reconstructed since the emergence of the *Kizilbas* in the late fifteenth century. The Sivas event particularly boosted Alevi politicisation and has had a homogenising and uniting effect on Alevi mobilisation, albeit not in Turkey, but in Europe. In 1993, almost all the Alevi associations in Germany were united under the Federation of Alevi communities of Germany (AABF: Almanya Alevi Birlikleri Federasyonu). However, the AABF did not come into being suddenly and abruptly immediately following the Sivas events. The idea of an Alevi federation had already been under discussion among Alevis in Germany since 1988 and we may observe that in 1990 certain Alevi associations had already started to come together under the name of the Federation of Alevi Communities (Alevi Cemaatlari Federasyonu), which was changed into the AABF in 1992. However the Federation only started to become an umbrella organisation from 1993 on. Almost at the same moment the emergence of the Federation of Alevi communities of the Netherlands came to the fore. Until 1998, even though there were lots of Alevi associations in almost every European country, only the German and Dutch ones were united in federation form. In 1998 the Federation of Alevi Communities of France (FUAF) and in 1999 the Federation of Alevi communities of Denmark (DABF) were founded. The AABF started to work on the project of a future Alevi confederation at a European level in 1997 and five years later the Alevi Federations of Germany, Netherlands, France, Denmark, Austria, Belgium, Switzerland and Sweden were united under the European Confederation of Alevi Communities (AABK: Avrupa Alevi Birlikleri Konfederasyonu or Avrupa Alevi Konfederasyonu), in 2002. The institutionalisation process at European level is considered to be an unfinished process by European Alevi leaders. During its general meeting in 2010, following a proposition by the FUAF, the AABK decided to adopt the FUAF's organisational structure, as defined by the French Alevis, as it had been initiated by them.

6.   The FUAF and the political participation of Alevis in France

Today in France the number of Alevis is estimated at approximately 200,000. Most of them immigrated to France between the late 1970s and the end of the 1980s and 80% of them have already acquired French nationality.[18] The history of the emergence of Alevi organisations in France is not very different from that of the other European Alevi organisation experiences. As of the beginning of the 1980s, we see the emergence of the first Alevi Cultural Centres in the north of France, especially in Strasbourg and in Metz (Alsace-Lorraine region) in parallel with the overtures of the first *Cem* houses. Two main activities of the first French Alevi Cultural Centres were in evidence: the organisation of religious meetings by inviting *dedes*, especially from Germany, and that of cultural events such as *saz*[19] concerts. Besides this, they had already started working on a more politically mobilised Alevi community in France, focusing on their claims towards Turkey. They also dealt with immigration issues regarding their community; they paid particular attention to these in order to gain French citizenship. Thus, in the French context, the emergence of different, mutually distinct types of Alevi associations was not initially observable. Even though the religious dimension of Alevism is still discussed among Alevis living in Turkey as well as by those in France, neither the religious nor the more politicised associations have hampered each other. Since 1998, all the Alevi cultural Centres of France, which number thirty, are gathered under the FUAF, which is structured according to the commission system. It is composed by a general assembly, an executive board, and by thirteen commissions such as: the logistics commission, the diplomacy and opening commission, the project and assistance commission, the media commission, the women and children's commission, the youth commission, the faith commission (*dedes'* commission), the arts and cultural commission; the education and research commission, the environmental commission, the economic and employers' commission and the advisory commission. Among these thirteen commissions only the *dedes'* commission is directly charged with religious issues, such as faith service, religious meetings, and the religious education of French Alevi youth through occasional seminars, during which opinions on faith issues are handed down. The president, vice-president, and all the members of the administrative board and the commission are elected by the congress of Alevi Cultural Centres.

The FUAF is not related to any political party in Turkey or in France nor is it affiliated to any party in Europe. The FUAF is opposed to the organisation of an Alevi political party because the Alevis generally state that they are a priori against the constitution of any political party formed on the basis of religious motives. However, one of the most important motivations of the federation, which has been reiterated on numerous occasions by the president and other members, is to politicise Alevis in France in terms of representative democracy. The federation facilitates gaining French citizenship for new immigrants and encourages them to learn more specifically about their rights and responsibilities as French citizens and especially to vote. As one of the FUAF leaders told us:

In fact the most important thing for us, which is as important as our claims regarding Turkey, is the naturalisation of Alevi immigrants. Because we are living here, we are part of France, so we should be able to vote here; we should also elect our governors. It is also very important for our claims concerning Turkey.[20]

During our research, none of the Alevis interviewed in France expressed any feeling of the existence of religious discrimination in French society, however they emphasised that their stigmatisation by certain Sunni groups continues, in France, especially through sermons delivered in some Sunni mosques. FUAF leaders and commission members underline that when they vote, they consider themselves firstly not as Alevi Muslims but as French citizens. Arguably due to the political incentive of the FUAF, there is high voter turnout among Alevis, with 82% of our sample voting regularly. Although it has already been speci-fied that FUAF is not affiliated to any political party in France, there is regu-larity in the voting behaviour of its members, and the French Socialist Party (PS) is the single most prominent party name which emerges during interviews. Indeed, the FUAF encourages Alevis to take part in the running of political parties at a local level; the only condition that the federation sets for this is that the political party should be left-wing. This is not imperative, but it is welcome, highly recommended. Each city that is a member of the FUAF has to nominate at least one Alevi candidate for municipal elections. Today in France there are ten elected Alevi officials in different municipal councils and one of them is the president of the Federation. By contrast, it is not recommended for the leaders of the Alevi movement to engage in politics at the national level in France. This is explained by the leaders of FUAF as being due to the neutrality principle of the umbrella organisation.

In this context, we can argue that the Alevi movement has adopted a pragmatic communitarian political attitude: local political practice, which is considered to be beneficial for the problems of the Alevi community at the local level, is recommended by the FUAF, while expanding this practice to the national level is not favoured since it is thought to entail the risk that FUAF and Alevi identity be associated with one single political party in France.

Generally speaking, the particularities of the French political field deter-mine the framework within which this political attitude has evolved. Alevi mobilisation in Europe is structured according to the opportunities offered by each national political context in which it evolves. It has been argued that Alevis recognised and made use of the political opportunities allowed for in the context of the proliferation of multicultural policies in 1980s Germany – established in order to accommodate and to support cultural pluralism, once it had been understood that immigrant workers and their families would not return to their countries. Purported use of this political opportunity was made by emphasising the cultural particularities of the Alevi identity and by separat-ing the latter from 'Turkish culture' (Massicard 2005: 284). This politicisation

of Alevi culture and identity shaped the future of Alevi mobilisation, which
has not evolved into a class-based social movement but rather into an identity-
based movement, despite the large-scale migration of radical left-oriented
Alevis to Germany after the 1980 military coup.

Aside from this, we may observe that the Alevi movement has made a
conscious effort to benefit from another opportunity, which the political
context indirectly offered: they highlighted, according to the Sunni communities in Germany, Alevi religious and cultural differences such as mixed-gender
worship and the fact that Alevi women do not wear headscarves. They also
underscored that Alevism is a branch of Islam opposed to both fundamentalism and Turkish nationalism. In 2004 the AABF acquired the status of 'religious community', which gave them the right to dispense their own religious
education, even if Alevis are generally against religious education in schools
(Massicard 2005: 295). They gained this status in four years, approximately,
whereas the Islamic Federation of Berlin acquired such a status only in 1998 at
the end of an eighteen-year-long struggle. The question can therefore be raised
whether the differential in representations between the Alevi and the Sunni
communities have not played a significant role in the political decisions taken
by the German state.

The accession to 'religious community' status in Germany can be contrasted
with the situation in France where it was impractical for Alevis to adopt the
same political strategies. In line with the *laïcité* law of 1905, imposing strict
separation of Church and State, the Alevi community has never attempted to
seek religious recognition as this is not possible within the French context.
However, the FUAF did claim to have the same rights as other religious communities existing in Alsace-Moselle, which is governed by a local law that
allows public subsidies for Roman Catholic, Lutheran and Calvinist denominational Churches and the Jewish religion. The FUAF demanded to benefit
from the positive interpretation and application of local law by the Strasbourg
municipality in favour of all religious communities in terms of the accommodation of religious diversity in the city. Furthermore, the FUAF continued to
seek cultural recognition for Alevism as constituting, for the time being, the
only possibility for recognition in France. For the FUAF, the 'recognition' of
Alevis and Alevism as a religion and a culture does not mean a direct official
recognition by the French state. The leaders of the FUAF state that:

> In France, when you talk about the Alevis, they can still look at you with a vacant
> stare and ask you if it is a type of insect. They don't mean it in a pejorative sense;
> they just don't know what it means. As Alevis, we want to be known and recognised
> in French society.[21]

Although Alevis consider that they are not currently suffering from any
oppression regarding their religious practices and the public expression of their

identity in France, they express their discontent concerning societal ignorance regarding Alevism per se. In order to solve this problem, the FUAF organised a meeting with the French Minister of National Education in 2010. During the meeting, they demanded the integration of Alevism, defined as a cultural phenomenon, into the course books of the French educational curriculum. At this juncture, the definition of Alevism again was at stake, and the ministry stated that in order to consider the claim, it would request an in-depth definition of Alevism. Consequently, the FUAF, which defines Alevism rather as a cultural phenomenon, than as a religious one, went to work on an 'official definition' of Alevism with *dedes*, scholars and historians. Each French Alevi Cultural Centre was also integrated into this process: they too were asked to provide a definition of their Alevism. To find the most global definition, incorporating each Alevi self-perception, has been the main goal of the FUAF in this enterprise. The FUAF has shown great interest in this issue, perhaps in part because the possible integration of 'Alevism' into school textbooks will be seen as an official recognition of Alevism in France. Among the three main objectives of the education and research commission of the federation, we may observe that the integration of Alevism into French school course books has the highest priority. Secondly, in continuity with the first demand, the FUAF also wants to integrate the future official definition of Alevism into the great French dictionaries like *Larousse*. Thirdly, a continuous improvement of instruction is demanded from the educators who will teach Alevism to French Alevis in Alevi Cultural Centres.

Even though organising seminars and meetings on Alevi culture and faith is one of the important activities of the FUAF, this has not been found to be sufficient for the instruction of the new generation by leaders of the movement in France. Recently the federation has taken the decision to develop a training programme in order to instruct Alevi educators so that they can educate young Alevis in a more uniform and systematic way. The FUAF, which decided to homogenise the form and content of Alevi education in France, will try to benefit from the German experience by bringing assistance from German Alevi educators on board in this project. There is no claim concerning the expansion of specific 'Alevi lessons' to schools, rather it is conceived as an educational practice on the level of Alevi associations. The leaders of the movement specify the considerable effort expended for the recognition of Alevism within the bounds of the French republican laic system.

7.   A redefinition of Alevism and the Alevi movement in Europe

This effort towards an eventual recognition of Alevism in French society and also at the state level through school textbooks is also directly related to Alevi claims concerning the Turkish political field. As we have already mentioned, while voting or taking part in a political party in France Alevis refrain from highlighting their Alevism, however their political claims are considerably structured by the expectations regarding their religious identity in Turkey. One of the points of commonality between the discourses of Alevi actors living in Turkey and in France is that they both think that the European Union figures large in the processes of the democratisation and secularisation of Turkey and that it should put political pressure on Turkey in questions concerning Alevis. They also consider that European countries offer the Alevi movement more favourable political contexts within which Alevi mobilisation can evolve in a more structured way. It can be also considered one of the reasons for the transfer from the Turkish to the European Alevi movement. A young Alevi from Istanbul states that:

> Here, it is almost impossible to politically achieve our claims because religion is still very important. If we were in Europe, everything would be easier; their legal system is based on human rights and the freedom of thought. Because of this Alevi associations in Europe should be bringing pressure to bear on Turkey. The Alevi mobilisation is not good enough here, in fact we don't have a real mobilisation consciousness.[22]

The European Alevi movement has tried to take over and assume the claims of Alevis generated according to need and a sense of discontentment experienced by Alevis living in Turkey. This direct connection to Turkey shows that European Alevis, over and above the perception of themselves as 'Muslims well-integrated into European societies', still consider themselves to be fundamentally Alevis of Turkey. Even though this may sometimes be formulated in different ways; the abrogation of the obligatory Sunni religious lessons and DIB and the official recognition of Alevis (as a Muslim community separate from the Sunnis) and the *Cemevi*s as their place of worship still constitute the primary political claims of the Alevi movement in Turkey and in Europe. The 'We vs Them', Alevi/Sunni dichotomy is still one of the dominant features of Alevi life histories in Turkey as well as in Europe. However, recently, the French Alevi movement has attempted to transform this meaning based on a process dependent on the victimisation of the Alevi community by the re-institutionalisation of the European Alevi movement. French Alevi leaders argue that the Alevi movement came into being as a 'reaction' to the 'sufferings' developed in an entangled organisational model. The president of the FUAF states that:

> As of the 1980s, the trade-unionists, the political militants, the village-based Alevis, all brought their political behaviour patterns and their understandings of mobilisation to Europe and shaped the Alevi movement. The only commonality of this heterogeneous mobilisation is that everybody is against the sufferings caused by injustice. This is no longer possible; it is a huge loss of energy and time. The time of reaction is over. Now we need an organisational model which can assess the potential of the Alevi people through religious, cultural and social mobilisation.[23]

In 2010, before that AABK adopted 'the commission model' proposed by FUAF, some conflicts had occurred within the confederation. However, before recommending its organisational model, the FUAF waited four years in order to see if it would work out well. In the meantime the number of Alevi Cultural Centres increased from fifteen to thirty in France. French Alevi leaders point out that among the other European Alevi federations the FUAF is the most active federation in terms of mobilising its community through religious, cultural and social activities. It is therefore to be observed that besides one of its main goals being to integrate Alevism as a concept into the French education system, the FUAF's interest is also largely focused on intra-community activities.

As the second step of this organisational renovation of the European Alevism, Durak Arslan, the president of FUAF, took the presidency of the institutionalisation commission of AABK.[24] In his new assignment he started to work on a project that he calls 'Global Alevi Unity' (KALB: Kuresel Alevi Birligi). In February 2010, almost simultaneously with the adoption of the commission model, Turgut Oker, the president of the AABK, had already mentioned for the first time that World Alevi Unity (DAB: Dunya Alevi Birligi) would be founded in a few years. The KALB is likely to attempt to boost the mobilisation of Alevi religious, cultural, economic and symbolic resources on a worldwide level through seven institutions: the Alevi Faith Centre, the Alevi Institute, the Alevi Confederation, the Alevi Artists' Unity, the Alevi Employers' Unity, the Alevi Media Unity and the Alevi Jurists' Unity. One of the main obstacles to a homogenous Alevi mobilisation is defined by Alevi leaders as the disunity of the Alevi faith so that the constitution of the Alevi Faith Centre, the first column of KALB, has been designated as the first task to be undertaken by the FUAF, which is working on the latter with Veliyettin Hurrem Ulusoy, the *postnisin*[25] of the *Dergah* of Haci Bektas Veli,[26] who has visited twenty-nine cities in Turkey in order to engage in discussions with the *dedes* of each Alevi community and to get their approval for faith unity under the KALB. So we observe that the structuring process of KALB is initially a European Alevi project although it will first be implemented in Turkey. Although the FUAF leaders emphasise that leadership by Veliyettin Ulusoy should be approved by the majority of Alevis; we have observed that a few Alevi communities have adopted a skeptical approach to KALB and to the imposition of a single Alevi faith leader. Cem Vakfi has remained outside KALB, however the FUAF has stated that the possible participation of Cem Vakfi, even if merely for approval, is likely to become an option in the future. As we mentioned above, the Cem Vakfi and PSADK are the two mains streams of the Alevi movement in Turkey. In this context, it can be argued that a future integration of Cem Vakfi into the Alevi Faith Centre could create a new conflict with Alevi communities leaning towards the PSADK, who have already opted to be united under it.

The KALB can thus be considered as a strategy of redefinition for Alevi mobilisation in both Europe and Turkey, aiming to overcome the absence of a well-defined institutional mechanism through a redefinition of Alevism, to promote a more homogenous Alevi movement. Such a tentative endeavour confirms the claim transfer made by Alevis of Turkey to the European Alevi movement and the continuous relationship of this movement with the Turkish religious and political fields.

8. Conclusion

The plural character of Alevi claims and multiple and divergent Alevi self-definitions confer a multifaceted nature onto the Alevi movement. Diverse Alevi self-definitions in France can be grouped into three major categories: Alevism as a religion, as a culture, and as a political attitude. The commonality of these self-definitions reflects the fact that the Alevi meaning-making process is largely dependent on self-perceptions and self-understandings in counter-distinction to Sunni interpretations of Islam. Whether Alevism is aligned to Islam or not is still a discussion point in Alevi communities. This Alevi-Sunni dualism and 'hero victim' imagery shows up regularly in actors' discourses in both Turkey and Europe. Today, one of the main objectives of Alevi leaders at a European level is to transform these meaning-making processes, which frame the claims and the movement itself, and which are highlighted by leaders as one of the main reasons for the organisational and political failure of the movement.

In fact it is apparent that the Alevi mobilisation in Europe represents an altogether more homogenous structure. The abrogation of mandatory religious lessons and DIB; the official recognition of Alevis (as a Muslim community in its own right independent from Sunnis) and the *Cemevi*s as their place of worship; the cessation of the construction of mosques in Alevi villages and of religious discrimination against Alevis in society and at state level are the main claims of the Alevi movement in Europe, which has been institutionalised under a single umbrella organisation, the AABK, since 2002.

According to the structuring of political arenas in different European countries, each Alevi community has established different political strategies in order to partake in the particular political arena of their country. The only common political strategy that Alevis have adopted in different European countries has been to emphasise their differences from other Muslim communities by illustrating their Alevism as a 'secular', and 'modern' form of Islam, opposed to fundamentalism and compatible with the values of European societies. In parallel, Alevis have also strategically chosen to enter into the religious field in terms of becoming a recognised religious community in Germany, where the acquisition of the status of 'a religious community' is one of the main challenges of the mobilisation of immigrant religious groups, especially among Muslims. In France Alevis avoid underlining their religious identity in political processes such as voting or taking part in a political party. In order to reassure the French republican secular tradition, the strategies of Alevi mobilisation are as follows: valorisation of the 'cultural' at the expense of the 'religious'; the depoliticisation of Alevi identity in France; the politicisation of the members of the Alevi community around the issue of French citizenship. Furthermore, societal recognition of Alevis and the integration of Alevism as a cultural phenomenon in school books in France are two of the main goals of the FUAF.

The politicisation of Alevism in Europe is 'always-already' tied to the Turkish political field. The dissatisfaction with the results of Alevi political demands regarding Turkey regularly constitute the first political motivation for Alevis wanting to integrate into European societies. This has occurred through a convergence of Alevi mobilisation at a European level in order to establish pressure groups with the capacity to influence Turkish political life. Recently we have witnessed, through a renovation of the organisational structure of the Alevi movement in Europe, European Alevi leaders attempting to reframe Alevi identity, i.e the main goals and the conscience of the Alevi movement. Their main objective is to overcome Alevi self-victimisation and to standardise and homogenise the movement. The FUAF is coordinating this re-institutionalisation process. It can be interpreted as another attempt to change the polarised structure of the Alevi movement which, seen from Turkey, is not unifiable. However, a considerable effort to redefine Alevism, in which each step of the process can take place under Alevi influence, is observable. Besides making demands on various European states to put pressure on Turkey in favour of Alevi claims, and trying to be an efficient actor in the European political field in view of Turkey, Alevi leaders seem also to be seeking to focus attention on intra-community activities. Nevertheless it should not be forgotten that this redefinition process is recent and ongoing. Attempts to construct a homogenous Alevi mobilisation have failed many times before, albeit in Europe this objective has been attained to a certain extent. In the final analysis, the evolution of both the Turkish and European political fields and their mutual interaction will influence the redefinition of the Alevi movement, which is significantly related to the redefinition of 'Alevism' by Alevi actors.

Notes

1. Alevis don't practise *salat*, ritual daily prayer, nor ritual fasting during the month of Ramadan; they do not attend mosques, their worship place is the *Cemevi*, the assembly house; they don't follow the *Jafari Fiqh*, which is the majority Twelver Shia school of jurisprudence. Today, the communality between Twelver Shiites and the Alevis is the belief in twelve imams and *Ahl al Bayt*, and the importance of the *Ashura*, the commemorations of the martyrdom of Hussein. In addition to this,

the Alevi actors who claim even their connection to *Ahl-al Bayt* and to the twelve imams, do not define themselves either as 'Shiite' nor as 'Jafari'.

2. Way, method, path; a general name for defining different schools in Sufism.
3. Red Heads, owing to their crimson headwear.
4. Derviche lodge.
5. A small Derviche lodge.
6. Alevi religious leader.
7. The public institution directly attached to the office of the prime minister, founded in 1924 by the National Assembly of Turkey after the abolition of the caliphate. It is the highest Islamic authority in the country.
8. Fieldwork conducted in Metz, in Strasbourg and in Istanbul in 2008 with 110 Alevis men and women aged between 15 and 80, from different economic levels, from different parts of Turkey and within FUAF, the Federation of Alevis of France; and then in Metz in 2011 with FUAF through a combination of research methods including: semi-structured interviews, structured interviews, life histories and focus group discussions.
9. Arabic-speaking Alevis should not be confused with Alawi Shias (Nusayris) centred in Syria nor with the Allawiya sufi order in Morocco.
10. Available at <http://ec.europa.eu/enlargement/archives/pdf/key_documents/2004/rr_tr_2004_en.pdf> (last accessed 14 November 2011).
11. *Ahl al Bayt* in Turkish.
12. All PSADs in Turkey are also united under the Alevi Bektashi Federation, which is the sister organisation of AABK (The European Confederation of Alevi Communities).
13. 'Official recognition' of *Cemevi* by the Turkish State means here the acquisition of the same legal status as the Sunni mosques in the country. It means also the attachment of Alevi places of worship and *dedes* to the DIB (Directorate of Religious Affairs).
14. *Cem* houses, Alevi places of worship.
15. Interview conducted in Strasbourg, February 2008.
16. Idem.
17. The Alevi religious ceremony.
18. Interview conducted with the President of FUAF, Metz, September 2011.
19. Alevi musical instrument.
20. Interview conducted in 2008, in Metz, France.
21. Interview conducted in Metz, September 2011.
22. Interview conducted in Istanbul, 2008.
23. Interview conducted in Metz, 2011.
24. After this article had been written, Erdal Kiliçkaya was elected as the new president of FUAF at the end of the seventh congress of Alevi Cultural Centres, which took place on 27 May 2012. The former president, Durak Aslan, retains the presidency of the institutionalisation commission of AABK and continues to work on the KALB project.

25. The supervisor of a *dergah* (the Sufi/Alevi convent), who is not a *dede*.
26. One of the main Alevi convents in Turkey, in Cappadocia.

References

Ayata, A. (1997), 'Identity Politics In Turkey', *New Perspectives*, no. 17, pp. 59–73.

Birge, J. K. (1937), *The Bektashi Order of Dervishes*, London: Luzac and Hartford Seminary Press.

Bozarslan, H. (2003), 'Alevism Myths of Research: The Need for a New Research Agenda', in P. J. White and J. Jongerden (eds), *Turkey's Alevi Enigma*, Leiden; Boston: Brill, pp. 3–17.

Bozarslan, H. (2000), 'L'alévism, la meta-histoire et les mtyhes fondateurs de la recherché', in Isabelle Rigoni (ed.), *Turquie: les milles viages. Politique, religion, femmes, immigration*, Paris: Syllepse, pp. 77–89.

Camuroglu, R. (1997), 'Some Notes on the Contemporary Process of Restructuring of Alevilik in Turkey', in K. Kehl-Bodrogi, B. Kellner-Heinkele and A. Otter-Beaujean (eds), *Syncretistics Religious Communities in the Near East*, Leiden: Brill, pp. 25–35.

Camuroglu, R. (1998), 'Alevi Rivivalism in Turkey', in T. Olsson and E. Ozdalga (eds), *Alevi Identity: Cultural, Religious and Social Perspectives*, Istanbul: Swedish Research Institute, pp. 79–84.

Erman, T. and E. Göker (2000), 'Alevi Politics in Contemporary Turkey', *Middle Eastern Studies*, vol. 36, no. 4 (October), pp. 99–118.

Frégosi, F. (2008), *Penser l'Islam dans la laïcité*, Paris: Fayard.

Kehl-Bodrogi, K. (2003), 'Ataturk and the Alevis: A Holy Alliance?', in P. J. White and J. Jongerden (eds), *Turkey's Alevi Enigma*, Leiden: Boston: Brill, pp. 53–71.

Kurzman, C. (2008), 'Meaning making in Social Movements', *Anthropological Quarterly*, vol. 81, no. 1 (Winter), pp. 5–15.

Lagroye, J. (2003), 'Les processus de politisation', in Lagroye J. (ed.), *La politisation*, Paris: Belin, pp. 359–73.

Massicard, E. (2005), *L'Autre Turquie : Le mouvement aléviste et ses territoires*, Paris: Presses Universitaires de France.

Mélikoff, I. (1993), *Uyur idik, Uyardilar : Alevilik, Bektasilik Arastirmalari*, Istanbul: Cem.

Mélikoff, I. (1998), *Hadji Bektasch: Un mythe et ses avatars: genèse et évolution du soufisme populaire en Turquie*, Leiden: Brill.

Nielsen, J. (2004), *Muslims in Western Europe*, 3rd ed., Edinburgh: Edinburgh University Press.

Sokefeld, M. (2008a), 'Difficult identifications: Debate on Alevism and Islam in Germany', in A. A. Hamarneh and J. Thielmann (eds), *Islam and Muslims in Germany,* Leiden: Brill, pp. 267–98.

Sokefeld, M. (2008b), *Struggling for Recognition: The Alevi movement in Germany and in Transnational Place*, New York: Berghahn.

Tarrow, S. (1992), 'Mentalities, Political Culture and Collective Action Frames: Constructing Meanings through Action', in A. D. Morris and C. McClurg Mueller (eds), *Frontiers in Social Movement Theory*, New Haven: Yale University Press, pp. 174–203.

Yaman, A. (2006), *Yesevilik, Alevilik, Bektasilik*, Ankara: Elips.

Vorhoff, K. (2003), 'The past in the Future: Discourses on the Alevis in Contemporary Turkey', in P. J. White and J. Jongerden (eds), *Turkey's Alevi Enigma*, Leiden: Boston: Brill, pp. 93–111.

Zacone, T. (2004), *La Turquie moderne et l'Islam*, Paris: Flammarion.

Zarcone, T. (2007), 'La communauté chiite de Turquie à l'époque contemporaine', in S. Mervin (ed.), *Les mondes chiites et l'Iran*, Paris: Karthala, pp. 135–63.

14

LEICESTER MUSLIMS: CITIZENSHIP, RACE AND CIVIL RELIGION

Carolina Ivanescu

It does not matter what I say I am: I am European and I am British. But it does matter how you see me. If you do not see me as a European, if you do not see me as a Brit, it does not matter what I say. Whatever I will say, I will be a Muslim. (interview, 26 July 2011)

In the 1970s newspaper advertisements from Leicester advised migrants to go elsewhere as the city was already 'full to the brim' after the acceptance of more than 14,000 Asian Indian refugees, more than half of the total number of people expelled from Uganda by Idi Amin: 'In your own interests and those of your family you should accept the advice of the Uganda Settlement Board and not come to Leicester, I think they said.' (interview, 26 July 2011). Leicester was overwhelmed by its increased population and was desperately hoping to stop more massive migration. However, by 1981 the migrant population had risen to 59,709 and by 2001 to 100,000 (Open Society Institute 2010: 32). By 2012 it is estimated that Leicester will become the first city in Britain to have a white minority (interview, 23 July 2011).

Leicester, a medium-sized city in the East Midlands is indeed on the way to becoming one of first British cities where former migrants will be a larger group than the native population. From 46.1% in 2001 (Census, 2001) the non-white population was estimated to rise to 51% by 2011 (ONS 2009) or to 55.6% by 2025 (Danielis 2007). As much of the ethnic minority population is Asian or Asian British, many 'double migrants' from African colonies, Leicester is a good example of a city where migration and the colonial past encounter discussions of ethnicity and race. Further, the largest and upcoming religious communities are Muslims, counted to 11.3% in 2001, expected to equal the number of Hindus, counted to 14.74% in 2001, by 2013. Because Leicester has essentially been one of the British cities of migration, populated by citizens with different ethnic origins, it is a place where diversity and a multitude of cultures is a given of everyday reality. Further, the local government of Leicester is proud of the multiculturalism of the city and believes its policies enhance plurality and the expression of difference. For all these reasons, it is a good place to see how Muslimness is defined at the intersection of citizenship and secularity regimes.

In the following part I will discuss how different uses of the concept of citizenship are and have been shaped by Britain as a state and as a nation, continuing the idea of the British Empire. Reconstructing historical changes within the idea of the state, nation and the people, I will point out how Britain has dealt in different time periods with inner and outer diversity, and issues relating to the territory of immigration and integration. In doing so, I will explain the main dimensions of the social and political imaginary in which religious migrants need to negotiate their place as reflected by policy documents at the national and local level. Further, expanding configurations of religion and multiculturalism in relation to ideas of race and ethnicity will be developed using the formation of Muslim collective identity and grassroots movements as interpretative collective action. In the second part of this chapter I will rely on ethnographic data collected in Leicester during the spring and summer of the year 2012 to point out how imaginaries of citizenship and secularity are mobilised and reinterpreted by local Muslim communities to their own advantage. In this, discourses of race and plurality are employed in creating space for religious collective identities, which have a specific local, national and transnational dynamic.

The British challenge after the last days of empire was management of its diversity and finding the right structure for the island state. These challenges were shaped by the needs of immigration control, in order to keep at bay the populations subject to the Queen but not part of the nation, and simultaneously managing internal diversity. A solution that was both conceptually rich and practical in nature was to be found in the concept of citizenship, linked to the idea of the nation imagined as a community.

Politically, citizenship and community have been historical points of struggle in British history, framed by a larger context of multiculturalism and its diverse positions: conservative, liberal, pluralist, commercial, corporate (Hall 2000: 210). This is further complicated by different positions as far as the relationship of culture to race, ethnicity and religion is concerned. In recent years, a concern with security has tightened the debate and a movement from a discourse of 'race to religion' can be observed (Allen 2005).

Although never quite disappearing, religion has in the last decade made a visible comeback both in the civil and in the political sphere in Britain, mostly through the attention given to Muslims and the active self-identification of different groups with the same label. The Rushdie affair caused an awareness of Muslims as a religious group which '(re)discovered a new community solidarity' (Modood 2005: 157). This collective force was effective as it could rest on the struggle for social and political recognition (Werbner 2002) and a consciousness of difference stemming from 'political blackness'.

If we consider the role and relevance of religion in present-day Britain we need to think about the way the concept of citizenship has historically allowed different forms of identification, while regulating the way the community/ communities were made relevant at different junctures. A context of narratives about Britishness joined by a historical vision on different citizenship regimes further needs to be considered in relation to external and internal diversity, through attention towards discourses and practices of immigration and integration.

1.   Migration and British citizenship

British citizenship has made a long journey from a contractual concept emphasising rights and duties to a 'deal' for active citizenship. As citizenship both tells us more about the balance between the interior and exterior of the state and of the nation, and at the same time it informs us about the boundaries across which the state and the nation cease to exist, in the following we will pursue changes in the concept of citizenship in relation both to migration and internal population management. In the case of Britain, collective migration history starts at the point where the legacy of the empire wanes and is connected with the British idea of the island as the nation.

The Alien Act of 1905 was innovative through its attempt to regulate immigration control upon entry to state territory (Wray 2006). The category of 'undesirable migrant' became salient from this moment onwards. Besides the terminology and categories on which the act is based, the most important effect of the act is the dichotomy between different population segments based on territorial belonging, which has been inherited by modern immigration control systems. So were also its inconsistencies and weaknesses, which stem from a contradiction in the forces that need to be managed by both immigration control and governments. Among these diverging forces should be mentioned the 'electoral desire for effective immigration control, the economic and other benefits of immigration, and the necessity of maintaining a public commitment to humanitarian principles' (Wray 2006: 303). The idea of a nation and of a community of people depends on the political climate and assessed gain from the immigration process, both balanced by a broad, ideological concept of moral, shared human values.

The beginnings of the British approach towards immigration control should be seen as managing the unexpected consequences of the empire. In the 1950s Britain considered itself too small to accommodate the population pouring onto the island from the various parts of the extensive territory that the British Empire had been. The result was increased immigration control and a shift in general attitudes towards race and colour (Freeman 1995). This was a response towards the equal legal, social and political rights of all citizens, understood as subjects of the Crown. The Marshallian take on citizenship will reformulate this royal allegiance and instead construct a pragmatic concept of citizenship, based on a need for addressing social imbalances. Marshall envisaged citizenship as a way of ensuring equality towards entitlements and as the protection of individuals from the vicissitudes of the labour market. As such it had little to do with duties and obligations, and it was little troubled by the distinction between public and private beyond the economic and social realm. It envisaged citizens as passive receptors of benefits needing equal chances, and thought of these benefits as formal rights rather than substantive benefits. The benefits were not conceived as an automatic guarantee of entitlement on the basis of citizenship, rather depended on three domains: work, war and reproduction. However, nationality continues to be understood in terms of monarchical allegiance, combined with a jus soli indifferent to race or religion (Everson 2010).

From 1962 onwards, through the Commonwealth Immigrants Act, differentiation between migrants was first introduced, in 1962 in terms of employment and skills, but from 1968 in terms of race (Murji and Solomos 2005). The post-war period already combined race relations, the interior management of populations of different provenance with migration control. The rationale was that by reducing diversity and restraining further migration, the integration of those already within the territory would become easier (Solomos 2003: 81). These shifts need to be seen in the light of Britain managing its internal diversity through reducing the number of new migrants while constructing a collective identification, a generic Britishness for the people already on the island, managed through the concept of race.

The period between 1960 and 1980 can be seen as one of rising social and political tension in regard to post-colonial migration. From 1973 onwards, limiting migration from beyond the European economic zone reinforced concerns with colour and race. It is important to note that Britain imposed immigration control a decade earlier than other European countries, which waited for the economic trouble of the early 1970s (Geddes 2005).

British citizenship was an almost inexistent concept until 1981, when the British Nationality Act (BNA) made a distinction between the native population and postcolonial migration from Commonwealth territories. The political and civic reaction to the British Nationality Act took the debate in two different directions, one towards the problem of immigration control, defining the nation in ethnic terms, while renouncing the civic basis of citizenship. Second, simultaneously, citizenship was understood as the prism through which Commonwealth citizens were assigned a status with full civil and political rights but no social rights. Built on the rationale of individual need, the British welfare state sought to take care of the rights of its citizens by selecting at entry and stratifying the population through different access to resources. While recognising racial difference, the principle of British citizenship maintains the tension between universal citizenship and (racial) group particularism. During the Labour 'equal opportunity policy' aiming at affirmative action, (racial) group particularism became a widespread assumption.

The year 1981 was a turning point for British citizenship, as it created 'aliens' both within and beyond the territory of the UK. As revocations of rights are characteristic of state building periods, we may consider 1981 the period from when we can talk of Britain as a state (Blitz 2006). The British Nationality Act broke with the Marshallian liberal tradition, based on an equilibrium of rights and duties with a focus on social justice, and made individuals responsible to earn the protection and care of the state (Tyler 2010: 71). Beyond this dynamic was the felt need to reinforce the British nation-state, through the including/excluding role of a layered citizenship. Hansen understands the changes initiated by the BNA as a process of clarification and rationalisation (2000). I would emphasise that this classification both defined the territory and decided the relations of equality and sovereignty. Persons with the right of abode were granted British citizenship, defined through its legal dimension. As such, British citizenship needs to be considered as a mechanism operating along migration and border control and integration and race management. This also implies that it is articulated along axes of neoliberal governing and multiculturalist legacies of management of diversity and plurality.

This double move has to be understood in the context of the intense and profound institutional reorganisation initiated by the Thatcher government, which implied the revocation of rights connected to citizenship and residence, and a turn towards a managerial state. The managerial turn in state administration meant the parallel bureaucratisation and professionalisation of the state, with increased privatisation, competition and restructuring and a shift of responsibilities from the public to the private (Clarke and Newman 1997). It had further implications for the labour market through the processes of privatisation and outsourcing, which were at the basis of many social and economic experiments (Wills 2010). This had implications for the tightening effect of the combined rhetoric on individual responsibility and the necessity to earn rights and the continued shrinkage of the welfare state, which further created divisions between the populations. The 'post-imperial class struggle over the resources of a diminished empire was underway' (Tyler 2010: 64), combining ethnic and racial hierarchies and superimposing them on existing class divisions.

But we may wonder how the nation was conceptualised in Britain during this time. By early 1980 citizenship in Britain distanced itself from the welfare state with its dynamics of social rights and class equality and was replaced with nationality, immigration and security. The shift towards a neoliberal nation state, cherished by the conservative Thatcher government created several categories of nationality and citizenship and created ethnic and racial boundaries between white and coloured populations (Baucom 1999). The boundaries gained validity not in the area of immigration but between fellow citizens, provoking waves of anger and unrest in cities with significant 'coloured' populations.

A multiculturalist discourse emerged aiming to include through state support and non-differential treatment both Commonwealth and British-born populations of migrant origin. Support was needed in order to remove 'distinctive barriers in their exercise of citizenship' (Meer and Modood 2009: 479). Multiculturalism accepted and recognised difference starting from the premise of independent cultures and cultural relativism influenced by British social anthropology (Heyck 1997).

Inequality as social exclusion became from 1997 onwards, due to Labour, a key policy focus addressed by the Social Exclusion Unit. In this period, a distinction was made between exclusion experienced at the general level of the society or 'wide' exclusion and 'deep' exclusion, which is experienced by a specific group of people, mostly minorities (Finn 2008). Policy responses to wide exclusion included from the mid-1990s onwards education, health, employment and access to information, resources and transport, while deep exclusion encountered policy responses that were more targeted and intensive. Towards the end of the 1990s and in the following decade, combating deep exclusion through targeting groups 'severely excluded' and 'at risk' was the preferred strategy of the British government. The larger context in which this shift of policies was taking place was the need to ensure citizenship participation through equality between individual citizens.

As the terms of the immigration policies have shifted, the national debate on multiculturalism has also been reconfigured, with New Labour as the main actor (Worley 2005). The link between national identity, democracy and immigration control, with a new emphasis on the concept of citizenship, had a direct effect on the way multiculturalism was perceived: the multiculturalist frames have been shifting, due to an increasing concern with immigration and national security, towards community cohesion and the importance of shared values, such as active citizenship (Rogers 2007). The 'community agenda', based on its identification of communities which led 'separate lives', not adhering to the community of the 'people' neither in thought nor in deed was a challenge to the philosophy of multiculturalism. Integration and hierarchical evaluation of ethnic, racial and cultural groups transformed the policy agenda, with repercussions in the political and civic articulation of multicultural ideas. Further, integration has been interpreted as a duty to be imposed on migrants through naturalisation, with an emphasis on language, knowledge about the UK and allegiance to the Queen.

The early years of the twenty-first century further took migration and citizenship policies in the direction of responsibility, both on an individual and at a collective level. As I have pointed out before, both individual migrants and their communities have been seen from the 1990s onwards as aliens and failed populations. However, from 2000 onwards we notice a shift from a preoccupation for living with and accommodating diversity to concerns for national security, with 'failed citizens and outsiders' seen as a threat to national identity. The moral opposition between good and failed citizens creates the collective body the British community, which aims at cohesion though ensuring its own security, expelling the problematic, 'failed' citizens. I agree with Tyler's argument that the failure of the 'failed' is contained by the dimensions of British citizenship, through a dialectical moral opposition between different categories of citizens (2010). Further, the oppositions articulated by the different layers of citizenship follow closely distinctions already present in British society: existing frames of difference between population groups defined in terms of race, ethnicity and later religion.

The 'failed populations' frames have been followed by the logic of 'dangerous populations', provoked by the riots around the Rushdie affair (1990) and the Bradford incidents (2005), which reinforced the perception of a conglomerate of social problems that could be associated with migrants and minorities in terms of race and religion related to problems of national identity, belonging and integration. Further, after 2001, global events culminating in the London bombings of 7 July 2005 have caused a vitriolic inflammation of the causal connection between failed multiculturalism and bad citizens, highlighted as problems with certain groups of the population radicalised by religion. These global incidents confirmed the fear of the failure of the multicultural model and echoed the changes taking place in other Western European countries. After 2001, in most of Europe we can observe a strict convergence of immigration and integration regulation (Joppke and Morawska 2003) and a change in attitude towards Muslims. The policy and political discourses shifted from a focus on the unification of the nation through citizenship integration and the maintenance of boundaries through immigration control towards an agenda of security concerns.

Citizenship plays a central role within the security discourse as it allows for certain population groups to be the legitimate target of security policies, drawing on the moral distinction between appropriate and inappropriate citizens. The consequence of securitisation is the criminalisation of segments of the population and the reinforcement of labels reproducing social and political stereotypes. The population of the nation-state is broken up in different groups labelled either as successful, as precarious or as failed (Tyler 2010). Whichever the label might be, the individuals are tightly connected to the nation-state that constructs the label through the inclusion/exclusion mechanism on which they depend. Butler and Spivak understand this mechanism as a proof of the impossibility of evading the nation-state (2007:17). Moreover, in spite of this process of splintering through top-down moral judgment, the appeal is made for a united community of citizens, based on a shared, self-defined morality. The nation needs a community that has a strong connection and commitment to Britain based on 'a range of proposals that touch every stage of an individual's life' and a common bond: citizenship (Goldsmith 2008, cited in Tyler 2010). Communities based on ethnicity, race and/or religion are considered proactive and voluntary forms of segregation from the national community. Further, the multicultural model of community of communities is questioned and policed.

However, in order to understand the impact of the changes in the understanding of the content and role of citizenship we need to consider historically the way diversity and plurality has been dealt with in Britain.

2. Race, plurality and multiculturalism

Colour and race are both at the basis of the framing of British immigration and integration policies. As a matter of fact, integration in the British context is seen as a way of improving relations between different population groups called communities, which are distinguished on the basis of race or colour (Favell 1998; Joppke 1999). Shifting in time from a multiculturalist discourse emphasising the equality between communities and cultures, to allegiance and subordination to the idea of one national community, Britain shows signs of convergence with current integration policies in other Western European countries (Joppke 1999). However, as I will point out, distinctions made upon race and culture remain important both for a definition of the national community in which the different communities need to dissolve as a form of self-identification and mobilisation for equality-based rights for groups within the national community.

Distinctions based on race and the early management of plurality have been an American export, taking place in the 1960s. The role of home secretary Roy Jenkins, the influence of the Harvard Law School and 'race relations' as analysed by the Chicago School need to be mentioned here (Bleich 2011: 61–2). According to the American model, differences in skin colour and, implicitly, cultures determine social conflict and problems, which can to be solved by civil law centred on the issue of discrimination (not criminal law). This 'colour racism' (Gilroy 1987) continues to be influential to this day, especially through the predominance of racial dualism in both legal and policy frameworks (Alexander 2002). The first Race Relations Acts from 1965 and 1968 were designed to ensure equality, helping migrants through providing welfare, while white communities were educated about the migrants. The idea was to stop discrimination between population groups and promote equality through equal chances (Solomos 2003).

A shift in thinking about race took place between 1968 and 1976 when the notion that policy in a plural society should not be colour blind gained terrain: racial prejudices were to be punished and affirmative action was to be introduced. This involved a change from thinking in terms of race relations to giving attention to acts of racism. In the 1970s race consciousness became coupled with issues of discrimination, linking the topic of race with that of gender (Sooben 1990; Bleich 2011: 65). Group-specific policy targets were introduced as a much-welcomed alternative to formal legal equality. Positive discrimination gained ground and race-conscious policies were given priority.

The 1990s saw the possibility of extension of race policies to Muslims. Collective claims were already voiced around the Rushdie affair: Muslims as a group need to be included under diversity categories. Through the Rushdie affair, Muslimness became a salient collective identity, which was increasingly being pushed forward both from the grassroots and from academia (Modood 1990; Asad 1990). The possibility for deeply ingrained patterns of exclusion, both discursive and institutional (related to a police incident where police discriminated based on skin colour) pointed to a need to shift away from multicultural rhetoric.

Muslims were firmly set apart, separated from other minority ethnic and faith communities (Ahmad and Evergeti 2010). The concept of islamophobia was used to describe a new form of racism, directed specifically against the Muslim population (Modood 1992). Formal rights were insufficient as inequality was strongly present in society, Muslims argued (interview, 24 July 2011). Further, Muslims felt the need to unite under a category that would encounter less discrimination than those based on race and ethnicity. Modood argued that discrimination is a sword with two edges, one making distinctions based on race, the other dividing based on culture (1992).

Until 2003, however, the courts did not accept Muslims as a group, although other religious groups such as Jews and Sikhs have been previously recognised. Discrimination of Muslims as Muslims was not punishable under the law up to that moment. Muslims could only apply for discrimination measures through indirect protection, as a member of an ethnic group, such as Pakistani, Arab, etc. This caused resentment and enhanced Muslim activism (Modood 2006). Along with the recognition of the group as such, collective identification became stronger, with the claim that difference was a right that needed to be accommodated by the government. Muslim assertiveness claimed recognition and argued that race relations are ineffective tools for accommodating religion.

Already beginning around the Rushdie affair, Muslims have been recognised as a religious group by civil society groups. The organisations that moderated between the government and Muslim representatives were in particular Anglican churches and not racially different groups (Modood 2006: 42). Public social recognition further shaped Muslims as a religious group, with religious claims in a specifically secular state, which discriminated on the basis of collective religion. However, Muslim voices at that moment were mixed, while claims were made in the name of Islam and argued around issues of blasphemy, some wanted recognition as a collective group in the name of religion in order to transgress ethnic and racial groups. A similar ambiguity can be found in the example of the Muslim Council of Britain formed in 1997 as a direct consequence of the Rushdie Affair, which had difficulties addressing with a unanimous voice both the government and the Muslim communities (McLoughlin 2005).

Muslimness was recognised as a valid category from the Rushdie affair on and remained a claim of accommodation for religion as religion, backed up by a community that wished to transcend other policy categories (interview, 26 January 2011). It is important to recognise that this concept of collective identity contrasts both the secular basis of the nation-state and the universalistic concepts of justice and resource management inherent in liberal citizenship. But it is just as important to recognise that the new collective identity formed through religion transgressed community and kin (for example *biraderi* networks) allegiances, and connected Muslims through adherence to Islam to the *ummah*. This new identification would prove especially salient in the British Muslim position regarding international conflicts, such as the positions towards the wars in Afghanistan and Iraq.

A sharp change in race relations can be further observed in the light of the security concerns that informed immigration and integration policies in the past decade. As a consequence of the 'race-riots' in cities with significant Pakistani and Bangladeshi populations, British social problems have already been in the 1990s increasingly packed in superimposed layers of different frames which equated violence with lack of integration, spatial segregation with separation and hate, while race, ethnicity and religion were often equated to each other. Moreover, as a consequence of 9/11 this easily translated into a global and national problem with Muslims, a claim which was met and contested by an increasingly aware and organised, but heterogeneous Muslim community.

3. Leicester Muslims – 'a pragmatic community'

In this part I will point out the specific instances that have grown out of grassroots initiatives in the city of Leicester. Besides the processes of collective identification, which have been triggered by national and local discourses and implementations of policies concerning race and citizenship, there are also efforts of embodiment taking place at the local level. For this I will follow closely the logic of the Prevent agenda (Home Office 2007) and Community Cohesion policies (Leicester City Council 2009), pointing out how specific interpretations of citizenship, race, religion and plurality affect the way Muslim groups organise and define themselves.

The Prevent agenda and the programmes focusing on community cohesion have been important for the Muslim community in Leicester. They singled out the Muslim community and focused on those Muslim groups considered moderate. The effect has been a competition between Muslim groups within the city for the limited resources provided under Prevent, and an uneasy feeling in regard to other faith communities that did not receive financial help (interview, 21 July 2011). Furthermore, Prevent came attached with the stigma of the special needs of the populations it was designed for, and the attention given to preventing terrorism. Muslims participating in one way or the other in Prevent needed to situate themselves actively in relation to issues of national security and the perceived Islamic danger, radicalisation.

The communitarian approach also caused difficulties for Muslims, though in a different manner to those caused by the Prevent agenda. This approach presented opportunities for engagement and funding but 'it is about religion or culture, but not about class and economy-related problems' (interview, 23 July 2011). As such it encouraged the claims of Muslims as a group, especially as a religious group, but it was not concerned with social class problems. Content with a cultural explanation for existing social inequalities, the community agenda did not go deep into tackling fundamental inequalities between different population segments.

The focus on culture and religion remained present during the Prevent policies. High profile community leaders and especially religious leaders are often exposed to actions informed by general security concerns. Being singled out for general security concerns is unpleasant: 'It is not easy to be on a plane and to be the only one singled out for special control out of 200 people. And that only because I have a beard and I look different.' (interview, 26 July 2011). These feelings are part of a more general perception that Muslims always have to defend themselves in the face of different forms of accusations, they need to react and respond to multiple social challenges: as a Muslim 'you have to prove all the time your intentions, your loyalty', a painful and exhausting experience both in the short- and long-run (interview, 23 July 2011).

However uncomfortable this focus on Muslims, it can also be seen and experienced in positive terms. Prevent also 'presents an opportunity, as the community receives funding, but also an entry point on cohesion and safety which can then be used to keep in touch with the municipality' (interview, 23 July 2011). Community leaders are aware of the advantages and disadvantages that policy attention brings with itself. Besides being aware, they are skillfully negotiating and employing the possibilities they have, using them as opportunities. The securitisation of religion repeatedly invites Muslims as a religious group to defend itself in the public scene and thus offers a possibility for visibility and audibility. Further, although policies come attached with certain forms of social stigma, they do provide access to resources, even if not to all parts of the Muslim communities.

The interaction between Muslims and local government has initiated a double process of change and accommodation, which can be seen in the context of the hope the two-sided process of integration Muslims expected. While Islam itself is not changing, the way it is understood and the way Muslims behave does (interview, 24 July 2011). This often means a creative process of interpretation and adjustment, triggered by the 'need to accommodate to the British society and this means that there are things which need to be understood in a different way than they were when the Qur'an was written' (interview, 23 July 2011). However, this creative and accommodated position makes Muslims fragile as they can be criticised from two different positions: first, from the point of view of the state ,which believes that Muslims could and should give up more of their identity, and second from the side of radical and traditionalist schools of thought, which say that European Muslims cannot be considered Muslims anymore, as they pervert the teachings (interview, 24 July 2011). For British Muslims this often implies a fear of not belonging, of not being accepted in society and a continuous doubt about the 'right way' (interview, 23 July 2011).

For some British Muslims the dilemma of accommodation involves the continuous need to be reflexive and assertive, a strong need for being responsive to society and it calls for a certain position of the believer in relation to the object of faith (interview, 23 July 2011). As such the contours and social relevance of Islam are changing. But can these changes be understood as a shift in religion under the pressure of regimes of secularity, or should they be seen as an organic process inherent in the nature of religion, as some Muslim practitioners suggest (interview, 21 July 2011) (also see Taylor 2007).

The process of adjustment is often about things that may seem insignificant. When elaborating on this point, one of my respondents talked about cultural rather than religious accommodation when explaining the adjustments needed for a dinner: in the seating arrangements neither a women dressed in *niqab* nor one dressed in a short skirt would be seated across from a Muslim man: the first one would not be able to eat without revealing her face, while the second would not be able to sit in a position which is not offensive. Similarly, he argued further, sensibilities need to be taken into account in society at large and accommodations need to be made (interview, 23 July 2011). In line with these thoughts, most Muslims believe that integration and accommodation needs to be a two-way process, organic and mutual in nature. While many are prepared to compromise, they feel the need to be assured that what is given will also be returned, even if in other ways (interview, 26 July 2011).

The community agenda, based on its identification of communities which lead 'separate lives', by not adhering to the national community neither in thought nor in deed presented a challenge to the philosophy of multiculturalism, as well as a challenge for Muslim communities. Multiculturalism converged on the idea expressed from the Muslim community of integration as a two-way process. However, both the focus on the community and on national security shifted the national and local discussion towards a reformulation in terms of integration as a one-way avenue. The dialectic of moral categories attached to citizenship alienated Muslims, as it demanded cooperation and input while giving little in return (interview, 21 July 2011). Also, the importance given to official representation enhanced the process of elite segmentation that is well captured by Bonney:

> From the perspective of the national debate over multiculturalism in 2006, two weaknesses might be observed. The first is that where the links between communities have developed, they were largely at the level of community leaders or opinion formers, not at the grassroots of the society. (Bonney and Le Goff 2007)

What is at stake is, from one side, the future of the multicultural legacy 'It is this vision of a "community of communities and citizens" which is now under attack by those who challenge the model of multiculturalism' (Bonney and Le Goff 2007), but also the shape Muslim communities can publicly take.

In Leicester integration takes on a specific dimension due to the demographics of the city. Because of the changing demography, the minority-majority balance in the city is likely to change in the near future. This feeds a continuous tension between different segments of the population within the city and a sense of fear for the white community: 'This is also why I think many people are getting scared, what will happen if it turns out in the coming census that Muslims are a majority in the city? I would expect quite a reaction' (interview, 24 July 2011). However, this dynamic based on demographics can also be expected to reverse. Just as Muslims live in the centre of Leicester as a consequence of the flight of the wealthier white population, as Muslims also become wealthier, they also move towards the periphery. In the near future it can be expected that the number of Muslims living in Leicester proper will diminish (interview, 17 July 2011).

Although scholars have shown that the Muslim community has made the greatest advances at the local political level (Joppke 2009: 455), in Leicester Muslims pride themselves more on civic initiatives. In Leicester, politics is not considered an important issue by representatives of the Muslim communities: Muslim identity is seen as better represented through initiatives stemming from grassroots, which provide a template for national and even international forms of Muslim identification and access to specific resources, such as the case of Muslim burial provisions, mediated through the Muslim Burial Council of Leicestershire. This institution is important for Muslims in Leicester because it builds on membership in the transnational *ummah*, without being political in nature. At the same time, it started as a grassroots organisation but is now active on the national level as the expert on Muslim burials and is consulted by other countries as well.

The sense of pride (this pride I have encountered only in Leicester) coming from the grassroots of the society is made clear in processes such as contributions from an Islamic engagement with the society as a whole, cooperation with other faiths and the development of a collective religious Muslim consciousness, which goes across sectarian divides and the development of specific Muslim provisions. The last-mentioned point is connected also with issues of cultural sensitivity towards specific religious needs and, as I will point out further on, is also an example of powerful connections between the local, national and global religious and (trans)national levels.

Muslims in Leicester are proud of the organisations they have, the institutions that work both on the local and the national level. Different organisational shapes have been tried over the years, from associations, councils and advisory groups to federations. However, from the point of view of Muslims in Leicester federations work best as an institutionalised form of the community because

> the federation has a structure where people are selected for two-year positions and then have committees underneath, which are thematic. Because it is elected it is responsible to the electorate and 50,000 Muslims in Leicester, there is transparency and the mandate to speak for the community. (interview, 23 July 2011)

Further, federations work across many smaller community organisations, unifying their voice and constructing a clear message. Because Muslim organisations are often co-opted in governing processes, or given specific tasks in inclusive policies such as Community Cohesion and Prevent, it is important for them to be able to claim legitimacy for the community they are representing. Thus, election of elites is taking place at all levels and a clear organisational structure is adopted. However, in Leicester most of the important functions are held by a handful of people, most of them managing multiple tasks. From such representatives it is expected to be critical, both towards the government but also towards their communities (interview, 21 July 2011). However, certain segments of Muslim communities are better represented at the elite level, and thus have a better chance of turning negotiations in the civil sphere in their favour.

Indeed, some Muslim groups feel neglected, not only because of the unequal distribution of material resources, but also because they feel left out from places of power. The smaller Ismaili community feels neglected both by the local government and the national branch office. Because they do not participate officially in policy implementation, they lack the necessary resources to make a visible social impact and they have less access to appropriate housing for their centre/mosque. Further, the national Ismaili community thinks of them as a provincial group, thus resources and control are refused, the local communities being excluded especially from the coordination and management of larger community events (interview, 15 February 2012).

Keeping together the communities requires effort 'because there are differences in every faith and there are differences in Islam as well, so we have to find a way to hold people together' (interview, 23 July 2011). An informal form of community bonding are football and cricket matches, with a team of Muslim imams playing against Christian clergy under the association of the Federation of Muslim Organisations and the St. Philips centre. In these events Muslim clergy have to form a team together, against 'sectarian divides' and play with representatives of other faith(s). The Muslim communities 'gel together' with the help of informal activities and this translates into a possibility for cooperation beyond the sports field. This model of Muslim community consolidation and interaction with other faith groups has been so successful that it has been exported to Sweden and Germany, across *ummah* networks (interview, 23 July 2011). These sports events are also organised between the police and imams so that 'fear of the role is removed, they are seen as human beings and not met only at the police station, when you have a need, when you have a problem' (interview, 24 July 2011).

Muslims in Leicester are positive about the role of religion in British society. In general, they believe that religion is considered a positive social force, in spite of society's secular character. 'Brits are not shy about religion, you can also see this from the big advertisements hanging visibly on churches with the time of the mass' (interview, 17 July 2011). The church has also proved to be an ally since the Rushdie affair, considering Muslims a religious group and sharing many inter-faith initiatives. However, Muslims often argue publicly that equal opportunities should be given to various religious groups. The historic heritage of the Anglican Church is something to be emulated by other faith institutions as well, through required equality in opportunities and treatment.

Besides the church, alliances are also forged on specific issues and in different power relations. The relationship between the Muslim communities and the Jewish community in Leicester is illustrative: they work together because

> ... our dietary requirements, our burials, our prayers and other issues like circumcision are common to both faiths. The Jewish community is very small, 450 people as compared to 50,000 Muslims, so we take the lead, but we work in cooperation with them to make sure we help them whatever their needs are. (interview, 21 July 2011)

Of course here, besides help and support, it also counts that an inter-faith or across-faiths claim is often more likely to succeed when considered by the secular nation-state and different governmental institutions.

Thus, Muslimness in the context of Leicester can be seen to evolve together with multiculturalist approaches arguing for equality (with other religions, lack of discrimination, inclusion). However, at the national level these Muslim claims are seen as 'politics of difference' that stress the exceptionality of Muslim communities. While often Muslims are perceived as going against both liberal individualism and secularism, from the example of Leicester we see that Muslims proceed according to British standards and discourses and engage with local policy frameworks. Those Muslim communities that do not actively take part in partner actions initiated by the local municipality are independent, manage themselves and raise their own funding. As Vertovec suggests, we can talk about a 'horizontal spread' of the Muslim community in Leicester, with diversity running both across a complexly organised and fractured community and a distinct pattern of localised need catering (1997).

4. Conclusion

The examples discussed so far suggest that religion in Leicester is more than a personal and private affair. As it is at the basis of a negotiated collective identity and informs a series of collective actions, it functions as civil religion (Bellah 1967). Muslims in Leicester are visible and active as Muslims, forging inter-faith alliances as well as providing mobilisation examples beyond the urban space they live in. The specific interpretation of the way civility is understood by Muslims in Leicester is filtered through policies at the local and national level. These policies, in their turn, build the concept of citizenship from a collective British imaginary of the nation and the people.

Muslims in Leicester are making use of local and national policies and through grassroots initiatives they interpret and actively engage with discourses of citizenship, race, ethnicity and multiculturalism. However, they see themselves, as do most Muslims in Britain, foremost as a religious group. As such they see both advantages and disadvantages in the way group-targeted policies work: on the one hand, through group-specific policies much needed resources are distributed and institutionalisation is enhanced, on the other hand, all benefits come at the cost of the stigma attached to the group: the stigma of being suspected of terrorism, radicalism and separatism.

The revival of religion, if we can call that the high social and political importance Muslimness enjoys in Leicester, has been made possible by the conceptual language of multiculturalism from the early 1970s onwards, especially the stress on equality. In the name of religion Muslims fight for equality, seen as evenhandedness between different religions and ethnic groups, but also for faith-specific rights, such as the right to die and be buried according to specific religious guidelines. Muslims also recognise the political significance of a collectivity united by religion and, thus, they are also active in the political sphere. Further, many organisations, local and national, populate the territory between civic and political, pointing out that faith is much more than an individual and personal affair.

Muslims fight for a lack of discrimination on the basis of religion: this aim has already been achieved in 2003 in the area of employment, while specific questions introduced in the Census point out that awareness of the importance of religion is growing. Further, through inter-faith activities and informal sports meetings between religious groups a collective idea of religion as an important part of social life is constructed, as community members argue, for the collective good.

References

Ahmad, W. and V. Evergeti (2010), 'The making and representation of Muslim identity in Britain: Conversations with British Muslim "elites"', *Ethnic and Racial Studies,* *33*(10), 1697–1717.

Alexander, C. (2002), 'Beyond black: Re-thinking the colour/culture divide', *Ethnic and Racial Studies, 25*(4), 552–71.

Allen, C. (2005), 'From race to religion: The new face of discrimination', in T. Abbas (ed.), *Muslim Britain: Communities under pressure*, London: Zed Books.

Asad, T. (1990), 'Ethnography, literature and politics: Some readings and uses of Salman Rushdie's *The Satanic Verses*', *Cultural Anthropology: Journal of the Society for Cultural Anthropology.*

Back, L., M. Keith, A. Khan, K. Shukra and J. Solomos (2002), 'New Labour's white heart: Politics, multiculturalism and the return of assimilation', *The Political Quarterly, 73*(4), 445–54.

Baucom, I. (1999), *Out of place: Englishness, empire, and the locations of identity*, Princeton: Princeton University Press.

Bellah, R. N. (1967), 'Civil religion in America', *Journal of the American Academy of Arts and Sciences*, 96 (1): 1–21.

Benhabib, S. (1992), *Situating the self: gender, community, and postmodernism in contemporary ethics*, New York: Routledge.

Bleich, E. (2011), 'Social research and "race" policy framing in Britain and France', *The British Journal of Politics and International Relations, 13*, 59–74.

Blitz, B. K. (2006), 'Statelessness and the social (de)construction of citizenship: Political restructuring and ethnic discrimination in Slovenia', *Journal of Human Rights, 5*(4), 453–79.

Bonney, R. and W. Le Goff (2007), 'Leicester's cultural diversity in the context of the British debate on multiculturalism', *International Journal of Diversity in Organizations, Communities and Nations, 6*(6), 45–58.

Butler, J. and G. C. Spivak (2007), *Who sings the nation-state? Language, politics, belonging*, London and New York: Seagull Books.

Census 2001, available at <http://www.leicester.gov.uk/ your-council-services/council-and-democracy/city-statistics/demographic-and-cultural> (last accessed 23 January 2012).

Clarke, J. and J. Newman (1997), *The managerial state: power, politics and ideology in the remaking of social welfare*, London and Thousands Oaks, CA: Sage.

Danielis, J. (2007), *Ethnic population forecasts for Leicester using POPGROUP,* unpublished MSc in Social Research Methods and Statistics, University of Manchester.

Everson, M. (2010), '"Subjects", or "citizens of erewhon"? Law and non-law in the development of a "British citizenship"', *Citizenship Studies,* 7(1), 57–83.

Favell, A. (1998), *Philosophies of integration: Immigration and the idea of citizenship in France and Britain,* New York: St. Martin's Press in association with the Centre for Research in Ethnic Relations, University of Warwick.

Freeman, G. P. (1995), 'Modes of immigration politics in liberal democratic states', *International Migration Review,* 29, 881–902.

Geddes, A. (2005), 'Getting the best of both worlds? Britain, the EU and migration policy', *International Affairs,* 81(4), 723–40.

Gilroy, P. (1991), *'There ain't no black in the union jack' The cultural politics of race and nation,* Chicago: University of Chicago Press.

Cantle, T. and Home Office (2001), *Community cohesion: a report of the independent review team,* London: Home Office.

Hall, S. (2000), 'Conclusion: The multicultural question', in B. Hesse (ed.), *Un/settled multiculturalism,* London: Zed Books.

Hansen, R. (2000), *Citizenship and immigration in post-war Britain the institutional origins of a multicultural nation,* Oxford and New York: Oxford University Press.

Heyck, T. W. (1997), 'After Tylor: British Social Anthropology 1888–1951 by George W. Stocking; The Expansive Moment: The Rise of Social Anthropology in Britain and Africa 1918–1970 by Jack Goody', *The American Historical Review,* vol. 102, No. 5, pp. 1486–88.

Joppke, C. (1999), *Immigration and the nation-state: The United States, Germany, and Great Britain,* Oxford and New York: Oxford University Press.

Joppke, C. (2009), *Veil : Mirror of identity,* Cambridge, UK and Malden, MA: Polity.

Joppke, C. and E. T. Morawska (2003), *Toward assimilation and citizenship: Immigrants in liberal nation-states,* Basingstoke and New York: Palgrave Macmillan.

Kundnani, A. (2002), 'The death of multiculturalism', *Race & Class,* 43, 67–72.

Lister, R. (2003), *Citizenship: Feminist perspectives,* New York: New York University Press.

McLoughlin, S. (2005), 'Mosques and the public space: Conflict and cooperation in Bradford', *Journal of Ethnic and Migration Studies,* 31(6), 1045–66.

Meer, N. and Modood, T. (2009), 'The multicultural state we're in: Muslims, "Multiculture" and the "Civic re-balancing" of British multiculturalism', *Political Studies,* 57(3), 473–97.

Modood, T. (2007), *Multiculturalism: A civic idea,* Cambridge, UK and Malden, MA: Polity Press.

Modood, T. (1990), *Muslims, race and equality in Britain: Some post-Rushdie affair reflections,* Birmingham: Centre for the Study of Islam and Christian–Muslim Relations.

Modood, T. and Runnymede Trust (1992), *Not easy being British: Colour, culture and citizenship,* Stoke-on-Trent: Runnymede Trust and Trentham.

Modood, T., A. Triandafyllidou and R. Zapata-Barrero (2006), *Multiculturalism, Muslims, and citizenship: A European approach*, London and New York: Routledge.

Modood, T., R. Hansen, E. Bleich, B. O'Leary and J. H. Carens (2006), 'The Danish cartoon affair: Free speech, racism, islamism, and integration', *International Migration*, 44(5), 3–62.

Murji, K. and J. Solomos (2005), *Racialization: Studies in theory and practice*, Oxford and New York: Oxford University Press.

Office for National Statistics (2011), available at <http://www.statistics.gov.uk/hub/index.html> (last accessed 3 March 2012).

Open Society Institute (2010), *Muslims in Leicester*.

Rogers, B. and R. Muir (2007), *The power of belonging: Identity, citizenship and community cohesion*, London: Institute for Public Policy Research.

Solomos, J. (2003), *Race and racism in Britain*, Basingstoke and New York: Palgrave Macmillan.

Sooben, P. N. (1990), The origins of the race relations act *Research Paper in Ethnic Relations no. 12*, Centre for Research in Ethnic Relations, University of Warwick.

Taylor, C. (2007), *A secular age*, Cambridge, MA: Belknap Press of Harvard University Press.

Tyler I. (2010), 'Designed to fail: A biopolitics of British citizenship', *Citizenship Studies*, 14(1), 61–74.

Vertovec, S. and C. Peach (1997), *Islam in Europe: The politics of religion and community*, New York: St. Martin's Press.

Werbner, P. (2002), *Imagined diasporas among Manchester Muslims: The public performance of Pakistani transnational identity politics*, Oxford and Santa Fe: James Currey, School of American Research Press.

Wills, J. (2010), *Global cities at work: New migrant divisions of labour*, London: Pluto Press.

Worley, C. (2005), '"It's not about race. It's about the community": New Labour and "community cohesion"', *Critical Social Policy*, 25(4), 483–96.

Wray, M. (2006), *Not quite white: White trash and the boundaries of whiteness*, Durham: Duke University Press.

PART FOUR

• • •

BREAKING THE BOUNDS

MUSLIMS AND ELECTORAL POLITICS IN BRITAIN: THE CASE OF THE RESPECT PARTY

Timothy Peace

1. Introduction

In comparison with many other European countries, Britain's ethnic minorities have been very successful at achieving political representation and making an impact on the political system. Whereas migrants and their descendants in other countries may have struggled for years to gain the right to vote and stand in elections, Commonwealth migrants to Britain from her former colonies were automatically given the right to citizenship, including full political rights. This even pre-dated the mass migration to Britain of the 1950s and 1960s, and three Members of Parliament (MPs) from the Indian subcontinent, though none Muslim, were elected to the House of Commons before World War II (Anwar 2001). Even today, citizens of the Commonwealth countries have full voting rights at all levels and can stand as candidates. Muslims have certainly played an important role in British electoral politics – be they migrants, British-born or even converts to Islam. The vast majority of Muslims in the UK trace their heritage to South Asia and it is they who have made the biggest impact. The first Muslim in Britain to hold elected office was Bashir Maan who emigrated from Pakistan to Britain in 1953. He became a City Councillor in Glasgow in 1970 and it was in that same city that Mohammad Sarwar was elected as the first Muslim MP in 1997. This was followed one year later by the first Muslim life peer in the House of Lords. Since then a number of British-born Muslims have also made an impact in politics, including Shahid Malik who in 2007 became the first Muslim Minister in the UK government when he was appointed as Parliamentary Under Secretary of State in the Department for International Development by then Prime Minister Gordon Brown. All of these pioneers were male and represented the Labour Party. Until quite recently, the overwhelming majority of all Muslim politicians, whether at local or national level, fitted this profile.

Parties across the political spectrum now make great efforts to connect with Muslims voters. Muslim communities are often geographically concentrated in certain neighbourhoods and it is widely assumed that they can affect the results of elections in a number of areas in the country. Over half of British Muslims live in just fifty parliamentary seats and in ten of these seats the Muslim population is over 20%. In the constituencies of Bethnal Green and Bow (East London) and Bradford West, the Muslim population approaches 40%. British local government authorities are split up into electoral districts called wards, which elect several councillors. Those wards with high numbers of Muslim residents usually elect fellow Muslims as their representatives and consequently over 200 Muslims are represented in British local government. As of 2012, the London Borough of Tower Hamlets has thirty local councillors who are Muslim, in Bradford there are twenty six and Birmingham city council has nineteen. There are eight Muslim Members of Parliament (six Labour and two Conservative), two British Muslim Members of the European Parliament, two Muslim Members of the Scottish Parliament and one Muslim Member of the National Assembly for Wales. Muslims have represented all the major political parties including the regional nationalist parties the Scottish National Party (SNP) and Plaid Cymru. Even if Muslim candidates have been elected for a variety of parties, it is still the Labour Party which most of them continue to represent. Labour also receives the most support in areas with a high concentration of Muslim residents. Indeed, constituencies with high numbers of ethnic minorities, whether Muslims or not, have traditionally represented 'safe seats' for the Labour Party. The relationship between Labour and Muslim communities has always been very strong and most Muslims who are members of political parties are also most likely to be associated with Labour. Purdham (1996: 133) even remarked that 'many local Labour parties in areas with a high Muslim population are now under Muslim control.'

The only party to make any significant impact on Labour's dominance in constituencies with large numbers of Muslims is the Respect Party. It has been noted for its electoral success in East London, Birmingham and Bradford, where large numbers of British Muslims reside. It managed to drastically reduce Labour's support in certain areas and achieved representation both within local government and in the lower house of the Westminster Parliament. This was a staggering achievement considering that minor parties in Britain have always been disadvantaged because of the 'winner takes all' voting system. As this chapter will show, the Respect Party concentrates on an essentially local campaigning strategy and uses civil society contacts in order to boost its electoral prospects. It is unique in Europe as the only party dominated by Muslim leaders and activists that has made an electoral breakthrough. This chapter provides an overview of the party and demonstrates how it has contributed to breaking down traditional ethnic politics that were exploited by the Labour Party. The empirical evidence is drawn from a series of semi-structured interviews with Respect councillors who were elected to Tower Hamlets London Borough Council as well as election material produced by the party. Additional material obtained from newspapers, party websites and other publications has also been used to inform the analysis. The chapter is divided into three sections; the first presents a history of the party and an examination of its electoral performance, it then details the specific dynamics at play within 'ethnic politics' in the UK before finally explaining how mosques, faith-based organisations and community groups helped Respect to gain support in the local community and representation in both local and national political institutions.

2. A brief history of Respect and its electoral performance

'RESPECT – The Unity Coalition' (hereafter Respect) was founded in January 2004.[1] It grew out of the British anti-war movement and the Stop the War Coalition (SWC), which organised the largest public demonstration in British history on 15 February 2003 to oppose the invasion of Iraq. The anti-war movement was crucial in the politicisation of a new generation of young people, especially British Muslims (Peace 2008). The unprecedented success of the movement, coupled with the widespread disappointment of many traditional Labour Party supporters, made the idea of forming an alternative party particularly attractive. This idea gained further credence when Labour performed poorly in local elections in Birmingham and Leicester in May 2003, results which were largely attributed to Muslim voters (BBC 2003). The project to form a party was spearheaded by the journalist and environmental campaigner George Monbiot, and Salma Yaqoob, a British Muslim woman who was the chair of the Birmingham chapter of the SWC. The MP George Galloway joined the fray after he was expelled from the Labour Party in October 2003. He would become Respect's figurehead and most well known personality (although he was never the party leader). The Socialist Workers Party (SWP), whose leaders were very active in the SWC, were also heavily involved in setting up Respect, which aimed to provide an outlet to voters angered by the war in Iraq but also to federate elements of the British radical left.[2]

Soon after its formation, Respect's leaders began campaigning ahead of the London Assembly and European parliament elections scheduled for 10 June 2004. They were well aware that a significant number of Muslim voters would be willing to switch their allegiance from Labour. The proportional voting systems employed also meant that this would be a golden opportunity to get Respect candidates elected. Many of these candidates were Muslims and election material actually advertised Respect as 'the party for Muslims'.

They also specifically billed the elections as a 'referendum on Blair and the war' in order to capture the vote of those angered by the invasion of Iraq (Figure 15.1). Given that the party had only been in existence for six months, its electoral performance was quite remarkable. In the European election, the party polled a quarter of a million votes. In the London region alone they received 91,175 votes, although this was not enough in order to elect an MEP. It also achieved 4.5% of the vote in the London Assembly contest but again narrowly missed out on a seat.[3] The breakdown of the vote showed that they had outperformed all other parties in the East London boroughs of Tower Hamlets and Newham, the two local authorities with the highest numbers of Muslim residents in the country.[4] One month later, the party won a local council by-election in Tower Hamlets and Oliur Rahman became Respect's first elected official. The party then set about preparing to elect its first MP. This would be no mean feat as the 'first past the post' plurality voting system in the UK makes it much harder for smaller parties to win seats than under proportional systems. It does however favour those parties whose support is geographically concentrated (Boucek 1998) and the residential segregation of many Muslim communities meant that those involved in Respect thought they might be able to capitalise on the weakness of Labour in some of its former strongholds. Respect were not the only group trying to exploit bitter feelings about the Iraq war amongst Muslim communities. There was also a campaign to unseat Labour MPs in the North West of England by the Muslim Public Affairs Committee (Russell et al. 2008).

The 2005 UK general election saw Respect put forward twenty-six candidates in England and Wales, again the majority of its candidates were Muslims. It was in East London where the party saw most potential for success as three of the four sitting Labour MPs had voted in favour of the invasion of Iraq. They also targeted other constituencies with large Muslim populations in places like Bradford, Birmingham, Manchester and Leicester. Respect candidates were however also fielded in places where very few Muslims live like Dorset and Neath. Its election manifesto made a stinging attack on the Labour Party and advocated for socialist principles:

> We believe that there is an alternative to imperialist war, unfettered global capitalism, and the rule of the market. We aim for a society where wealth is used to meet the needs of the people, not the profits of the corporations. We aim to organise opposition to all forms of inequality and injustice. We actively oppose the destruction of the environment, inherent in the profit system, which threatens the future of the planet. Our aim is to create a socially just and ecologically sustainable society. As we have seen over the war on Iraq, there is a huge democratic deficit in Britain. Millions marched against the invasion and millions more opposed it. Yet their wishes were ignored, while those of George Bush were dutifully carried out. At the last two elections, millions voted for Labour candidates, expecting them to improve their

lives. Not many would have expected tuition fees, privatisation, wars, attacks on the disabled and asylum seekers, and massive handouts to big business. (Respect 2005)

Respect put most of its resources into trying to elect candidates in East London and amassed an army of volunteers to canvass potential electors and persuade them to give their vote to a party that many had never even heard of. To the surprise of many political commentators, George Galloway was subsequently elected as MP for the constituency of Bethnal Green and Bow, overturning a Labour majority of over 10,000. Two other Respect candidates in the area finished second to Labour and Salma Yaqoob also came second in the Birmingham Small Heath and Sparkbrook constituency. The party won on average 6.9% of the vote nationwide in the constituencies it contested and performed quite poorly in most areas outside of London and Birmingham, indeed seventeen of their candidates lost their deposit, i.e. gained less that 5% of the vote. Success in these two areas was no doubt linked to the fact that the anti-war movement had been strong and Respect had a base on which to build. Following the 2005 election results, a number of local councillors from both Labour and the Liberal Democrats decided to defect to Respect.

At local elections in May 2006, the party fielded over 150 candidates and went on to elect a total of sixteen local councillors, twelve of whom were for Tower Hamlets Council. In 2007 it also elected an additional two councillors, bringing the nationwide total to eighteen. Until this moment the party had been making steady progress but events later that year would lead to a sharp decline in its fortunes. In late 2007 there was a split, not uncommon in parties of the radical left, and those connected with the SWP left the coalition. The effect on its electoral scores was devastating. It performed poorly in the 2008 London Assembly elections and did not even put forward candidates for the 2009 European elections. In 2010, the party had only eleven parliamentary candidates for the general election that was held on 6 May that year. They failed to elect any candidates and lost the seat previously held by George Galloway. They also lost most of their local councillors who were repre-sented in Tower Hamlets, Newham and Birmingham. Galloway attempted to get elected to the Scottish Parliament in May 2011 but received just 3% of the vote. Many assumed the party was destined for the history books but at the by-election for the Bradford West constituency in March 2012 the party pulled off its biggest win to date. George Galloway returned as an MP with a stunning 56% of the vote. This result shocked the whole political establish-ment and Galloway called it 'The Bradford Spring' (BBC 2012). In local elec-tions the following month the party won five seats on Bradford City Council gaining well over 50% of the vote in the Manningham and City wards. Respect's previous best performances came at a time when the Iraq war was still a very salient issue. Its success had been interpreted by most as an anti-war protest vote. The victory in Bradford showed that the reasons were perhaps

George GALLOWAY
Fighting for Muslim rights!

আজ গ্যালোওয়ে মুসলমানের অধিকারের জন্য লড়ে চলেছেন!

چارج گیلوے سلمانوں کے حقوق کے لیے جنگ لڑ رہے ہیں!

جورج جالاواي يكافح من أجل حقوق المسلمين!

A referendum on Blair and the war....

OUR CHOICE

YES✓   **NO** X

100,000 VOTES ELECTS GALLOWAY FOR LONDON
Say NO to the war, NO to the occupation, NO to Blair

VOTE *RESPECT* JUNE 10

জুন ১০ রেসপেক্টে ভোট দিন

جون 10 کو ریسپیکٹ کو ووٹ دیں

يوم 10 في RESPECT لصوتك إعط

Published by L Smith, Respect Winchester House, London NW1 1SPA. Printed by East End Offset, London E3

How to vote and make a difference

IF YOU WANT GEORGE GALLOWAY TO REPRESENT YOU, GIVE US YOUR VOTE ON THE WHITE BALLOT PAPER FOR THE EUROPEAN ELECTIONS.

Respect – The Unity Coalition (George Galloway) George, Galloway, Unjan Mirza, Ken Loach, Elaine Graham-Leigh, Paul Foot, Rita Carter, Vanessa Brittain, Gerry MacFarlane.	X

যদি আপনি চান গ্যালোওয়ের প্রতিনিধিত্ব চান। ইয়োরোপীয় নির্বাচন নামা ভোটপত্রে আপনার ভোট আমাদের দিন।

اگر آپ چاہتے ہیں کہ جارج گیلوے آپ کی نمائندگی کرے تو یورپی انتخابات کے سفید بیلٹ پیپر پر ہمیں ووٹ دیں۔

إذا رغبت أن يمثلك جورج جالاواي، أعط صوتك على ورقة الإنتخابات الوروبية البيضاء.

To elect RESPECT members to the Greater London Assembly vote RESPECT on the ORANGE London Assembly ballot paper. This is crucial.

HE STOOD UP FOR MUSLIMS, NOW IT'S OUR TURN TO STAND UP FOR HIM!

What you can do

We do not have the money or the media coverage that the big parties have. Our strength is you. We need you to contact us and take leaflets to your local mosque, study circle, community organisation etc. Take posters to put up in your house or local shops. Make sure you tell your friends and family to vote on June 10.

What we stand for

Action to tackle Islamophobia, racism and discrimination... End to the occupation of Iraq and Palestine... Low-cost public housing... Reliable, cheap and safe public transport for all... Against tuition fees.... Pensions linked to earnings.... Equal pay and employment rights for all workers.... An end to the destruction of the environment...

GEORGE GALLOWAY FIGHTING FOR MUSLIM RIGHTS

☐ I would like to help in the Muslim campaign to elect George Galloway
☐ I would like to join RESPECT and I enclose £10. Make cheques payable to Unity Political Fund.
☐ I would like to make a donation to the campaign– amount £.............

First name	Surname	(Capitals please)
Address		
	Postcode	
Phone	Email	

George Galloway RESPECT MP – Room 333, House of Commons, London SW1A 0AA.
Contact the Galloway campaign team on 07956 210 332, email: muslimsgalloway@yahoo.com

RESPECT – the party for Muslims

RESPECT emerged from the anti-war movement and includes many of its leading members. Our candidates include many leading Muslim and non-Muslim activists from trade unions, community and religious organisations.

Some of our candidates for the European Parliament and the Greater London Assembly

রেসপেক্ট – মুসলমানদের পার্টি

যুদ্ধ বিরোধী আন্দোলন থেকে উঠিয়ে রেসপেক্ট রয়েছে যা আন্দোলনের বেশ কিছু প্রধান নেতা। আমাদের প্রার্থিদের মধ্যে আছ সবাই, সাম্প্রদায়িক ও ধর্মীয় সংস্থার অনেকগুলি প্রথিতযশা মুসলমান এবং অমুসলমান সক্রিয় কর্মী আছে।

(RESPECT) - ﺳﭙﯿﮑﭧ ﭨﯽ ﻣﮑﺲﻻﻧﺰ ﮐﮯ ﻟﯿﮯ ﺳﭙﯿﮑﭧ ﭘﺎﺭﭨﯽ

ﺍﯾﺪﻭﺭﺍﺭﺍﻥ ﮐﮯ ﻟﯿﮯ

ﺍﻟﺤﺰﺏ ﻷﺟﻞ ﺍﻟﻤﺴﻠﻤﯿﻦ - RESPECT

ﻧﺸﺄ ﺣﺰﺏ ﻣﻜﺎﻓﺤﺔ ﺍﻟﺤﺮﺏ RESPECT ﻣﻦ ﺃﻋﻀﺎﺋﻬﺎ ﺍﻟﺒﺎﺭﺯﯾﻦ. ﻭﻣﻦ ﺍﻹﺗﺤﺎﺩﺍﺕ ﺍﻟﺘﺠﺎﺭﯾﺔ ﻭﺍﻟﺠﺎﻟﯿﺎﺕ ﻭﺍﻟﻤﻨﻈﻤﺎﺕ ﺍﻟﺪﯾﻨﯿﺔ.

RESPECT Call us now on **020 7170 4030/1** or go to **www.respectcoalition.org**

A referendum on Blair and his war

In the last election 86% of Muslim voters gave their votes to New Labour but:

● Blair ignored us on Afghanistan
● Blair ignored us on Kashmir
● Blair ignored us on imprisoning Muslims without charge or trial
● Blair ignored us on Palestine
● Blair ignored us on Iraq

On June 10 don't let Blair claim that we are happy with his policy of support for George Bush and Ariel Sharon. Don't let him ignore us any more.

Can we win? – YES we can!

It takes 100,000 votes to get an MEP elected. It is a London-wide election by proportional representation – so every one of our votes count.

George Galloway – a fighter for Muslims.

For over 30 years he has dedicated his life to the struggle for justice by the peoples of Palestine, Iraq, Bangladesh and Pakistan.

Married to a Palestinian doctor; teetotal, he has strong religious principles about fighting injustice. He was expelled by Blair because he refused to apologise for his anti-war stance. Our Muslim MPs stayed silent or supported the war. Who do you want to be our voice?

Liberal Democrats – is it a vote against Blair and the war?

They supported the war once it began and still support the occupation of Iraq. Tens of thousands of Iraqi men, women and children were killed and are still dying today. Others face humiliation, torture and rape on a daily basis.

Only RESPECT says 'No to the war; No to the occupation, Freedom for Iraq'.

Sarah Ludford MEP leads the Lib-Dem list on June 10 and is a proud member of 'Friends of Israel' whilst Jenny Tongue MP was sacked because she expressed sympathy about Palestine.

Only RESPECT says 'No to the Israeli occupation, Freedom for Palestine'.

Figure 15.1 Respect election material (RESPECT 2004)

more complex than that. Yet again, the party had shaken up the electoral landscape in an area with a large Muslim population that was considered to be a Labour heartland. One of the ways it achieved this was by challenging the manipulation of minority communities and the political process that was hitherto commonplace.

3. Ethnic politics in Britain

The link between the Labour Party and the communities of post-colonial migrants and their descendants has traditionally been very solid and constituencies with high numbers of ethnic minorities have always been bastions of Labour support. In his groundbreaking study *Race and Party Competition in Britain*, Anthony Messina (1989: 151) summed up the situation thus: 'Asian and Afro-Caribbean electors constitute a solid voting bloc; and these constituencies are extremely loyal to Labour. By virtually all indices, Labour is the party of, if not unambiguously for, non-whites.' Indeed, for many years support for the Labour Party from these sections of the electorate was seen as natural because most migrants (and their descendants) formed part of the working class and Labour had also supported ethnic minorities by promoting race relations and anti-discrimination legislation. Labour had also taken a more active role in using pillars of such communities to stand as candidates in elections, although this practice has since been adopted by all the main parties. In comparison with many other countries in Western Europe, actively selecting ethnic minority candidates may appear particularly progressive. However, this has often involved many perverse aspects. Minority communities, in particular South Asian communities, have been commonly used as vote banks in a pattern of co-optation of 'community leaders'. In his study into the politics of ethnic minorities and the Labour Party in Birmingham, Garbaye (2005) identified three main styles of co-optation: patronage, radical activist and ethnic community. The patronage model involves candidates receiving favours for their community in return for securing election victory for Labour. However, they are not given access to decision-making processes and merely expected to deliver votes for the party from their community. Radical activists were more involved in the party and often came from the second generation who were more politically savvy than their parents. Their candidacy was often supported by other left-wing activists within the Labour Party. In the ethnic community model, councillors built political careers on resources drawn from their communities and merely used Labour as a structure without much interest in party discipline. These three models have tended to overlap and operate simultaneously in areas with high numbers of ethnic minorities in Britain.

This situation has led to undemocratic practices as electors from minority communities, particularly those of South Asian origin, are often encouraged to vote according to family or kinship relations. This is a situation that is prevalent in many Muslim communities. Glynn (2008: 71) describes how patronage worked within the Bengali community in East London:

> Clan politics is often explained as an Asian import, but it is probably more accurate to say that a close community with strong patriarchal structures allows for the most efficient use of those non-party ties and networks that are exploited by politicians of all backgrounds. The importance of patronage relations was strengthened by communication difficulties that left those who could translate English and Bengali (and understood political procedure) in a powerful position. Existing patterns of patronage that are found in many ethnic minority communities will inevitably be exploited in politics, and possibly reinforced. Bengali members would refer to others as 'my members'; and when Labour canvassers went round Spitalfields they did not bother to knock on every door – Bengali party members knew where to find the community leaders who would be able to deliver perhaps twenty votes.

The Bengali community in East London is very prominent due to a specific history of chain migration from Bangladesh, in particular the region of Sylhet (Eade 1989). In other cities such as Birmingham and Bradford it is the Pakistani community that dominates, in particular those with family ties to Mirpur in Pakistan-administered Kashmir. In these communities the *biraderi* (extended family) has often been used to secure votes for a particular candidate, be they Muslim or non-Muslim. The Labour Party in particular has exploited this situation for many years and has knowingly 'allowed *biraderi* politics to flourish' (Lewis 2007: 52).[5] Kingsley Purdham studied Muslim councillors in the mid-1990s and discovered that:

> 74 per cent of councillors interviewed for this research stated that in their experience individuals have attempted to invoke loyalties along kinship/caste/*biraderi* lines in their appeals to Muslims at the local level. 13 per cent of the Muslim councillors interviewed refused to comment, a denial which may suggest an even higher overall percentage. (Purdham 2001:151)

This kind of politics occasionally leads to outright corruption, such as the Birmingham postal vote scandal in 2004 which led to three Muslim Labour councillors being ousted and banned from standing for office by an election commissioner who found them guilty of corrupt and illegal practices (Stewart 2006).[6] The Respect Party as a whole, and George Galloway in particular, campaigned against vote-rigging through the postal voting system and indeed an end to postal voting on demand (BBC 2005). It saw this as a means for Labour to siphon off some of its potential support and it lodged a petition on 31 May 2005 which challenged the general election result in the constituency of Birmingham Sparkbrook and Small Heath because of suspicion of electoral fraud. Respect also resisted pressure from community leaders to select candidates based purely on their family background, as former leader Salma Yaqoob explains:

> It is for the reasons that *biraderi* (extended clan) networks can exert undue influence that we have been campaigning in Birmingham against postal votes. Women in particular have been disenfranchised. Postal votes are filled out in the 'privacy' of one's own home. But it is not private when family members, candidates or supporters, can influence – subtly or otherwise – the way you complete your vote . . . Last year in Birmingham Sparkbrook we came under considerable pressure when we selected a candidate whose family were originally from the same village in Pakistan as the sitting Lib Dem councillor. It was alleged we were splitting the *biraderi* vote. And that we could not win by so doing. We resisted those pressures, just as we resisted pressures when the same people said we could never win by standing a woman candidate. (Yaqoob 2008)

Pressure to vote according to kinship ties is a concern for many younger Muslim voters who have in the past decided not to vote as a form of protest. In the wake of the by-election victory in Bradford West, the media quickly picked up on the importance of the *biraderi* system even if they underestimated just how ingrained the use of kinship ties has been in British politics (Akhtar 2012). Journalists reported that many young people they spoke to in Bradford admitted they had gone against the wishes of their parents or the community elders to vote for Galloway. Therefore the Respect Party challenged many of the prevailing orthodoxies associated with British ethnic politics and has reaped the benefits.

Respect was often criticised for being 'communalist', i.e. only campaigning for one particular ethnic/religious group. Respect never aimed to base itself exclusively on Muslim voters, even though its support was disproportionately from the Muslim community. In reality, all the major parties try to appeal to a Muslim electorate, both through their policies and candidates. Nevertheless, it is inaccurate to talk of a 'Muslim vote' in the sense of one homogeneous voting bloc. Muslim voters are usually split according to several different cleavages whether related to family ties, theological affiliations or simply the kind of socio-economic cleavages that separate all voters.[7] Parties need to do much more than gain a hypothetical Muslim vote. They need to deal with both local political concerns as well as taking into account diaspora politics imported from abroad. For some British Muslim councillors, 'political involvement with the country of departure can extend into British politics and into active involvement in political causes or political parties of their departure country. Activists can therefore maintain a foot in two countries' (Purdham 2000: 53). The Kashmir issue has been very important in British politics because of the sheer number of people who still have strong family ties to this area (Ellis and Khan 1998). In Birmingham for example, the People's Justice Party (PJP) was formed in 1998 to campaign on this issue and even elected a handful of local councillors. In the 2001 general election it gained 13% of the vote in the Birmingham Sparkbrook and Small Heath constituency. Unsurprisingly, Respect's Salma Yaqoob has always spoken out about events in Kashmir and campaigned against the actions of the Indian security services by, for example, picketing the Indian consulate. Galloway too never failed to mention Kashmir in his campaign in Bradford, as well as the issue of Palestine.[8]

In Tower Hamlets, there is an Islamist/secularist cleavage amongst the Bengali community, which relates to the Bangladesh Liberation war of 1971.[9] The politics of Bangladesh have also been transported to Britain, leading to:

> A complicated interweaving of political struggles between (1) the major parties (Awami League, Bangladesh National Party and Jatiya Party) and Islamist pressure groups in Bangladesh and (2) British political parties. Political struggles between Bangladeshi activists in Tower Hamlets operated at several levels, therefore – at the level of formal British political discourse and practice, as well as at formal and informal levels where Bangladeshi political issues were more important. These different levels influenced elections and debates in the Tower Hamlets political arena, so that support for a particular political party and its policies could not be taken at face value. (Begum and Eade 2005: 184)

Many of the elected politicians from the Bengali community in this area have links with parties in Bangladesh and it is through such links that they have been able to build up their political capital. When George Galloway ran for MP in 2005, he was taken by Respect members on a tour of Sylhet in order to garner support for his candidacy.[10] A Respect councillor explains this decision:

> We said to George 'go and visit those poor areas, family members will appreciate that, they will then phone up and canvass for you from Bangladesh' and that's what happened. People phoned up telling their family members to 'give this gentleman a chance'. Also, we needed to divide the voters as soon as possible because we also have the Bangladeshi politics to deal with too. This meant trying to make friends with all the political parties over there, giving them hope and aspiration, providing neutrality as an MP and to serve the interests of Bangladesh. This helped to neutralise the [Bangladeshi] political parties who would normally have affiliated themselves with the Labour Party.[11]

Such divide and conquer tactics demonstrate an astute political awareness of the likely voting patterns amongst the local community. Respect activists were very shrewd in taking into account both local politics and what was happening back in South Asia.

Respect also received criticism for only using Muslim election candidates.

Again, this is slightly unfair as the party has put forward candidates from a variety of ethnic and religious backgrounds and its leaders have often been keen to point out that their candidates are the most diverse, not only regarding ethnicity but also in terms of age and gender.[12] It is a simple fact that in areas of high Muslim population, parties are most likely to select candidates who are also Muslim. This has been the case at the local level for quite some time and is now also becoming more common for parliamentary elections. For example, in 2010 the Conservative, Labour and Liberal Democrat parties put forward only Muslim candidates in the parliamentary constituencies of Bethnal Green and Bow and Birmingham Ladywood. In the past, parties (in particular Labour) encouraged ethnic minorities to serve at the local level in order to control a particular council but made it more difficult for them to stand for parliamentary seats. Indeed many prominent government ministers have been elected in such constituencies, which are seen as 'safe seats'. Councillors representing wards with a large ethnic minority population are inevitably members of ethnic minorities themselves, irrespective of their party affiliation. Respect usually elected councillors in wards that had a high proportion of Muslim residents such as Sparkbrook in Birmingham, Green Street West in Newham and Shadwell in Tower Hamlets.

4. The role of mosques, faith-based organisations and community groups

Respect provides an interesting case study of the relationship between political parties and civil society as it evolved directly from a social movement. Such a trajectory represents a somewhat anomalous path for modern day parties but is of course not novel in the history of Western European democracies where mass parties often started as 'a movement from society towards the state' (Biezen 2005: 169). From the outset Respect was, by its very nature, already embedded in a host of civil society organisations and networks connected to the anti-war movement but also to the wider movement against neo-liberal globalisation (Peace 2008).[13] Its platform included issues that could be readily identified with the radical left such as opposing neo-liberalism, renationalising public services and promoting trade unionism a well as a commitment to 'social justice'. Specific manifesto pledges included opposition to privatisation policies, higher taxes aimed at businesses and high earners, the repeal of 'anti-union' legislation, safeguarding the National Health Service (NHS), defending civil liberties and raising the minimum wage (Respect 2005, 2010). International issues such as government foreign policy have also been used as key mobilising themes, even for local elections. Opposition to Britain's military presence in Iraq and Afghanistan has been central to this, but Respect candidates also attempt to mobilise the electorate around other issues close to the heart of many Muslims such as the Israeli-Palestinian conflict. Respect candidates combine this with a strong focus on local issues. One Respect councillor who was interviewed stressed that he wanted to make a point of winning by operating at the grassroots level. It is through their links with mosques, faith-based organisations and community groups that they are able to gain support for their candidates despite the stiff electoral competition from more established parties.

The party is, in fact, at a massive disadvantage regarding both human and financial resources in relation to the established parties, a fact it readily admitted in its campaign literature: 'We do not have the money or the media coverage the big parties have. Our strength is you. We need you to contact us and take leaflets to your local mosque, study circle, community organisation, etc.' (Respect 2004). The mosques and local community groups (which may not necessarily have a religious focus) are the two most important aspects of civil society that Respect has relied on in order to achieve electoral success. Such a strategy is commonplace in ethnic politics and is also employed by competing politicians, many of whom are also from the ethnic minority community in question. In Tower Hamlets for example, former Bengali youth activists occupy a pivotal role in the community organisation sector and many have entered the local authority through either Labour or the Liberal Democrats and subsequently succeeded in securing funding for cultural and community projects (Eade and Garbin 2006: 185). Community organisations are dependent on council funding, which encourages a patron-client relationship with local councillors and the party they represent. Respect candidates were thus forced to innovate and bypass some of the traditional structures, or in some cases create new rival organisations.

In areas of high numbers of Muslim residents, mosques and other faith-based organisations are some of the most visible and influential civil society players. These organisations have become even more important in recent years as both national and local governments seek to engage faith groups in order to facilitate regeneration, provide consultation on policy making and service delivery as well as generally promoting 'community cohesion' through inter-faith activity (McLoughlin 2005). The leading mosques in East London are involved in partnerships with local authorities to carry out social welfare functions and faith-led groups are heavily involved in preventive work on drugs, youth homelessness, teenage pregnancy and anti-social behaviour (Begum and Eade 2005). The East London Mosque (ELM) has developed a particularly dominant role in this respect and works in close collaboration with the health authorities, job centre and local schools (Glynn 2008). It is seen as a key power broker in the local political arena, so much so that every local politician is obliged to speak with its leadership and publicly visit the mosque if they want to stand a chance of being elected.[14]

The East London Mosque has been highly successful at building alliances with local government officials, and its recent expansion that resulted in the creation of the

London Muslim Centre (used for prayers, recreational facilities and housing) has strengthened its position at a time when funding for secular groups significantly declined. (Eade and Garbin 2006: 188)

It has also become an important actor through its membership of Citizens UK, which unites over one hundred different civil society organisations across the city campaigning on various social issues.[15]

Mosques do not usually openly support one particular candidate at election time as this could be divisive and also counter-productive. Some are strictly apolitical and avoid involvement in party politics altogether.[16] The description that Schmitt-Beck and Farrell (2008: 14) provide about organised interests is certainly apt concerning the more political mosques such as ELM:

> Often, they refrain from clearly taking sides at elections, for fear of alienating members who no longer automatically come from the same political background, but also in order to prevent their relations to government officials from being entirely dependent on the fickle electoral fate of just one particular party. On the contrary, they generally try to stay on friendly terms with several parties at the same time. Sometimes they avoid clear party political statements and refer to more subtle techniques of signalling to their members what the best electoral choices are.

Likewise, faith-based organisations are often registered charities and this too means that they are legally not permitted to endorse political parties or display partisan affiliation. However, it is widely acknowledged that leaders within both mosques and related organisations hold the ability to sway the opinions of many voters and so local politicians often enter into negotiations with them. As one Respect councillor simply put it, 'they need our help and we need their votes'. To this end, Respect candidates and supporters would often leaflet outside mosques after Friday prayers and on certain occasions were allowed to address those inside. In Newham, the link between local mosques and Respect candidates was very close. Respect's candidate for the parliamentary seat of East Ham in 2005 was Abdul Khaliq Mian, a local community organiser and part of the Newham Muslim Alliance (NMA), a coalition of leaders from twenty-five local mosques. He organised several hustings, debates and fundraising events at venues such as Muslim faith schools and his selection was endorsed by other mosque leaders: 'Before I stood we called a meeting of the elders from the mosques and explained the process. They endorsed me' (Taylor 2005). The Respect candidate for mayor of Newham in 2006 was Abdurahman Jafar, a human rights barrister and vice-chair of the legal affairs committee of the Muslim Council of Britain (MCB). Both candidates were able to mobilise large numbers of voters in Newham, despite coming second in both contests.[17] These links have also been important in Birmingham, another area where Respect has made an electoral breakthrough. Salma Yaqoob is a spokeswoman for Birmingham Central Mosque and also secured the backing of several Muslim scholars for her campaigns (Figure 15.2).

In his campaign for election in Bethnal Green and Bow in 2005, George Galloway made a point of visiting all the mosques in the area and spoke to their trustees. 'Their support was crucial for George's campaign; all the mosques helped George because he did the right thing. He went and visited them all and talked to the leadership. They gave him advice and he took it.'[18] Indeed, although it is difficult to gauge just how vital this support was, it is widely assumed that institutions such as ELM and faith-based organisations close to it such as Islamic Forum Europe (IFE) were instrumental in his election victory. So much so that Bangladeshi politicians from the secularist Awami League were urging their supporters in London to vote Labour in spite of the Iraq issue (Hussain 2007).[19] IFE and its youth wing the Young Muslim Organisation (YMO) are inspired by the Islamist political party Jama'at-i-Islami.[20] Respect came in for a lot of criticism because of its links with activists from IFE. When questioned on this subject, a Respect councillor defended this strategy:

> We have to speak to everyone. You can't say 'OK we're going to support Awami League and exclude Jama'at-i-Islami.' Jama'at is very powerful in Bangladesh, all the business sector in Sylhet is controlled by Jama'at and there is big support for Jamaat in Tower Hamlets.[21]

The journalist Andrew Gilligan has repeatedly criticised the IFE and its role in local politics, even claiming that it exercised significant control over the council in Tower Hamlets (Gilligan 2010).[22]

Community groups, whether they are religious or ethnic in character, are useful for local politicians who often maintain direct links with them and provide their revenue through council funding. In his study of Muslim councillors, Purdham (2000: 49) noted that they had 'voluntary experience in various anti-racist agencies, community action groups and advice centres'. Respect candidates were no different and also had connections with different grassroots community groups and drew on these connections for their campaign. Community workers were also encouraged to come on board and take part in campaigning for Respect. Thus a lot of time was devoted to these groups because:

> In the Bangladeshi community there are so many associations linked to their particular village or geographical area and the whole cultural psyche is linked to that. They do a lot of projects and fundraising . . . if you understand that well you can utilise it to your advantage.[23]

Once elected into office in 2006, a number of Respect councillors in Tower Hamlets used the tactic of setting up local community groups in the

GODSIFF'S SHAME...

HE VOTED FOR THIS:

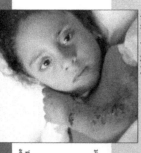

Roger Godsiff has relied on people's ignorance of his true record for too long. It's time for the truth to be exposed.

- On 18th March 2003, on the final and crucial vote to authorize war, Godsiff voted *FOR* the war in Iraq.
- He is deliberately deceiving voters by claiming to be anti-war because he voted for a previous anti-war amendment.

This hypocritical deception is a shameful disgrace. Don't let him get away with it any more.

A US bombing raid destroyed Aysha's house in Fallujah on 6th October 2004 killing eight members of her family, including her pregnant mother and three year old brother. Aysha was the only survivor.

Aysha Saleem, 4 year old orphan

DO NOT ACCEPT:

- Over 100,000 Iraqis killed (Lancet, 2005).
- Torture and sexual humiliation in Abu Ghraib prison.
- Godsiff voted for the Terrorism Bills in 2001 and 2005 - supporting detention without trial, leading to Guantanamo Bay style imprisonment in Belmarsh, UK.

NOR FORGET:

- Godsiff also supported the war in Afghanistan. He said: "I support the actions of the international coalition" on 1st November 2001 in Parliament".
- Over 20,000 people were killed.

ON MAY 5TH YOU CAN BE THEIR VOICE

7	Salma YAQOOB *RESPECT*	X

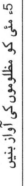

راجر گاڈسف کی .... بے ترگی

راجر گاڈسف کی

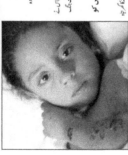

حلیمہ سلیم، چار سالہ یتیم بچی

معاف نہ کیجئے:

مت بھولئے:

7	Salma YAQOOB *RESPECT*	X

MUSLIM SCHOLARS ENDORSE SALMA YAQOOB

At this vital time of the General Election, we the undersigned wish to express our support for Salma Yaqoob, the Respect Candidate in the areas of Sparkbrook, Small Heath, Sparkhill and Fox Hollies in Birmingham. We feel she is the best candidate in the constituency for the following reasons:

- She stood up and campaigned against the wars in Afghanistan and Iraq in a brave and consistent manner. Even when others were not prepared to speak out, she has been a voice of principle.
- The Labour MP pretends he is anti-war but on the final and crucial vote to authorise war he voted in the House of Commons **FOR** war to begin. The Liberal Democrat candidate has no record of campaigning around this vital issue.
- Our community very much needs people of ability who can speak on our behalf in the House of Commons where decisions affecting the lives of millions of people are taken.
- She has shown herself to be a capable representative as she has been effective in not only mobilising large numbers of people in demonstrations for just causes, but has spoken in front of millions of people in speeches and the media – both in this country and around the world.

- She has brought to the forefront the issues of Kashmir and Palestine to non-Muslims and lobbied to defend the hijab – challenging the stereotypes and demonisation of Islam that has made life difficult for countless Muslims.
- She is a voice of reason who is respected by all the different communities – Muslim and non-Muslim, presenting a positive image, whilst remaining true to the values of Islam.
- She would be an MP we would all be proud of.

Not using the vote simply reinforces the hands of oppressive rulers and their unjust policies. It is the duty of every Muslim to support those people who stand for truth and justice –whoever they are. We urge the community to break away from the tradition of simply supporting those they have personal links with – representation and competency are the real issues. Allah says in the Quran:

"O you who believe! Stand up for justice, as witnesses to Allah, even if it goes against yourselves or your parents and relatives. Whether they are rich or poor, Allah is nearer to both (than you are). Do not follow your own desires and deviate from the truth. If you twist or turn away, Allah is aware of what you do." (4:134)

Signed by: Mufti Abdul Majid Nadeem, Mohammad Sarfraz Madni, Maulana Abdul Hadi, Qazi Zakiullah Saleem, Maulana Sher Khan Jamri Al-Azri, Maulana Dr Abdul Rub Saqib, Allama Mohammad Khalid, Maulana Abdul Salaam Rashidi, Qari Mohammad Toyyab, Hafiz Mohammad Arif, Maulana Karamatllah Al Khairi, Maulana Abdul Karim Saqib, Maulana Dr Akhtar Al-Zaman Ghauri and others.

Campaign Hotline 07841 617 532   www.respectcoalition.org

"Vote for an MP who will be YOUR voice"

It's time for change
...vote *RESPECT*...vote Salma Yaqoob

"People are fed up with dishonest and corrupt politics. Roger Godsiff has been complacent for too long. It's time for change… You can judge me on my record, not just my promises. I helped to form the "Stop the War Coalition" in September 2001 to oppose the wars in Afghanistan and Iraq and to organise 11 national demonstrations including the 2 million march on February 15th 2003. I am also fighting for local people to get a better deal on Pensions, Education and Council Services. On May 5th I am asking for your support."

Only Respect can beat New Labour, we had over 9,000 votes in this area in the European elections in 2004. The Lib Dem candidate is no alternative he has no record of speaking out on any of these issues.

Campaign Hotline 07841 617 532   www.respectcoalition.org

Figure 15.2 Election flyer for Salma Yaqoob in 2005

wards they represent. Respect put forward a number of female candidates and they worked particularly hard to gain a female vote for the party, something that is often neglected by mainstream parties that tend to focus on male community leaders. Former Respect Councillor Lutfa Begum attributed her election victory and that of her daughter Rania Khan to the support of women's groups that met in the mosque.[24] In Bradford, female voters were also cited as one of the reasons why George Galloway was able to win with such a large percentage of the vote in 2012 (Pidd 2012). This kind of canvassing is not limited to the South Asian communities. Pensioner's groups were also approached, as they contained many residents who were upset by the shift away from traditional working class values by Labour. In its manifestos, Respect targeted these voters by calling for a rise in the basic state pension, free long term care for pensioners and an extension of their free local bus travel privileges to be extended to include rail services (Respect 2005, 2010). Tenants and Residents Associations (TRAs) were also another way for Respect candidates to gain support in the local community, particularly through the campaign to stop councils selling off their remaining housing stock.

Local campaigning against the wars in Iraq and Afghanistan contributed the most to Respect's successes in its early years. Tower Hamlets Stop the War (THSW), was one of the largest local branches of the SWC. Many of those who were candidates for Respect were involved in this branch and its success and implantation into the local community also helps to explain why Tower Hamlets became the heartland of the party. Once Respect started campaigning as a political party it could rely on the pre-existing networks that had been built up with various sections of civil society as a solid base for support. It also meant that the party had at its disposal a virtual army of volunteers ready to help the campaign, including many young people who had become politicised through the anti-war movement.

> We had a lot of volunteers. On the Saturday before the election 400 went out. That was exceptional, but there were regular teams from other parts of London. We had local Respect supporters and attracted more during the campaign, including lots of Bengali kids. They provided lots of canvassers. On the day of the election there were banners hanging from windows and across streets.[25]

Many youth groups had been involved in THSW and Abjol Miah who was elected as a councillor in 2006 had previously worked for Tower Hamlets council as a youth leader. This gave him a significant amount of political capital amongst the local youths and those voting for the first time. Tower Hamlets has a young population and the youth vote itself was extremely important for Respect. Respect's task was facilitated because those born and brought up in Britain are more likely to reject the traditional pattern of the father dictating the political direction of the family and delivering bloc votes to a particular candidate. Labour was still relying on this *modus operandi*, which younger voters often oppose and perceive as archaic.[26] The same factor was at work in Bradford in 2012 where the youth vote was seen as one of the keys to the by-election victory.

5. Conclusion

This chapter has shown how Muslims in Britain became involved in electoral politics with the Respect Party which rode on the back of the success of the anti-war movement. The association with this movement has been both a blessing and a curse. It gave the impetus for its creation and also provided it with a base within civil society from which it could subsequently draw support. The invasion of Iraq was a central issue on which the party could campaign given that many voters, particularly Muslims, were angered by this foreign policy decision. Since the anti-war movement became less influential, it has become harder for the party to mobilise potential supporters. As Poguntke (2002: 49) has remarked, 'while good links with new social movements may be a significant (though highly contingent) electoral asset during phases of high protest mobilization, it is of little value in quiet times.' British troops have now left Iraq and will soon leave Afghanistan so Respect will need to lose its tag as a mere 'anti-war party' and attempt to re-invent itself. Until very recently it seemed like this was not going to be possible and the party was in the doldrums after the electoral disappointments of 2010 and 2011. However, the return of George Galloway to Westminster in 2012 has re-invigorated the party and hopes are high that the 'Bradford Spring' can be extended to other parts of the country. It is difficult to predict whether Respect can build on the shock by-election victory, but the results of the subsequent local elections did give them cause for optimism.

Although the party has not been able to expand its influence outside of East London, Birmingham and now Bradford, it changed the political landscape in these areas. It forced mainstream parties to re-think their own electoral strategies in response to its success. This is particularly true in Tower Hamlets, where the party was instrumental in campaigning for a referendum for a directly elected mayor.[27] Activists in Bradford are hoping they can shake up the way local government works there too. Respect has also made an impact in another important way. It has campaigned for an end to the corruption of 'ethnic politics' that had been exploited by the larger political parties. Although this will continue to persist for many years to come, young British Muslims in particular have shown their disdain for this by-passing of democracy. Respect has in fact brought to the fore a new generation of young British Muslim political activists and leaders, particularly women, many of whom will continue to play an important role in British politics. These young activists will be the ones taking the party forward into the future and its continued success will depend on them.

Notes

1. 'RESPECT' is a recursive acronym standing for Respect, Equality, Socialism, Peace, Environmentalism, Community, and Trade Unionism. The official name is now The Respect Party, see <http:// http://www.respectparty.org> (last accessed 25 May 2012). For a more detailed history of the founding and development of the party see Peace (2013).
2. The SWP is a Trotskyist party and the largest organisation on the far left in Britain, see <http://www.swp.org.uk> (last accessed 25 May 2012).
3. Parties must win at least 5% of the party list vote in order to win any seats in the London Assembly.
4. The 2001 census indicated that Tower Hamlets has 71,389 Muslims, 36.4% of the overall population. In Newham there were 59,293 people who identified themselves as Muslim (24.3%).
5. It is not however limited to the Labour party. In fact, the Conservative party has 'unsuccessfully attempted to divide the Muslim Labour vote by highlighting the *biraderi* identities of Muslim Labour candidates and selecting rival *biraderi* Conservative candidates' (Purdham 2001: 151).
6. For extensive details of cases of electoral fraud and postal voting in the UK see White and Moulton (2009).
7. For example, many Muslim businessmen will naturally vote Conservative. The party has responded to this new electorate by setting up a Muslim Forum, available at <http://www.conservativemuslimforum.com> (last accessed 25 May 2012).
8. Respect and George Galloway played a leading role in the Viva Palestina aid convoy, see <http://www.vivapalestina.org> (last accessed 25 May 2012). Respect councillors also called for the boycott of Israeli products.
9. For more details see Glynn (2002) and Eade and Garbin (2006).
10. This is where most Bangladeshis in East London trace their origins and links between the villages of this area and first generation migrants are still important.
11. Interview with Respect councillor for Tower Hamlets Council.
12. Almost half of their candidates (33 out of 68) were female for the 2004 European elections. At the 2005 general election 9 out of 26 candidates (34.6%) were female and in 2010 it was 3 out of 11 (27%).
13. Often referred to as the 'anti-globalisation movement' or by its supporters as the 'Global Justice Movement'.
14. Interview with Respect councillor in Tower Hamlets.
15. The East London Communities Organisation (TELCO) was launched in 1996 and eventually developed into a London-wide initiative, see <http://www.citizensuk.org> (last accessed 25 May 2012) and Jamoul and Wills (2008).

16. Interestingly, 85% of the Muslim councillors that Pudham (2000) interviewed believed that mosques should not be involved in politics.

17. It is not only Muslims in Newham who utilise faith-based organisations. The Christian Peoples Alliance (CPA) is a party that has also elected councillors and seeks support from churches. It received 70,294 votes for the London Assembly elections in 2008, beating both Respect and the United Kingdom Independence Party (UKIP). See <http://www.cpaparty.org.uk> (last accessed 25 May 2012).

18. Interview with Respect councillor in Tower Hamlets.

19. The Awami League led the struggle for the independence of Bangladesh from Pakistan. They are deeply opposed to the ELM as some of the trustees are accused of war crimes from 1971.

20. Founded in 1941 by Abul Ala Maududi, it competes in elections in both Pakistan and Bangladesh.

21. Interview with Respect councillor in Tower Hamlets.

22. See also the documentary that Gilligan made with the Channel 4 Dispatches programme entitled 'Britain's Islamic Republic', first aired on 1 March 2010. Respect activist Abjol Miah was accused by Gilligan of being an IFE activist which he has always denied. Miah subsequently sought recourse from the Press Complaints Commission which concluded that *The Daily Telegraph* had breached clause 1 (accuracy) of the Editors' Code.

23. Interview with Respect councillor in Tower Hamlets.

24. Purdham (2000: 48) also discovered that female Muslim councillors are contacted more often by female members of their electoral ward.

25. Sean Doherty, Respect election agent for Bethnal Green and Bow in 2005, quoted in Taylor (2005).

26. Interview with Respect councillor in Tower Hamlets.

27. Residents voted in favour of this proposal in 2010 and so power has effectively been taken away from the Labour party, which benefited from the traditional Cabinet system. Respect leaders would argue that the Executive Mayoral System, now in place, gives greater power and accountability to the residents of the borough. They did not put forward their own candidate for Mayor but instead supported the Independent candidate, Lutfur Rahman, who had been deselected by Labour. He went on to win the Mayoral election, which Respect considered to be a tactical victory. Voters in Bradford and Birmingham voted against introducing a directly elected mayor on 3 May 2012.

References

Akhtar, P. (2012), 'British Muslims and local democracy: after Bradford', *openDemocracy*, 20 April, available at <http://www.opendemocracy.net/idea/parveen-akhtar/british-muslims-and-local-democracy-after-bradford> (last accessed 25 May 2012).

Anwar, M. (2001), 'The participation of ethnic minorities in British politics', *Journal of Ethnic and Migration Studies*, 27(3), pp. 533–49.

BBC (2003), 'Did Muslim vote cost Labour?', *BBC News*, 2 May, available at <http://news.bbc.co.uk/1/hi/uk_politics/2994309.stm> (last accessed 25 May 2012).

BBC (2005), 'Respect action over postal vote', *BBC News*, 18 April, available at <http://news.bbc.co.uk/2/hi/uk_news/politics/vote_2005/frontpage/4455635.stm> (last accessed 25 May 2012).

BBC (2012), 'George Galloway wins Bradford West by-election', *BBC News*, 30 March, available at <http://www.bbc.co.uk/news/uk-politics-17549388> (last accessed 25 May 2012).

Begum, H. and J. Eade (2005), 'All Quiet on the Eastern Front? Bangladeshi Reactions in Tower Hamlets', in T. Abbas (ed.), *Muslim Britain: Communities Under Pressure*, London: Zed Books, pp. 179–93.

Biezen, I. V. (2005), 'On the theory and practice of party formation and adaptation in new democracies', *European Journal of Political Research*, 44(1), pp. 147–74.

Boucek, F. (1998), 'Electoral and parliamentary aspects of dominant party systems', in J.-E. Lane and P. Pennings (eds), *Comparing party system change*, London: Routledge, pp. 103–24.

Eade, J. (1989), *The politics of community: the Bangladeshi community in East London*, Aldershot: Gower Publishing.

Eade, J. and D. Garbin (2006), 'Competing visions of identity and space: Bangladeshi Muslims in Britain', *Contemporary South Asia*, 15(2), pp. 181–93.

Ellis, P. and Z. Khan (1998), 'Diasporic mobilisation and the Kashmir issue in British politics', *Journal of Ethnic and Migration Studies*, 24(3), pp. 471–88

Garbaye, R. (2005), *Getting into Local Power: The Politics of Ethnic Minorities in British and French Cities*, Oxford: Blackwell.

Gilligan, A. (2010), 'Radicals with hands on the levers of power: the takeover of Tower Hamlets' *The Sunday Telegraph*, 28 February.

Glynn, S. (2002), 'Bengali Muslims: The New East End Radicals?' *Ethnic and Racial Studies*, 25(6), pp. 269–88.

Glynn, S. (2008), 'East End Bengalis and the Labour party – the end of a long relationship?', in C. Dwyer and C. Bressey (eds) *New Geographies of Race and Racism*. Aldershot: Ashgate, pp. 67–82.

Hussain, D. (2007), 'Globalization, God and Galloway: The Islamisization of Bangladeshi Communities in London', *Journal of Creative Communications*, 2(1&2), pp. 189–217.

Jamoul, L. and J. Wills (2008), 'Faith in Politics', *Urban Studies*, 45(10), pp. 2035–56.

Lewis, P. (2007), *Young, British and Muslim*, London: Continuum.

McLoughlin, S. (2005), 'The State, New Muslim Leaderships and Islam as a Resource for Public Engagement in Britain', in J. Cesari and S. McLoughlin (eds), *European Muslims and the secular state*, Aldershot: Ashgate, pp. 55–69.

Messina, A. (1989), *Race and Party Competition in Britain*, Oxford: Oxford University Press.

Peace, T. (2008), 'L'impact de la «participation musulmane» sur le mouvement altermondialiste en Grande-Bretagne et en France', *Cultures & Conflits*, 70, pp. 109–28.

Peace, T. (2013), 'All I'm asking, is for a little Respect: Assessing the performance of Britain's most successful radical left party', *Parliamentary Affairs*, 66(1).

Pidd, H. (2012) 'How women won it for George Galloway', *The Guardian*, 4 April.

Poguntke, T. (2002), 'Party organizational linkage: parties without firm social roots?', in K. R. Luther and F. Müller-Rommel (eds), *Political Parties in the New Europe: Political and Analytical Challenges*, Oxford: Oxford University Press, pp. 43–62.

Purdam, K. (1996), 'Settler Political Participation: Muslim local councillors', in W. A. R. Shadid and P. S van Koningsveld (eds), *Political participation and identities of Muslims in non-Muslim states*, Kampen: Kok Pharos, pp. 129–43.

Purdham, K. (2000), 'The political identities of Muslim councillors in Britain', *Local Government Studies*, 26(1), pp. 47–64.

Purdam, K (2001), 'Democracy in Practice: Muslims and the Labour Party at the Local Level', *Politics*, 21(3), pp. 147–57.

Respect (2004), *George Galloway: Fighting for Muslim rights*, London: Respect. Available at <http://web.archive.org/web/20040809045950/www.respectcoalition.org/pdf/310504_ma_ggmr.pdf> (last accessed 25 May 2012).

Respect (2005), *Peace, Justice, Equality. The Respect Manifesto for the May 2005 Election*, London: Respect. Available at <http://news.bbc.co.uk/1/shared/bsp/hi/pdfs/RESPECT_uk_manifesto.pdf> (last accessed 25 May 2012).

Respect (2010), *Homes, Jobs and Peace: Manifesto for a Hung Parliament*, London: Respect. Available at <http://gmrespect.org.uk/resources/Respect_Manifesto_2010.pdf> (last accessed 25 May 2012).

Russell, A. et al. (2008), 'Non-Party Activity in the 2005 UK General Election: "Promoting or Procuring Electoral Success"?', in D. M. Farrell and R. Schmitt-Beck (eds) *Non-party actors in electoral politics: the role of interest groups and independent citizens in contemporary election campaigns*, Baden-Baden: Nomos, pp. 103–25.

Schmitt-Beck, R. and D. M. Farrell (2008), 'Introduction: The Age of Non-Party Actors', in D. M. Farrell and R. Schmitt-Beck (eds), *Non-party actors in electoral politics: the role of interest groups and independent citizens in contemporary election campaigns*, Baden-Baden: Nomos, pp. 13–24.

Stewart, J. (2006), 'A Banana Republic? The investigation into electoral fraud by the Birmingham Election Court', *Parliamentary Affairs*, 59(4), pp. 654–67.

Taylor, I. (2005), 'Respect: the view from below', *International Socialism*, 108, available at <http://www.isj.org.uk/index.php4?id=137> (last accessed 25 May 2012).

White, I. and M. Moulton (2009), 'Postal voting and electoral fraud', *House of Commons Library Standard Notes*, 3667, available at <http://www.parliament.uk/commons/lib/research/briefings/snpc-03667.pdf> (last accessed 25 May 2012).

Yaqoob, S. (2008), 'The SWP takes a step backwards', in G. Galloway et al., *Respect: Documents of the Crisis*, London: IMG publications.

CHAPTER

16

CLICHÉS ARE FUNNY AS LONG AS THEY
HAPPEN ON STAGE: COMEDY AS POLITICAL
CRITICISM

Riem Spielhaus

1. Introduction

The topic of the evening: Elections are just around the corner. Federal elections in Fatihland[1]! What will happen? Recently politics has recognized foreigners as a voting bloc. But now the question is – we are enlightened democrats here – the question is therefore: 'What do *we* Germans actually know about *us* Turks?' Tell me! Tell me! [applause].[2] (Çevikkollu 2009)

This opening sequence of a stand-up performance by Fatih Çevikkollu, a German actor and comedian born to Turkish parents in Cologne, introduces a contestation of ethnic stereotypes in everyday life. Çevikkollu is committed to the German tradition of political cabaret and frequently appears in established TV shows. His performance *Moslem TÜV*[3], which he published as a book and took to comedy stages around Germany, criticises a citizenship test from 2006 aimed at scrutinising Muslim applicants' values. Besides, Çevikkollu supports campaigns for participation in elections like the one by the German Federal Agency for Civic Education for the federal elections in 2009. The political content of his shows, as well as his personal engagement for political partici-pation, distinguish Çevikkollu as an entertainer with both political awareness and a voice.

Stand-up comedy and other creative political interventions of Muslims or individuals of Muslim background have largely been neglected within research on political participation in this field. Most surveys on political participation concentrate on active and passive elective participation, the measurement of trust in legal and political institutions, adherence to liberal-democratic values, degrees of organisation, and protest movements. This chapter, however, approaches political satire and other subversive strategies that allow subalterns

[322]

to address injustice, discrimination and structural exclusion from the political field as a form of political activism. In an atmosphere of suspicion and verbal taboos, political satire can play a significant role by addressing and criticising attempts at domestication and securitisation.

With *Allah made me funny, Little mosque in the prairie* and *Moslem TÜV* Muslim comedy and satire entered mainstream entertainment in North America but also in some western European countries, especially after the Danish Muhammad cartoon crisis. With Fatih Çevikkollu this chapter focuses on a specific Muslim comedian but also opens its view to other performers of Muslim background and their position in the German comedy scene. The chapter is first of all interested in comedians who perform at a professional level and present themselves as Muslims, or as individuals with a Turkish or Muslim background, while taking a stance on Islam and integration debates in their performances. It departs from the notion that Muslims' contributions to politically grounded satire, the field of humour, of absurdity, ridicule, and subversion are worth examining in terms of their content as well as of their political strategies to address the unspeakable.

2. Academic literature on Muslim minority comedy

While satire and comedy in general appear to be themes of literature and media analysis rather than of studies in political science, a growing awareness can be observed concerning the political relevance and impact of stand-up, late night commentators and even sit-coms in the North American context (Willett 2008; Gray et al. 2009). Satire is attributed the ability to energise civic culture, engage audiences, inspire public political discussion and draw citizens enthusiastically into the realm of the political. It can say things that other players in the field, like the press, are 'too timid to say, proving itself a more critical interrogator of politicians at times and a more effective mouthpiece of the people's displeasure with those in power, including the press itself' (Gray et al. 2009: 4).

In North America we can also see an academic interest in Muslims who are active in the production of comedy and satire and new formats of explicitly Islamic comedy that follows a public interest in Muslim comedy (Bilici 2010; Amarasingam 2010; Michael 2011). In his article 'Laughter is the best medicine' about Muslim American comedy, Amarnath Amarasingam characterises their resort to humour as a way to challenge and effectively critique popular culture representations of Muslim and Arab Americans with the aim of introducing new opinions and counter-hegemonic ideas into society's 'common sense' (Amarasingam 2010: 466). Also Jaclyn Michael sees the aim to challenge stereotypes and misperceptions of Muslims and Islam in North America as a reason for the rise of different Muslim stand-up groups who tour throughout the US and beyond. Hence, the new and negative associations with being Muslim in America, Bilici calls them 'negative charisma', are the impulse and therefore the prerequisite for Muslim responses in the form of public stand-up humour (Bilici 2010). As Michael concludes, Muslims continue the American minority tradition of engaging with American social life through public humour.

> As the newest minority to gain national relevance as a source of social anxiety, Muslim Americans continue a historical tradition of using stand-up comedy as a way of lending their voices to the discourses of what it means to be a minority and an American at a critical moment in American social history. (Michael 2011: 5)

Humour is of course only one of many instruments to challenge negative stereotypes on Muslims. However, Amarasingam discloses the notion among some comedians he interviewed that speaking seriously does not change anything at the moment because nobody is listening anyway, 'So the only way to do it is to be funny about it' (Ahmed Ahmed quoted in Amarasingam 2010: 474). For Muslim comedians the comedy club is therefore an ideal place to challenge assumptions (Amarasingam 2010: 468).

Jaclyn Michael develops a particular interest in the social functions of humour for the social group of Muslim Americans. Drawing on studies of humour in philosophy, linguistics and psychology, he highlights the three major explanations – superiority, relief and incongruity – for how humour works. The superiority theory sees an important trope of humour in the perception of superiority in the context of social life. It therefore points at the key power dynamic between the subject and object of ridiculing laughter. When subordinate social groups joke about themselves and the society that discriminates against them, it is the reversal of the hierarchical relationship that provides the tension for laughter. The comedy stage hence serves as a space for resistance to oppressive power relations and social positions. The laughter of relief, on the other hand, theorises humour from a psychological perspective as a mechanism to release social tensions and to cultivate kinship with the audience using a 'laughter of recognition' that expresses shared cultural associations. According to Michael, the social bonding potential of humour and laughter can explain why socially critical Muslim American comedians deliberately encourage the laughter of relief to promote positive group association. Finally, laughter based on the perception of incongruity is premised on the difference between expectations and result. This includes ideas and images that are or seem to be inconsistent, inappropriate, absurd or inverted. However, a condition for the humour of incongruity is shared knowledge or common presumptions, which can then serve as a basis for the tension of jokes and accordingly be challenged by them. Following Michael, these three theoretical explanations for laughter can help us understand the social functions and subversive capacities that qualify humour as an instrument for subordinate social groups to challenge social assumptions and re-imagine social life (Michael 2011: 9–10).

Comedy constructs a counter-world to the world of ordinary life. Because the everyday world has become extraordinary, the Muslim (an oddity in American life) has become funny when he appears 'ordinary'. (Bilici 2010: 205)

It is hence the apparent incongruity between what, for Muslims, seems ordinary, namely being a follower of Islam and a truthful citizen, that serves as the simple basis for laughter according to this observation by Muhacit Bilici. Mainstream media representations of the community and Islam contribute to what, from the perspective of Muslims, is a distorted reality that provokes the need to 'rectify and reassert their own sense of what is real' (Bilici 2010: 205).

As former actors, many contemporary comedians have been part of the production of these negative media representations but at some point they decided to turn their backs on the movie business, where they could not find any roles but those of terrorists. They then switched to stand-up comedy in order to mock the very roles they once played (Bilici 2010: 205).

Within the North American context, researchers attribute to Muslim comedy a function as a mediator between Muslim and non-Muslim audiences but also as an educator and medium of raising awareness among Muslim communities (Amarasingam 2010; Michael 2011). Jeanette Jouili describes how Muslim comedians in the UK cater to their communities not only with tailored jokes but a *halal* environment that distinguishes itself from comedy clubs that serve alcohol. Their audiences will be assured that no immoral jokes will be made. However the specific humour then does directly address serious and unpleasant problems within the community. In that way comedians addressing the in-group appear to be much more critical of issues like domestic violence than they would choose to be when performing in front of a general audience (Jouili 2010).

3. In reality clichés aren't funny – challenging stereotypes on stage

In a closer look at the German comedy scene we will see some similarities with the North American and UK context, however there are also striking differences. One is that ethnicity here (still) prevails over religious affiliation in the identity markers chosen by comedians for their stage personas. As we shall see, only one performer explicitly positions himself and his shows in the context of the Islam debate, while other comedians of Muslim background do refer to dominant public debates but challenge them on a subtle level by confronting the images of Turks and Arabs without directly addressing religion. Another striking difference is that these comedians have entered the established channels of German comedy. They therefore primarily address general audiences. A particularly Muslim or even Islamic comedy scene that caters most of all to the Muslim community seems to be just in the making.[4] A great similarity to what has been observed with regard to the US, UK and Canada are the

motivation and functions of stand-up and other forms of humour as educators
to challenge misperceptions and encourage social cohesion.

The performances of Fatih Çevikkollu provide various examples for this:

> What do *we* Germans actually know about *us* Turks? [applause] Tell me! What do
> we know? Do we live in a society? Are there several? If yes, which one was first?
> Who is guest, who is host? Who has no clue about any of these? Do we participate in
> a modern society? Do Turks go onto the Internet? If yes, *how*? [audience laughing]
> Of course they go onto the Internet, but not like *you*! They might not be able to go
> on SPIEGEL-Online[5]. Not possible! Their keyboard has only *ü*'s. [pause] Is *that* our
> knowledge? [applause] Is that our *knowledge*? If that is our knowledge, these are
> clichés. Clichés are, as you just realised, funny. As long as they happen on stage. In
> reality clichés aren't funny.[6] (Çevikkollu, 2009)

Still, Çevikkollu carries on. He mentions fictitious websites Muslims would
frequent like rent-a-burqa.de, mullah-space.com or talibanscout24. At first
he seems to encourage his audience to laugh, but once they really get going
he looks at those laughing the most with a pedagogical attitude: 'Jokes at the
cost of minorities and you are laughing. Super!' Just to continue as if it was all
right to laugh:

> Of course we go onto the Internet. Yesterday, I sat at the Internet and quickly shot
> me a used suicide vest. [Audience laughs, Çevikkollu looks cross] I'll report this to
> SPIEGEL-Online! [Turns away and makes note on his palm]. Germans are laughing
> about suicide-vest-joke. Have we come that far again? [long pause].[7] (Çevikkollu,
> 2009)

Fatih Çevikkollu continues to make jokes about ethnic minorities, especially Turks, referring to the Taliban, terrorism or foreigners' lack of knowledge of the German language, every now and then criticising the audience for
laughing. While making fun of ethnic minorities, the comedian repeatedly
interrupts his performance to affront them for laughing at his increasingly
racist jokes. In this subversive way he reflects upon open and hidden racism
and senses of superiority while turning his experiences of being under surveillance as a Muslim against the spectators. Every now and then he stops his performance to makes notes of their behaviour on his palm. Holding his audience
accountable for the jokes they laugh at and making sure that his derogatory
jokes about East Germans, Vietnamese, Blacks and Turks are not meant to be
demeaning but rather to serve as teaching material. Çevikkollu manages to
present himself as gradually understanding the prejudices underlying his own
jokes and thinking, thus inviting the audience to reflect on ethnic and religious
stereotypes and notions of superiority in connection with class and economic
might.

4. The contemporary German comedy scene

The tradition of political cabaret, founded in the early 1900s, was characterised by political satire and gallows humour, sharing with French cabaret the
atmosphere of intimacy. Its main ingredients were sketches, satirical mono-
logues and parodies targeting mainly political and social topics of a rather
serious nature with a critical stance using techniques like cynicism, sarcasm
and irony, with Kurt Tucholsky as a key figure. After Hitler determined that
the *Kabarett* was a 'political enemy' of the Third Reich, the genre saw a rebirth
right after the end of the war. Television included political cabaret in its pro-
grams with shows like *Scheibenwischer* (English: windscreen wiper), *Satire
Gipfel* (English: satire summit) or *Die Heute Show* (English: the daily show).
Starting in the 1990s, researchers record a fundamental change in the German
TV landscape, driven by the increasing importance of different comedic
formats for audience ratings (Knop 2007). German comedy TV certainly has
been influenced and took up influences from US American comedy, such as the
format of late night shows. This led to the development of humourous mass
TV products, often referred to as Comedy TV. Present-day televised cabaret
and comedy have both been nourished by two traditions: that of political and
literary *Kabarett* and that of political satire as an element of popular *Karneval*.
While today comedy is the domain of private channels that are competing for
the most audacious shows and performers, public broadcasters uphold the
tradition of more sophisticated and critical political cabaret (Casadevall 2007).

Taking a look at the developments within Turkish German contributions to
political cabaret, Karin Bower observes a thematic continuity.

> What connects early Turkish German cabaret performers and satirist-comedians of
> more recent vintage is their palpable frustration with the cyclical nature of integra-
> tion debates that reify cultural differences while obscuring similarities between Turks
> and Germans and the transformations that have already occurred in German society.
> (Bower 2012: 194)

While comedians who migrated to Germany or migrants who turned to
comedy did not get any long-term access to established cabaret shows and
clubs, the contemporary comedy scene is becoming more diversified. The
children of immigrants are invited to perform in public service broadcasters' tradition-steeped satire shows and the Comedy TV of private channels,
as well as on known stages of political cabaret. A few like Bülent Ceylan are
even filling stadiums with audiences for their solo shows. In a twisted way
and not at all explicitly, it appears that the Mohammad cartoon crisis fostered a growing interest in Muslim comedians and performers with a Muslim
background. The debate about the lack of or even aversion to humour among
Muslims hence might have contributed to this diversification of a hitherto

rather homogenous German comedy scene that was dominated by male actors without a migration background.

Fatih Çevikkollu is far from the only successful comedian with a background from a Muslim majority country. One of the first comedians of Turkish background who recurrently appeared in mainstream TV was Uğur Bağışlayıcı, who began his career in satire in the 1990s under the pseudonym Django Asül (English: Django Asylum). Among German comedians he stands out not only with his Mediterranean physiognomy but his Bavarian dialect. Another very successful comedian with a strong local dialect is Bülent Ceylan, who performed his first solo show 'Döner for one' in 2002. In 2011 the private broadcasting agency RTL aired his own comedy show *The Bülent Ceylan Show* with six episodes. Ceylan presents a range of stage personas with a dialect specifically from the South German region around the city of Mannheim, among them the caretaker Mompfred, the Turkish Macho Hassan, and the wannabe society lady Annelies from the southern province, who believes she speaks standard German. While the comic tension in the performances of Django Asül and Bülent Ceylan lies in the combination of the seemingly incompatible elements of being of Turkish descent and at the same time showing a strong regional rooting in a German dialect, the performances of Murat Topal are based on the apparent absurdity of a Turk in the function of a police officer. Before entering the comedy business, Topal worked as policeman in Berlin Kreuzberg. With his ability to impersonate various accents of immigrants, Topal performs parodies from the daily experiences of a Turkish policeman in a so-called problematic district (*Problembezirk*). The actor, musician, theatre director and satirist Serdar Somuncu attracted notorious attention with his commented readings from Adolf Hitler's book *Mein Kampf,* which led to controversies with social democratic politicians and bomb threats from right-wing groups.[8] His understanding of ridiculing performance, where subversion and parody serve as an invitation for a discussion, appears to resemble civic education rather than entertainment. He stopped his tour with *Mein Kampf* in September 2001 and developed a new programme called *Der Hassprediger liest BILD* (English: The preacher of hate is reading *BILD*[9]). Çevikkollu, Asül and Ceylan have all been invited onto primetime talk shows, however Serdar Somuncu is increasingly becoming a favourite invitee to debates about integration or Islamic and other forms of extremism. Among the less established comedians is Idil Baydar, the only woman of Turkish background, who posts performances of her favorites character, Jilet Ayse, since 2011 on her YouTube channel and has attracted the interest of newspapers and cultural commentators.[10] Abdelkarim, a young comedian of Moroccan background who started performing on stage in 2007 and appeared in major TV shows in 2010, is the first successful German comedian with Arab parents.

Comedy, cabaret and political satire, however, constitute only one field of humour in contemporary German culture. Actors, authors, and characters with a Turkish or other backgrounds from a Muslim majority country also appear much more often and regularly than about a decade ago in other fields, such as television series or humourous columns in newspapers. A major result of this development appears to be the questioning and weakening of ingrained notions of culture (Koch 2008: 221).

5.   Muslim, Turkish-German or postmigrant?

The German comedians mentioned in this chapter are discussed under various terms in the academic literature, but mostly under the term Turkish-German. While Yesilada (2011) argues that Turkish-German authors and comedians are increasingly depicted and perceived as Muslims and so this term is therefore problematic, the label Turkish-German[11] seems to be well established within German literary studies (see Adelson 2005; Yesilada 2011; Specht 2011; El-Hissy 2012). More recently the term 'postmigration' has been suggested to characterise the emerging literary production. Shermin Langhoff, the artistic director of a local theatre in Berlin-Kreuzberg, uses this term to describe a new creative scene that is conscious and reflective about past migration that characterises society in the present.

A great part of Turkish-German comedy thematically does not refer to aspects of migration itself or even its direct effects but to a specific postmigratory scenario, as Theresa Specht argues. The focus is not on the situation of being a stranger. In fact, the newly established comedians are unmistakably socialised in this society. Nevertheless their German identity is questioned because of their family's migration, their 'foreign' physiognomy or names. This dominant theme in stand-up performances and other artistic productions is addressed with the attribute postmigratory (Specht 2011). The term explicitly does not pertain to a person's situation or history as a new word for difference in physiognomy, accent or family history, but rather to current society's obsession with migration and integration that perpetually locates parts of the population outside of the national imaginary.

The protagonists of what Specht describes as postmigratory or transcultural humour are hence not migrants but perhaps children or grandchildren of migrants. Despite a Muslim background they are not necessarily Muslims. However, they do answer to and engage with the highly interrelated debates about migration, integration and Islam in Germany. Many comedians with a background in Turkey do not 'speak as Muslims' as several prominent individuals with a (recognisable) background in Muslim majority countries did during the last decade, and thereby reject the 'assigned . . . role of the Muslim' (Spielhaus 2010: 23). The characters played by the comedians often do not make any reference to their religious affiliation, except the one by Fatih Çevikkollu. In his frequent but mostly vague references to faith Çevikkollu subtly indicates the religious difference between audience and presenter.

6.   Between stage and audience

Good evening [applause]. Thank you. I want to introduce myself, my name is Fatih Çevikkollu. That is Turkish and in German this means Fatih Çevikkollu [audience laughs]. I am Muslim [silence]. Did you realise? You say 'Muslim' and the tension in the room changes immediately.[12] (Çevikkollu, 2008)

Today, as a Muslim you are representing a risk. Fear prevails. Is there fear of Muslims? Yes. The German nation freezes in fear of the Muslim. Hence, they want to protect *you* [points at the audience] from *me* [points at himself]. And they developed the most hilarious methods.[13] (Çevikkollu, 2006)

This is the introduction to Çevikkollu's critical comment on the implementation of a questionnaire testing would-be citizens from Muslim majority countries on their attitudes to the constitution in Baden-Wuerttemberg, a South-German state.

For example: Baden-Wuerttemberg has launched the attitude test. [. . .] The attitude test is designed especially for all Muslims, people of Muslim faith, who want to have the German citizenship. That means a faith community is put to the test, and controlled for their attitude. It is not the first time that a faith community in Germa . . . well, anyway . . . There are questions in this, questions, you don't believe it! I want to quote the original questions. Something like: [speaks seriously and very slowly] 'You come to know that some of your neighbours or friends have carried out a terrorist attack or are planning to do so. How do you react?' [Mimics picking up his mobile phone and dialing. Screams into the virtual speaker] 'Mohamed! Mohamed . . . why? Why do I have to learn this from the newspaper? Allah Allah'. They could have done this the easy way: 'Are you terrorist?' 'Yes, No, Maybe.' Such things.[14] (Çevikkollu, 2006)

With comments like these Çevikkollu clearly positions himself within the tradition of German political cabaret. He performed in established programmes like the *Satire Gipfel* and *Neues aus der Anstalt*. After finishing school in Cologne, Fatih Çevikkollu worked at a local theatre and later on studied acting at the *Ernst Busch Academy of Dramatic Arts* in Berlin from where he was recruited for the *Schauspielhaus Düsseldorf*. His breakthrough came in 1999 with a leading role in the sitcom *Alles Atze,* where he played the Turkish kiosk vendor Murat. According to Çevikkollu the character was intended to be a lower class Turk who spoke broken German, but he persuaded the writers to let his character be the only person in the show who speaks standard German. Çevikkollu acted in several movies before he started his first solo tour, *Fatihland,* in 2005, which was followed by *Komm zu Fatih* (English: Come to Fatih) and *Fatih unser* (English: Our Fatih/ Our Father[15]).

In an interview with a German newspaper Fatih Çevikkollu explained that he chose comedy instead of classical theatre because classical theatre does not offer opportunities for self-determination and is badly paid.

> In television, the dependence is even greater. Casting agencies have Turk cabinets, for the less privileged two-bit processor that carries gold chains and grabs his crotch. That does not interest me at all. I want to tell stories. I do not need to act goofy.[16]
> (Çevikkollu quoted in Rennefanz, 2008)

Here Çevikkollu presents his choice of comedy as a decision for self-determination and a rebellion against the characters that actors with a Turkish look are assigned in the mainstream media. As a comedian he can determine his preferred themes and is able to find the style of performance that suits him best. While other comedians use a variety of stage personas, Çevikkollu usually comes on stage as himself and feeds his shows with personal stories and experiences.

> The political and satirical texts that I write are usually very personal, they aim to educate, while being entertaining and charming. They shall bring joy to people's hearts. Again and again religion plays a role, for example the 'Muslim-TÜV' is part of my programme. This is about the test for integration in Baden-Württemberg. I am just writing a book entitled *Muslim-TÜV* that reflects upon social change, religion and questions such as: Yesterday a Turkish bastard, today a top terrorist, what happened?[17] (Çevikkollu 2008: 45)

In his book *Der Moslem-TÜV* Çevikkollu explains that he has observed a change in the perception of Turks. While they used to be looked down upon as unskilled guest workers from Anatolian villages, they are now suddenly confronted with the image of a high-level terrorist. Not without irony he calls this 'steep social climbing, but well at the margin'[18] (Çevikkollu 2010: 18–19). When Çevikkollu characterises the content of his shows, it sounds very similar to the observations of Muhacit Bilici on the English speaking comedy scene.

> In my programmes I portray things in the way they are and that has an effect on people. I don't like malicious tones; I want to connect people emotionally with each other and with me. That is my goal.[19] (Çevikkollu 2008: 45)

Çevikkollu has the impression that he needs to share his experiences of reality, since his everyday world has become extraordinary to his surrounding and his audience. In an interview he reflects upon his shows as possibilities for his audience to get into direct contact with daily matters in the life of Turks in Germany.

People remained strangers to one another during the past fifty years. Imagine, many people got their first emotional insight into Turkish life in my programme.[20] (Çevikkollu quoted in Rennefanz 2008)

Thus, not without a critical tone, Çevikkollu uses his position on stage to explain the confusion and also fear among Muslims that has arisen as a result of the measures taken by European states to fight terrorism:

And what happens now? The whole nation is in fear, and how about the Muslims? The common Muslim like you and me ... is standing there and only wants to live for the day and is simply lost. There are 1.3 billion Muslims in the world. A few commit terror in the truest sense of the word, something we all condemn, we agree about this, but the rest: totally confused, disoriented. 'May I now go to the mosque or is this already a terrorist act? Can I follow my religion or am I already observed by the intelligence?' Total confusion, disorientation to the core.[21] (Çevikkollu 2008)

7.   The ambivalence of staging stereotypes

The little excerpt from the programme by Fatih Çevikkollu that introduced this chapter alludes to both the funny quality and the serious reality of ethnic stereotypes. Ambivalence and the dangers of staging stereotypes of ethnic or religious minorities are not only discussed in academic literature about comedy and satire but are taken up directly by comedians. Writers and comedians like Serdar Somuncu recurrently criticise the affirmative performance of clichés by some Turkish actors.

There are even Turks, who play Turks in a way, that they think that Turks are, so that others, who do not know how Turks actually are, think that Turks are like they are played by Turks, who themselves do not know how they actually should be. (Somuncu 2009: 34–5)[22]

Even though Bülent Ceylan engages in comedy that is devoid of serious or explicitly political content and is geared to attract tens of thousands of people at a time, his reflections on his stage personas and performances show a highly developed political conscience. With Hasan, the Macho-Turk, he brings a stereotype on stage but he aims to allow the audience to develop empathy if not even sympathy with this character.

Sometimes people laugh and then they are a bit embarrassed for laughing at something one is not supposed to make jokes about in Germany. 'Better not be racist!' people think. But I think that you can actually make a fool of racism. [...] I am against racism, but I'm a comedian, I do not make documentaries, but entertainment.[23] (Ceylan 2009)

Despite their very different formats of comedy and satire, the basic strategy shared by Çevikkollu, Somuncu and Ceylan is to bring stereotypes or even racist representations on stage, thereby bringing them to the awareness of the audience, and, finally, to wipe them away with shared laughter.

While current public debates maintain the antagonism of Turkish versus German identities, young German-Turkish comedians self-consciously present themselves as Turkish and German, while skillfully performing (their) multiple identities. Fatih Çevikkollu, Murat Topal and Bülent Ceylan enter the stage bound to specific German cities or regions like Cologne, Berlin or Mannheim, using strong regional dialects, which hold enough tension to be regarded as funny. Serdar Somuncu uses a different strategy to present himself as German. Reading the writings and speeches of national-socialists such as Hitler and Goebbels, Somuncu engages with Germany's darkest past and with contemporary fear-mongering by reading leading German and Austrian tabloids, critically reflecting on the language and content of this material.

Even though the stage persona of Fatih Çevikkollu often refers to himself as being Muslim and even though other comedians are taking up the debate about Islam in Germany, ethnic identity appears to overrule religious identity on the stages of German comedy clubs and in German TV shows. The target group of actors such as Çevikkollu, Ceylan, Topal and Somuncu is clearly the broad public, i.e. largely non-Muslim or non-Turkish audiences. However, the rather recent YouTube videos of Idil Baydar and her alter ego Jilet Ayse appear to appeal to a smaller group of people who share a discomfort with exclusive debates and structures in German society. In contrast to the performances of her established male colleagues, Jilet Ayse can hardly be seen as a pedagogical programme for others. Baydar rather probes identity strategies to confront dominant stereotypes on her own terms.

8. Conclusion

This chapter has examined political satire and other subversive strategies as a form of political activism and participation. With this perspective comedy and political cabaret can clearly be understood as attempts to take an active role vis-à-vis subjectification by government and society. Comedians like Çevikkollu take on the role of both commentators on social developments and daily politics as well as of mediators between populations with limited contact. Whether marked as members of a religious or ethnic minority, comedians invert given social hierarchies just by the act of stepping on stage. They are not the ones joked about but become the agents behind the humour. In some cases this alone seems to be strange and therefore funny and critical at the same time. The Turkish policeman displays such an incongruity. However it remains debatable whether this incongruity is perpetuated with every performance or can be really challenged by joking about it. In any case, comedy stages serve as spaces for resistance to oppressive power relations and confining social positions. The performers mentioned here use this space in order to affiliate with the audience. Therefore shared cultural associations and experiences that cross religious belonging and ethnic differences are central to their performances. As the examples above show, comedy is a relevant field of political intervention for Muslims and people with a background in Muslim majority countries in which the social functions and subversive capacities that qualify humour are used as instruments by a subordinate social group to challenge assumptions and re-imagine social life.

Notes

1. The comedian frequently plays on the similarity between his Turkish first name Fatih and the German diminutive 'Vati' for father. The name of his first show, *Fatihland,* then plays on the double meaning of Fatih's land and fatherland. Also his other programme titles *Komm zu Fatih* (English: *Come to Fatih)* and *Fatih unser* (English: *Our father)* draw on this wordplay.

2. All quotations from German comedy performances are translated by the author. 'Das Thema des Abends: Die Wahlen stehen vor der Tür, was passiert? Bundestagswahlen in Fatihland. In der Politik hat man jetzt den Ausländer als Wahlgruppe, als Wahlmannschaft? . . . Stimmen, als Stimmen entdeckt. Und jetzt die Frage ist doch – wir sind doch hier aufgeklärte Demokraten. Die Frage ist doch: "Was wissen *wir* Deutsche eigentlich über *uns* Türken?" Sag ma! Sag ma! [applause].' (Çevikkollu, 2009)

3. TÜV is a German acronym that no German-registered road vehicle may be operated on public roads without. It stands for *Technical Inspection Association,* the body that 'validates the safety of products of all kinds to protect humans and the environment against hazards'. Fatih Çevikkollu applies the term to the securitisation of Muslims in citizenship tests and to racial profiling.

4. The initiative *I,SLAM, a Muslim poetry slam* is a rather recent but also the most noticeable forum for satire and comedy organised by Muslims for young Muslims in Germany today. Available at <http://i-slamm.de> (last accessed 27 August 2012).

5. SPIEGEL-Online is the Internet platform of the established German weekly news magazine *Der Spiegel*, a publication known as the forerunner of investigative journalism in Germany.

6. 'Was wissen *wir* Deutsche eigentlich über *uns* Türken?' Sag ma! Sag ma! [applause] Was wissen wir? Leben wir in einer Gesellschaft? Sind es mehrere? Wenn ja welche war zuerst da? Wer ist Gast, wer ist Geber? Wer hat von beidem keine Ahnung? Nehmen wir teil an einer modernen Gesellschaft? Gehen Türken ins Internet? Wenn ja, wie? Natürlich gehen die ins Internet, aber nicht so wie Du. Das geht ja gar nicht! Die können vielleicht gar nicht auf Spiegel-Online gehen. Das ist gar nicht möglich. Die Tastatur hat ja nur ü's! Ist *das* unser Wissen? Ist das unser

Wissen? Wenn das unser Wissen ist, sind das Klischees. Und Klischees sind, gerade selber gemerkt, lustig. Solange sie auf der Bühne stattfinden. In der Realität sind Klischees nicht lustig.' (Çevikkollu, 2009)

7. 'Natürlich gehen wir ins Internet. Gestern abend noch im Internet gesessen, mir bei Ebay noch schnell 'nen gebrauchten Sprengstoffgürtel geschossen. [Publikum lacht, Çevikkollu schaut böse] Das schreib ich SPIEGEL-Online! [Dreht sich weg und macht Notizen auf seiner Handfläche]. Deutsche lachen über Sprengstoffgürtelgag. Sind wir schon wieder so weit? [long pause].' (Çevikkollu, 2009)

8. Kathrin Bower gives a detailed description of Serdar Somuncu's performance of *Mein Kampf* and his argument that public access to the text and critical engagement with it is a prerequisite for its demystification while it is banned in Germany (Bower 2012).

9. *BILD* is the biggest German tabloid newspaper. During shows in Austria Serdar Somuncu read from the *Kronenzeitung*, the biggest Austrian tabloid.

10. Available at <http://www.youtube.com/user/IdilBaydar?feature=watch> (last accessed 27 August 2012).

11. In the area of literature the label 'Turkish-German' appears to me to be just as imputing as the labels 'migrant' or 'Muslim' literature. Firstly, do immigrants and their descendants from Turkey ethnically identify in diverse ways as Turks, Kurds, etc. Secondly, especially when born and raised in Germany, they often identify as German and, finally, it remains questionable whether their family background has such a formative effect as to justify a separation from other literary and cultural productions.

12. 'Guten Abend. Vielen Dank. Ich darf mich kurz vorstellen. Mein Name ist Fatih Çevikkollu [publikum lacht]. Das ist Türkisch und auf Deutsch heißt das Fatih Çevikkollu. Ja, ich bin Moslem [stille]. Hast Du das gemerkt? Du sagst Moslem und die Spannung im Raum ändert sich direkt.' (Çevikkollu 2008)

13. 'Heute stellst Du als Moslem ein Risiko dar. Es herrscht Angst im Raum. Gibt es Angst vor Moslems? Ja! Die Angst ist so groß . . . Die deutsche Nation ist erstarrt vor Angst vor dem Moslem. Also man will Dich [zeigt auf das Publikum] schützen vor mir [zeigt auf sich]. Und da gibt's dann die wahnsinnigsten Methoden dafür.' (Çevikkollu 2006)

14. 'Zum Beispiel Baden-Württemberg haben die eine Gesinnungsprüfung rausgehauen. Diese Gesinnungsprüfung ist für alle Moslems, Menschen muslimischen Glaubens, die die deutschen Staatsbürgerschaft haben wollen. Also da wird eine Glaubensgemeinschaft auf den Prüfstand gestellt und kontrolliert nach Gesinnung. Es ist nicht das erst mal das eine Glaubensgemeinschaft in Deut . . . , egal. Da sind Fragen drin, da sind Fragen drin, das glaubst Du gar nicht. Ich will das nur mal zitieren. Das sind Originalzitate aus dem Test: [spricht ernst und sehr langsam] Sie erfahren, dass Leute aus ihrer Nachbarschaft oder Bekannte oder Freunde einen Anschlag begangen haben oder planen. Wie reagieren Sie? [Mimt das er zum Handy greift und wählt. Schreit in den vorgestellten Hörer] Mohamed! Mohamed . . . warum? Warum muss ich das aus der Zeitung erfahren? Allah, Allah! Das

hätten sie auch leichter haben können: "Sind Sie Terrorist?" "Ja, Nein, Vielleicht." Solche Dinge.' (Çevikkollu 2009)

15. The wordplay refers to both the comedian's name and the Lord's Prayer and thereby alludes to the religious content of the show.

16. 'Beim Fernsehen ist die Abhängigkeit noch viel größer. Es gibt bei Castingagenturen Türkenschränke, für den minderbemittelten Zwei-Bit-Prozessor, der Goldkettchen trägt und sich in den Schritt greift. Das interessiert mich alles nicht. Ich will Geschichten erzählen. Ich muss nicht auf doof machen.' (Çevikkollu quoted in Rennefanz 2008)

17. 'Die politisch-satirischen Texte, die ich mache, sind meistens sehr persönlich, sie sollen aufklären, dabei unterhaltsam und charmant sein – sie sollen den Zuschauern Freude im Herzen bereiten. Religion spielt immer wieder eine Rolle, ich habe zum Beispiel einen "Moslem-TÜV" im Programm, dabei geht es um den Test zur Integration in Baden-Württemberg. Ich schreibe auch gerade ein Buch mit dem Titel "Moslem-TÜV", da geht es um gesellschaftliche Veränderungen, um Religion, um Fragen wie: Gestern noch Kümmeltürke, heute schon Topterrorist, was ist da passiert?' (Çevikkollu 2008: 45)

18. 'ein steiler sozialer Aufstieg, aber immer schön am Rand entlang.' (Çevikkollu 2010: 18–19)

19. 'Ich stelle in meinen Programmemen die Dinge dar, wie sie sind, das bewegt schon etwas bei den Leuten. Gehässige Töne liegen mir nicht, ich möchte, dass sich die Leute emotional miteinander und mit mir verbinden, das ist mein Ziel.' (Çevikkollu 2008: 45)

20. 'Man ist sich in den vergangenen fünfzig Jahren sehr fremd geblieben. Stellen Sie sich mal vor, viele Leute haben in meinem Programm zum ersten Mal einen emotionalen Einblick in das türkische Leben bekommen.' (Çevikkollu quoted in Rennefanz 2008)

21. 'Und was passiert jetzt? Die ganze Nation hat Angst und was ist mit dem Moslem? Der gemeine Moslim wie Du und ich, der steht da und will den lieben Gott nur einen guten Mann sein lassen und weiß nicht weiter. Es gibt 1.3 Milliarden Moslems auf der Welt. Ein paar machen Terror im wahrsten Sinne des Wortes, das verurteilen wir alle, da brauchen wir gar nicht drüber reden, aber der Rest, total verunsichert. Orientierungslos. Darf ich jetzt in die Moschee gehen oder ist das schon ein terroristischer Akt? Kann ich jetzt meiner Religion folgen oder werde ich schon vom Verfassungsschutz beobachtet? Totale Irritation, Orientierungslosigkeit bis ins Mark.' (Çevikkollu 2008)

22. 'Es gibt sogar Türken, die Türken so spielen, wie sie glauben, dass Türken sind, damit andere, die nicht wissen, wie Türken eigentlich sind, denken, dass Türken so sind, wie sie gespielt werden von Türken, die selbst nicht wissen, wie sie eigentlich sein müssten.' (Somuncu 2009: 34–5)

23. 'Manchmal lachen die Leute und dann ist es ihnen ein bisschen peinlich, dass sie über etwas gelacht haben, worüber man in Deutschland eigentlich keine Witze machen soll. "Bloß nicht rassistisch sein!" denken die Leute. Ich meine aber,

dass man Rassismus auch lächerlich machen kann. Ich glaube sogar, wenn man Hitler ausgelacht hätte und Witze über ihn gemacht, dann hätte ihn das richtig fertig gemacht. Ich bin gegen Rassismus, aber ich bin Comedian, ich mache keine Dokumentationen, sondern Unterhaltung.' (Ceylan 2009)

References

Amarasingam, A. (2010), 'Laughter the Best Medicine: Muslim Comedians and Social Criticism in Post-9/11 America', *Journal of Muslim Minority Affairs*, 30(4), pp. 463–77.

Bilici, M. (2010), 'Muslim ethnic comedy: inversions of Islamophobia', in A. Shryock (ed.), *Islamophobia/Islamophilia: Beyond the Politics of Enemy and Friend*, Indiana University Press, pp. 195–208.

Casadevall, G. (2007), 'Political satire in Germany: from the political Kabarett of the thirties to Comedy TV', *Quaderns del CAC*, 27(1), pp. 79–86.

Çevikkollu, F. (2008), 'Kümmeltürke oder Terrorist?', in *Spiegel Spezial* 2/2008.

Çevikkollu, F. (2010), 'Elections in North Rhine-Westphalia', in *Satire-Gipfel*, season 2, episode 7.

Çevikkollu, F. (2009), 'Alles außer Hochdeutsch', in *3Satfestival*, episode 3.

Çevikkollu, F. (2008), 'Der Moslem-TÜV', in *Ottis Schlachthof*.

Çevikkollu, F. (2006), 'Der Gesinnungstest', in Prix Pantheon Gala.

Çevikkollu F. and S. Mysorekar (2010), 'Der Moslem-TÜV. Deutschland einig *Fatihland*', Reinbek bei Hamburg: Rowohlt.

Ceylan, B. (2009), 'Rassismus lächerlich machen – Interview mit Bülent Ceylan', in *Rhein-Neckar-Zeitung*, 27 May.

El-Hissy, M. (2012), *Getürkte Türken. Karnevaleske Stilmittel im Theatre, Kabarett und Film deutsch-türkischer Künstlerinnen und Künstler*, Bielefeld: Transcript.

Gray, J., J. Jones and E. Thompson (2009), *Satire TV: Politics and Comedy in the Post-Network Era*, New York: New York University Press.

Jouili, J. (2010), 'Muslim artists and practices of dialogue in post 7/7 UK', Paper at the workshop *Dialogue and Law as tools of Muslim integration into European societies,* Utrecht University, 14–15 January 2010.

Knop, K. (2007), *Comedy in Serie. Medienwissenschaftliche Perspektiven auf ein TV-Format*, Bielefeld: Transcript.

Koch, L. (2008), 'Das Lachen der Subalternen – Ethno-Comedy im deutschen Film und Fernsehen' in Wara Wende (ed.), *Wie die Welt lacht – Interkulturelle Formen von Welterschließung und Selbstbildung im Witz*, Würzburg: Verlag Königshausen & Neumann, pp. 208–23.

Michael, J. (2011), 'American Muslims stand up and speak out: trajectories of humor in Muslim American stand-up comedy', *Contemporary Islam*, doi:10.1007/s11562-011-0183-6.

Rennefanz, S. (2008), 'Ich bin ein Bundestürke. Interview mit Çevikkollu, Fatih', in *Berliner Zeitung*, 1 November.

Somuncu, S. (2009), *Der Antitürke*, Reinbek bei Hamburg: Rowohlt.

Spielhaus, R. (2010), 'Media making Muslims: the construction of a Muslim community in Germany through media debate', *Contemporary Islam*, 4 (1), pp. 11–27.

Willett, C. (2008), *Irony in the Age of Empire: Comic Perspectives on Democracy and Freedom*, Bloomington: Indiana University Press.

Yesilada, K. E. (2011), 'Gotteskrieger-Konfigurationen des radikalen Islam in der deutschsprachigen Gegenwartsprosa', *Jahrbuch Türkisch-Deutsche Studien 2010*, Göttingen: V&R Unipress, pp. 197–208.

NOTES ON THE CONTRIBUTORS

Jonatan Bäckelie holds an MA in Religious Studies and is currently a doctorate student at the University of Gothenburg. His research focuses on how young people active in religious organisations and/or political parties view the intersection between religion and politics.

Alessia Belli is currently a research fellow at Sant'Anna School of Advanced Studies (Pisa, Italy) where she obtained her PhD in Politics, Human Rights and Sustainability. Her work includes: 'She Who Disputes: Muslim women activists in Italy and the UK speak for themselves' in Haleh Afshar (ed.); *Women and Fluid Identities: Strategic and Practical Pathways Selected by Women* (2012); and her PhD dissertation *Progressive Multiculturalism and Fluid Identities: the Case of Muslim Women Activists in Italy and the United Kingdom* (2012).

Salima Bouyarden is a French PhD research student in the Department of Arab, Mediterranean and Eastern studies, University of Strasbourg, who is currently working on French and British Muslims and the emergence of a European Islam. Her wider research interests include the nature of democracy and the nation-state, transnationalism and identity formation.

Maike Didero is research assistant at the department of geography at RWTH Aachen University, Germany. Her thesis deals with the image of Islam in the German media and its impact on the identity construction and everyday lives of Moroccan migrants and their descendants living in Germany (NRW). Further research interests include socio-economic and political developments in Egypt and Morocco, discourse analysis and qualitative methods in social studies. She has recently published on 'Cairo's informal waste collectors', *Erdkunde* 2012/1.

Franck Frégosi is Senior Research Fellow at the research centre PRISME-Société, Droit et Religion en Europe, Centre National de la Recherche Scientifique (CNRS), University of Strasbourg, where he is currently teaching, and in the Institute of Political Science, Aix-en-Provence. His publications include *La Formation des cadres religieux musulmans en France. Approches sociojuridiques* (1998); *Le Religieux dans la commune. Les régulations locales du pluralisme religieux en France* (with J.-P. Willaime, 2001); *Lectures contemporaines du droit islamique. Europe et Monde arabe* (ed. 2004); *Penser l'islam dans la laïcité* (2008, 2nd ed. 2011); and *Bruno Etienne, le fait religieux comme fait politique* (2009).

Carolina Ivanescu is a cultural anthropologist affiliated to the Departments of Public Administration and Sociology and is a member of the CIMIC research network of Erasmus University, Rotterdam. Since February 2012 she has been working as a postdoctoral researcher on the European-Integration-Fund-financed project IMPACIM, which analyses the impact of integration restrictions encountered by family migrants. She has published in *Culture and religion, Ethnic and Racial Studies* and *Social Anthropology.*

Adil Hussain Khan is Assistant Professor of Islamic Studies at Loyola University, New Orleans. He holds a PhD from the School of Oriental and African Studies (SOAS), University of London. Most recently, he was a Visiting Assistant Professor in the Department of Religion at the University of Illinois at Urbana-Champaign. Prior to this, he conducted postdoctoral research on the History of Islam in Ireland at University College Cork. His research interests include sectarian reform movements in nineteenth-century South Asia and unconventional expressions of Islam. He is also interested in aspects of contemporary Islam, Muslim identity, and Islam's intellectual tradition.

Deniz Koşulu is a PhD candidate at CHERPA, L'Institut d'Etudes Politiques d'Aix-en-Provence. Her PhD thesis is entitled 'The politicisation of identity claims of Twelver Shia and Alevi minorities in contemporary Turkey: modes of claims, relation to the state'. She previously held a research position at PRISME, CNRS, Strasbourg. Her research interests include social movements, identity construction, the politicisation of religious minorities, Shia Islam, Turkish politics, and the Muslim world in Europe.

Göran Larsson is Professor of Religious Studies at the University of Gothenburg, Sweden. He has published a large number of publications on Islamic Theology and Muslims in Europe and his most recent publication is *Islam in the Nordic and Baltic Countries* (2009) and *Muslims and the New Media: Historical and Contemporary Debates* (2011). He is also responsible for the section on Sweden in the *Yearbook of Islam in Europe* (2009 ff.).

Lasse Lindekilde is Associate Professor at the Department of Political Science, University of Aarhus, Denmark. He has a PhD from the European University Institute, Florence, for a thesis on the reactions of Danish Muslims to the publication of the Muhammad cartoons. Currently he is researching radicalisation prevention policies in Europe and questions of tolerance vis-à-vis the political participation of minorities. His recent publications include 'Neo-liberal governing of "radicals": Danish radicalisation prevention policies and potential iatrogenic effects', *International Journal of Conflict and Violence*, 6(1), 2012; and 'Soft repression and mobilization: The case of transnational activism of Danish Muslims during the cartoons controversy', *International Journal of Middle East Studies*, 42(3), 2010.

Agata S. Nalborczyk is Assistant Professor at the Department for European Islam Studies, Faculty of Oriental Studies, University of Warsaw. She holds a PhD in Arabic and Islamic Studies. Agata is the author of numerous articles published in a wide variety of journals and books, including: *Islam and Christian-Muslim Relations*, *Global Change, Peace and Security*, *Islamochristiana*, *TRANS*, *Jahrbuch Polen*, in *Muzułmanie w Europie* vol. 1. ed. by A. Parzymies (2005). She is Editor of *Muzułmanie w Europie* vol. 2 (2012), and contributor to the *Yearbook of Muslims in Europe* since 2009.

Jørgen S. Nielsen is Danish National Research Foundation Professor of Islamic Studies and Director of the Centre for European Islamic Thought, Faculty of Theology, University of Copenhagen. He has previously held academic positions in Beirut, Birmingham (UK), and Damascus. Major recent publications include *Muslims in Western Europe* (1992, 3rd ed. 2004); *Shari'a as Discourse: Legal Traditions and the Encounter with Europe*, (joint ed., 2010); *Islam in Denmark: The Challenge of Diversity* (ed., 2012). He has been chief editor of the *Yearbook of Muslims in Europe* since 2009.

Z. Fareen Parvez is Assistant Professor of Sociology at the University of Massachusetts, Amherst. She received her PhD in sociology from the University of California at Berkeley. She is currently working on a book manuscript that will draw on her dissertation, a comparative ethnography of the politics of Islamic revival movements in France and India, for which she conducted participant observation in the working-class suburbs of Lyon, France, and in poor neighbourhoods and slums in Hyderabad, India. She has published in *Qualitative Sociology* and *Gender & Society*.

Timothy Peace is a postdoctoral fellow at the Alwaleed Centre of the University of Edinburgh. He completed his PhD at the European University Institute and previously held a research fellowship at the Université du Québec à Montréal.

His work has been published in journals such as *Patterns of Prejudice* and *Parliamentary Affairs*.

Egdūnas Račius is Professor of Middle Eastern and Islamic studies and Head of the Department of Regional Studies of Vytautas Magnus University, Kaunas, Lithuania. He is a co-editor and contributing author of the *Yearbook of Muslims in Europe* (2009 onwards) and reviews editor of the *Journal of Muslims in Europe*. Račius wrote the chapter on 'Islam in Lithuania' in Göran Larsson (ed.) *Islam in the Nordic and Baltic Countries* (2009), and 'Muslims in Catholic Lithuania: between the status quo and alternatives', in Milda Ališauskienė and Ingo W. Schröder (eds), *Religious Diversity in Lithuania: Ethnographies of Hegemony and Pluralism* (2011).

Riem Spielhaus is research fellow at the Centre for European Islamic Thought, University of Copenhagen, where she studies the formation and configuration of knowledge on Muslims within academia on the basis of a comparison of quantitative national and multinational polls. Her main area of research is Muslim minority studies with a focus on the production and dissemination of Islamic knowledge, identity politics, the institutionalisation of Islam, and the religious practice of Muslims in Europe. Her thesis 'Who is a Muslim anyway?' was awarded the Augsburg Science Award for Intercultural Studies in 2010.

Fatima Zibouh is a researcher in political and social science at the Université de Liège (Centre of Ethnic and Migration Studies) in Belgium. Her doctoral research is centred on the political participation of ethnocultural minorities through different forms of artistic expression. She has published *La participation politique des élus d'origine maghrébine*, Louvain-La-Neuve: Academia-Bruylant, 2010.

INDEX